Scalable Application Development with NestJS

Leverage REST, GraphQL, microservices, testing,
and deployment for seamless growth

Pacifique Linjanja

Scalable Application Development with NestJS

Group Product Manager: Kaustubh Manglurkar
Publishing Product Manager: Chayan Majumdar
Book Project Manager: Srinidhi Ram
Senior Content Development Editor: Feza Shaikh
Technical Editor: Simran Ali
Copy Editor: Safis Editing
Indexer: Tejal Soni
Production Designer: Ponraj Dhandapani
DevRel Marketing Coordinator: Nivedita Pandey

First published: January 2025

Production reference: 2301025

Published by Packt Publishing Ltd.
Grosvenor House
11 St Paul's Square
Birmingham
B3 1RB, UK.

ISBN 978-1-83546-860-9

www.packtpub.com

To my parents, my sisters, and my brothers for their love and support.

– Pacifique Linjanja

Contributors

About the author

Pacifique Linjanja is a skilled software engineer known for building enterprise-level applications with technologies such as NestJS. He has led diverse development teams globally, delivering scalable, efficient software solutions across multiple projects. In addition to his work, Pacifique actively contributes to open source communities, sharing his expertise and insights through technical talks and coding workshops. He enjoys mentoring new developers and continues to broaden his knowledge by exploring various fields beyond technology, believing in the importance of learning and giving back to the tech community.

I want to thank the people who have been close to me and supported me, especially my brother Ansima and my parents.

About the reviewer

Piyush Kacha is the co-founder of Anwit, where technology becomes a canvas for creativity and innovation is the brush. He graduated with a Bachelor of Engineering from Gujarat Technological University in 2019. While still in college, he joined Kevit Technologies in 2018 as a backend engineer and advanced to team lead over four years. In 2022, driven by an entrepreneurial spirit, he co-founded Anwit to craft IT solutions that not only work but also bring joy. A lifelong learner, he is currently exploring Gleam, a functional programming language designed to eliminate runtime errors. Piyush is passionate about transforming challenges into opportunities, continually pushing the boundaries of innovation in the tech world.

I owe my deepest gratitude to my family and colleagues for their unwavering support and belief in my vision. Your encouragement has been the cornerstone of my journey, inspiring me to overcome challenges and strive for excellence. A heartfelt thank you to the incredible teams at Kevit Technologies and Anwit for fostering an environment where innovation thrives. This accomplishment would not have been possible without all of you.

Table of Contents

Part 1: Introduction to NestJS and Scalable Application Architecture

1

Overview of NestJS   3

2

Understanding Scalable Application Architecture Principles and Design Patterns   25

3

Setting Up Your NestJS Environment and Exploring NestJS – Building a Robust App   49

4

Advanced Concepts – Modules, Controllers, Providers, Exception Filters, Pipes, Guards, and Decorators   73

Part 2: REST APIs and GraphQL in NestJS

5

Building and Optimizing REST APIs with NestJS   129

6

Unleashing the Power of GraphQL and the Apollo Federation Architecture in NestJS   173

Part 3: Testing and Debugging APIs in NestJS

7

Testing and Debugging REST APIs in NestJS   201

8

Testing and Debugging GraphQL APIs in NestJS   237

Part 4: Scaling with Microservices and NestJS

9

Deep Dive into Microservices: Concepts and Architectural Styles   261

10

Building Scalable Microservices with NestJS 273

11

Testing and Debugging Microservices in NestJS 309

Part 5: Real-World Application Examples and Case Studies

12

Case Study 1 - E-commerce Application   341

13

Case Study 2 – Social Networking Platform   405

14

Case Study 3 – Enterprise Resource Planning System   443

Part 6: Deployment, DevOps, and Beyond

15

16

17

NestJS Performance Optimization

18

NestJS Security Best Practices

Appendix

Concluding Remarks and Next Steps   557

Preface

NestJS is a powerful framework for building efficient, scalable, and maintainable server-side applications. With its modular architecture and native TypeScript support, NestJS allows developers to streamline the process of building REST APIs, GraphQL APIs, and microservices. This book, *Scalable Application Development with NestJS*, is a complete guide to using NestJS to develop robust applications that can grow with your business needs. Through practical examples, you'll learn how to integrate testing strategies, deploy seamlessly with CI/CD pipelines, and scale effortlessly in production environments.

Who this book is for

If you are a software engineer, developer, or tech lead aiming to gain a deeper understanding of how to build scalable applications using NestJS, REST, GraphQL, and microservices, this book is for you. Whether you're new to NestJS or a seasoned developer, this guide provides a comprehensive approach to leverage NestJS for your next big project. It's also ideal for project managers and other IT professionals seeking insights into enterprise-level efficient development, testing strategies, and deployment processes. Even technology enthusiasts will find this book enlightening.

What this book covers

Chapter 1, Overview of NestJS, is an introduction to what NestJS NestJS is and what it is capable of.

Chapter 2, Understanding Scalable Application Architecture Principles and Design Patterns, dives into the principles of scalable application architecture and the essential design patterns and best practices used for building scalable applications in NestJS. This chapter covers the fundamental concepts of scalability, such as load balancing, caching, and horizontal scaling.

Chapter 3, Setting Up Your NestJS Environment and Exploring NestJS – Building a Robust App, is a comprehensive guide to setting up the development environment for NestJS and exploring the framework by building a robust application. It covers the installation of NestJS and NestJS, along with the configuration of essential tools such as npm and TypeScript.

Chapter 4, Advanced Concepts – Modules, Controllers, Providers, Exception Filters, Pipes, Guards, and Decorators, delves deeper into NestJS and its advanced features. You will discover modules, controllers, providers, exception filters, pipes, guards, and decorators – all crucial components for building scalable and efficient NestJS applications.

Chapter 5, Building and Optimizing REST APIs with NestJS, covers the process of building and optimizing REST APIs using NestJS. You will gain an understanding of best practices when designing REST APIs, including versioning, pagination, and error handling.

Chapter 6, Unleashing the Power of GraphQL and the Apollo Federation Architecture in NestJS, explores the powerful world of GraphQL and explains how to build efficient GraphQL APIs using NestJS. This chapter will also cover the Apollo Federation architecture, enabling the creation of scalable and modular GraphQL APIs in a microservices-friendly environment.

Chapter 7, Testing and Debugging REST APIs in NestJS, covers various strategies, techniques, and tools for testing and debugging REST APIs developed in NestJS, providing them with the skills necessary to ensure the robustness of their APIs.

Chapter 8, Testing and Debugging GraphQL APIs in NestJS, covers testing and debugging strategies for GraphQL APIs in NestJS. It covers unit testing, **end-to-end** (E2E) testing, and common debugging techniques for GraphQL.

Chapter 9, Deep Dive into Microservices: Concepts and Architectural Styles, dives into microservices, introducing key concepts and architectural styles. You will learn about the benefits and challenges of microservices and gain an understanding of key architectural styles such as event-driven, database per service, and API gateway.

Chapter 10, Building Scalable Microservices with NestJS, shows how to use NestJS to build scalable microservices. You will learn how to define and implement microservices, how to communicate between microservices, and how to use the NestJS Microservices package.

Chapter 11, Testing and Debugging Microservices in NestJS, provides insights into testing and debugging microservices built with NestJS. You will learn how to write unit and integration tests for microservices, how to debug microservices, and how to handle common issues in a microservices environment.

Chapter 12, Case Study 1 - E-commerce Application, explores a case study of building an e-commerce application using NestJS. It covers architectural considerations, data modeling, implementing REST APIs, handling user authentication, and integrating payment gateways.

Chapter 13, Case Study 2 - Social Networking Platform, presents a case study of building a social networking platform using NestJS. It covers designing the application structure, implementing GraphQL APIs, managing user relationships, integrating real-time features, and handling user-generated content.

Chapter 14, Case Study 3 - Enterprise Resource Planning System, provides a case study of building an **Enterprise Resource Planning** (ERP) system using NestJS. It covers designing the system architecture, implementing microservices, managing data synchronization, and handling complex business processes.

Chapter 15, Deploying NestJS Applications, explains how to deploy NestJS applications to various environments, including local servers, Docker, and cloud platforms such as AWS, Google Cloud, and Render.

Chapter 16, Embracing DevOps: Continuous Integration and Continuous Deployment for NestJS, discusses **Continuous Integration and Continuous Deployment (CI/CD)** in the context of NestJS. You will learn about various CI/CD tools, and how to implement a CI/CD pipeline for a NestJS application.

Chapter 17, NestJS Performance Optimization, delves into performance optimization for NestJS applications, discussing techniques for improving speed, efficiency, and reliability.

Chapter 18, NestJS Security Best Practices, deals with security best practices for NestJS applications. It discusses strategies for ensuring data security, handling authentication and authorization, and preventing common security threats.

Appendix, Concluding Remarks and Next Steps, offers a summary of key concepts learned throughout the book and suggests the next steps if you want to continue your journey with NestJS.

To get the most out of this book

Chapter 3 explains how to install all the required software and packages. You will need to have NestJS installed on your computer – any version above 16.0.0 – to get started. All code examples have been tested using NestJS 10 on macOS. However, they should work on any operating system where NestJS 10 and future version releases are installed.

Software/hardware covered in the book	Operating system requirements
NestJS 10	Windows, macOS, or Linux
TypeScript 4.0 and above	
Client Application (Postman or a Web browser)	

If you are using the digital version of this book, we advise you to type the code yourself or access the code from the book's GitHub repository (a link is available in the next section). Doing so will help you avoid any potential errors related to the copying and pasting of code.

Download the example code files

You can download the example code files for this book from GitHub at `https://github.com/ PacktPublishing/Scalable-Application-Development-with-NestJS`. If there's an update to the code, it will be updated in the GitHub repository.

We also have other code bundles from our rich catalog of books and videos available at `https:// github.com/PacktPublishing/`. Check them out!

Conventions used

There are a number of text conventions used throughout this book.

Code in text: Indicates code words in text, database table names, folder names, filenames, file extensions, pathnames, dummy URLs, user input, and Twitter handles. Here is an example: "Inside your `src/` directory, create a new sub-directory named `users`."

A block of code is set as follows:

```
// ... existing imports
import { UsersModule } from './users/user.module';
// ... existing code
imports: [UsersModule], // Add this line
// ... the rest of the code
```

Any command-line input or output is written as follows:

```
$ nest new user-management-graphql
```

Bold: Indicates a new term, an important word, or words that you see onscreen. For instance, words in menus or dialog boxes appear in bold. Here is an example: "Create a new environment, choose **Web Server Environment**, and select Docker as the platform"

> **Tips or important notes**
> Appear like this.

Get in touch

Feedback from our readers is always welcome.

General feedback: If you have questions about any aspect of this book, email us at customercare@packtpub.com and mention the book title in the subject of your message.

Errata: Although we have taken every care to ensure the accuracy of our content, mistakes do happen. If you have found a mistake in this book, we would be grateful if you would report this to us. Please visit www.packtpub.com/support/errata and fill in the form.

Piracy: If you come across any illegal copies of our works in any form on the internet, we would be grateful if you would provide us with the location address or website name. Please contact us at copyright@packt.com with a link to the material.

If you are interested in becoming an author: If there is a topic that you have expertise in and you are interested in either writing or contributing to a book, please visit authors.packtpub.com.

Share Your Thoughts

Once you've read *Scalable Application Development with NestJS*, we'd love to hear your thoughts! Scan the QR code below to go straight to the Amazon review page for this book and share your feedback.

https://packt.link/r/1835468608

Your review is important to us and the tech community and will help us make sure we're delivering excellent quality content.

Free Benefits with Your Book

This book comes with free benefits to support your learning. Activate them now for instant access (see the "*How to Unlock*" section for instructions).

Here's a quick overview of what you can instantly unlock with your purchase:

PDF and ePub Copies

Next-Gen Web-Based Reader

Access a DRM-free PDF copy of this book to read anywhere, on any device.

Multi-device progress sync: Pick up where you left off, on any device.

Use a DRM-free ePub version with your favorite e-reader.

Highlighting and notetaking: Capture ideas and turn reading into lasting knowledge.

Bookmarking: Save and revisit key sections whenever you need them.

Dark mode: Reduce eye strain by switching to dark or sepia themes

Part 1:
Introduction to NestJS and Scalable Application Architecture

This part introduces you to the NestJS world and helps you understand the spirit behind the framework, its architecture, and the design pattern used internally.

This part includes the following chapters:

- *Chapter 1, Overview of NestJS*

- *Chapter 2, Understanding Scalable Application Architecture Principles and Design Patterns*

- *Chapter 3, Setting Up Your NestJS Environment and Exploring NestJS – Building a Robust App*

- *Chapter 4, Advanced Concepts – Modules, Controllers, Providers, Exception Filters, Pipes, Guards, and Decorators*

1

Overview of NestJS

As the world of server-side development continues to evolve, the demand for robust, scalable, and easily maintainable frameworks grows ever greater. Enter NestJS—a progressive Node.js framework that combines elements of **Object-Oriented Programming (OOP)**, **Functional Programming (FP)**, and **Functional Reactive Programming (FRP)** to deliver a unique development experience. By embracing TypeScript and providing a highly modular architecture, NestJS opens the door to clean, efficient, and secure server-side applications.

In this chapter, you will immerse yourself in the intricate world of NestJS. We will guide you through the foundational aspects, starting with what NestJS is and the problems it aims to solve. You will learn about its philosophy and design patterns, its robust ecosystem, and how TypeScript amplifies the development experience. By the end of this chapter, you will have gained a comprehensive understanding of why NestJS has emerged as a developer favorite for creating scalable and maintainable server-side applications.

In this chapter, we're going to cover the following main topics:

- Introduction to NestJS
- The power of TypeScript
- Key features of NestJS
- The ecosystem of NestJS
- Why choose NestJS?

> **Free Benefits with Your Book**
> Your purchase includes a free PDF copy of this book along with other exclusive benefits. Check the *Free Benefits with Your Book* section in the Preface to unlock them instantly and maximize your learning experience.

Technical requirements

The code files for the chapter can be found at `https://github.com/PacktPublishing/Scalable-Application-Development-with-NestJS`

Introduction to NestJS

In the rapidly evolving world of web development, developers continuously seek tools and frameworks that provide efficiency, structure, and scalability. As applications grow more complex, a robust and adaptable framework becomes vital. NestJS, a progressive Node.js framework, stands out as a prominent solution for building server-side applications that are maintainable and scalable.

Historical context

The landscape of backend development has undergone seismic changes since the early days of the web. Starting from simple CGI scripts to monolithic architectures and evolving to RESTful services and microservices, each phase has brought its own set of challenges and solutions. NestJS emerges as a framework designed to address the complexities of modern applications, providing a structured way to build scalable, efficient, and robust server-side applications.

NestJS was created by Kamil Myśliwiec and officially released in 2017. It was designed with the aim of empowering developers with a versatile toolset that merges the capabilities of OOP, FP, and FRP. Inspired by Angular, NestJS builds on the strong foundations of TypeScript, allowing developers to write more robust and error-free code.

Myśliwiec was working as a software engineer at a company that was using Angular for frontend development. He was impressed with Angular's architecture and wanted to create a similar framework for backend development.

NestJS is built on top of Express, a popular Node.js framework. It adds a number of features that make it easier to develop scalable and maintainable applications, such as dependency injection, routing, and middleware.

NestJS has quickly become one of the most popular Node.js frameworks. It is used by a number of large companies, such as Adidas, GitLab, and Decathlon.

Here is a timeline of the key events in the history of NestJS:

- 2016: NestJS is created by Kamil Myśliwiec

- 2017: NestJS 1.0 is released

- 2018: NestJS 5.0 is released, which introduces a number of new features, such as support for TypeScript 3.0 and asynchronous routing

- 2019: NestJS 6.0 is released, which introduces a number of new features, such as support for WebSockets and GraphQL

- 2020: NestJS 7.0 is released, which introduces a number of new features, such as support for TypeScript 4.0 and serverless deployments

- 2021: NestJS 8.0 is released, which introduces a number of new features, such as support for TypeScript 4.3 and asynchronous event emitters

- 2022: NestJS 9.0 is released, which introduces a number of new features, such as support for TypeScript 4.5 and asynchronous pipes
- 2023: NestJS 10.0 is released with support for TypeScript 4.8

NestJS is a rapidly evolving framework that is constantly being updated with new features, with a fast-growing community that keeps maintaining the framework, which is maturing every single day. It is a popular choice for building scalable and maintainable Node.js applications.

Problem statement – the need for NestJS

The server-side landscape is littered with a myriad of frameworks and libraries. However, many of them offer a limited structure for application design, leading to maintenance nightmares as projects scale. Additionally, with the increasing demands for real-time processing and microservices architectures, a well-structured, scalable solution is more needed than ever. Enter NestJS, a framework that brings modularity, scalability, and strong typing into the picture.

Node.js is a popular platform for building scalable and efficient web applications. However, it can be difficult to develop large and complex applications using Node.js alone.

NestJS is a TypeScript framework that provides a number of features that make it easier to develop large and complex Node.js applications. These features include the following:

- **Dependency injection**: Dependency injection is a design pattern that allows you to decouple your code from its dependencies. This makes your code more modular and easier to test.
- **Routing**: NestJS provides a powerful routing system that makes it easy to define the endpoints for your application.
- **Middleware**: Middleware is code that is executed before or after a request is handled by your application. NestJS provides a variety of middleware that you can use to add common functionality to your application, such as authentication and logging.
- **Testing**: NestJS provides a number of features that make it easy to test your application. These features include a built-in testing framework and support for mocking dependencies.

NestJS is a powerful framework that can help you develop large and complex Node.js applications more easily. If you are looking for a framework that can help you build scalable and maintainable Node.js applications, then NestJS is a great option.

NestJS versus other frameworks – a comparative analysis

Express provides the bare minimum for building applications; it leaves the architecture largely up to you, including choosing whether to use NestJS or competitors such as Koa, Sails.js, and hapi. NestJS goes a step further by providing a well-defined structure for your application. It's not merely a collection of libraries but an integrated system offering a consistent development methodology.

The following table provides a simplified comparison of NestJS and these other frameworks:

Feature	NestJS	Express	hapi	Fastify	Koa
Native programming language	TypeScript	JavaScript	JavaScript	JavaScript	JavaScript
Dependency injection	Yes – built-in	Yes – needs to be implemented	Yes – needs to be implemented	Yes – needs to be implemented	Yes – a few built-in utilities
Routing	Yes	Yes	Yes	Yes	Yes
Middleware	Yes	Yes	Yes	Yes	Yes
Error handling	Yes	Yes	Yes	Yes	Yes
Testing	Yes – plenty of built-in tools	Yes	Yes	Yes	Yes
GraphQL support	Yes – plenty of built-in tools	Yes	Yes	Yes	Yes
Microservise support	Yes – plenty of built-in tools	Yes	Yes	Yes	Yes
Community	Large and active	Large and active	Large and active	Active	Active
Documentation	Excellent	Good	Good	Good	Good
Performance	Excellent	Not bad	Good	Excellent	Good
Scalability	Excellent	Good	Good	Good	Good
Maintainability	Good	Good	Good	Good	Good

Table 1.1: NestJS vs other framework

As you can see, NestJS is a feature-rich framework that is comparable to other popular Node. js frameworks. It offers a number of advantages, such as its use of TypeScript, its large and active community, and its excellent documentation.

However, it is important to note that there is no "best" framework for every application. The best framework for you will depend on your specific needs and requirements.

Here are some additional things to consider when choosing a framework for your next project:

- **The size and complexity of your project**: If you are building a small project, then a simple framework such as Express may be sufficient. However, if you are building a large or complex project, then you may need a more feature-rich framework such as NestJS.

- **Your team's experience and skills**: If your team is already familiar with a particular framework, then that may be the best choice for your project. However, if your team is new to Node.js, then you may want to choose a framework that is known for its ease of use.

- **Your project's requirements**: Some frameworks are better suited for certain types of projects than others. For example, if you need to build a RESTful API, then you will need a framework that supports routing. If you need to build a real-time application, then you will need a framework that supports WebSocket.

Ultimately, the best way to choose a framework is to research your options and choose the framework that is the best fit for your specific needs.

NestJS by numbers

As of October 2024, NestJS boasts a vibrant community with over 67k GitHub stars, 2M weekly downloads from npm, and more than 400 contributors. These numbers are a testament to its growing popularity and adoption in the developer community.

The philosophy of NestJS

The philosophy of NestJS is based on the following principles:

- **Convention over configuration**: NestJS uses a convention-over-configuration approach, which means that many of the settings and options are predefined and can be overridden as needed. This makes it easier to get started with NestJS and build consistent applications.

- **Dependency injection**: NestJS uses dependency injection to manage dependencies between components. This makes it easier to test and maintain applications, and it also helps to promote loose coupling.

- **Modular architecture**: NestJS applications are organized into modules, which makes it easier to find and understand code. Modules can be imported and exported as needed, which makes it easy to reuse code and build scalable applications.

- **Reactive programming**: NestJS supports reactive programming, which makes it easier to build event-driven applications. Reactive programming is based on the idea of streams, which are sequences of data that can be processed asynchronously.

- **TypeScript**: NestJS is built on TypeScript, which is a superset of JavaScript that adds type safety. Type safety helps to prevent errors and to make code more readable and maintainable.

The philosophy of NestJS is designed to make it easier to build scalable, maintainable, and testable Node.js applications.

Key advantages of using NestJS

In this section, we'll uncover the core advantages that make NestJS a compelling choice for server-side development. Whether you're concerned about reducing boilerplate code, maintaining a scalable application, or tapping into an active developer community, NestJS has got you covered. Let's delve into the features that not only simplify development but also elevate it.

- **Convention over configuration**: One of the defining features of NestJS is its opinionated architecture, advocating a "convention-over-configuration" paradigm. This reduces boilerplate and decision fatigue, helping you focus more on the business logic.

- **Strong typing with TypeScript**: NestJS strongly encourages the use of TypeScript, offering static type-checking and self-documenting code, thereby reducing bugs and making the code base more maintainable.

- **Scalability – more than just handling requests**: Scalability in NestJS is not just about handling an increased number of requests. It also pertains to the modularity and ease of feature additions, making it the go-to choice for growing projects.

- **A community-driven approach**: NestJS is backed by an active community, evidenced by its thriving ecosystem, frequent updates, and extensive documentation. This ensures that the framework stays relevant and continuously evolves to meet emerging challenges.

Now that we have explored the foundational elements, philosophies, and advantages of using NestJS for scalable server-side development, it's time to delve into one of its cornerstone technologies. Up next, we'll discuss the power and benefits of using TypeScript in the NestJS framework, illuminating why it's considered more than just a "nice-to-have" feature.

The power of TypeScript

In a landscape where JavaScript dominates server-side development, TypeScript offers a unique edge with its robust type-checking and object-oriented capabilities. This section will shed light on why TypeScript is not just a beneficial choice but almost an essential one when working with NestJS.

Why TypeScript?

JavaScript, while ubiquitous and versatile, leaves much to be desired in terms of type safety and self-documenting code. TypeScript, a superset of JavaScript, was developed by Microsoft to address these issues. When used in the context of a server-side framework such as NestJS, TypeScript's features shine even brighter.

The value proposition – what does TypeScript offer?

TypeScript brings static typing to JavaScript, allowing you to define data types at compile time. This feature provides several key advantages:

- **Error reduction**: Catching type-related errors at compile time, rather than runtime, can save significant debugging time and prevent potential system failures

- **Code quality**: Static typing often leads to more readable and self-documenting code, making it easier for team members to understand the code base

- **IDE support**: Modern IDEs provide better IntelliSense and autocomplete features when TypeScript is used, making development faster and more efficient

Figure 1.1 explains how TypeScript works. It first compiles `.ts` files via its compiler, ts-loader, and then writes its equivalent code before all the `.js` code gets bundled into a single-entry point via a bundler.

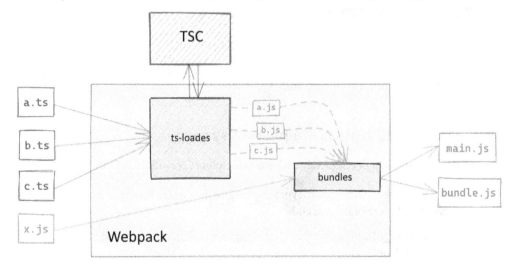

Figure 1.1: Diagram of how TypeScript compiles into plain JavaScript and the type-checking process

Code snippet – TypeScript in action

Consider this JavaScript code that has a bug:

```javascript
// javascript code
function add(a, b) {
  return a + b;
}
console.log(add(5, "10"));   // Output: 510
```

Now, let's see how TypeScript can help us:

```typescript
// typescript code
function add(a: number, b: number): number {
  return a + b;
}
console.log(add(5, "10"));   // Error: Argument of type
                             // 'string' is not assignable
                             // to parameter of type
                             // 'number'.
```

Notice how TypeScript catches the type mismatch at compile time, reducing the chances of bugs making their way into the production code.

> ⚒ Try it out!
>
> What happens when you try to compile the preceding TypeScript code with the type mismatch? Experiment and note down your observations.

TypeScript and NestJS – a perfect synergy

TypeScript's features align seamlessly with the principles of NestJS. Here's how:

- **Decorators**: Both NestJS and TypeScript utilize decorators for metadata reflection, leading to cleaner and more organized code

- **Strong typing:** This ensures that your NestJS controllers, services, and other classes are robust and maintainable

- **Modularity**: TypeScript's namespace and module system help in organizing code, making it scalable and thus aligning with NestJS's modular architecture

Code snippet – NestJS with TypeScript

Let's create a simple NestJS service with TypeScript:

```typescript
// typescript code
import { Injectable } from '@nestjs/common';

@Injectable()
export class AppService {
  getData(): string {
    return 'Hello, NestJS!';
  }
}
```

In this snippet, the `@Injectable()` decorator and the `**: string**` return type are both examples of how TypeScript enhances NestJS development.

By integrating TypeScript, NestJS offers a development environment that is robust, efficient, and less prone to errors. TypeScript's static typing, enhanced IDE support, and compatibility with modern programming paradigms make it a crucial part of the NestJS ecosystem.

Now that we've seen how TypeScript elevates the NestJS development experience, let's delve deeper into the framework itself. In the next section, we'll explore the key features that make NestJS a powerful choice for building scalable applications.

Key features of NestJS

NestJS is not just another framework; it's a complete ecosystem for building scalable, maintainable, and robust server-side applications. It incorporates a range of features that facilitate quick development without sacrificing quality. Let's explore these key features.

Modularity

NestJS is a modular framework, which means that applications are organized into modules. Modules are self-contained units of code that can be imported and exported as needed. This makes it easy to find and understand code, reuse code, and build scalable applications.

There are two types of modules in NestJS:

- **Root modules**: The root module is the main module for your application. It imports all of the other modules in your application and bootstraps your application.

- **Feature modules**: Feature modules are modules that contain code for a specific feature of your application. They can be imported and exported as needed, which makes it easy to reuse code and build scalable applications.

NestJS modules are organized in a tree structure. The root module is at the top of the tree, and the feature modules are nested below the root module. This makes it easy to find and understand the code in your application.

NestJS modules are also loosely coupled. This means that modules are not tightly dependent on each other. This makes it easy to test and maintain applications, and it also makes it easy to change or update modules without affecting other modules in your application.

NestJS modularity is a powerful feature that makes it easy to build scalable, maintainable, and testable applications.

The following are the benefits of NestJS modularity:

- **Decoupled code**: Modules encourage the separation of concerns, leading to more maintainable code

- **Reusability**: Build once and use across multiple parts of your application or even in different projects

- **Improved scalability**: Modules can be scaled independently, which makes it easy to scale your application as needed

- **Improved testability**: Modules are loosely coupled, which makes them easier to test

- **Improved maintainability**: Modules make it easier to make changes to your application without affecting other parts of your application

Here is a typical module definition in a NestJS application. This is an integral part of the framework that allows for modularization of functionalities. Let's look at the code and then break it down:

```typescript
// typescript code
@Module({
  imports: [UsersModule, OrdersModule],
  controllers: [AppController],
  providers: [AppService],
})
export class AppModule {}
```

Here's a step-by-step explanation of the preceding code:

- `@Module({...})` `Decorator`: In NestJS, decorators are special functions that provide metadata about the class they decorate. Here, `@Module` is a decorator that tells NestJS that `AppModule` is a module.

  The following are the properties within the `@Module` decorator:

  - `imports`: This is an array where you list other modules that this module will need. In the snippet, `AppModule` requires `UsersModule` and `OrdersModule`. These might be modules that handle user data and order data, respectively.

- `controllers`: Controllers handle incoming requests and return responses to the client. In this snippet, `AppController` is listed, indicating that this module uses it to handle certain routes and actions.

- `providers`: Providers can be a lot of things in NestJS – services, repositories, factories, and so on. They often handle the logic and data manipulation behind the scenes. Here, `AppService` is listed as a provider, which could be responsible for some business logic or data fetching.

We will look into this further in *Chapter 3*.

- `export class AppModule {}`: This is the declaration of the `AppModule` class. By itself, this class doesn't do much. However, combined with the `@Module` decorator, it provides NestJS with the information it needs to understand the structure and dependencies of the application.

Modules in NestJS allow you to organize your application into logical and functional sections. As your application grows, you'll have more controllers, providers, and even other modules. Organizing them using modules ensures that you can keep track of all these parts, making your application more maintainable and scalable.

> **⁇ Interactive task**
>
> Try creating a new module for handling products in an e-commerce application. What controllers, providers, and services might you need?

Dependency injection

Dependency injection is a design pattern that allows us to create loosely coupled code. Loosely coupled code is code that is not tightly dependent on other pieces of code. This makes code easier to test, maintain, and reuse.

In NestJS, dependency injection is implemented using the `@Injectable()` decorator. The `@Injectable()` decorator marks a class as being injectable. This means that the class can be injected into other classes using dependency injection.

To inject a dependency into a class, we use the `@Inject()` decorator. The `@Inject()` decorator takes the name of the dependency as an argument. The dependency will be injected into the class constructor when the class is instantiated.

Benefits

The benefits are as follows:

- **Testability**: Makes unit testing easier as dependencies can be easily mocked

- **Loose coupling**: Classes are not hardwired but are provided as needed

Here is a common example of a dependency injection code snippet used in NestJS. The following service will be injected into a module. We will explore and understand how in *Chapter 3*:

```typescript
// typescript code
@Injectable()
export class UsersService {
  constructor(
    private readonly userRepository: UserRepository
  ) {}
}
```

> **? Quick challenge**
>
> Refactor the preceding code to inject another dependency named `OrdersRepository`. How would you modify the constructor?

Decorators

Decorators are a powerful feature of NestJS that can be used to modify the behavior of classes, methods, and properties. Decorators are declared using the @ symbol, followed by the name of the decorator.

There are many different types of decorators available in NestJS, each with its own specific purpose. Some of the most common decorators include the following:

- `@Injectable`: This decorator is used to mark a class as being injectable. This means that the class can be injected into other classes using dependency injection.

- `@Controller`: This decorator is used to mark a class as being a controller. Controllers are responsible for handling HTTP requests and responses.

- `@Get`: This decorator is used to mark a method as being a GET endpoint. GET endpoints are used to retrieve data from the server.

- `@Post`: This decorator is used to mark a method as being a POST endpoint. POST endpoints are used to create data on the server.

- `@Put`: This decorator is used to mark a method as being a PUT endpoint. PUT endpoints are used to update data on the server.

- `@Delete`: This decorator is used to mark a method as being a DELETE endpoint. DELETE endpoints are used to delete data from the server.

We will have more time to revisit all of them practically as we dive deeper into the practical sides of the book.

Benefits

Here are the most important benefits we get when using Decorators:

- **Metadata reflection**: Attach metadata to classes/functions easily
- **Cleaner code**: Less boilerplate and more declarative code
- **Improved code readability**: Decorators make it easy to understand the purpose of a class, method, or property
- **Increased code flexibility**: Decorators can be used to modify the behavior of classes, methods, and properties at runtime
- **Improved code maintainability**: Decorators can be used to centralize changes to the behavior of classes, methods, and properties
- **Reduced code duplication**: Decorators can be used to avoid duplicating code that modifies the behavior of classes, methods, and properties

Code snippet

In the following example, we have used some built-in decorators from NestJS:

```typescript
// typescript code
@Get('profile')
async getProfile(@Req() request: Request) {
  return this.usersService.find(request.userId);
}
```

Guards

In NestJS, guards play an important role. When building professional applications, they determine whether the request will be handled by the route, based on certain criteria or conditions. These conditions can be role-based, permission-level-based, and so on, often referred to as authorization.

Guards, in NestJS, are classes annotated with the `@Injectable()` decorator. They must implement the `CanActivate` interface and have access to the execution context of the request, which makes them smarter than the usual middleware in traditional Express applications.

Benefits

Wit the use of Guards, we get:

- **Centralized authorization logic**: Guards allow you to define authorization logic in one place, making it easier to manage access control across multiple routes.

- **Reusable security policies**: Once created, guards can be reused across different controllers or services, promoting code reuse. This is especially useful when you have recurring security policies, such as ensuring a user is authenticated or has certain roles, which can be applied to multiple routes without rewriting the logic.

- **Enhanced security**: Guards help in strengthening security by controlling access at the very beginning of the request life cycle. They intercept incoming requests before they reach the route handler, ensuring that only authorized requests proceed, thereby preventing unauthorized access to sensitive resources.

- **Context-aware authorization**: With access to the execution context (which includes the request, response, and other relevant data), guards can perform complex, context-sensitive authorization checks. For example, you can examine request headers, tokens, or even the user's role to make dynamic decisions about whether to allow or deny access.

- **Integration with other features**: Guards integrate seamlessly with other NestJS features, such as dependency injection and middleware. This allows for highly flexible and scalable architectures where guards can work alongside services or other components, making your security layer more maintainable and adaptable to change.

Code snippet

The following is an example code snippet:

```
@Injectable()
export class AuthGuard implements CanActivate {
  canActivate(
    context: ExecutionContext,
  ): boolean | Promise<boolean> | Observable<boolean> {
    const request = context.switchToHttp().getRequest();
    return !!request;
  }
}
```

The preceding code snippet is a sample of a guard called `AuthGuard`, and as you can see, the `canActivate()` method takes the `context` parameter. We then return `true` if the request is present; otherwise, we return `false`. In a typical guard, the `canActivate()` function should return a Boolean. When it returns `false`, the request will be rejected; otherwise, it is passed to the route handler.

Exception filters

NestJS provides a layer to handle exceptions across your application uniformly.

Benefits

When using Exception filters, we get:

- **Centralized error handling**: Manage errors in one place
- **Custom responses**: Craft user-friendly error messages

Code snippet

Combining the dependency injection and decorator features we have seen before, here is an example of an exception filter in a NestJS app. These filters can be imported from a built-in NestJS library or customized by the developer:

```typescript
// typescript code
@Catch(NotFoundException)
export class NotFoundExceptionFilter implements
ExceptionFilter {
  catch(
    exception: NotFoundException,
    host: ArgumentsHost
  ) {
    const ctx = host.switchToHttp();
    const response = ctx.getResponse();
    const status = exception.getStatus();

    response.status(status).json({
      statusCode: status,
      message: "Not Found!",
    });
  }
}
```

NestJS has a built-in layer for handling exceptions, allowing developers to catch and manage exceptions in a uniform manner throughout the application. This specific code demonstrates how to use **exception filters** for this purpose.

Here's a breakdown of the code:

- **Annotation** – @Catch(NotFoundException):
  - This is a decorator provided by NestJS
  - It indicates that the filter is specifically designed to catch exceptions of the NotFoundException type

- Whenever `NotFoundException` is thrown within the application, this filter will catch it and execute the logic inside the `catch` method

- **Class declaration** – `NotFoundExceptionFilter`:

  - This class implements the `ExceptionFilter` interface from NestJS

  - By implementing this interface, we're promising that this class will have a method called `catch` that follows a certain structure

- **The catch method**:

  - This is where the actual exception handling occurs

  - It takes two parameters:

    - `exception`: The exception being caught, in this case, an instance of `NotFoundException`

    - `host`: An instance of `ArgumentsHost`, which provides access to the arguments of the method that threw the exception

- **Switching contexts** – `host.switchToHttp()`:

  - This line is used to retrieve the HTTP context in which the exception was thrown

  - With this, you can get access to both the request and response objects of the HTTP cycle

- **Getting the response** – `ctx.getResponse()`:

  - This retrieves the HTTP response object, allowing manipulation of the response being sent to the client.

- **Retrieving exception status** – `exception.getStatus()`:

  - Since `NotFoundException` is an HTTP exception, it carries with it a status code. This method retrieves that status code.

- **Setting the response**:

  - The response object's `status` method sets the HTTP status code for the response

  - The `json` method then sends a JSON response to the client with the given status code and the `Not Found!` error message

This code demonstrates a custom exception filter in NestJS that catches `NotFoundException` and sends back a consistent, user-friendly JSON error message to the client. This not only enhances error handling in the application but also ensures a better user experience.

⟨?⟩ **Quiz**

How would you modify the filter to handle `BadRequestException`?

Pipes

Pipes are a powerful feature of NestJS that can be used to transform data as it flows through your application. Pipes are declared using the `@Pipe()` decorator.

There are many different types of pipes available in NestJS, each with its own specific purpose. Some of the most common pipes include the following:

- **Validation pipes**: Validation pipes can be used to validate data before it is processed by your application
- **Transformation pipes**: Transformation pipes can be used to transform data into a different format
- **Logging pipes**: Logging pipes can be used to log data as it flows through your application
- **Error-handling pipes**: Error-handling pipes can be used to handle errors that occur as data flows through your application

Pipes can be chained together to create more complex behavior. For example, the following pipe chain validates the data, transforms it into a different format, and logs it:

```typescript
// typescript code

@Pipe({name: 'myPipe'})
export class MyPipe {
  constructor(private readonly logger: Logger) {}
  transform(value: any) {
    this.logger.log('The value is: ' + value);
    return value;
  }
}
```

Pipes are a powerful tool that can be used to improve the flexibility and maintainability of your NestJS applications.

Here are some of the benefits of using pipes in NestJS:

- **Flexibility**: Pipes can be used to transform data in a variety of ways, making it easy to adapt your application to different needs
- **Maintainability**: Pipes can be easily reused and updated, making it easy to maintain your application as it evolves

- **Performance**: Pipes are executed asynchronously, which helps to improve the performance of your application

Interceptors

Interceptors allow you to inspect and transform HTTP requests/responses in your app.

Interceptors are a powerful feature of NestJS that can be used to intercept requests and responses as they flow through your application. Interceptors are declared using the @Interceptor() decorator.

There are many different types of interceptors available in NestJS, each with its own specific purpose. Some of the most common interceptors include the following:

- **Logging interceptors**: Logging interceptors can be used to log requests and responses as they flow through your application
- **Error-handling interceptors**: Error-handling interceptors can be used to handle errors that occur as requests and responses flow through your application
- **Security interceptors**: Security interceptors can be used to secure requests and responses as they flow through your application
- **Caching interceptors**: Caching interceptors can be used to cache requests and responses as they flow through your application

Benefits

Using Interceptors, you get:

- **Aspect-oriented programming**: Separate cross-cutting concerns such as logging or transforming response
- **Flexibility**: Modify requests or responses as required

Code snippet

Let's delve into a practical implementation of an interceptor. The following code snippet showcases a basic interceptor that transforms the response structure:

```typescript
// typescript code
@Injectable()
export class TransformInterceptor implements
NestInterceptor {
  intercept(context: ExecutionContext, next: CallHandler):
  Observable<any> {
    return next.handle().pipe(
      map(data => ({ result: data })))
```

```
        );
    }
}
```

In this interceptor, named `TransformInterceptor`, the response data is enveloped in an object with a key named `result`. This allows for consistent response structures throughout the application.

⚒ **Try it**

Can you modify the interceptor to log the duration of each request? Hint: Use `Date.now()` to get the current timestamp.

❓ **Review questions**

Why is modularity crucial in NestJS? How do pipes enhance data validation in NestJS? What is the core purpose of interceptors in NestJS?

We've just explored the core features and functionalities that make NestJS a standout framework. As we move on, our next focus will be on the vast **ecosystem of NestJS**, diving into the libraries and tools that further enhance its capabilities.

The ecosystem of NestJS

In software development, an ecosystem refers to the environment in which a technology or framework resides. This includes everything from community support to third-party libraries, tools, and services that complement the core offering. A rich ecosystem is often a sign of a mature and sustainable framework, and NestJS is no exception.

Third-party modules

The modularity of NestJS enables seamless integration with various third-party libraries. The following are some examples:

- **TypeORM**: For database interaction
- **GraphQL**: For building GraphQL APIs
- **Passport**: For authentication
- **Swagger**: For API documentation

Nest CLI

NestJS provides a powerful **Command-Line Interface** (**CLI**) tool that streamlines the development process.

Benefits

Leveraging the Nest CLI, here are the benefits you get:

- **Code scaffolding**: Easily generate modules, services, and controllers
- **Build and serve**: Compile and run your app with simple commands

Code snippet

Using the Nest CLI, here are some commands you can use to get started with a simple Nest project:

```bash
# bash code
$ nest new my-new-project
$ nest generate module users
```

The first command will help you set up a basic NestJS project with the name `my-new-project`. The second one will generate a new model under the created project. Before running it, you need to be in a NestJS directory.

These are only two commands provided by the Nest CLI. We will explore this further in *Chapter 3* of the book.

Community support

A strong community ensures a framework's sustainability. NestJS has an active community that contributes to the following:

- Documentation
- Tutorials
- Third-party modules

Engagement activity

Search for a NestJS community forum or a Discord/Slack channel. Participate in a discussion and share your insights there.

The official NestJS's discord channel can be found here `https://discord.gg/G7Qnnhy`

Review questions

What third-party modules commonly complement NestJS? How does the Nest CLI enhance the development workflow? Why?

The ecosystem surrounding NestJS is both rich and growing, making it an excellent choice for robust and scalable applications. With community support, third-party modules, and a user-friendly CLI, you're well equipped to handle any challenge. Let's now wrap everything up by exploring the core reasons why NestJS is an ideal choice for building scalable and maintainable applications in the next section.

Why choose NestJS?

By this point, you've gathered enough information about NestJS, but the lingering question remains: why choose NestJS over other backend frameworks?

- **Strong architecture**: NestJS enforces a strong architectural pattern that ensures your application is scalable and maintainable

- **TypeScript support**: Type safety and IntelliSense support through TypeScript integration offer a superior development experience

- **Flexibility**: NestJS is flexible and unopinionated, allowing you to choose your own libraries for databases, authentication, and so on

- **Strong ecosystem**: As we've seen, the ecosystem surrounding NestJS is robust, providing you with all the tools needed for enterprise-grade applications

- **Community and enterprise support**: An active community and the backing of enterprise solutions ensure the framework's sustainability

> ⚒ **Decision-making exercise**
>
> List your current project requirements and see how many of them can be directly addressed by NestJS features and its ecosystem. Share your insights.

Choosing a backend framework is a significant decision that will affect your project's future scalability, maintainability, and overall success. NestJS offers a compelling suite of features, backed by a strong ecosystem and community, making it an excellent choice for various types of projects—from start-ups to large enterprises.

> ❓ **Review questions**
>
> How does NestJS ensure that your application is maintainable? What role does TypeScript play in NestJS? How does the NestJS ecosystem contribute to its viability as a framework of choice?

Summary

In this chapter, we've embarked on an exciting journey exploring NestJS, a robust framework designed to make server-side development seamless and scalable. We began by introducing you to the framework, discussing its origins, and outlining its core philosophies. We then delved into the transformative power of TypeScript in a NestJS environment, elucidating how strong typing can improve code maintainability and reduce errors. Furthermore, we examined the key features of NestJS that make it a highly modular and scalable choice for modern web development, such as its opinionated architecture and community-driven approach.

Get This Book's PDF Version and Exclusive Extras

Scan the QR code (or go to `packtpub.com/unlock`). Search for this book by name, confirm the edition, and then follow the steps on the page.

Note: Keep your invoice handly. Purchase made directly from packt don't require one.

2

Understanding Scalable Application Architecture Principles and Design Patterns

Welcome to *Chapter 2*, where we'll dig deep into the architectural principles and design patterns that empower you to build scalable applications with NestJS. NestJS is an incredibly powerful framework, but wielding that power effectively requires a solid understanding of key concepts such as caching, design patterns, and asynchronous programming. If you've ever wondered how to elegantly manage global state, optimize performance, or write code that gracefully scales, this chapter will be the place to get your answers.

By the end of this chapter, you'll have a theoretical understanding of various caching strategies to boost your app's performance. You'll also become proficient in using design patterns that contribute to the scalability and maintainability of your application. However, it doesn't stop there; you'll learn why NestJS prefers certain patterns over others and how to apply asynchronous programming effectively for high-scale applications. These lessons will equip you with the skills and knowledge to build applications that not only function well but also stand the test of scalability.

In this chapter, we're going to cover the following main topics:

- Principles of scalable applications
- Caching strategies for performance optimization
- Design patterns for building scalable NestJS applications
- Understanding asynchronous programming for scalability
- Best practices for building scalable applications

Navigating these topics will provide you with a holistic approach to application architecture, ensuring that you're well-equipped to tackle the challenges of building enterprise-level, scalable applications with NestJS.

Technical requirements

The code files for the chapter can be found at `https://github.com/PacktPublishing/ Scalable-Application-Development-with-NestJS`

Principles of Scalable Application Architecture

Ever dreamed your application will become so popular that it'll be the talk of the tech world? We all have, but dreams alone don't scale. Your architecture does. So, what is this magical thing called "scalable architecture"? In technical terms, scalability is the capability of a system to handle a growing amount of work, or its potential to accommodate growth.

Your app as a growing city

Picture this: your application is a small, cozy town. It has basic amenities—a grocery store, a park, and a few houses. Now, what if this town suddenly had to accommodate an influx of newcomers? Two options are offered to you:

- **Option A**: You scramble to build more houses, but they're all over the place. Now the town is a messy labyrinth.

- **Option B**: You had a well-planned blueprint from the start. Each new addition fits neatly into its designated spot. Voilà—your small town gracefully transforms into a bustling city!

Scalable architecture is like that well-planned blueprint for your application. It ensures that as your app gains traction, it doesn't turn into a jumbled mess. Instead, it scales up smoothly, like a well-planned city:

Figure 2.1: Which city would you rather live in? Your app's architecture works the same way

The three Ss of scalability

Let's dig a bit deeper into the three Ss of scalability:

- **Speed**: Can your application handle more requests per minute as the user base grows? Nobody likes a slow app!

- **Storage**: Can it store more data without choking up? More users mean more data.

- **Simplicity**: Can you easily add new features without breaking existing ones? Your users will always want something new and shiny!

The importance of modular design – a double-edged sword

When you hear "modular design," you might think, "Ah yes, splitting my application into smaller, manageable pieces—easy!" Well, hold on a bit. While modularization is generally a good idea, it can also be a double-edged sword. Let's explore the ins and outs.

Why go modular?

First off, why even bother with modules? Here's why: they give your code structure, making it easier to manage. Modules logically separate your code base, making it easier to test, debug, and extend. Think of modules as departments in a company; each has its own set of responsibilities.

Code snippet 1

```
// In a NestJS app, creating a module for handling user
// authentication
@Module({
  imports: [],
  controllers: [AuthController],
  providers: [AuthService],
})
export class AuthModule {}
```

In the previous code snippet, we have a simple module class called AuthModule, and we are using the @Module decorator to make it a NestJS class. In the essence of modular thinking, this one will only manage the authentication logic, and the implementation part of it will depend on the business logic.

The risks – when modules go wild

Here's the kicker: having too many modules can lead to a host of problems. Imagine a company having a department for every little task; chaos would ensue! Similarly, excessive modularization can make your code harder to follow and debug, and can even impact performance. Figure 2.2 shows how we should decide to create a module or not:

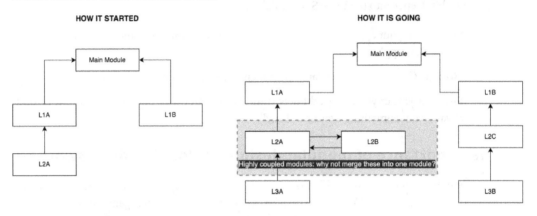

Figure 2.2: As your application scales, deciding on when to go modular
or not can help your team maintain the project easily

The decision-making process – to module or not to module

So, how do you decide when to create a module? Ask yourself the following:

- **Is the feature standalone?** — Can it function independently of other features?
- **Is it complex?** — Does it involve multiple components, providers, and so on?
- **Will it be reused?** — Is this functionality you'll need in other parts of your application or in future projects?
- **Is it a separate concern?** — Does it represent a unique area of responsibility within your application?

If you answer "yes" to most of these questions, it's a good indicator that a separate module could be beneficial.

Code snippet 2

```
// Example of when NOT to create a new module in NestJS
@Injectable()
export class LoggingService {
  log(message: string): void {
    console.log(message);
  }
}
```

In the previous code snippet, we have a simple `LoggingService` class that only prints out in the console. This service is simple and will likely be used across modules, so it might not need its own module.

> **Quick exercise**
>
> Review some of your recent Node.js applications or the last program you worked on. Identify a part of the code that you think should have been a separate module and another part that should not.

Statelessness – the cornerstone of horizontal scaling

Here is a quick question: do you remember what you ate for lunch three Wednesdays ago? No? That's okay; your server shouldn't remember stuff like that either! In the tech world, a short memory is often appreciated, especially when it comes to servers.

Why be stateless?

Let's pretend your server is like a super-efficient food truck. It serves up tasty orders (data) to people (clients) all day. However, imagine if the truck started remembering each person's previous orders, allergies, and whether they were a "no pickles" kind of person. That's a lot to juggle, right?

Being stateless means your food truck—uh, server—doesn't care who you are or what you ordered last time. You ask for a burger, it gives you a burger, end of transaction. It's this forgetfulness that makes it easy to replicate this food truck all around the city (horizontal scaling) without worrying about syncing who likes what.

Code snippet 3 follows:

```
// A simple example to bring home the point.
import { Controller, Get } from '@nestjs/common';
@Controller('stateless')
export class StatelessController {
  @Get()
  statelessEndpoint(): string {
    return 'Hello, anonymous human! Enjoy your stateless
            interaction.';
  }
}
```

In the previous code snippet, we implemented a simple stateless controller. Since this controller doesn't worry about the sender of the request, it only returns a string, no matter who made the request, and this is an example of being stateless.

Database scalability – sharding, replication, and partitioning

Databases are like the wizards behind the curtain. However, even wizards need to scale their magic, sometimes, through techniques such as sharding, replication, and partitioning, which will be discussed later in the book.

Microservices and scalability

Ever heard of the saying "divide and conquer"? That's the spirit behind microservices. Each microservice has its own role and can be scaled independently. We have a chapter dedicated especially to microservices, and we will get to discuss this useful architecture that allows us to scale applications later, in *part 4* of the book.

The social network of microservices – event-driven architecture

Picture a bustling cocktail party, where everyone's mingling and having great conversations. Now imagine if, instead of walking over to talk to someone directly, you had to announce your news loudly for everyone to hear (awkward, right?). That's the gist of event-driven architecture.

Why events over direct calls?

In traditional setups, one service might make a direct API call to another service to get something done—a bit like walking over and tapping someone on the shoulder to talk. However, what happens if that person is already deep in conversation? They can't multitask and your important message gets delayed.

Now imagine instead that you simply announce: "Hey, I've got free pizza here!" You've just emitted an "event." Anyone interested in pizza (and let's face it, who isn't?) will come over to you. You don't need to go to each person one by one; they react to the event you emitted.

Breaking it down – events and listeners

In an event-driven architecture, one part of your application triggers or emits an "event" and other parts listen for it. When they hear it, they execute some code—like a gaggle of pizza enthusiasts flocking to the snack table.

Code snippet 4

```
// Let's see this social event in action with this NestJS
// code snippet
import { Injectable } from '@nestjs/common';
```

```
import { EventEmitter2 } from '@nestjs/event-emitter';
@Injectable()
export class EventsService {
  constructor(private eventEmitter: EventEmitter2) {}
  triggerEvent(): void {
    this.eventEmitter.emit('user.created', {
      /* payload */
    });
  }
}
```

In the previous code snippet, we are using the `EventEmitter` class from `@nestjs/event-emitter` to create a simple event. This event will then be processed by a listener for further computing. In the chapter dedicated to microservices, we will learn how to process these events and make sure data stays consistent, no matter the order of events.

Figure 2.3 shows a perfect illustration of an event-driven architecture where an event can trigger a series of events and make sure the user gets the right update on the flow of the events while they are being processed:

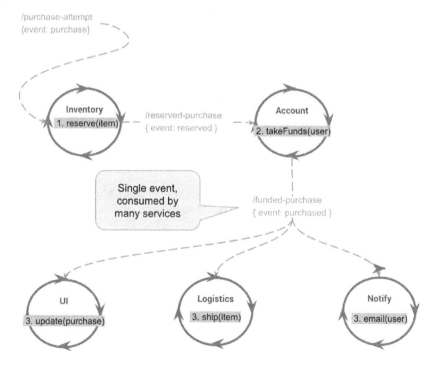

Figure 2.3: An illustration of an event-driven architecture

(copyright: `https://www.confluent.io/blog/journey-to-event-driven-part-1-why-event-first-thinking-changes-everything/`)

With an event-driven architecture, you can create a more dynamic, responsive, and scalable system, a bit like ensuring everyone at your party is well-fed and entertained without having to check in with each person individually.

Take a deep breath. We've covered a lot of ground. These principles are not only theoretical; we have shared a couple of code snippets for illustration and we will dive into more practical exercises later in this book.

In this section, we have discovered the principles of scalable architecture, including what it means to design an event-driven architecture and its importance. In the next section, we will see how to manage the growth of the application and how to deal with highly demanding processes with a load balancing mechanism.

Load balancing and horizontal scaling

Have you ever been to a concert or a big sports event? Think of those traffic cops or event staff, efficiently directing a horde of excited fans to their respective seats or exits without causing chaos. In our digital arena, that's the role of a load balancer!

Why all the hype about load balancers?

Imagine your application is hosting a grand virtual concert. Thousands of users (fans) are rushing in to get the best experience. If they all went to the same entrance (server), things would quickly get chaotic, right?

A load balancer acts like that super-efficient event staff, ensuring fans (users) are distributed to multiple entrances (servers) so that everyone gets a seamless experience. Whether it's 100 or 100,000 fans, the load balancer ensures everyone has a memorable night without crashing the party!

Balancing is an art and a science

It's not just about evenly distributing the load. A good load balancer is smart. It knows which server entrances are less crowded, which ones are closer to the fans, and sometimes even which entrances offer the quickest access to snacks (important data).

Horizontal what now?

Oh, you caught that new term, did you? "Horizontal scaling" is like clone-a-trooper for servers. Instead of making one server super buff and powerful (that's vertical scaling), you clone it. Now you have multiple servers, all equally capable of handling requests without having to know each other's business. Magic!

> **Quick exercise**
>
> All right, pop quiz time! 📝 Envision your perfect concert experience. What three qualities would you want from the event staff directing traffic? Jot them down. Now, translate those qualities to a load balancer. Did we strike the right note?

Now that we have discovered what load balancing is and its importance in a scalable architecture, let's talk about something often underrated: caching strategies. Why would someone even need it to improve their app's performance? The answer is in the next section.

Caching strategies for performance optimization

Ever walked into a room and forgotten why you're there, only to walk back and remember instantly? It's frustrating to do the same thing twice for no reason, right? Computers can also feel that way (metaphorically speaking). Caching is like the not in the notepad that helps you remember why you walked into that room.

In technical terms, caching is the process of storing copies of frequently accessed data in a "cache" so future requests can be served more quickly. With caching, you essentially save time and resources, making your application faster and more efficient.

Types of caching – knowing your tools

Just like you have different types of notepads—sticky notes, digital notes, pocket notebooks—there are different types of caches, too. Let's explore some of them:

- **In-memory caching**: Like Post-it notes on your computer screen, it's quick to write and read, but disappears when you shut down
- **Database caching**: More like a pocket notebook, this type of cache is stored in the database and is a bit more permanent
- **Content caching**: Think of this as taking a screenshot of a web page to quickly look at it later without reloading the entire thing

The ABCs of caching strategies

Remembering everything isn't helpful; you want to remember the right things. Here are the ABCs of different caching strategies:

- **Least recently used (LRU)**: If your notepad is full, you'll erase the note you haven't looked at for the longest time.
- **Time to live (TTL)**: Sticky notes with expiration dates. After a set period, they self-destruct!

- **Cache invalidation**: Sometimes, your notes become outdated or incorrect. You'll need to replace them with new, accurate information.

When caching goes wrong – pitfalls and how to avoid them

Imagine writing down your grocery list and then forgetting to update it when someone else picks up the milk. You end up with too much milk and no coffee! Caching isn't foolproof. Here are some pitfalls:

- **Cache staleness**: When the cache is outdated and serves old data
- **Cache thrashing**: When data keeps getting evicted before it's used, essentially defeating the purpose of caching
- **Cache complexity**: When you overdo it and end up with a complicated cache infrastructure that's hard to manage

> **Quick exercise – time to reflect on your cache**
>
> Take a moment to consider the last application you built. Can you identify places where implementing a cache would have improved performance? How about places where caching might introduce problems? Jot these down.

Caching in the NestJS universe

Since this book has a special focus on NestJS, let's look at a quick code snippet to implement simple caching in a NestJS app.

Code snippet 5 follows:

```
// Caching a response in a NestJS service
import {
  Injectable,
  CACHE_MANAGER,
  Inject,
  CacheStore
} from '@nestjs/common';
@Injectable()
export class AppService {
  constructor(
    @Inject(CACHE_MANAGER) private cacheManager: CacheStore
  ) {}
  async cacheThis(): Promise<string> {
    let value = await this.cacheManager.get('my-key');
    if (value) {
      return `From cache: ${value}`;
```

```
    }
    value = 'some expensive operation result';
    await this.cacheManager.set(
      'my-key',
      value,
      { ttl: 600 }
    );
    return `Processed: ${value}`;
  }
}
```

In the previous code snippet, we are caching an expensive operation in a service within a NestJS application to improve performance by reducing the need to repeatedly execute a costly process. Here's the breakdown of the rest of the code:

- **Import statements**: The code imports `Injectable`, `CACHE_MANAGER`, `Inject`, and `CacheStore` from `@nestjs/common`. These are provided by NestJS to facilitate dependency injection and caching functionality.

- **Service decoration**: The `@Injectable()` decorator marks the `AppService` class as a provider that can be managed by NestJS's dependency injection system. This allows it to be injected into controllers or other services.

- **Service class**: Export class `AppService` defines a new service class named `AppService` that will contain logic that can be shared across the application.

- **Constructor and dependency injection**: The constructor of the `AppService` class uses the `@Inject` decorator to inject the cache manager. The `CACHE_MANAGER` token is used to tell NestJS's dependency injection system to provide an instance of `CacheStore`.

- **Cache operation method**: The `Async cacheThis(): Promise<string>`: This method is an asynchronous function that promises to return a string once the operation is complete.

- Within the method, it first attempts to retrieve a value from the cache using the `my-key` key via `this.cacheManager.get('my-key')`.

- If a value is found (`if (value)`), it means the expensive operation's result is already cached. The method then returns that value prefixed with `From cache:`, indicating the response was served from the cache.

- **Caching logic**: If the cache does not have a value for `my-key`, the code proceeds to simulate an expensive operation by assigning `'some expensive operation result'` to the value.

- **Return processed value**: After caching the value, the method returns a string with a prefix of `Processed:`, indicating that the operation had to be processed and was not served from the cache.

This caching strategy can greatly improve the performance of your application by avoiding the need to perform the expensive operation every time the `cacheThis` method is called. Instead, it serves the precomputed result from the cache whenever available, thus saving time and resources.

We've covered the what, why, and how of caching, and even seen it in action with some NestJS code. Understanding caching is crucial to building scalable systems, which ties back to our discussion on the principles of scalable architecture and load balancing.

Up next, we're diving into design patterns that'll further bulletproof your NestJS applications for scale.

Design patterns for building scalable NestJS applications

Design patterns, in the realm of software development, are proven solutions to common problems. They're like architectural blueprints for building software. When it comes to the NestJS framework, certain design patterns emerge as particularly effective for ensuring scalability and maintainability. Let's delve into these patterns and the reasoning behind NestJS's architectural choices.

Why design patterns matter

Imagine constructing a building without a plan. Not only would the process be chaotic, but also, the result might be unstable. Similarly, neglecting design patterns in software can lead to messy code, unscalable systems, and a host of unforeseen issues.

In a framework such as NestJS, designed for scalability and flexibility, following recognized design patterns isn't just a recommendation—it's a cornerstone of its design philosophy.

The singleton pattern for managing global state

In essence, the singleton pattern ensures that a class has just one instance and provides a point of access to that instance from any other class.

Why NestJS prefers the singleton pattern

NestJS heavily uses the singleton pattern, particularly for services. Why? Because services often manage tasks such as database connections, caching, and configuring data—operations that you don't want multiple instances interfering with.

A quick look at the singleton pattern in NestJS

Code snippet 6

```
@Injectable()
export class MyService {
  // This service will be instantiated once and shared
  // across modules
}
```

With `@Injectable()`, NestJS ensures that the service remains a singleton across modules, promoting consistency and reducing potential data conflicts.

The factory pattern for object creation

This pattern deals with the problem of creating objects without specifying the exact class of object that will be created.

Why NestJS uses the factory pattern

In NestJS, providers aren't just limited to services. They can be anything: objects, strings, numbers, and so on. To offer this flexibility without forcing the developer to hardcode object creation, NestJS employs the factory pattern.

Code snippet 7 follows:

```
{
  provide: 'MY_FACTORY_TOKEN',
  useFactory: (connection: Connection) => {
    return new MyCustomClass(connection);
  },
  inject: [DbConnectionToken],
}
```

Here, `useFactory` is an example of the factory pattern in action, allowing dynamic object creation based on dependencies.

Dependency injection for loose coupling

Dependency injection (DI) is a technique whereby one object supplies the dependencies of another object, rather than having them constructed internally. It's pivotal to achieving inversion of control and promotes loose coupling.

Why NestJS swears by DI

NestJS's entire ecosystem revolves around DI. By embracing DI, NestJS ensures that systems are modular, testable, and scalable. Components, whether services or controllers, aren't tightly bound but interconnected through a well-defined system.

Witnessing DI in NestJS

The following code is an example of a commonly used DI in NestJS applications:

```
constructor(private myService: MyService) {}
```

Here, instead of creating an instance of `MyService` inside the component, NestJS injects it, ensuring that the component isn't directly dependent on `MyService`.

Figure 2.4 shows an illustration of loosely coupled modules all working together to accomplish a certain task:

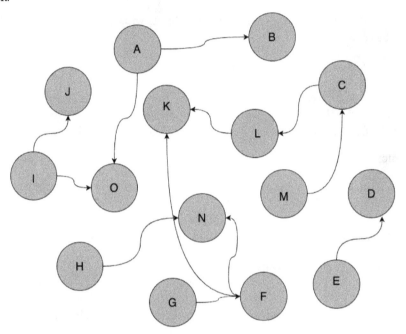

Figure 2.4: Loosely coupled modules working in synchrony

The decorator pattern for extending functionality in NestJS

In the realm of design patterns, the decorator pattern serves a unique purpose: it allows developers to add new functionalities to objects without altering their structure. This type of design pattern comes under structural patterns as it acts as a wrapper to existing classes.

Why NestJS is built on the decorator pattern

NestJS utilizes decorators to gather metadata about your classes, functions, and properties. This metadata can be utilized at runtime to do a range of tasks—whether it's setting up an HTTP route, injecting dependencies, or establishing a WebSocket gateway. Metadata reflection is a cornerstone of NestJS, and it's what powers the framework's extensibility.

Modularity and clean code

By using decorators, NestJS enables developers to write cleaner, more modular code. Decorators abstract away a lot of boilerplate, allowing developers to focus on writing business logic. This enhances readability and maintainability, making the code base more manageable as it scales.

Enhanced functionality with minimal intrusion

Decorators in NestJS add layers of functionality to your code without requiring you to alter the core logic. For instance, the `@Roles()` decorator can quickly add role-based access control to a method without requiring you to modify the method's implementation. The non-intrusive nature of decorators makes them ideal for scalable applications.

Strongly typed system

The use of decorators often goes hand-in-hand with TypeScript's type checking, enhancing development-time type safety. For example, the `@Body()` decorator not only extracts properties from the request body but can also enforce type constraints if used in conjunction with **data transfer object (DTO)** classes.

NestJS decorators in action

In a RESTful API, the `@Controller` and `@Get/@Post/@Put/@Delete` decorators set up routes, transforming classes and methods into request handlers almost magically.

Code snippet 8 follows:

```
@Controller('cats')
export class CatsController {
  @Get()
  findAll() {
    return 'Returns all cats';
  }
}
```

This simple code snippet shows an example of a controller that is handling a GET request; thanks to the `@Get` decorator, there is no need to specify which metadata is supposed to be part of the request, since the function already knows.

Request payload extraction

Decoratorsrequesting" such as `@Query`, `@Param`, and `@Body` streamline the process of extracting parameters, query strings, and request bodies, making the controller methods cleaner and more focused.

Code snippet 9

```
@Get('find')
findCat(@Query('name') name: string) {
  return `Returns cat with name ${name}`;
}
```

Custom decorators

NestJS also allows for the creation of custom decorators, offering endless extensibility options. For instance, you could create a @Sanitize decorator that automatically cleanses incoming data to prevent **Structured Query Language (SQL)** injection attacks.

Code snippet 10

```
export const Sanitize = createParamDecorator(
  (data, req) => {
    return sanitize(req.body); // fictional sanitize
                               // function
  },
);
```

DI

With @Injectable, @Inject, and custom provider decorators, NestJS turns DI into a sleek, painless process.

Code snippet 11

```
@Injectable()
export class CatsService {
  constructor(
    @Inject('DATABASE_CONNECTION')
    private dbConnection: Connection
  ) {}
}
```

NestJS without decorators versus with decorators

Here, we'll observe how things would look in a hypothetical NestJS world without decorators and compare it to how decorators simplify the development process.

Routing and controllers

In a world without decorators, setting up a simple route might involve a less elegant configuration, using direct method calls and manual route mapping.

Code snippet 12

```
export class CatsController {
  constructor(
    private readonly expressApp: Express.Application
  ) {
    this.expressApp.get('/cats', this.findAll.bind(this));
  }
  findAll(req: Request, res: Response) {
    res.send('Returns all cats');
  }
}
```

Using decorators, the process is streamlined, enhancing code readability, like the one shown in the code snippet 13 below

Code snippet 13

```
@Controller('cats')
export class CatsController {
  @Get()
  findAll() {
    return 'Returns all cats';
}}
```

Request payload extraction

Without requesting" decorators, you'd need to manually extract request parameters, which can be cumbersome.

Code snippet 14

```
export class CatsController {
  constructor(
    private readonly expressApp: Express.Application
  ) {
  this.expressApp.get('/find', this.findCat.bind(this));
  }
  findCat(req: Request, res: Response) {
    const name = req.query.name;
    res.send(`Returns cat with name ${name}`);
  }
}
```

Now with a decorator such as @Query, we simplify the parameter extraction process, as shown in the code snippet 15 below.

Code snippet 15

```
@Get('find')
findCat(@Query('name') name: string) {
   return `Returns cat with name ${name}`;
}
```

DI

Handling dependencies manually without decorators could look cumbersome and would require extra bootstrap code.

Code snippet 16 follows:

```
export class CatsService {
   private dbConnection: Connection;
   constructor() {
      // some singleton pattern
      this.dbConnection = DatabaseConnection.getInstance();
   }
}
```

With decorators

By using @Injectable and @Inject, DI becomes sleek and painless.

Code snippet 17

```
@Injectable()
export class CatsService {
   constructor(
      @Inject('DATABASE_CONNECTION')
      private dbConnection: Connection
   ) {}
}
```

Why decorators make NestJS outstanding

The extensive use of decorators in NestJS is not a mere design choice, but a calculated decision for facilitating development across various domains—whether it's web, mobile, or desktop applications. Decorators offer a harmonious blend of elegance, functionality, and extensibility, making NestJS a robust framework for building scalable, maintainable, and enterprise-grade applications.

By using the decorator pattern, NestJS allows developers to focus on what truly matters: solving complex problems without worrying about the plumbing. It provides a layer of abstraction that enriches development, from initial setup to large-scale feature implementation.

In conclusion, design patterns are the backbone of any well-structured application, and NestJS champions this philosophy. By understanding and leveraging these patterns, developers can harness the true power of NestJS, ensuring scalable, maintainable, and efficient applications.

In our upcoming sections, we will dive deeper into asynchronous programming, which is another cornerstone of building scalable systems, especially in a Node.js environment such as NestJS.

Understanding asynchronous programming for scalability

Asynchronous programming might sound like a complex term straight out of a computer science textbook, but understanding it is crucial for building scalable applications, particularly in a JavaScript-based framework such as NestJS. As the famous saying goes, "Scalability is to performance what agile is to development." Let's demystify this concept and discuss why embracing asynchronous programming can be a game-changer for your NestJS applications.

What is asynchronous programming?

In the simplest terms, asynchronous programming allows multiple operations to execute concurrently but not necessarily at the same instant. In a synchronous model, operations are performed one after the other, blocking subsequent actions until the current one is completed. Asynchronous programming, on the other hand, allows operations such as I/O-bound tasks to be offloaded, freeing up the main thread to handle other tasks.

Why asynchrony is important for scalability

In a server-side application, you can't afford to have idle resources while waiting for database queries, API calls, or other I/O-bound operations to complete. Asynchrony ensures that your resources are used optimally.

Improved user experience

Users don't like to wait. Asynchronous programming ensures that your application remains responsive even when it's performing tasks that take time. This responsiveness directly translates into a better user experience.

Easier to scale

Applications that make effective use of asynchronous programming are generally easier to scale horizontally. By efficiently using the available resources, you can handle more users without adding more hardware.

Asynchronous programming in NestJS

NestJS, being built on top of Node.js, naturally supports asynchronous patterns. Let's take a look at how NestJS leverages this power.

Using Promises and async/await

NestJS promotes the use of Promises and the async/await syntax for handling asynchronous operations elegantly. For example, let's say you have a service that fetches user data from a database. Code snippet 18 shows how the implementation should look without the `async/await` syntax.

Code snippet 18

```
getUserById(id: string) {
  return this.database
    .query(`SELECT * FROM users WHERE id = ${id}`)
    .then(user => user)
    .catch(err => {
      throw new Error(err);
    });
}
```

Now using the `async/await` syntax, we get the version shown in the code snippet 19 below.

Code snippet 19

```
async getUserById(id: string) {
  try {
    const user = await this.database.query(
      `SELECT * FROM users WHERE id = ${id}`
    );
    return user;
  } catch (err) {
    throw new Error(err);
  }
}
```

The `async/await` version is not only more readable but also easier to reason about and debug.

Event loop and non-blocking I/O

NestJS capitalizes on Node.js's event-driven architecture, which is inherently non-blocking and well-suited to scalable applications. The event loop handles all asynchronous tasks and ensures smooth execution.

Reactive programming with RxJS

NestJS also integrates seamlessly with RxJS, a library for reactive programming that makes it easier to compose asynchronous or callback-based code. This further adds to the capabilities of building scalable, reactive services.

In conclusion, asynchronous programming isn't just a feature; it's a foundational element for building scalable applications. NestJS leverages asynchronous programming to its fullest extent, providing developers with the tools they need to build applications that are both scalable and performant.

Understanding and employing asynchronous programming practices in NestJS will set you on the path to creating applications that are responsive, efficient, and ready to grow.

So, the next time you find yourself contemplating the scalability of your NestJS application, remember that understanding and utilizing asynchronous programming is like equipping your application with a turbocharger. It's all about getting more done, faster and more efficiently.

In the next section, we will bring it all together and discuss best practices for thinking about scalable applications.

Best practices for building scalable applications

As we approach the end of this chapter, it's time to bring everything together. You've explored the architecture and design patterns, and even delved into the nitty-gritty of asynchronous programming in NestJS. However, knowing all these individual components is like having all the ingredients for a gourmet dish—you still need the recipe. So, let's get down to the actionable best practices that will serve as your blueprint for building scalable applications in NestJS.

Code organization is key

Consider the following good practices for a better code organization:

- **Modular design**: Split your application into well-defined modules. NestJS makes this easy with its module system. Keeping related functionalities together simplifies both development and scaling.

- **Clean code**: The importance of writing clean, maintainable code cannot be overstated. Stick to conventions, be consistent in naming, and above all, make your code self-explanatory.

Optimizing data storage and retrieval

When dealing with a large dataset, consider including the following features:

- **Database indexing**: Ensure your databases are properly indexed. Indexing speeds up the data retrieval process, thereby making your application faster and more scalable.

- **Caching**: As discussed earlier, caching is essential for performance optimization. Utilize caching strategies to serve frequently accessed data, significantly reducing database load.

Embracing microservices for decoupling

Microservices architecture isn't just a buzz phrase; it's a best practice for large-scale applications. By decoupling various parts of your application, microservices allow individual components to scale independently.

Automating testing and deployment

Consider adding the following capabilities to your future applications:

- **Continuous integration**: Setting up a **continuous integration/continuous delivery (CI/CD)** pipeline automates the testing and deployment processes, ensuring that your application is always in a deployable state.

- **Automated testing**: Invest in automated testing. It not only improves the quality of your code but also makes sure that scaling doesn't introduce new bugs.

Making use of middleware and interceptors

Middleware and interceptors in NestJS act as the perfect control points for logging, measuring, or modifying requests and responses, which are often crucial activities when scaling an application.

Don't neglect security

Among various security considerations, here are the most common to consider:

- **Rate limiting**: Protect your application from abuse by implementing rate limiting on your APIs.

- **Validation and sanitization**: Always validate and sanitize data. An application that is secure is easier to scale since you don't have to constantly put out security fires.

Leveraging load balancing

As you learned earlier, load balancing effectively distributes incoming network traffic across multiple servers. This ensures high availability and reliability, making your application inherently more scalable.

Using application metrics for insights

Consider the following metrics to get useful insights on your application's state:

- **Logging and monitoring**: Keep an eye on your application metrics. Tools such as Grafana and Prometheus can give you insights that are crucial for scaling.

- **Performance metrics**: Response times, error rates, and other **key performance indicators (KPIs)** should be monitored to understand how well your application is scaling.

Summary

Scalability isn't a standalone feature or a checkbox item; it's a complex interplay of best practices, design patterns, and architectural choices. These elements must work in harmony to create a scalable application.

And there you have it—the cornerstone practices that transform your theoretical understanding of scalability into actionable insights in the context of NestJS. You're now more than just a follower of industry trends; you're equipped with the conceptual toolkit that sets the foundation for building truly scalable applications. These aren't just best practices; they're your North Star in the sometimes foggy landscape of application development.

However, understanding is only the first step; implementation is the key. Are you ready to get your hands dirty with some real code? Brace yourself, because our next chapter, will take you from zero to hero in actually applying these best practices. We will set up your development environment and dive straight into constructing a robust, high-performance application with NestJS.

So, keep your **Integrated Development Environment (IDE)** ready and your thinking cap on; you're about to translate the abstract best practices into concrete actions. The next chapter promises to be a hands-on deep dive into the practical side of things. Let's keep the momentum going and start building that marvel of an application you're now more than prepared to develop.

3

Setting Up Your NestJS Environment and Exploring NestJS – Building a Robust App

NestJS is a standout framework for building scalable and maintainable server-side applications. This chapter provides a comprehensive guide to help you unleash its full potential.

To set the foundation, we'll initiate the installation of Node.js and NestJS, including the necessary **command-line interface (CLI)** tools. This ensures you have all you need to begin your development journey. Subsequently, we'll configure essential tools such as npm and TypeScript, smoothing out your development process.

With your environment ready, we'll introduce you to the structure of a NestJS project, giving you the confidence to explore and understand its components. The journey continues with practical insights into creating and managing modules, controllers, and providers. Discover how to gracefully handle exceptions using filters and maintain data integrity through validation with pipes and guards.

By the chapter's end, you'll possess a suite of essential skills: setting up a NestJS environment, organizing your application effectively, and crafting applications ready to meet real-world challenges. These capabilities not only elevate your server-side application prowess but also set the stage for best practices in subsequent chapters.

Key topics in this chapter include the following:

- Installing Node.js and NestJS
- Scaffolding a new NestJS project
- Understanding the NestJS project structure
- Creating and managing modules
- Building controllers to handle requests

- Implementing providers for business logic
- Gracefully handling exceptions with filters
- Data validation using pipes and guards

Prepare to equip yourself with the tools and knowledge for building robust, scalable, and maintainable NestJS applications. Let's get started!

Technical requirements

The code files for the chapter can be found at `https://github.com/PacktPublishing/Scalable-Application-Development-with-NestJS`

Installing Node.js and NestJS

To commence your NestJS journey, it's imperative to set up your development environment accurately. In this section, we'll guide you through installing both Node.js and NestJS—the bedrock of robust server-side applications.

Node.js serves as the runtime environment that enables JavaScript execution on the server. NestJS complements it by simplifying the process of architecting scalable Node.js applications. Together, they're an unmatched pair in the realm of modern web development.

Here's a breakdown of the installation.

Step 1 – Install Node.js

For those already equipped with Node.js (version 16 or higher), feel free to skip ahead. If not, let's gear up:

1. **Download Node.js**: Navigate to the official Node.js website (`https://nodejs.org/`) and secure the **Long-Term Support** (**LTS**) version tailored to your OS.

2. **Run the installer**: Launch the downloaded installer, following its prompts. This not only installs Node.js but also npm by default.

3. **Verify installation**: Confirm Node.js and npm installations by unveiling their versions via your terminal:

```
$ node -v
$ npm -v
```

Step 2 – Install the NestJS CLI

To install the NestJS CLI before getting started, you need to follow these simple steps:

1. **Install NestJS CLI**: With Node.js in place, install the NestJS CLI system-wide. This CLI offers robust tools for NestJS applications:

    ```
    $ npm install -g @nestjs/cli
    ```

2. **Verify installation**: Ascertain the CLI's installation by revealing its version:

    ```
    $ nest --version
    # or use
    $ nest info
    ```

Bravo! You've laid the groundwork with the Node.js and NestJS CLI installations. The framework offers a runtime environment, while the latter presents vital tools for sculpting NestJS apps.

Up next, we'll refine your development space by configuring npm and TypeScript, fortifying it for NestJS development. Your server-side application development is about to receive a boost!

Scaffolding a new NestJS project

Now that you have Node.js, npm, and nest-cli ready to go, it's time to create your first NestJS project. NestJS provides a convenient command-line tool to scaffold a new project with all the necessary boilerplate. In this section, we'll walk through the process of creating a new NestJS application, step by step.

> **Important note**
> TypeScript is automatically included when you initialize a NestJS project, so there's no need to configure it separately.

Creating a new NestJS project

With Node.js, npm, and nest-cli primed and waiting, the stars have aligned for you to embark on creating your maiden NestJS project. NestJS rolls out the red carpet with a user-friendly command-line tool, ensuring your project gets off the ground without a hitch. Together, we'll navigate this process, making sure every move is clear and precise.

> **Quick byte**
> NestJS already packs TypeScript under its hood when you kickstart a project. That's one less thing to worry about!

The birth of a NestJS project

Now, let's create our first project using the following simple steps.

Step 1 – Set the stage

From your desired terminal, navigate to the folder where you need to put your NestJS project. Let's say I want the project to be under Documents/nestjs.

Step 2 – Command your creation into existence

Invoke the NestJS CLI's power with the following command. Replace my-nest-app with a name that resonates with your vision:

```
$ nest new my-nest-app
```

As the command runs, the NestJS CLI will prompt you with a couple of choices: package manager preference and a starter app's inclusion. For this odyssey, we're siding with yarn and embracing the sample app.

Figure 3.1 shows how the terminal should look when initializing a new NestJS project:

```
⚡  We will scaffold your app in a few seconds..

? Which package manager would you 💜 to use? yarn
CREATE my-nest-app/.eslintrc.js (663 bytes)
CREATE my-nest-app/.prettierrc (51 bytes)
CREATE my-nest-app/README.md (3347 bytes)
CREATE my-nest-app/nest-cli.json (171 bytes)
CREATE my-nest-app/package.json (1952 bytes)
CREATE my-nest-app/tsconfig.build.json (97 bytes)
CREATE my-nest-app/tsconfig.json (546 bytes)
CREATE my-nest-app/src/app.controller.spec.ts (617 bytes)
CREATE my-nest-app/src/app.controller.ts (274 bytes)
CREATE my-nest-app/src/app.module.ts (249 bytes)
CREATE my-nest-app/src/app.service.ts (142 bytes)
CREATE my-nest-app/src/main.ts (208 bytes)
CREATE my-nest-app/test/app.e2e-spec.ts (630 bytes)
CREATE my-nest-app/test/jest-e2e.json (183 bytes)

✓ Installation in progress... 🍵

🚀  Successfully created project my-nest-app
👉  Get started with the following commands:

$ cd my-nest-app
$ yarn run start


                    Thanks for installing Nest 🦁
        Please consider donating to our open collective
                to help us maintain this package.


              🍷  Donate: https://opencollective.com/nest
```

Figure 3.1: Your terminal after initializing a new NestJS project

Step 3 – Dive into the labyrinth of your project

The scaffolding ritual is complete. Now, journey into the heart of your project:

```
$ cd my-nest-app
# Pop open your favorite IDE to behold the structured elegance NestJS
offers.
```

Figure 3.2 shows approximately how the project structure should look:

Figure 3.2: The new NestJS project structure

Allow me to be your guide as we tour this digital realm:

- **src/**: The epicenter that houses your application's soul—this consists of modules, controllers, providers, and more, all aligned with the TypeScript philosophy

- **dist/**: The fruits of your labor—transpiled JavaScript files rest here once you command your app to face the world

- **node_modules/**: The toolbox—every cog, wheel, and screw (read: dependencies) that makes your project tick is here

- **test/**: Your proving grounds—tests that ensure your app's might and resilience find their home here

- **tsconfig.json & nest-cli.json:** The rulebooks—these are configuration blueprints for TypeScript and the NestJS CLI, respectively

Step 4 – Ignite your sample application

Before we move forward, let's see what the application we just created looks like when we start it, using the following command from the project root directory:

```
$ npm run start:dev
```

Observe as your NestJS application initializes on the assigned port, typically port 3000 by default. Let your browser be the window to this new world at `http://localhost:3000`. Revel in the warm welcome your sample app extends. This makes a simple GET request to the API you just created.

Figure 3.3 shows how your terminal should look when running the `start:dev` script:

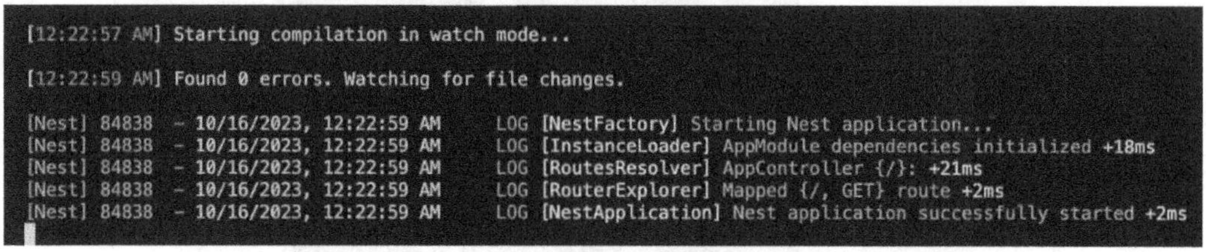

```
[12:22:57 AM] Starting compilation in watch mode...

[12:22:59 AM] Found 0 errors. Watching for file changes.

[Nest] 84838  - 10/16/2023, 12:22:59 AM     LOG [NestFactory] Starting Nest application...
[Nest] 84838  - 10/16/2023, 12:22:59 AM     LOG [InstanceLoader] AppModule dependencies initialized +18ms
[Nest] 84838  - 10/16/2023, 12:22:59 AM     LOG [RoutesResolver] AppController {/}: +21ms
[Nest] 84838  - 10/16/2023, 12:22:59 AM     LOG [RouterExplorer] Mapped {/, GET} route +2ms
[Nest] 84838  - 10/16/2023, 12:22:59 AM     LOG [NestApplication] Nest application successfully started +2ms
```

Figure 3.3: Your terminal when starting the server – beautiful, right? :)

Figure 3.4 shows the request to the API from the web browser:

Hello World!

Figure 3.4: NestJS says hi

Victory! 🎉 You've not only scaffolded but also breathed life into a brand-new NestJS project. The horizon is filled with adventures—modules, controllers, providers, and best practices that'll mold your project into a beacon of excellence.

We've just embarked on our NestJS journey by successfully scaffolding a new project, familiarizing ourselves with its initial setup, and running our sample application. With this foundational step complete, we're poised to dive deeper.

Up next, let's unravel the intricacies of the NestJS project structure and truly understand the backbone of our application.

Understanding the NestJS project structure

Stepping into the heart of NestJS, one immediately recognizes its unique blend of elegance and purpose-driven design. Every directory and every file has a place and a purpose. Understanding the NestJS project structure is paramount, not just for the sake of navigation but also to truly grasp its philosophy.

Why is NestJS's project structure important?

NestJS takes inspiration from mature languages and tools, aligning closely with Angular's modular design (https://angular.io/guide/feature-modules). This approach aims to keep your code base maintainable, scalable, and organized, allowing developers—both novices and experts—to easily locate files and understand the flow and relationships within the application.

Refer to *Figure 3.2* to get an overview of how the project is structured by default. As the application grows, the structure may evolve, but keep in mind that the role of each directory will make our lives easier:

The src/ directory

Arguably the most accessed directory, `src/` is where the magic happens. Herein reside your modules, controllers, providers, and the core logic of your application:

- **Modules**: These encapsulate specific application domains, fostering clean separation of concerns. Think of them as distinct sections of your app that can operate independently but are part of the whole. All the modules' entry points should be named like `*.module.ts` by convention; this will help in terms of maintenance and code readability.

- **Controllers**: These handle incoming HTTP requests and route them to their corresponding service functions. All the controller files should be named like `*.controller.ts` by convention.

- **Providers**: These represent a combination of services, repositories, factories, and more. They perform the actual business logic, keeping controllers slim and focused.

Currently, our app has a unique module (the app module) and its entry point is `app.module.ts`. In a real-world application, we will most likely have more than one module. Keeping it all in a single folder (`src/` as it is by default) can make our `src/` folder hard to maintain. It's recommended to create more sub-folders under `src/` and maintain each module separately. *Figure 3.6* shows an example of a `src/` folder with a bunch of modules versus another one with a well-organized structure. Remember, NestJS only gives us direction, but the way we organize it will mostly be in our hands.

Figure 3.5 shows the current `src/` folder created by nest-cli when we initialized the project:

Figure 3.5: The initial src/ folder

When our project grows, NestJS gives us the flexibility to structure the `src/` folder. However, to stay in the philosophy of NestJS and follow its native structure, we can use the CLI to generate resources for the app so NestJS takes care of putting those components in the right place.

Figure 3.6 shows two different project structures. The first one shows only mixed modules and their components together within the same `src/` folder, while the second one separates concerns in grouping components together, using the NestJS CLI. We may end up having the second structure and you can clearly see how easy it can be to maintain the second one instead of the first one:

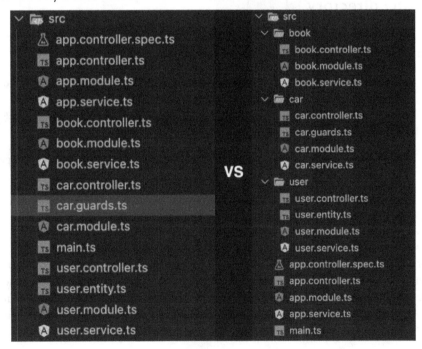

Figure 3.6: Separating modules into different folders under the src/
folder makes our code structure more readable

Additionally, and so importantly, in the `src/` folder, we have our main entry point into the app, which is the `main.ts` file. Currently, here is what the file looks like:

```
import { NestFactory } from '@nestjs/core';
import { AppModule } from './app.module';

async function bootstrap() {
  const app = await NestFactory.create(AppModule);
  await app.listen(3000);
}
bootstrap();
```

This is simply a JavaScript function that we run, allowing us to set a port. When we get to specific case studies, we will see when, why, and how we can improve this initial file to match a certain project's requirements.

The dist/ directory

Every time you prepare your application for deployment or whenever you start your project, the TypeScript code gets transpiled into JavaScript, and the results are stored in the `dist/` directory. This is the version of your application that will be run, and we will probably never touch or maintain it since the folder gets generated on runtime. The folder will usually be ignored by Git since it's useless to have it pushed to any environment.

The node_modules/ directory

A common sight in Node.js projects, `node_modules/` is where all your project's dependencies reside. Each package you install via npm or yarn has its own spot in this directory.

The test/ directory

True to NestJS's philosophy of building robust applications, the `test/` directory is where your unit and **End-to-End (e2e)** tests live. It's a testament to the framework's commitment to quality and reliability.

Each business logic file under the `src/` folder (such as the service files, controller, etc.) can have its own testing files nested into it. For unit tests and integration tests, we have a full chapter on testing, and we will explain this in detail when we get to *Chapter 7*.

Configuration files – tsconfig.json and nest-cli.json

Every application requires a bit of configuration. The `tsconfig.json` file caters to TypeScript's needs, defining rules and specifics for the transpiration process. On the other hand, `nest-cli.json` provides configuration for the NestJS CLI, fine-tuning how the CLI behaves and interacts with your project.

By appreciating the thought process behind NestJS's directory structure, you align yourself with its ideology. A well-structured project is akin to a well-organized library: each book has its place, and finding what you need becomes a seamless task. With this understanding, you're not just coding; you're crafting art that aligns with NestJS's philosophy.

As we venture further, remember that every part of NestJS is purposefully designed, echoing its commitment to developer productivity and application maintainability. Ready to delve deeper? Let's move on and explore the intricacies of creating modules, building controllers, and implementing providers.

Creating and managing modules

NestJS thrives on its modular architecture. If you've ever marveled at a well-constructed building with each room having a distinct purpose, that's the beauty NestJS brings to the world of backend development. This chapter aims to make you the master architect of your NestJS applications, so let's delve deep into the art and science of modules.

What are modules in NestJS?

At its core, a module is a class adorned with the `@Module()` decorator. Just like rooms in a building, modules encapsulate distinct features of your application, ensuring a clean separation of concerns. They play a pivotal role in maintaining organization, scalability, and readability, making it easier to add, modify, or remove features as your application evolves.

The role of the root module

Among all the modules, there's one that stands out—the root module. Think of it as the main entrance of a building. The root module is where the application begins its journey, pulling in other modules and setting the stage for the entire application. Its importance cannot be understated; it's where modules, middleware, and even third-party modules get registered, orchestrating the entire app.

Figure 3.7 shows how modules are structured around the root module (application module) and is taken from NestJS's official documentation (`https://docs.nestjs.com/`):

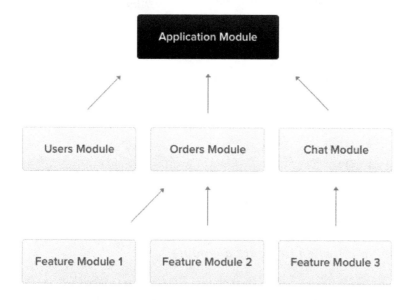

Figure 3.7: Module organization across a NestJS application

Creating a new module

NestJS architecture gives you the ability to create your modules as you want. You can either decide to generate modules using the CLI or manually create them. Letting the CLI create them for you will come with a couple of benefits, such as placing the module in the right place, or importing it automatically in the root module, resulting in connecting your new module to the whole application. The following explains how you can use both methods.

Using the NestJS CLI

The CLI, being a Swiss Army knife for NestJS developers, provides a convenient command to generate a new module:

```
$ nest generate module <module-name>
```

In shorthand, it is as follows:

```
$ nest g mo <module-name>
```

This command not only creates a new module file but also automatically registers it in the nearest parent module (or app module).

Manually creating a module

For those who enjoy manual craftsmanship, see the following:

1. Create a new file named `<module-name>.module.ts`.

2. Populate it with the basic structure:

    ```
    import { Module } from '@nestjs/common';

    @Module({
      imports: [],
      controllers: [],
      providers: [],
    })
    export class <ModuleName>Module {}
    ```

3. Import and register the module in your desired parent module (or the root module).

Decision time – when to create a module

A common question that arises is when one should carve out a new module. The answer lies in the **single responsibility principle** (**SRP**). If a feature or domain has a distinct responsibility that can operate independently or be thought of as a standalone unit, it's a prime candidate for a new module. Think user management, payments, or notifications—each of these can be a module. We discussed a lot about modular design in the first chapter, so don't hesitate to go back to that chapter if a refresh is needed.

Quiz time

To the following questions, write down corresponding answers:

*   What does the root module orchestrate in a NestJS application?

*   What's the primary command to create a module using the NestJS CLI?

*   When is it ideal to consider creating a new module?

> **Important note**
> Always remember that modules are not just for separation; they help in creating reusable chunks. A well-defined module can be easily imported into another module or even other NestJS projects.

Managing modules

Modules, once created, often need to interact. Whether you're sharing a service between two modules or setting up routes, managing the relationships between modules is crucial. Here are the `@Module` decorator's properties that help us manage the relationship between modules:

- **Imports**: In the `@Module()` decorator, the `imports` array lets one module use the exported providers of another module.

- **Exports**: To make providers, guards, or filters available for other modules, use the `exports` array in the `@Module()` decorator.

- **Controllers and providers**: Controllers define routes and handle incoming requests, while providers encapsulate the logic. They're declared in the `controllers` and `providers` arrays, respectively.

In the initial NestJS project, we have an example of interaction between modules even if we have a single module. See what we have in the `app.module.ts` file:

```
import { Module } from '@nestjs/common';
import { AppController } from './app.controller';
import { AppService } from './app.service';

@Module({
  imports: [],
  controllers: [AppController],
  providers: [AppService],
})
export class AppModule {}
```

As this code suggests, the app module works itself for now and doesn't have any module imported. The imports array will certainly become bigger as we point more modules to the root module.

Modules form the architectural backbone of a NestJS application. With a clear understanding of their creation and management, you're well on your way to mastering NestJS's ideology. As we construct our application, always keep in mind the modular nature of NestJS. It ensures clarity, maintainability, and scalability.

Ready for the next level? Let's dive deeper into controllers and their fascinating world.

Building controllers for handling requests

Every web application has a front door, a place where guests (or, in our case, client requests) are greeted and directed to the right location. In the grand mansion of our NestJS application, controllers are the door attendants, ensuring every request is handled efficiently and directed to the right service. If you're eager to design these crucial gatekeepers, you're in the right place. Buckle up, because we're about to delve deep into the realm of controllers!

What is a controller in NestJS?

Controllers in NestJS are responsible for taking incoming requests, handling them, and returning responses to the client. They're typically adorned with the `@Controller()` decorator and contain handler methods for different routes.

Crafting your first controller

Creating a controller is a breeze, especially if you've mastered modules already! You can either generate it with the CLI or manually, as we did for the module. Here is how.

Using the NestJS CLI

Just like with modules, the CLI is here to simplify our lives:

```
$ nest generate controller <controller-name>
```

For the shortcut lovers, see the following:

```
$ nest g co <controller-name>
```

This command crafts a new controller file and registers it in the associated module. Additionally, it generates a test file alongside the controller file by default. Optionally, if you don't want to create the test file, you can pass the `--no-spec` flag to the command.

Manually building a controller

If you're a hands-on developer, see the following:

1. Create a new file named `<controller-name>.controller.ts`.
2. Frame it with the basic structure:

```
import { Controller, Get } from '@nestjs/common';

@Controller('<route-name>')
export class <ControllerName>Controller {
  @Get()
```

```
    findAll(): string {
      return 'This is a sample response!';
    }
  }
```

This is a basic controller that shows how a minimal NestJS controller should look.

3. Then, import and register the controller in the respective module.

Handling requests with decorators

NestJS provides a myriad of decorators to make handling different request types a piece of cake:

- @Get(): This is for handling GET requests.

- @Post(): Eager to receive POST requests? This is your go-to.

- @Put(): This is ideal for updating resources.

- @Delete(): When something needs to go, use this.

Not only can you specify the request type, but also the route, passing a string as a parameter as in the following code snippet:

```
@Get('details')
fetchDetails(): string {
  return 'Fetching the details for you!';
}
```

> **Important note**
> Each handler method in a controller corresponds to a specific route and its purpose should be singular and clear. Adhering to this ensures scalability and maintainability.

Quiz time

To the following questions, write down the corresponding answers:

- What's the primary role of controllers in a NestJS application?

- Which decorator is used to handle DELETE requests?

- How do you specify a particular route for a handler method?

Dynamic routes and parameters

Sometimes, you'll want to design routes that are dynamic, such as when fetching the details of a user based on their ID. NestJS has got you covered—here is how:

```
@Get('users/:userId')
fetchUserDetails(@Param('userId') userId: string): string {
   return `Details for user with ID: ${userId}`;
}
```

The @Param() decorator grabs the dynamic part of the route, making it available within your handler method.

As you sculpt your NestJS application, remember that controllers are the frontline soldiers, greeting every request and ensuring they're catered to. With a robust set of controllers, you're setting the foundation for a resilient, scalable, and efficient application.

Now that our gates are well-guarded, it's time to explore the majestic halls within—the services and providers that do the heavy lifting!

Implementing providers for business logic

Picture a bustling kitchen in a grand mansion. While the controllers are the door attendants who greet the guests, providers are the skilled chefs behind the scenes, meticulously preparing every dish with finesse and expertise. In the context of our NestJS mansion, providers encapsulate the core business logic, ensuring our app not only looks good on the outside but also functions seamlessly on the inside. Ready to don your chef's hat and whip up some stellar business logic? Let's dive in!

What is a provider in NestJS?

At its core, a provider in NestJS is a class that acts as a source of something—whether it's how to obtain data, run specific tasks, or perform any other action that's integral to your application. Decorated with the @Injectable() decorator, providers are cornerstones of NestJS's powerful dependency injection system.

Crafting your first provider

The birth of a provider in NestJS is an affair both elegant and straightforward. As the controller and the module, NestJS gives you two ways of creating your amazing providers.

Using the NestJS CLI

For those who love automation, see the following:

```
$ nest generate service <service-name>
```

The shorthand is as follows:

```
$ nest g s <service-name>
```

This command whips up a new service file that's ready to house your business logic.

Manually building a provider

For the artisans who prefer manual craftsmanship, see the following:

1. Create a fresh file named `<service-name>.service.ts`.

2. Sketch out the foundational structure:

```
import { Injectable } from '@nestjs/common';

@Injectable()
export class <ServiceName>Service {
  performTask(): string {
    return 'Executing the core task!';
  }
}
```

3. Make sure to import and register the service within its associated module.

We have created our custom module, controller, and providers. Basically, these three pieces will most likely be the *must-have* for your NestJS application.

Now, let's dive a little bit deeper into the design pattern that makes NestJS so robust: dependency injection.

Dependency injection – the magic behind providers

One of NestJS's strongest suits is its robust **dependency injection** (**DI**) system. With DI, you can easily inject one provider into another, fostering modular and maintainable code. It's like having a sous-chef ready to assist whenever needed!

For instance, if `UserService` needs the capabilities of `DatabaseService`, here is how you can make it happen:

```
import { Injectable } from '@nestjs/common';
import { DatabaseService } from './database.service';
```

```
@Injectable()
export class UserService {
  constructor(
    private readonly databaseService: DatabaseService
  ) {}

  fetchUserData(): string {
    return this.databaseService.getData('user');
  }
}
```

In the previous code example, we have injected the capabilities of databaseService into the UserService class. This dependency needs to be injected into the constructor class, making sure that the instance of the database will be available from the UserService initiation, everywhere we have a UserService instance.

> **Important note**
>
> Always remember the tenet of single responsibility. Each provider should manage a singular, distinct functionality. This ensures clarity and ease of maintenance.

Quiz time

To the following questions, write down corresponding answers:

- How do you mark a class as a provider in NestJS?
- What is the primary role of the @Injectable() decorator?
- How do you inject one provider into another?

Custom providers – beyond classes

While classes are the most common providers, NestJS isn't limited to them. With custom providers, you can also employ values, factories, and more as providers. They provide added flexibility in managing your application's dependencies.

With adept providers in place, our NestJS mansion's kitchen is buzzing with activity, churning out delicious dishes (or, in our case, executing flawless business logic). However, a mansion is not complete with just a kitchen. As we progress, we'll venture into more chambers, each vital to crafting a holistic and efficient NestJS application. Next stop? Middleware and interceptors!

Handling exceptions with exception filters

Imagine you're a skilled juggler, gracefully managing multiple tasks. However, occasionally, a ball might drop. It's in those moments that we require a safety net. Within our NestJS realm, **exception filters** serve as that very safety net, gracefully catching any unforeseen issues. In *Chapter 4*, we will discuss advanced concepts of NestJS, including exceptions, with real examples.

What are exception filters?

Exception filters give you control over exceptions thrown by your application. By extending the `ExceptionFilter` base class, you can define custom responses for when things go awry.

Crafting a basic exception filter

Let's briefly see how this works with the following example:

```
import {
  Catch,
  ArgumentsHost,
  HttpException,
  ExceptionFilter
} from '@nestjs/common';
import { Response } from 'express';

@Catch(HttpException)
export class HttpExceptionFilter implements ExceptionFilter {
  catch(exception: HttpException, host: ArgumentsHost) {
    const ctx = host.switchToHttp();
    const response = ctx.getResponse<Response>();

    response.status(exception.getStatus()).json({
      message: exception.message,
      timestamp: new Date().toISOString(),
    });
  }
}
```

Let's break this code down and see how it works:

- `Imports`:

  - We're importing `Catch`, `ArgumentsHost`, and `HttpException` from `@nestjs/common`.

  - The `Response` object is taken from `express`, which NestJS uses under the hood.

- `@Catch(HttpException)`:

  - The `@Catch()` decorator tells NestJS which exceptions our filter should catch. In this case, it's set to catch all exceptions of type `HttpException`.

- The `catch` method:

  - Within our filter, the `catch` method is responsible for handling the exception.

  - The `exception` gives us access to the thrown exception object.

  - The `host` lets us switch to different contexts. Here, we use it to access the underlying express `Response` object.

- `Response building`:

- We're sending a JSON response with the status of the exception (`response.status(exception.getStatus()).json(...)`) and additional data such as the exception message and a timestamp.

This filter serves as a foundation. With it, any thrown `HttpException` instance type will be transformed into a more readable and standardized response format.

Next, let's talk about validation. Do you remember the *never trust the user input* rule?

Validating data with pipes and guards

Pipes and guards are like the keen-eyed bouncers at a prestigious club, ensuring every guest (all data, in our case) meets the requisite criteria before entry.

Pipes – transforming and validating

Pipes operate in two main capacities: **data transformation** and **data validation**. By chaining multiple pipes, you can ensure data integrity and uniformity across your application.

See the following for a brief overview:

```
import {
  PipeTransform,
  Injectable,
  ArgumentMetadata
} from '@nestjs/common';
```

```
@Injectable()
export class SamplePipe implements PipeTransform {
  transform(value: any, metadata: ArgumentMetadata) {
    // Validation or transformation logic here
    return transformedValue;
  }
}
```

We can break this code down as follows:

- `Imports`:

    - The `PipeTransform` instance is a contract that our custom pipes will adhere to.

    - The `Injectable` and `ArgumentMetadata` instance types are imported from `@nestjs/common`. These are core concepts in NestJS that aid in the creation of pipes and the understanding of the context in which the pipe is used, respectively.

- `@Injectable()`:

    - The `@Injectable()` decorator marks our `SamplePipe` class as a provider that can be managed by NestJS's DI system.

- `Implementing PipeTransform`:

    - Our `SamplePipe` class implements the `PipeTransform` interface, which mandates the presence of a `transform` method in our class.

- `The transform method`:

    - This is where the magic happens. The `transform` method takes in two arguments:

    - `value`: The original value being processed

    - `metadata`: Provides additional metadata about the argument such as the type (`'body'`, `'query'`, etc.)

    - Within this method, you can introduce your validation or transformation logic. The `transformedValue` instance type returned will then replace the original `value` instance type in the data being processed.

This simple yet powerful structure facilitates a myriad of use cases. From converting string numbers into actual JavaScript numbers to ensuring that a received payload adheres to a specific **data transfer object** (**DTO**), the possibilities with pipes are truly expansive.

Guards – protecting routes

Guards are the sentinels of NestJS that determine whether a request should proceed to its route handler. In NestJS, a guard will always implement the canActivate method. A basic guard might look like this:

```
import {
  CanActivate,
  ExecutionContext,
  Injectable
} from '@nestjs/common';

@Injectable()
export class SampleGuard implements CanActivate {
  canActivate(context: ExecutionContext): boolean {
    // Logic to determine whether the request should
    // proceed
    return true;
  }}
```

We can break this code down as follows:

- Imports:

  - The CanActivate instance type is an interface that, when implemented, acts as a guard deciding whether to allow the request to continue.

  - The ExecutionContext and Injectable instances are imported from @nestjs/common. These help in understanding the context in which the guard is used and making our guard a provider, respectively.

- @Injectable():

  - The @Injectable() decorator marks the SampleGuard class as a provider that can be managed by NestJS's DI system.

- Implementing CanActivate:

  - Our SampleGuard class implements the CanActivate interface. This necessitates the definition of a canActivate method in our class.

- The canActivate method:

  - This method is the heart of our guard. It takes in an ExecutionContext object, which encapsulates details of the in-flight request.

- The method must return a Boolean. If it returns `true`, the request continues to the route handler. If `false`, the request is denied.

- The `// Logic to determine whether the request should proceed` comment is a placeholder where you'd implement the logic to decide whether the request should continue. This could involve checking for authentication tokens, user roles, and more.

Using guards, you can craft intricate access control mechanisms, ensuring that every request accessing your routes is legitimate and authorized.

> **Note**
> Pipes and guards are broad topics. We'll explore these in a subsequent chapter to understand them in depth.

Now that we have almost everything it takes to build a robust NestJS application, we are ready to build actual applications. This is what we are going to do together in the next two chapters.

Summary

This chapter provided a thorough guide to utilizing NestJS to create scalable and maintainable server-side applications. It began by guiding you through the installation of Node.js and NestJS, along with the necessary CLI tools. The chapter ensured a smooth development process by showing you how to configure essential tools such as npm and TypeScript.

We then introduced the structure of a NestJS project, which lays the foundation for understanding its components. The chapter progressed with practical insights into creating and managing modules, controllers, and providers, essential elements of NestJS applications. It also covered how to handle exceptions with filters and maintain data integrity through validation using pipes and guards.

By the end of the chapter, we have acquired essential skills in setting up a NestJS environment, organizing an application effectively, and developing applications that can address real-world challenges. These skills are crucial for elevating one's proficiency in server-side application development and laying the groundwork for the best practices that will be covered in subsequent chapters.

In the next one, let's take the skills we gained in this chapter to another level, exploring the advanced features of NestJS. Everything we learned here will serve us as we master the key pieces of the NestJS ecosystem.

Get This Book's PDF Version and Exclusive Extras

UNLOCK NOW

Scan the QR code (or go to `packtpub.com/unlock`). Search for this book by name, confirm the edition, and then follow the steps on the page.

Note: Keep your invoice handly. Purchase made directly from packt don't require one.

Advanced Concepts – Modules, Controllers, Providers, Exception Filters, Pipes, Guards, and Decorators

Welcome to *Chapter 4*, where we embark on an exhilarating dive into NestJS's advanced playground. If you've ever wondered what lies beneath the surface of this renowned framework, guiding it to be so extensible and adaptable, you're about to have an enlightening experience. As we journey deeper, we'll uncover the intricate machinery — from modules to decorators — that empowers developers such as you to create applications that are not only functional but also masterpieces of scalability and efficiency.

You've already glimpsed the foundational pillars of NestJS. Now, imagine those foundational concepts as the roots of a tree. In this chapter, we will climb its branches, exploring advanced facets that allow the tree to touch the sky, weather storms, and adapt to changing seasons.

Here's a roadmap for our ascent:

- Diving deeper into modules
- NestJS controller essentials and advanced practices
- Understanding providers in depth
- Request lifecycle

By the time we reach the end of this chapter, you'll have not only a deep theoretical understanding but also the hands-on skills to weave these advanced concepts into your applications. You'll be equipped to design NestJS apps that aren't just efficient and scalable but also a testament to outstanding software architecture. So, are you ready to ascend to new heights? Let's begin this exciting climb!

Technical requirements

The code files for the chapter can be found at `https://github.com/PacktPublishing/Scalable-Application-Development-with-NestJS`

Diving deeper into modules

In the intricate tapestry of software design, the notion of modularity has always stood out as an emblem of both elegance and efficiency. Within the paradigms of NestJS, modules emerge as the linchpin, unifying disparate elements into a cohesive and powerful whole. But to truly appreciate their role, we must embark on a deeper exploration, diving into the philosophy and pragmatism of modular thinking. Ready to uncover the layers? Let's begin.

The essence of modular thinking

Before the age of modern programming, software was often written as monolithic structures — colossal blocks of code where functionalities were intertwined. It worked, but as applications grew, so did the chaos. Enter modular programming. Born out of the need for order in the midst of growing complexity, modular programming championed the idea of dividing software into distinct, manageable parts, or "modules." This wasn't just a technical shift; it was a transformative approach to problem-solving, urging developers to see applications not just as code but as a symphony of interconnected yet independent pieces.

Figure 4.1 illustrates the difference between a monolith structure that only has one block, which gets bigger the more we add functions to it, versus a modular structure that has multiple blocks connected together and working in harmony:

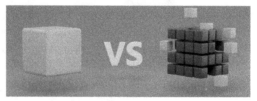

Figure 4.1: Monolith structure versus modular structure – copyright `coinmarketcap.com`

Why it's more than just organization

While at first glance, modular thinking might seem like mere organization, it's a paradigm that goes beyond neatness. It's about creating clear boundaries, fostering reusability, and ensuring each module can evolve without causing ripples across the entire application. In the world of NestJS, this becomes all the more paramount. With each module acting as a cornerstone for specific functionalities, understanding their role means appreciating the intricate balance between independence and interdependence.

Modules in NestJS aren't just a structural element; they're a reflection of a deeper philosophy. As we journey further, we'll explore how this philosophy manifests in the design and functionality of Nest applications. Up next, we delve into tangible aspects of modules in NestJS, breaking down their roles and responsibilities.

The fundamental role of modules in NestJS

As we set foot into the intricacies of NestJS, it becomes evident that modules aren't just a byproduct of the framework's design; they are its beating heart. Modules play a pivotal role in forming the underlying structure and ensuring the seamless orchestration of the myriad elements within an application. To discern their significance, let's peel back the layers.

The cohesive binder of an application

Modules in NestJS act like the glue that binds the various components of an application together. At their core, they serve as **organizational units** (**OUs**), allowing related functionalities to be grouped together, resulting in a more intuitive and structured code base. When you think of modules, envision a well-organized library where each section or shelf houses a specific genre of books. In the realm of NestJS, these "genres" are your controllers, providers, and other elements of the application, as illustrated in *Figure 4.2*:

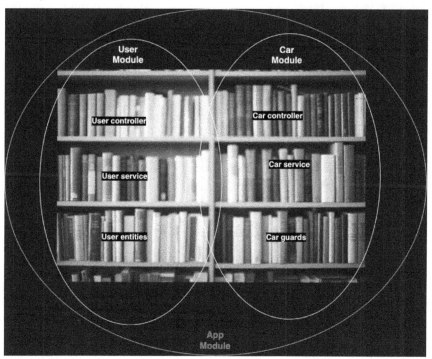

Figure 4.2: Illustration of NestJS modules

A conduit for scalability and maintainability

The role of modules isn't confined to organization alone. As applications grow, so does their complexity. Modules act as a conduit, ensuring that this growth is sustainable. They facilitate scalability by allowing developers to add, modify, or remove functionalities without disrupting the entire application's equilibrium. This modular design inherently supports maintainability. When updates or fixes are required, developers can pinpoint the exact module responsible and make changes without wading through a sea of unrelated code. Think of it like updating one section of our earlier library without causing a commotion in the other sections.

Modules, in their essence, are the unsung heroes of NestJS, quietly yet effectively ensuring that applications remain structured, scalable, and maintainable. As we move forward, we'll delve into the mechanics of creating and initializing these modules, giving you a hands-on insight into their configuration and deployment.

Creating and initializing a module

Diving deeper into the realm of NestJS modules, it's crucial to understand not just their role but also their anatomy. Creating and initializing a module isn't just about invoking a decorator or adding a few lines of code. It's about understanding the various components that constitute a module and how they interplay to ensure the module functions optimally. Let's unravel this intricate dance.

The anatomy of a module

Every NestJS module is a class characterized by a set of properties, each serving a distinct purpose. These are defined using the `@Module()` decorator. Let's dissect this decorator to understand its key properties:

- `controllers`: Here, you list a set of controllers defined in the module. Controllers are responsible for handling incoming requests and returning responses to the client. In the following code snippet, we have a module decorator with a single controller; note that this array can take multiple controllers handling different HTTP requests, by their paths or verbs:

    ```
    @Module({
        controllers: [AppController],
    })
    ```

- `providers`: These are entities that can be injected into constructors due to Nest's **dependency injection** (**DI**). Providers can be services, repositories, factories, and more. In the following code snippet, we have an example of an `AppModule` with a single provider, `AppService`:

    ```
    @Module({
        providers: [AppService],
    })
    ```

- imports: This property allows modules to import other modules, thereby enabling shared functionalities. It ensures that the providers of the imported module become part of the module it's being imported into, as shown in the following code snippet:

```
@Module({
    imports: [SharedModule],
})
```

- exports: When you want a module's providers (or the imported module's providers) to be accessible and shared across multiple modules, they need to be exported using the exports property of the @module decorator, as in the following code snippet:

```
@Module({
    exports: [SharedService],
})
```

A cautionary tale: While the flexibility offered by these properties is empowering, misuse can lead to pitfalls. For instance, failing to export a needed service might result in errors or not having the necessary functionalities in another module that relies on it. Generally, Nest will catch such errors and notify the developer through logs.

First steps – your first custom module

Taking that first step to create your custom module is both thrilling and foundational in your NestJS adventure. Let's start with a basic template:

```
import { Module } from '@nestjs/common';
import { CustomController } from './custom.controller';
import { CustomService } from './custom.service';

@Module({
  imports: [],
  controllers: [CustomController],
  providers: [CustomService],
})
export class CustomModule {}
```

Here, our CustomModule class encompasses a CustomController module and a CustomService module. As it stands, there are no imports—this module is self-contained, not relying on any other modules, and likewise, nothing is exported, ensuring its services and controllers are unique to this module.

But what happens when our `CustomModule` class needs to interact with other modules? Let's examine a scenario where it depends on two other modules—`UserModule` and `AuthModule`:

```
import { Module } from '@nestjs/common';
import { CustomController } from './custom.controller';
import { CustomService } from './custom.service';
import { UserModule } from './user.module';
import { AuthModule } from './auth.module';

@Module({
  imports: [UserModule, AuthModule],
  controllers: [CustomController],
  providers: [CustomService],
})
export class CustomModule {}
```

In this evolved version, `CustomModule` imports `UserModule` and `AuthModule`. This means it can now use any services or components from these imported modules that have been exported by them. If, for instance, `UserModule` had a service that `CustomModule` needed, it would first need to be exported from `UserModule` to be accessible here.

> **Key insight**
>
> By importing other modules, we're not just linking them—we're weaving a web of dependencies. This interlaced structure should be crafted with care to avoid circular dependencies and ensure that the application remains scalable and maintainable.

As our exploration into the modular architecture of NestJS continues, it's evident that modules aren't just building blocks. They're intricately designed components that shoulder the responsibility of defining and managing the boundaries and interactions of our application's functionalities.

The application module graph

Every NestJS application, at its heart, is fundamentally a collection of modules. These modules encapsulate distinct functionalities and interact to form a coherent application. Think of them as pieces of a puzzle; while each piece has its unique shape and picture, it's the interlocking of these pieces that completes the overall image.

Visualizing module interactions

At the very core of every NestJS application lies the **root module**, typically known as the `AppModule`. It's the entry point of your application—the central hub that ties all other modules together. Every NestJS project has this primary module, which acts as the foundation upon which other modules are added.

To fully understand the application's architecture, one must visualize its module graph, a depiction of how modules interlink and depend on each other. If you've wondered about the data structure NestJS uses to represent these connections, it's a directed graph. Why a graph? Because it allows for a clear representation of dependencies and relationships, facilitating the understanding of data flow and module interactions.

Nest's module system ensures that each module is a single unit of responsibility. As modules become dependent on one another, they form a **directed acyclic graph** (**DAG**) that paints a clear picture of your application's architecture. This visualization aids in the following aspects:

- **Problem diagnosis**: Easily identifying which modules might be affected when a single module encounters an issue

- **Optimized refactoring**: Recognizing which modules can be independently refactored without disturbing the application's overall functionality

- **Enhanced scalability**: Strategically adding new modules or expanding existing ones based on the current module graph

Understanding inter-module dependencies

Connecting modules is straightforward — one module declares its dependencies on others via the imports array in the @Module decorator. For instance, if ModuleA needed functionalities from ModuleB, it would simply import ModuleB as shown in the following code:

```
@Module({
   imports: [ModuleB],
})
export class ModuleA {}
```

However, simply importing doesn't make functionalities available. ModuleB should explicitly export the required services or controllers, making them accessible to other modules, like the following:

```
@Module({
   providers: [ServiceFromModuleB],
   exports: [ServiceFromModuleB]
})
export class ModuleB {}
```

Here's where intricacies come into play:

- **Isolation of modules:** One might ponder if it's possible to have a standalone module, disconnected from the root module or any other module. In practice, this isn't feasible. Every module in a NestJS application invariably connects, either directly or indirectly, to the root module. Isolated modules would remain inert and wouldn't contribute to the application's functionality.

- **Exporting functionalities**: Remember — simply importing a module doesn't guarantee access to its services or controllers. The supplying module should explicitly export the required functionalities. If `ModuleB` provides a service that `ModuleA` needs, this raises an essential question: Can a module be accessed directly without being exported? The answer is nuanced. While you can utilize the functionalities within the module they're declared, to share them across multiple modules, they must be exported. Think of exports as giving "permission" to other modules to utilize specific services or controllers.

- **Optimal number of modules**: There isn't a strict number of modules an application should have. However, each module should encapsulate a specific functionality or domain of your application. Having clearly defined modules aids in maintainability and scalability.

- **The decision to export**: Not all modules need to be exported. The decision hinges on whether you foresee other modules needing the functionalities contained within a specific module. If a module is solely supportive and doesn't offer services or controllers that others might require, there's no need to export it.

Understanding the module graph's intricacies and the logic behind inter-module dependencies provides architects and developers with the insights needed to craft scalable and maintainable applications. It's the harmony between modules, each performing its part, that produces a cohesive and efficient NestJS application.

In the subsequent sections, we will explore potential pitfalls, such as circular dependencies, and strategies to ensure a smooth, error-free module interaction.

DI – the silent orchestrator

In software development, one can't overstate the value of managing dependencies well. The arrangement, accessibility, and lifetime of an application's components significantly influence its adaptability, maintainability, and testability. Enter DI — a design pattern that graces NestJS with its prowess. But what if NestJS opted not to employ this design pattern? The consequences would reshape the framework's essence, with ripples affecting scalability, maintainability, and testing ease.

Principles and power of DI

To understand the power of DI in a framework such as NestJS, here is what things could look like without it:

- **Tighter coupling**: Imagine a world where each class instantiates its dependencies. This design would not only lead to tighter coupling between components but would also restrict modularity. Testing would be a challenge, as mocking dependencies for isolated testing would be cumbersome.

- **Less reusability**: Without DI, changing a component's behavior by swapping out a dependency would demand modifying the component itself, greatly diminishing code reusability.

- **Compromised configurability**: Flexibility in configuring applications, especially at runtime, would take a hit. You'd be bound to hardcoded dependencies, making the system rigid.

With DI, the following can be achieved:

- **Separation of concerns (SoC)**: DI champions the principle of SoC. Instead of classes being responsible for sourcing their dependencies, an external system (the injector) provides them. This separation boosts modularity and makes components more interchangeable.

- **Improved testability**: With DI, testing becomes more straightforward. Since dependencies can be injected, you can easily substitute real implementations with mocks or stubs, facilitating isolated unit tests.

- **Dynamic dependency resolution**: DI empowers applications with dynamic dependency resolution, letting developers modify system behavior by altering the provided dependencies without changing the classes using them.

In essence, DI streamlines the architectural flow, allowing developers to focus on crafting logic without being bogged down by the intricacies of dependency management.

Nest's hierarchical injector

NestJS not only leverages DI but also elevates it with its hierarchical injector system. This system works in layers, ensuring that each module and its components get their dependencies from the closest injector, be it module-specific or global.

For instance, when `ServiceA` requests a dependency, the injector first checks within its module. If it doesn't find it there, it climbs up the hierarchy, examining parent modules, all the way to the root module or global scope.

This hierarchical approach offers several advantages:

- **Scoped instances**: It enables scoped instances of providers. A service can have different instances in different modules, allowing for module-specific configurations and behaviors.

- **Enhanced modularity**: The hierarchical system encourages clear boundaries between modules, reinforcing modularity.

- **Fallback mechanism**: The layer-based lookup provides a built-in fallback mechanism. If a local module doesn't provide a dependency, the system can fall back to a parent module or the global scope.

In conclusion, NestJS's decision to harness DI, complemented by its hierarchical injector, is strategic. It offers developers a seamless experience, ensures optimal application structuring, and inherently boosts testability and modularity. It's hard to imagine the NestJS we love without its silent orchestrator.

Circular dependencies – the loop you don't want

Circular dependencies are a common challenge, especially in a modular system such as NestJS. When left unresolved, they can lead to unexpected behaviors and can complicate the initialization process of your application modules and services. Identifying and resolving them becomes crucial to ensure the robustness of your application.

Identifying potential circular dependencies

The first step in managing circular dependencies is spotting them. Typically, they manifest when two classes, services, or modules are interdependent. Here's a classic example:

Example 1: Service interdependency

```
// cat.service.ts
import { Injectable } from '@nestjs/common';
import { DogService } from './dog.service';

@Injectable()
export class CatService {
  constructor(private dogService: DogService) {}
}

// dog.service.ts
import { Injectable } from '@nestjs/common';
import { CatService } from './cat.service';

@Injectable()
export class DogService {
  constructor(private catService: CatService) {}
}
```

Here, the `CatService` class injects `DogService` into its constructor, meaning it depends on `DogService`. In parallel, `DogService` is injecting `CatService`, thereby depending on it. This mutual dependency creates a cyclical reference. For the Nest framework to instantiate `CatService`, it requires an instance of `DogService`, but `DogService` cannot be instantiated without an instance of `CatService`. This cyclic nature makes it unclear which should be initialized first, leading to a deadlock in the initialization process.

Another common scenario is when modules rely on each other, as in the following example:

Example 2: Module interdependency

```typescript
// cat.module.ts
import { Module } from '@nestjs/common';
import { DogModule } from './dog.module';

@Module({
  imports: [DogModule],
})
export class CatModule {}

// dog.module.ts
import { Module } from '@nestjs/common';
import { CatModule } from './cat.module';

@Module({
  imports: [CatModule],
})
export class DogModule {}
```

The situation is analogous at the module level in this example. The CatModule class imports DogModule, which means it relies on some functionalities provided by the latter. Conversely, DogModule imports CatModule, indicating its dependence on the former. This mutual importing spawns a circular dependency.

During the initialization process, the NestJS framework will struggle to determine which module should be initialized first, as each module is waiting for the other. This cyclical dependency, just as in the service example, leads to ambiguity in initialization order.

> Tip
>
> You can use the Madge (https://github.com/pahen/madge) tool to check if you are running into a circular dependency error or to know exactly where is it happening using the following commands:

```
$ npx madge dist/main.js --circular
$ npx madge dist/main.js --image graph.png
```

The first command will print No circular dependency found! if you don't have a circular dependency in your project, as shown in *Figure 4.3*; and the second one will generate a file with the specified name in the project root that looks like *Figure 4.4*:

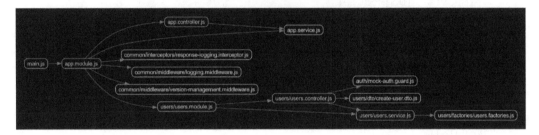

Figure 4.3: No circular dependency found

Figure 4.4: Application graph printed by Madge

Strategies to avoid and resolve circular dependencies in NestJS

Here are a few strategies NestJS suggests to avoid circular dependencies:

- **Forward reference**: NestJS provides a mechanism called forwardRef() that allows you to reference classes before they are defined, hence resolving the cyclic dependency issue.

  Using our CatService and DogService classes from the earlier example, here's how you can resolve the circular dependency using forwardRef():

```
// cat.service.ts
import {
  Injectable,
  forwardRef,
  Inject
} from '@nestjs/common';
import { DogService } from './dog.service';

@Injectable()
export class CatService {
  constructor(
    @Inject(forwardRef(() => DogService)) private
    dogService: DogService
  ) {}
}
```

With this, `DogService` is not directly imported in the constructor but instead referenced through the `forwardRef()` function, thus deferring its instantiation and resolving the cyclic dependency.

- **Service refactoring**: Sometimes, circular dependencies signal a design issue. Consider refactoring your services or modules to adhere to the **Single Responsibility Principle** (**SRP**). This may involve splitting a service or module into smaller, more focused units or reconsidering the relationships between them.

- **Dependency abstraction**: Introduce an intermediary service or module that both conflicting services or modules can depend on. This intermediary can abstract out the common functionalities needed by both, eliminating the direct cyclical reference.

By understanding the potential sources and challenges of circular dependencies and leveraging the tools and design principles provided by NestJS, developers can ensure a smoother, more efficient application initialization process.

Sharing modules across the application

Building scalable applications is not just about breaking down your application into modules but also about efficiently sharing functionalities across different parts of your application. Enter the power of exports and global modules in NestJS.

Why exports matter

Every module has a private context. Services, controllers, or any other component defined in a module are encapsulated within. However, there might be situations where a service or component needs to be shared with other parts of the application.

Let's consider a logging service. This service might be required in numerous other modules for consistent logging mechanisms.

Without the ability to export this service, we'd end up either duplicating the service (bad for maintainability and memory footprint) or moving everything into one mega module (bad for scalability).

In NestJS, the `exports` array in a module's metadata specifies which providers from this module should be shared and can be used in other modules:

```
@Module({
  providers: [LoggingService],
  exports: [LoggingService],
})
export class SharedModule {}
```

With this setup, any module that imports `SharedModule` will also have access to `LoggingService`, promoting **Don't Repeat Yourself (DRY)** principles and centralized logic management.

Global modules – available everywhere

While exporting modules is powerful, NestJS takes it a notch higher with global modules. Once defined as global, a module doesn't need to be imported into other modules; its providers and controllers become instantly accessible everywhere:

```
import { Global, Module } from '@nestjs/common';

@Global()
@Module({
  providers: [ConfigService],
  exports: [ConfigService],
})
export class ConfigModule {}
```

Such global modules are particularly useful for core services such as configuration management, logging, or database connections that are pervasive across the application.

Modular organization for large-scale applications

As applications grow, so does the complexity. Proper modular organization ensures that this growth remains manageable and doesn't turn your code base into an intertwined mess.

Structuring for growth – feature modules

It's advisable to think of modules in terms of business features or domains. Each feature or domain can have its own module, making it easier to reason about, develop, and test.

For example, in an e-commerce application, we could have the following:

- `UserManagement` could be a separate module
- `ProductManagement` is another module
- `OrderandCheckout` could be another module

Such a setup not only modularizes the code but also the team. Different teams can work on different modules without stepping on each other's toes.

Over time, certain modules can become bloated. Periodic assessments should be done to ensure modules are focused and not taking on too many responsibilities. A rule of thumb is if a module is doing too much, it might be time to split it.

Remember — the main goal is to ensure that each module has a single responsibility and is a cohesive unit. This approach ensures that modules remain maintainable, understandable, and, when needed, reusable.

Final thoughts on Nest's modular philosophy

Nest's approach to modularity isn't an afterthought. It's at the very core of its design philosophy.

Modularity in NestJS draws inspiration from age-old software design principles, coupled with modern-day application needs. The aim is to offer developers a way to create structured, scalable, and maintainable applications without feeling restricted.

Modules in NestJS are like building blocks—each block serves a purpose, and together they form the complete application. This vision encourages developers to think in terms of boundaries, responsibilities, and collaborations.

The modular approach ensures that as your application grows, it doesn't grow out of control. Instead, it grows in a structured manner. Each module you add, each service you create, and each controller you define fits into a larger, well-defined puzzle.

When you embrace this modular thinking, you're not just writing code for the present. You're architecting your application for the future, ensuring it remains agile, adaptable, and, above all, a joy to work on.

Alright – we have covered the most important aspects of modules in NestJS; with a lot of practice in the upcoming chapters, we will make sure all this theoretical knowledge is useful in building for real. Now, let's talk about another important core concept of NestJS in the next section.

NestJS controller essentials and advanced practices

In the realm of web applications, controllers play a pivotal role in managing incoming requests and producing relevant responses. NestJS, with its well-architected patterns, elevates this role to a symphony of organized code. In this section, we're going to unveil the mysteries of controllers in NestJS, from their foundational aspects to crafting your very first one.

At the heart of every NestJS application lies a critical component: the controller. Acting as the nexus between the client and the server, controllers handle incoming requests, route them to the appropriate services, and send back responses. They form the bridge that connects your application's functionality to the outside world.

Imagine your NestJS application as a bustling train station. The controllers are akin to the stationmasters, guiding trains (or requests) to the correct platform (or service) and ensuring everything runs smoothly. Without them, the station would descend into chaos!

Creating your first controller

Setting up a controller in NestJS is straightforward. The framework's CLI provides a convenient way to scaffold one. Here's how:

```
$ nest generate controller users
# or use its shortcut
$ nest g co users
```

This command generates a `users` controller, creating a `users.controller.ts` file within the `users/` directory. If this directory doesn't exist, the Nest CLI will create one for you. Here's a simplified look at what the file contains:

```
import { Controller } from '@nestjs/common';

@Controller('users')
export class UsersController {}
```

The `@Controller()` decorator tells Nest that `UsersController` is a controller and can handle HTTP requests. The `users` argument specifies that this controller will handle requests to the `/users` endpoint.

> **Important note**
>
> In the way NestJS architecture has been designed, a controller shouldn't exist without a module; a `UsersModule` module is required, which will then be connected to the root module so that our created routes are registered in the application context.

Basic routing in controllers

Routing is foundational to controllers. It's the mechanism that tells the application which controller method should handle which HTTP request. NestJS uses decorators to make this routing declarative and easy to understand.

At the core of routing are route handlers. These are methods within a controller that handle specific routes. NestJS provides a set of decorators—such as `@Get()`, `@Post()`, and others—that correspond to HTTP request methods.

Consider the following code:

```
import { Controller, Get } from '@nestjs/common';

@Controller('users')
```

```
export class CatsController {
  @Get()
  findAll() {
    return 'This action returns all users';
  }
}
```

In the preceding example, the @Get() decorator without any arguments specifies that the findAll() method should handle GET requests to the /users endpoint.

But what if you wanted more granularity? What if you wished to have separate routes under the 'users' endpoint? That's where paths come into play:

```
import { Controller, Get } from '@nestjs/common';

@Controller('users')
export class UsersController {
  @Get('details')
  findDetails() {
    return 'Details about users';
  }

  @Get('images')
  findImages() {
    return 'Images of various users';
  }
}
```

In this updated example, the @Get('details') decorator directs GET requests of the /users/details endpoint to the findDetails() method, while the @Get('images') decorator directs GET requests of the /users/images endpoint to the findImages() method.

By using paths with route decorators, you can organize and structure your application routes more efficiently, allowing for greater flexibility and scalability as your application grows.

Parameterized routes

Web applications often deal with dynamic content, where the data you want might depend on some variable—such as the ID of an item. This is where parameterized routes come into play. Instead of having static endpoints such as /users, you'd have something such as /users/:id where :id can be any value representing the **unique identifier** (UID) of a user.

To handle such dynamic routes, NestJS introduces the @Param decorator. This decorator allows you to extract parameters from the URL, making them available to the controller methods.

Introducing the @Param decorator

The @Param decorator in NestJS is used to extract and bind the route parameters to the controller method parameters. When a client sends a request to a URL containing route parameters, NestJS binds the values from the URL to the method's parameters using this decorator.

For instance, in the /users/:id route, id is a route parameter. When a client sends a request to /users/123, 123 is the value of the id parameter.

Let's see this in action:

```
import { Controller, Get, Param } from '@nestjs/common';

@Controller('users')
export class UsersController {
  @Get(':id')
  findOne(@Param('id') id: string) {
    return `This action returns a user with ID ${id}`;
  }
}
```

In this example, the following takes place:

- The route is defined as @Get(':id'), indicating that it expects an id parameter in the URL
- Inside the findOne() method, the @Param('id') decorator is used to extract the id parameter from the URL
- The value of the id parameter is then bound to the id argument of the findOne() method
- The method returns a string that includes the value of id, showing the ID of the cat being fetched

This mechanism allows your application to respond to a multitude of potential URLs with a single route, extracting the required data from the URL itself.

Handling multiple parameters

NestJS allows for the definition of multiple parameters within a single route. Suppose you want to filter users by id, sex, and minAge, with the possibility of an optional query parameter, salary. The route could look something like this: /users/:id/:sex/:minAge.

Here's how you would define and handle it:

```
import {
  Controller,
  Get,
  Param,
  Query
} from '@nestjs/common';

@Controller('users')
export class UsersController {
  @Get(':id/:sex/:minAge')
  filterUsers(
    @Param('id') id: string,
    @Param('sex') sex: string,
    @Param('minAge') minAge: number,
    @Query('salary') salary?: number
  ) {
    return `Fetching users with ID: ${id},
            Sex: ${sex},
            Minimum Age: ${minAge},
            and Salary: ${salary || 'Not Specified'}`;
  }
}
```

In the preceding example, the following takes place:

- The `@Get(':id/:sex/:minAge')` route specifies three parameters.

- The `@Param()` decorator is used three times, once for each parameter, to extract their values from the URL. Nest will automatically bind these values from the request body; omitting them will result in undefined variables and may break the logic of your controller.

- An optional `salary` query parameter is handled using the `@Query('salary')` decorator. If the client does not provide this query parameter, the value will default to `undefined`.

It's important to note that in the `/users/123/male/2?salary=10000` route, we have the following:

- `123` corresponds to `id`

- `male` corresponds to `sex`

- `2` corresponds to `minAge`

- The `salary=10000` query parameter corresponds to `salary`

This versatility allows NestJS applications to cater to various filtering, sorting, and querying needs in real-world scenarios.

With parameterized routes, multiple parameters, and the powerful combination of @Param and @Query decorators, NestJS equips you with the flexibility to design dynamic routes for a broader range of requests in your application.

Scaling your controllers

In the realm of NestJS, as with any structured backend framework, keeping controllers lean, focused, and maintainable becomes essential, especially as your application scales. Next are strategies to ensure your controllers effectively manage HTTP traffic without becoming bloated or convoluted:

- **Separate concerns**: Adhering to the SRP can make a significant difference. A controller's primary function should be to handle HTTP requests and delegate further logic elsewhere. If you find your controller managing both users and their orders, for instance, consider breaking them into UsersController and OrdersController.

- **Utilize modules**: Think of modules as individual containers of related functionality. As you introduce more controllers, services, or other providers into your application, consider grouping them using modules. For example, a UsersModule module can encompass everything related to users, making the application's structure clearer and more modular.

- **Middleware and interceptors**: Before delving deeper into more advanced NestJS features, it's good to know that there are tools available for handling common tasks (such as logging, data transformation, or minor validations) either before the request reaches the controller or right after it leaves. Middleware and interceptors play a pivotal role here, ensuring that the controller doesn't get burdened with responsibilities outside of handling the request-response cycle.

- **Leverage service classes**: The real power of keeping controllers slim comes from service classes. Let's assume you're building functionalities around users. Instead of placing the logic to fetch, modify, or delete a user directly in the controller, you delegate these tasks to a service class.

Here's a simplified example:

```
@Controller('users')
export class UsersController {
    constructor(private usersService: UsersService) {}

    @Get(':id')
    findUserById(@Param('id') id: string) {
        return this.usersService.findById(id);
    }
}
```

```
      // ... other methods ...
  }
```

In this snippet, `UsersController` merely directs the task of fetching a user by ID to `UsersService`. The service then contains the actual logic, perhaps querying a database or making API calls. This separation ensures that controllers only handle traffic, delegating business logic to services.

To sum it up, the goal is to keep your controllers as streamlined as possible. The aforementioned strategies provide a roadmap to that end, ensuring that as your application grows, its structure remains coherent, organized, and efficient. Controllers should act as traffic managers, channeling requests to appropriate services or providers that handle the business logic.

Refined request handling

In NestJS, as your application becomes more sophisticated, merely handling HTTP requests isn't enough. You need techniques to refine this process, ensuring efficient, secure, and scalable request handling. This section unlocks the secrets behind such refined techniques, ensuring that your controllers are not just gatekeepers but also effective traffic managers.

In web applications, understanding the incoming request is pivotal to effective response handling. The `Request` object in NestJS acts as a window to this essential information, granting you insight into various details of the incoming request.

The anatomy of the Request object

The `Request` object in NestJS is a rich source of information. Coming from the underlying Express or Fastify instance, it contains data about the client, the HTTP request, headers, and more:

```
import { Controller, Get, Req } from '@nestjs/common';
import { Request } from 'express'; // if you use Fastify,
                                   // import from 'fastify'

@Controller('info')
export class InfoController {
  @Get()
  extractReqInfo(@Req() request: Request) {
    return {
      method: request.method,
      url: request.url,
      headers: request.headers
    };
  }
}
```

In the preceding snippet, the following takes place:

- We're importing the `Request` object type from Express.

- The `@Req()` decorator provides access to the underlying `Request` object. We extract attributes such as `method`, `url`, and `headers` from this object.

Extracting metadata

One of the primary use cases of the `Request` object in a web application is to access the metadata associated with the incoming request. This metadata provides valuable information, ranging from headers and cookies to client details and more.

In NestJS, extracting this information is straightforward, and the `@Req()` decorator is pivotal in achieving this.

Headers are used to send additional information from the client to the server. This might encompass authentication tokens, content type specifications, information about the kind of response the client can handle, and so forth.

Let's take a look at how we can access these headers:

```
@Get('headers')
showHeaders(@Req() request: Request) {
  return request.headers;
}
```

In the preceding code, the following takes place:

- We use the `@Get('headers')` decorator to specify that this method should handle `GET` requests to the `/headers` endpoint.

- The `@Req()` decorator is employed to inject the full `Request` object into the `showHeaders()` method.

- The `request.headers` instance is an object that contains all the incoming headers. We simply return it, making it possible for us to inspect every header sent with the request.

By harnessing the power of the `Request` object and decorators such as `@Req()`, you can effortlessly fetch and utilize metadata, enhancing the responsiveness and adaptability of your application.

Advanced request manipulation

Web applications often require intricate request handling. While at times, it's about reading from a request, there are scenarios where you'll need to add, modify, or even delete certain aspects of the incoming request before passing it down to services or other parts of your application. This enables you to enforce business logic, manage custom metadata, or even enhance request data for improved processing downstream.

Consider a scenario where you'd like to annotate incoming requests with additional metadata, perhaps for logging, analytics, or any custom business need. Here's how you can achieve this:

```
@Get('annotate')
annotateRequest(@Req() request: Request) {
  // Adding custom metadata
  request['customMetadata'] = {
    timestamp: new Date(),
    userAgent: request.headers['user-agent'],
    route: request.route.path
  };
  // Further processing...
}
```

Let's break down the preceding code snippet:

- The @Get('annotate') decorator specifies that this method should handle GET requests made to the /annotate endpoint.
- We use the @Req() decorator to inject the full Request object.
- A new property, customMetadata, is added to the Request object. This property is an object containing the following:
  - The current timestamp, which showcases when the request was received.
  - The user agent from the headers, which indicates the client's software and version (for example, browser or app).
  - The accessed route path.

Now that you've enriched the Request object with custom metadata, it can be used in various parts of your application, such as services or middleware.

Imagine you have a logging service that tracks user activity:

```
@Injectable()
export class LoggingService {
  logActivity(request: Request) {
    const metadata = request['customMetadata'];
    console.log(
      `Accessed route: ${metadata.route} at
      ${metadata.timestamp} via ${metadata.userAgent}`);
  }
}
```

In your controller, after adding metadata to the request, you can pass the request to `LoggingService` for further action:

```
constructor(
  private readonly loggingService: LoggingService
) {}

@Get('annotate')
annotateRequest(@Req() request: Request) {
  // ... [Metadata addition code]

  this.loggingService.logActivity(request);
}
```

By employing advanced request manipulation techniques, developers can imbue their applications with heightened functionality, ensuring data is processed efficiently and intelligently.

To gain insights such as the client's IP address or even geolocation, you can rely on the `Request` object:

```
@Get('client-info')
clientInfo(@Req() request: Request) {
  return {
    ip: request.ip,
    // you could use a service to derive geolocation from
    // IP, etc.
  };
}
```

In this snippet, we extract the client's IP address. Using this IP, one could further integrate geolocation services if needed.

Advanced Data Transfer Objects and validation pipelines

As you deal with more complex data in a growing application, **Data Transfer Objects** (**DTOs**) become a crucial tool. They define the shape and expectations of the data you'll be working with, ensuring type safety and validation.

There are scenarios where the data structure you're working with isn't flat. A user, for instance, might have an address, and that address might have multiple properties. To handle this, you can create nested DTOs:

```
import {
  IsString,
  IsNotEmpty,
  IsNumber,
  ValidateNested
} from 'class-validator';

class AddressDTO {
  @IsString()
  @IsNotEmpty()
  street: string;

  @IsNumber()
  houseNumber: number;
}

export class UserDTO {
  @IsString()
  @IsNotEmpty()
  name: string;

  @ValidateNested()
  address: AddressDTO;
}
```

In the provided code snippet, the following applies:

- We start by importing necessary validators from the `class-validator` package
- The `AddressDTO` class represents a user's address
- The `street` attribute must be a string and cannot be empty, ensured by `@IsString()` and `@IsNotEmpty()` respectively
- The `houseNumber` attribute should be a number, as verified by `@IsNumber()`
- The `UserDTO` class describes a user with a name and an address
- The `name` attribute needs to be a string and cannot be empty
- The `@ValidateNested()` decorator ensures that the `address` property complies with the `AddressDTO` structure

Conditional validation with validation groups

Your application might encounter situations where data validation needs to vary based on the operation being performed. For example, when updating a user's data, not all fields might be mandatory. Validation groups allow you to apply validations conditionally. You can see an example of this in the following code snippet:

```
import {
  IsString,
  IsNotEmpty,
  IsOptional
} from 'class-validator';

export class UpdateUserDTO {
  @IsString()
  @IsNotEmpty({ groups: ['create'] })
  name: string;

  @IsString()
  @IsOptional()
  bio?: string;
}
```

In the preceding code snippet, the following applies:

- The `UpdateUserDTO` class is imported alongside the necessary validators.
- The `name` attribute must be a string, ensured by the `@IsString()` decorator.
- When creating a user, the name is mandatory, represented by `@IsNotEmpty({ groups: ['create'] })`. However, for other operations such as updates, the name might not be necessary.
- The `bio` attribute is optional and can be a string. The `@IsOptional()` decorator indicates this optionality, and `@IsString()` confirms that if present, it should be a string.

By integrating advanced DTO structures and validation techniques, you bolster your application's data integrity, ensuring that operations are conducted on clean, validated, and expected data structures.

Custom validation decorators

While `class-validator` provides a comprehensive set of validation decorators, there will be instances where you need a custom validator specific to your application's requirements.

Consider you need to validate if a given string is a palindrome. Instead of manually checking this in multiple places, you can encapsulate this logic in a custom validation decorator:

```
import {
  registerDecorator,
  ValidationOptions
} from 'class-validator';

export function IsPalindrome(
  validationOptions?: ValidationOptions)
{
  return function (object: Object, propertyName: string) {
    registerDecorator({
      name: 'IsPalindrome',
      target: object.constructor,
      propertyName: propertyName,
      options: validationOptions,
      validator: {
        validate(value: any) {
          return typeof value === 'string' &&
            value === value.split('').reverse().join('');
        }
      }
    });
  };
}
```

Here's an explanation of the preceding code:

- We begin by importing `registerDecorator` and `ValidationOptions` from `class-validator`.
- We then define an `IsPalindrome` function, which takes in `validationOptions`. These options allow us to customize validation error messages or specify groups, among other settings.
- Inside this function, another function is returned that uses the `registerDecorator()` method. This method is pivotal for creating custom decorators in `class-validator`.
- The `name` attribute specifies the name of the decorator.
- The `target` and `propertyName` attributes help pinpoint the exact location where our decorator is used.
- The `validator` key holds an object with a `validate()` method. This method contains our custom logic: in this case, checking if a value is a palindrome.

With this custom validator in place, you can now decorate properties in your DTOs with @IsPalindrome(). When the validation pipeline runs, it checks if the decorated property's value is a palindrome.

After defining our custom validation decorator, the next logical step is to incorporate it into our DTOs. This ensures that incoming or outgoing data adheres to our custom validation logic.

Imagine a DTO for a linguistic service that studies palindromes. A requirement for one of the endpoints is that a provided word or phrase should indeed be a palindrome. Here's how you might structure such a DTO:

```
import { IsNotEmpty } from 'class-validator';
import {
  IsPalindrome
} from './path-to-your-decorator-file';

export class PalindromeDTO {
  @IsNotEmpty()
  @IsPalindrome({
    message: 'The provided word or phrase is not a
    palindrome.'
  })
  word: string;
}
```

In the preceding code snippet, the following applies:

- We start by importing necessary validators, including our custom @IsPalindrome decorator.

- In the PalindromeDTO class, we have a property named word that will hold the string we wish to validate.

- We first ensure that the word attribute is not empty with @IsNotEmpty().

- Next, we use the @IsPalindrome() decorator. Additionally, we've provided a custom error message using the message attribute in case the validation fails.

With this DTO in place, when a user submits data to an endpoint expecting a PalindromeDTO instance, the NestJS validation pipeline will verify that the submitted word attribute is not empty and is a palindrome. If it's not a palindrome, the pipeline will return an error with a "The provided word or phrase is not a palindrome." message.

By integrating custom validation decorators within DTOs, you centralize your validation logic and maintain cleaner, more intuitive controllers and services.

Transforming data

Post-validation, there might be a need to transform the validated data. The `class-transformer` package helps with this:

```
import { Transform } from 'class-transformer';

export class UserDTO {
  @IsString()
  name: string;

  @Transform(value => value.toUpperCase())
  favoriteColor: string;
}
```

Here, the `@Transform()` decorator ensures that the `favoriteColor` value is stored in uppercase.

Response transformation – interceptors in action

Interceptors play a significant role in the NestJS architecture. At a high level, interceptors allow developers to inspect and transform HTTP requests and responses. They can act before or after a route handler (controller method) executes, making them versatile tools for tasks such as logging, transformation, or measuring performance.

The fundamental job of an interceptor is to allow operations both before and after the execution of a method. Let's delve into an example:

```
import {
  Injectable,
  NestInterceptor,
  ExecutionContext,
  CallHandler
} from '@nestjs/common';
import { Observable } from 'rxjs';
import { map } from 'rxjs/operators';

@Injectable()
export class UppercaseInterceptor implements
NestInterceptor {
  intercept(
    context: ExecutionContext, next: CallHandler):
    Observable<any>
  {
    return next.handle().pipe(
```

```
      map(data =>
        (typeof data === 'string' ? data.toUpperCase() :
          Data
        )
      )
    );
  }
}
```

In the preceding code snippet, the following applies:

- `@Injectable()` declares that `UppercaseInterceptor` can be managed by Nest's DI system.

- The `intercept()` method is where the magic happens:

  - The `context: ExecutionContext` instance provides details of the current request cycle, allowing you to access the request, response, or even metadata about the currently executing route.

  - The `next: CallHandler` instance represents the next processor in the request flow. By calling `next.handle()`, you pass control to the next interceptor or the route handler itself.

- Within the `map` operator, we check if the response data is a string. If it is, we convert it to uppercase. Otherwise, we return the data as is.

Response mapping

Beyond simple transformations, interceptors can restructure the entire response body. Consider this interceptor, which wraps responses:

```
@Injectable()
export class ResponseInterceptor implements NestInterceptor
{
  intercept(
    context: ExecutionContext, next: CallHandler):
    Observable<any>
  {
    return next.handle().pipe(
      map(data => ({ status: 'success', data })
      )
    );
  }
}
```

Now, irrespective of what your route handlers return, every response will be an object containing a `status` field with a `'success'` value and a `data` field holding the original response.

In the next section, we will explore how to intercept requests and make sure users certain criteria are met before a request can access specific endpoints. So, buckle up, and let's dive deeper into the world of NestJS!

Middleware – the uncelebrated controller companions

In the architecture of modern web applications, middleware functions are the unsung heroes working behind the scenes. They have the unique capability to intercept and process incoming requests before they reach your route handlers (controllers) and after a response has been sent by your application. In NestJS, middleware takes on the form of a function that has access to `Request` and `Response` objects, as well as the next function, which is a part of the request-response cycle.

Middleware functions can perform a variety of tasks, such as the following:

- Modifying `Request` and `Response` objects
- Ending the request-response cycle
- Calling the next middleware in the stack
- Logging, authentication, and much more

In NestJS, middleware functions are constructed to work in harmony with the modular structure of the framework, thereby offering a robust and organized approach to handling side tasks.

One of the most fundamental uses of middleware is logging. By capturing each incoming request, a logging middleware can help keep track of how the system is being used, as well as help in debugging.

For example, here's how you might write a simple logging middleware in NestJS:

```
import {
  Injectable,
  NestMiddleware
} from '@nestjs/common';
import { Request, Response, NextFunction } from 'express';

@Injectable()
export class LoggingMiddleware implements NestMiddleware {
  use(req: Request, res: Response, next: NextFunction) {
    console.log(
      `[${new Date().toISOString()}]
      Request made to: ${req.path}`);
    next();
  }
}
```

In this snippet, the following takes place:

- We create a LoggingMiddleware class that implements the NestMiddleware interface; this automatically transforms this class into a middleware in addition to the @Injectable decorator.

- The use() method is where we define what the middleware does. Here, it logs the current date and the requested path.

- The next() function is called to pass the request to the next middleware (or to the route handler if it's the last middleware in the stack).

After the execution of your middleware, a short conclusion is drawn about the request, giving valuable insights into the traffic your application is receiving.

Building custom middlewares in NestJS

To build a custom middleware in NestJS, we first define a class that implements the NestMiddleware interface. Let's walk through creating a middleware that checks for a specific header in the request:

```
import {
  Injectable,
  NestMiddleware
} from '@nestjs/common';
import { Request, Response } from 'express';

@Injectable()
export class HeaderCheckMiddleware implements
  NestMiddleware
{
  use(req: Request, res: Response, next: NextFunction) {
    if(req.headers['x-custom-header']) {
      console.log('Header is present');
      next();
    } else {
      res.status(400).send('Missing custom header');
    }
  }
}
```

Let's break down the code:

- Our HeaderCheckMiddleware class looks for x-custom-header in the request headers

- If the header exists, we log a message and proceed by calling next()

- If the header is missing, we terminate the request by sending a 400 response

This middleware is a great example of intercepting and validating requests for specific requirements before they reach your controllers.

Enhanced middleware configuration

To leverage the middleware concept in NestJS, here are some important points to consider:

- **Applying global middleware**: In NestJS, global middleware is applied to every incoming request, regardless of the route. This is especially useful for functionality that needs to be executed across the entire application, such as **cross-origin resource sharing (CORS)** handling or general logging.

    Here's how to set up global middleware in your main application file (usually `main.ts`):

    ```
    import { NestFactory } from '@nestjs/core';
    import { AppModule } from './app.module';
    import {
      LoggingMiddleware
    } from './logging.middleware';

    async function bootstrap() {
      const app = await NestFactory.create(AppModule);
      app.use(new LoggingMiddleware().use);
      await app.listen(3000);
    }
    bootstrap();
    ```

    Here, `app.use(new LoggingMiddleware().use)` registers `LoggingMiddleware` as a global middleware.

- **Chaining multiple middlewares**: NestJS allows chaining multiple middlewares on the same route. This can be useful when you want to perform several operations in sequence, such as validating a request, then logging it, and perhaps modifying it before it reaches the controller.

    Let's add another middleware to our chain:

    ```
    consumer
      .apply(
        FirstMiddleware,
        SecondMiddleware,
        LoggingMiddleware
      )
      .forRoutes('*');
    ```

    In the `apply` function, multiple middleware can be passed in the order they should be executed.

Utilizing functional middleware

While class-based middleware is common in NestJS, sometimes a simpler approach using functional middleware is preferable, particularly for lightweight tasks.

A functional middleware is simply a function that doesn't need an @Injectable() decorator and can be used directly:

```
export function SimpleLogger(req, res, next) {
  console.log('Simple log:', req.path);
  next();
}
```

It's applied as follows:

```
consumer.apply(SimpleLogger).forRoutes('*');
```

The MiddlewareConsumer class offers methods to fine-tune the routes that middleware is applied to:

- exclude(): This method allows you to specify routes that the middleware should not apply to:

```
consumer
    .apply(LoggingMiddleware)
    .exclude(
      {
        path: 'health',
        method: RequestMethod.GET
      },
      {
        path: 'metrics',
        method: RequestMethod.ALL
      }
    )
    .forRoutes('*');
```

  Here, LoggingMiddleware is applied globally except for the /health GET requests and all /metrics requests. The RequestMethod class can be imported from the @nestjs/ common package.

- forRoutes(): This method is used to apply middleware to specific routes. It can take strings, route paths, controllers, and even methods of controllers:

```
consumer
  .apply(AuthenticationMiddleware)
  .forRoutes(
```

```
    { path: 'users', method: RequestMethod.ALL }
);
```

AuthenticationMiddleware is now only applied to routes under /users.

Middleware sequence and execution flow

Middlewares in NestJS are executed in the order they are configured. This sequence is crucial because it determines how the request is processed and potentially transformed before reaching the controller. Understanding this sequence is essential to avoid unexpected behaviors in your application's logic.

To ensure middlewares do not create bottlenecks, it's important to keep them lean and efficient, delegating any heavy processing to services or background tasks when possible.

While powerful, middleware isn't always the right tool for every job. For instance, when you need to guard routes based on authentication or authorization, you would be better off using guards. Middleware is great for tasks that do not involve decision-making concerning the continuation of the request-response cycle based on business logic.

As a closing thought on middleware, remember that while they're not always at the forefront of development conversations, they play a vital role in the robustness and reliability of your application.

As we wrap up this section on middleware, it's clear that these components serve as critical checkpoints within the request lifecycle, facilitating tasks that are orthogonal to your business logic. Their correct usage ensures a clean and maintainable code base.

Before diving into our next topic, let's visualize a middleware flow as shown in *Figure 4.4*:

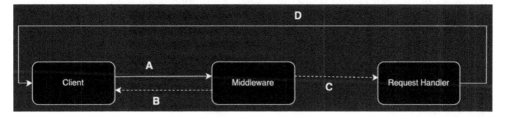

Figure 4.5: Request flow

In *Figure 4.4*, we can see the following:

- When a client makes an HTTP request (*A*), the request is first intercepted by the middleware, which can make some computations and checking such as logging, verifying the token, verifying the presence of certain information in the request, or even modifying the Request object before passing it to the handler

- If the request doesn't satisfy a certain number of criteria (*B*), the middleware itself will respond to the client, with a proper error message

- If the request is correct (*C*), the middleware will pass it to the next step by calling the `next()` function; by then, the request can be handled by another middleware in the queue or the request handler, which is, in Nest context, the controller

- Next, the controller will send back a response to the client (*D*)

Middleware in NestJS is a powerful feature allowing for a granular approach to request handling. From setting up global middleware to chaining and customizing routes with `MiddlewareConsumer` methods, we have the tools to control the flow of our application in a sophisticated manner. As we apply these principles, we ensure that our application not only performs its primary tasks effectively but also handles auxiliary operations with precision and elegance.

With the middleware landscape detailed, we'll pivot to *Deep dive into route guards*, building upon our knowledge of request handling. Guards offer a different perspective on traffic management, with a focus on authorizing access to routes, ensuring that our application remains secure and user access is correctly managed.

Deep dive into route guards

Route guards are a fundamental part of the NestJS framework, crucial for ensuring that a certain set of logic is fulfilled before a route handler is executed. These guards are particularly vital for implementing authorization and authentication logic in an application.

At its core, a route guard in NestJS is a class annotated with `@Injectable()` that implements the `CanActivate` interface. This interface requires the `canActivate()` function, which NestJS calls to determine whether the current request is allowed to proceed.

Figure 4.5 illustrates how guards work in a NestJS application:

Figure 4.6: Guards in NestJS – credit https://docs.nestjs.com/guards

Working principles of guards

Guards have the power to control the request pipeline. They can decide either to pass the request through to the next stage (by returning `true`) or to block it (by returning `false`). Guards operate by examining the `ExecutionContext` class, which provides details about the request, response, and execution context.

Let's begin with a simple example. Here's a guard that blocks every request:

```
import {
  Injectable,
  CanActivate,
  ExecutionContext
} from '@nestjs/common';

@Injectable()
export class BlockGuard implements CanActivate {
  canActivate(context: ExecutionContext): boolean {
    // In a real scenario, you'd implement some logic here
    return false;
  }
}
```

In this code snippet, the canActivate() method always returns false, meaning no routes will be accessible when this guard is active. The ExecutionContext argument gives you access to the request details, although it's not used here.

Using guards for authentication and authorization

Authentication is the process of verifying who a user is, while authorization is about determining what they are allowed to do. Guards are an excellent place to perform these checks.

Here's an example of an authentication guard:

```
@Injectable()
export class AuthGuard implements CanActivate {
  canActivate(context: ExecutionContext): boolean |
    Promise<boolean> | Observable<boolean>
  {
    const request = context.switchToHttp().getRequest();
    return validateRequest(request);
  }
}

function validateRequest(request: Request): boolean {
  // Authentication logic here
  return request.headers.authorization ? true : false;
}
```

This guard checks for the presence of an authorization header in the request, a common way to implement token-based authentication.

Role-based access control with guards

For applications with different user roles, guards can enforce **role-based access control** (**RBAC**). Here's an example of an RBAC guard implementation:

```
@Injectable()
export class RolesGuard implements CanActivate {
  canActivate(context: ExecutionContext): boolean {
    const request = context.switchToHttp().getRequest();
    const user = request.user;
    return user && user.role === 'admin';
  }
}
```

This guard checks if the user object in the request has the role of 'admin'. Only users with an 'admin' role can access the route.

Dynamic guards – context-based guard execution

Dynamic guards are adaptable and can modify their behavior based on the request or context. For example, you might have a guard that allows access during certain hours of the day:

```
@Injectable()
export class TimeBasedGuard implements CanActivate {
  canActivate(context: ExecutionContext): boolean {
    const currentHour = new Date().getHours();
    // Allow access only during office hours
    return currentHour >= 9 && currentHour <= 17;
  }
}
```

This guard grants access to a route only if the current time is within the specified range.

Guard composition – combining multiple guards

NestJS allows applying multiple guards to a route, and they will be resolved in a logical AND manner. This means all guards must return true for the request to proceed:

```
@UseGuards(AuthGuard, RolesGuard)
@Get('admin-panel')
findAdminPanel() {
  // Admin panel data
}
```

In this case, a request must pass both `AuthGuard` and `RolesGuard` to access the `admin-panel` route.

Global guards

A global guard applies to every route in the application. You can set up a global guard in the main application file:

```
async function bootstrap() {
  const app = await NestFactory.create(AppModule);
  app.useGlobalGuards(new AuthGuard());
  await app.listen(3000);
}
bootstrap();
```

In this setup, `AuthGuard` is applied globally, so all routes require authentication.

> **Important note on execution order**
>
> Before we conclude our exploration of guards in NestJS, it's crucial to understand their place within the request processing pipeline. In the typical flow of a NestJS application, middlewares always execute before guards. This sequence is by design, allowing middleware to perform its duties, such as request logging, body parsing, or even authentication, before any guard decides on whether to allow or deny a request to proceed to a route handler. Remember—the middleware's job is to prepare and qualify requests for further handling downstream, while guards are the gatekeepers, making the final call on access control based on the preparatory work done by middlewares.

By keeping this order in mind, developers can architect their applications with clarity, ensuring that each component of the request pipeline does its job effectively and at the correct stage. This clear delineation of responsibilities is one of the strengths of NestJS, providing a robust structure for developing scalable and maintainable server-side applications.

Guards are indispensable in NestJS, serving as the gatekeepers of routes and ensuring that only valid requests proceed. By leveraging guards, developers can enforce authentication, authorization, and a myriad of custom access control policies in their applications.

Transitioning from this understanding of guards, we will now explore how NestJS facilitates data persistence with robust database integration techniques, ensuring that your application's data layer is as reliable as its error handling.

Streaming data with NestJS controllers

Data streaming is a method of continuously transferring data from a sender to a receiver, allowing the receiver to start processing the data before the entire payload has arrived. This approach contrasts with traditional data transfer methods, which require all data to be available before any processing can begin.

In web applications, streaming can be used to handle large files, live video, or real-time data feeds. It is beneficial for improving user experience by reducing wait times and enhancing performance by decreasing memory usage on the server.

The main advantages of streaming in web applications include the following:

- **Efficiency**: Processes data on the fly without needing to store the entire content in memory

- **Scalability**: Handles large or infinite data sources, such as live media feeds

- **Responsiveness**: Provides users with immediate feedback, which is crucial for video streaming and online gaming

The role of streams in NestJS

NestJS leverages Node.js streams to efficiently handle data transfers. This integration ensures that NestJS applications can manage large amounts of data or data that is continuously produced without overwhelming server resources.

Node.js provides four types of streams:

- **Readable**: Streams from which data can be read (for example, `fs.createReadStream`)

- **Writable**: Streams to which data can be written (for example, `fs.createWriteStream`)

- **Duplex**: Streams that are both readable and writable

- **Transform**: Duplex streams that can modify or transform the data as it is written and read

Implementing a basic data stream

Before diving into code, let's set the scene. Imagine a scenario where we want to stream a large dataset from the server to a client, such as sending a large CSV file containing user data.

We start by creating an endpoint in a NestJS controller that will stream the data:

```
import { Controller, Get, Res } from '@nestjs/common';
import { Response } from 'express';
import { createReadStream } from 'fs';
import { join } from 'path';

@Controller('data')
export class DataController {
```

```
@Get('stream')
streamData(@Res() res: Response) {
  const filePath = join(__dirname, 'large-dataset.csv');
  const stream = createReadStream(filePath);

  stream.pipe(res);
}
}
```

In this code snippet, the following takes place:

- We import the necessary modules and decorators
- We create a `DataController` class with a `streamData()` method
- Inside the method, we use Node.js's `createReadStream` function to read a file from the filesystem
- We then pipe this read stream directly to the `Response` object, which is a writable stream, using `stream.pipe(res)`

This method streams the file to the client, sending data in chunks as soon as it is available, instead of waiting for the entire file to be read into memory.

The `.pipe()` method is used to take the data from the readable stream and send it to the `Response` object, which is a writable stream. This method is efficient because it only processes small pieces of the file at a time.

Using RxJS Observables for streaming

NestJS is built with RxJS, a library for reactive programming using Observables. To implement streaming with Observables, we can do the following:

```
import { Controller, Get } from '@nestjs/common';
import { Observable } from 'rxjs';
import { createReadStream } from 'fs';
import { join } from 'path';
import { map } from 'rxjs/operators';

@Controller('data')
export class DataController {
  @Get('observable-stream')
  streamWithObservable(): Observable<any> {
    const filePath = join(__dirname, 'large-dataset.csv');
    const stream = createReadStream(filePath);
```

```
      return new Observable(observer => {
        stream.on('data', (chunk) => observer.next(chunk));
        stream.on('error', (err) => observer.error(err));
        stream.on('end', () => observer.complete());
      }).pipe(
        map(chunk => ({ data: chunk.toString() })),
      );
    }
  }
```

Here, we've wrapped the stream in an `Observable` instance and mapped each chunk to an object with a `data` property. This approach gives us more control over the streaming process, allowing for complex operations such as filtering and error handling.

Best practices for streaming data

While implementing streams in NestJS, here are a couple of best practices to follow:

- **Error handling in streams**: Always listen for the `error` event on streams to prevent crashes and properly handle exceptions
- **Performance considerations**: When dealing with large streams, monitor resource usage and adjust the stream's chunk size to optimize for memory and speed

Streaming data is a powerful feature in NestJS that enables efficient, real-time data handling for applications. By understanding and implementing streams properly, developers can build responsive and scalable web applications that handle data gracefully and efficiently.

In the next section, we will explore other advanced NestJS controller features that further enhance the capabilities of your applications.

Advanced WebSocket patterns

In the world of real-time applications, WebSockets play an integral role in facilitating immediate and persistent communication between the client and the server. NestJS, with its scalable architecture, offers sophisticated patterns for leveraging WebSocket technology. In this section, we dive deep into advanced WebSocket patterns, exploring how they can be implemented within NestJS to build highly interactive and real-time applications.

Before delving into the patterns, let's establish an understanding of WebSockets. WebSockets enable a full-duplex communication channel that remains open for as long as needed, allowing messages to be passed back and forth while keeping the connection alive. This is particularly useful for any application where real-time updates are crucial.

Benefits of using WebSockets in real-time applications

Real-time applications such as chat systems, live news feeds, or online gaming platforms benefit immensely from WebSockets due to their ability to facilitate instant data transfer without the typical request-response model of HTTP, making the user experience smooth and responsive.

With this foundational knowledge, let's see how NestJS equips us with the tools to implement WebSocket servers.

Setting up WebSockets in NestJS

Let's dive into setting up Websocket in your NestJS application.

NestJS simplifies the complexity of real-time backends with its `@nestjs/websockets` module, which is built on top of robust libraries such as `Socket.IO` or `ws`, providing seamless integration for WebSocket functionalities.

To kickstart our WebSocket journey, we begin by setting up a basic server. NestJS uses the concept of a gateway to handle WebSocket connections. This gateway acts as a bridge between your clients and the server, managing incoming and outgoing messages.

Have a look at the following code snippet:

```
import {
  WebSocketGateway,
  SubscribeMessage,
  WebSocketServer
} from '@nestjs/websockets';
import { Server } from 'socket.io';

@WebSocketGateway()
export class AppGateway {
  @WebSocketServer()
  server: Server;

  @SubscribeMessage('message')
  handleMessage(client: any, payload: any): string {
    return 'Hello world!';
  }
}
```

In this snippet, the following takes place:

- We declare an `AppGateway` class with the `@WebSocketGateway()` decorator, which initializes a WebSocket server
- The `@WebSocketServer()` decorator injects the underlying server instance, allowing direct access to the native server API
- The `@SubscribeMessage('message')` decorator listens for incoming messages with the `'message'` event name and provides a simple handler that responds with `'Hello world!'`

This setup is the starting point for enabling WebSocket communication in a NestJS application.

Next, we'll discuss patterns that can be used to organize data flow and handle more complex scenarios in WebSocket communication.

Organizing data flow with namespaces and rooms

Namespaces in `Socket.IO`, which NestJS can utilize, allow you to segment WebSocket communication into different paths or contexts, which is similar to having multiple WebSocket servers and is useful for dividing the application into features or functionalities.

Rooms are a feature within namespaces that lets you further organize WebSocket connections. This is especially useful for broadcasting messages to a subset of clients, such as in a chat room or a multiplayer game lobby.

Have a look at the following code snippet:

```
@WebSocketGateway()
export class ChatGateway {
  @SubscribeMessage('joinRoom')
  handleRoomJoin(client: any, room: string) {
    client.join(room);
    client.emit('joinedRoom', room);
  }

  @SubscribeMessage('leaveRoom')
  handleRoomLeave(client: any, room: string) {
    client.leave(room);
    client.emit('leftRoom', room);
  }
}
```

Here, the following takes place:

- The `handleRoomJoin()` method allows a client to join a specific room
- The `handleRoomLeave()` method is the counterpart for leaving the room
- The client is notified upon joining or leaving the room with an event

With these methods, you can manage the flow of communication in a granular way, ensuring messages are delivered to the right recipients.

Coming up next, we'll explore how to secure our WebSocket channels with authentication and authorization practices.

Authentication and authorization in WebSockets

While WebSockets are great for real-time data, they also open up a direct line of communication that, if not secured, could be exploited. Therefore, it's crucial to implement authentication and authorization to verify the identity of users and control access to various WebSocket channels.

NestJS allows for the integration of standard auth strategies, such as **JSON Web Token** (**JWT**) or **Open Authorization** (**OAuth**), with WebSockets. This can be achieved through middleware or guards, which can inspect the handshake or connection process to ensure the validity of a client's credentials.

Have a look at the following code snippet:

```
@WebSocketGateway()
export class AuthGateway {
  @SubscribeMessage('authenticate')
  handleAuthentication(client: any, token: string) {
    try {
      // Logic to validate the token
      const user = validateToken(token);
      client.user = user;
      client.emit('authenticated');
    } catch (e) {
      client.error('Authentication failed');
    }
  }
}
```

In this example, the following takes place:

- A message listener for `'authenticate'` is used to process the client's token
- The `validateToken` function is a hypothetical function that would validate the token and return the user's information
- Upon successful authentication, the `user` object is attached to the client, and the client is notified

This pattern ensures that only authenticated users can access and interact with the WebSocket server.

To wrap up this section, we'll summarize the key points and the role of advanced WebSocket patterns in NestJS applications.

WebSockets offer a powerful means to enable real-time, bi-directional communication between clients and servers. By mastering the advanced patterns provided by NestJS, developers can build complex, real-time applications with efficient data flow management, secure connections, and scalable architectures. This exploration of advanced WebSocket patterns in NestJS demonstrates the framework's commitment to providing developers with the tools needed to handle real-time communication at scale.

As we conclude this section, remember that WebSocket communication is just one of many advanced features NestJS offers. By combining these practices with the other aspects of NestJS, you can craft robust, efficient, and highly interactive applications.

Understanding providers in depth

Providers are the cornerstone of NestJS's architecture. They are at the heart of NestJS's DI system, serving as a powerful pattern for managing class dependencies. Essentially, providers can be anything that can return a value, such as a service, factory, value, or class. NestJS treats these providers as first-class citizens, meaning they're fundamental to the structure and operation of any NestJS application.

In NestJS, providers are responsible for various tasks such as the following:

- Defining a set of functions that various components of an application might need
- Encapsulating complex logic
- Accessing data from a database
- Performing computational operations

The beauty of providers lies in their versatility and reusability, which lead to cleaner, more efficient code.

Brief recap – providers and modules

Before diving deeper into providers, let's quickly recap their relationship with modules. In NestJS, modules are the tapestry where providers are declared and assembled. Each module encapsulates providers, creating a clear and organized application structure.

Modules in NestJS serve as an organizational framework that allows us to group related functionalities together. When we define a provider, it must be associated with a module. This association tells NestJS's DI system about the provider's scope and its availability to be injected into other components such as controllers and services.

What constitutes a provider in NestJS?

Providers in NestJS are broadly defined as classes that encapsulate business logic and are annotated with a decorator, typically @Injectable(). These classes can be injected into other classes via the constructor, allowing for a modular and testable approach to development.

There are several types of providers in NestJS:

- **Services**: Classes that handle business logic and data retrieval
- **Factories**: Functions that return a provider instance dynamically
- **Values**: Hardcoded values that can be injected
- **Classes**: When a class itself can be a provider

This flexibility allows developers to choose the right tool for the job, ensuring that the application's components are loosely coupled and highly modular.

Services, factories, values, and more

The most common provider is a service. Let's take a look at a simple service provider:

```
import { Injectable } from '@nestjs/common';

@Injectable()
export class CatsService {
  findAll(): string[] {
    return ['Whiskers', 'Tom', 'Felix'];
  }
}
```

In this snippet, we define a service named CatsService. By using the @Injectable() decorator, NestJS understands that this class is a provider and can be used in the DI system. This service has a single method, findAll, which returns an array of cat names.

How DI works in NestJS

DI is a design pattern that NestJS utilizes to provide components with their dependencies rather than creating them internally. DI allows for greater modularity and ease of testing. In NestJS, DI is accomplished by using decorators to "inject" providers into classes that require them.

Here's an example of DI in action:

```
import { Controller } from '@nestjs/common';
import { CatsService } from './cats.service';

@Controller('cats')
export class CatsController {
  constructor(private catsService: CatsService) {}

  findAll() {
    return this.catsService.findAll();
  }
}
```

In the `CatsController` class, `CatsService` is injected through the constructor. NestJS's runtime system takes care of creating an instance of `CatsService` and passing it to the `CatsController` class when it's instantiated.

Injecting providers into modules, controllers, and other providers

Providers can be injected into any class that NestJS manages, including other providers, modules, and controllers. When a provider is injected, NestJS looks up the provider tree to find the closest instance that matches the required dependency.

Scope and lifetime of providers

By default, providers in NestJS are singletons. This means that a single instance of the provider is shared across the entire application, ensuring efficient memory usage and consistent data management. Here's an example of this:

```
// Singleton provider, the default in NestJS
@Injectable()
export class SingletonService {
  // Service logic here
}
```

This singleton provider is instantiated once and the same instance is used wherever the provider is injected.

Request and transient scopes

Apart from the default singleton scope, NestJS also offers request and transient scopes for providers:

- **Request scope**: A new instance of the provider is created exclusively for each incoming request
- **Transient scope**: A new instance is created every time a provider is injected, which is useful for stateful services that are not shared

You can see an example of both in the following code snippet:

```
// Request scoped provider
@Injectable({ scope: Scope.REQUEST })
export class RequestScopedService {
  // Service logic here
}

// Transient scoped provider
@Injectable({ scope: Scope.TRANSIENT })
export class TransientService {
  // Service logic here
}
```

Providers in NestJS are powerful and flexible components that serve as the backbone of the framework's DI system. They promote a clean and modular application structure, ensuring that components are easily testable and maintainable. As we proceed, we will explore custom providers and their configurations, further expanding on the capabilities of NestJS's DI system. We'll see how custom providers can be tailored to specific application needs, enhancing the versatility of your NestJS applications.

Custom providers

NestJS allows for a range of custom provider types, enabling developers to tailor the DI to their specific needs. These are defined in the module where they'll be used.

The useFactory key allows you to create a provider dynamically. This is particularly useful when the creation process involves some logic.

Have a look at the following code example:

```
{
  provide: 'ASYNC_CONNECTION',
  useFactory: async () => {
    const connection = await createConnection();
    return connection;
  },
}
```

In this example, an asynchronous operation is required to create a database connection. The factory function can also inject dependencies by providing an `inject` array.

When you want to provide a class that can be instantiated, use the `useClass` syntax.

Here's an example of this:

```
{
  provide: 'Connection',
  useClass: DatabaseConnection,
}
```

Here, `DatabaseConnection` would be a class that provides the necessary logic for managing a database connection.

You can provide a constant value or a set of configurations using `useValue`.

Here's an example of this:

```
{
  provide: 'CONFIG',
  useValue: {
    host: process.env.DB_HOST,
  },
}
```

This is useful for injecting configuration objects or constants that don't require any instantiation logic.

With `useExisting`, you can map providers to use the instance of another already created provider.

Here's an example of this:

```
{
  provide: 'AliasConnection',
  useExisting: DatabaseConnection,
}
```

This creates an `AliasConnection` alias that points to the same instance as `DatabaseConnection`, ensuring only one instance is maintained.

Asynchronous providers

Async providers are useful when some initialization steps are asynchronous, such as database connections or API calls.

Have a look at the following example:

```
{
  provide: 'ASYNC_RESOURCE',
  useFactory: async (): Promise<ResourceType> => {
    const resource = await someAsyncFunction();
    return resource;
  },
}
```

Here, the provider will wait for `someAsyncFunction` to resolve before becoming available for injection.

Practical scenarios include setting up database connections, initializing third-party services, or fetching configuration settings from a remote server during the application startup.

In NestJS, providers can be private to a module unless explicitly exported. Private providers can only be injected into components that are also within the same module.

Exporting providers from modules

To make a provider available outside of its declaring module, you must export it.

Here's an example of this in action:

```
@Module({
  providers: [CatsService],
  exports: [CatsService],
})
export class CatsModule {}
```

`CatsService` is now accessible to any module that imports `CatsModule`.

Enhancers as a special kind of provider

Enhancers, as with interceptors, filters, guards, and pipes, are treated as providers in NestJS, but they are used for extending the framework's behavior rather than providing data or services.

Have a look at the following example:

```
@Injectable()
export class LoggingInterceptor implements NestInterceptor
{
  intercept(context: ExecutionContext, next: CallHandler):
    Observable<any>
```

```
{
  console.log('Logging...');
  return next.handle();
  }
}
```

Here, `LoggingInterceptor` acts as a provider that intercepts request handling and logs a message.

Enhancers are registered in a similar way to providers and can inject dependencies through their constructors.

Advanced techniques and best practices

When building your providers, here are a couple of best practices to follow:

- **Dynamic modules and providers**: NestJS supports dynamic modules that can create providers based on external parameters

  Have a look at the following example:

  ```
  @Module({})
  export class DynamicModule {
    static forRoot(options: DynamicModuleOptions):
      DynamicModule
    {
      return {
        module: DynamicModule,
        providers: createProviders(options),
      };
    }
  }
  ```

  This module can be customized based on `options` passed to `forRoot`.

- **Design patterns**: Developers can create custom decorators to simplify the injection of providers or to associate tokens with providers for easier identification

Since we have gathered a deep understanding of what providers are, it's time to wrap everything up by exploring the request lifecycle in NestJS in the next section.

Understanding request lifecycle

It's been a long journey, and we've learned a lot. Before we conclude, let's consolidate our understanding of the request lifecycle. We've already seen how a NestJS application consists of various components such as modules, controllers, and providers. But how does a request navigate through these components to generate a server response? To clarify this, we've included a diagram that explains it more effectively.

Figure 4.6 summarizes everything you need to know about the request lifecycle, from the initial client request to the server's response. The diagram uses green lines to show the normal request flow—if everything goes as planned—and red lines to indicate what happens if something unexpected occurs, such as a middleware blocking a request or a guard denying access. Before the response is sent back to the client, interceptors process the `Response` object to ensure the client receives the correct response. Depending on the specifics of your application, some components might be omitted or additional elements such as an exception filter or a `catchError()` method in the interceptor might be included. The chart may vary slightly, but the underlying logic remains the same:

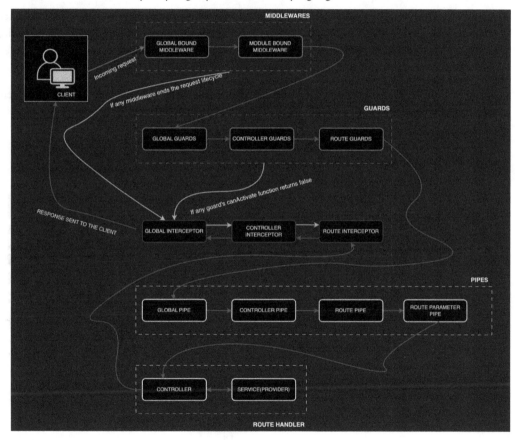

Figure 4.7: Request lifecycle

Summary

Wrapping up *Chapter 4*, we've journeyed through the heart of NestJS, unlocking the secrets behind its advanced features. We've climbed from the foundational modules that structure our apps with grace and efficiency through the nuanced world of controllers and providers that breathe life into our code. Along the way, we've navigated essential guards and pipes that keep our applications secure and our data validated, and we've adorned our classes with powerful decorators to extend their capabilities effortlessly.

This deep dive has not only expanded our theoretical understanding but also armed us with practical tools to sculpt applications that are robust, scalable, and beautifully architected. With this knowledge, we stand on the brink of practical application: building a RESTful API that harnesses the full potential of NestJS.

As we step into the next chapter, we're ready to apply these advanced concepts to real-world challenges, shaping our NestJS applications into works of technical art. Ready to roll up your sleeves and bring theory into action? Let's leap into this together!

Get This Book's PDF Version and Exclusive Extras

UNLOCK NOW

Scan the QR code (or go to `packtpub.com/unlock`). Search for this book by name, confirm the edition, and then follow the steps on the page.

Note: Keep your invoice handly. Purchase made directly from packt don't require one.

Part 2:
REST APIs and GraphQL
in NestJS

This part helps you build basic RESTful and GraphQL APIs and understand the versatile nature of NestJS.

This part includes the following chapters:

- *Chapter 5, Building and Optimizing REST APIs with NestJS*
- *Chapter 6, Unleashing the Power of GraphQL and the Apollo Federation Architecture in NestJS*

Building and Optimizing REST APIs with NestJS

Welcome to an exciting chapter where we'll transform knowledge into practice! After delving deep into the intricacies of NestJS in the previous chapters, we're now ready to apply our skills and build something tangible and impactful. This chapter is all about crafting and fine-tuning REST APIs using NestJS while leveraging the powerful features and best practices we've uncovered so far.

Are you geared up for some real-world coding? Here's what we'll embark on together in this chapter:

- Introduction to REST APIs in NestJS
- Building a basic REST API in NestJS
- Versioning your API
- Error handling
- Documenting your API

By the end of this chapter, you'll not only have a solid understanding of REST API development with NestJS but also hands-on experience in building one. So, without further ado, let's dive in and start building.

Technical requirements

The code files for the chapter can be found at https://github.com/PacktPublishing/Scalable-Application-Development-with-NestJS

Introduction to REST APIs in NestJS

Remember how we kicked things off in *Chapter 3* by crafting a simple NestJS application? Well, now it's time to peel back another layer. We were able to make a **GET** request to the **application programming interface (API)** we created back then because, by default, NestJS supports the **REpresentational State Transfer (REST)** architectural style.

So, what's this REST thing, anyway? And how's it different from being *RESTful*? This question may have arisen as you read this paragraph, and it's great as it calls out your curiosity! Think of REST as more than a set of tools; it's a philosophy for designing applications that communicate over a network. It's all about simplicity, using stateless operations, and providing a uniform way to address resources, often over our good old friend, HTTP. On the flip side, when we talk about something being RESTful, we're referring to an API that's a walking, talking example of these REST principles and uses familiar HTTP methods such as GET, POST, PUT, and DELETE in a way that's both scalable and user-friendly.

Let's consider a real-world scenario. Take PayPal, for instance. Its backbone is built on REST principles, ensuring everything ticks along nicely. Meanwhile, it offers RESTful APIs for the world to connect with its services, sticking closely to those same principles.

Now, let's get back to NestJS. This framework doesn't just *support* REST; it's practically married to it. This means that when you whip up a basic NestJS application, you're already playing in the REST playground.

And guess what? We're not just going to chat about these ideas; we're going to roll up our sleeves and make them come to life. Next, we'll learn how to build our basic REST API using NestJS. There, you'll step into the shoes of a builder, piecing together your very own REST API using NestJS. It's time to turn those concepts into something you can see, touch, and interact with. Let's jump right in and start piecing this puzzle together!

Building a basic REST API

As we embark on this exciting phase of building a REST API, let's refresh our memory of the core concepts we've learned so far. Remember the environment setup from *Chapter 3* and the deep dive into modules, controllers, providers, exception filters, pipes, guards, and decorators in *Chapter 4*? We're about to bring all these elements into play.

Setting up your REST API project

Whether you're continuing with the NestJS application from *Chapter 2* or starting afresh, the principles remain the same. Let's begin by setting up our project environment:

- **For a new project**, run nest new project-name in your terminal.
- **For an existing project**, navigate to your existing project directory.

- **Understanding the structure**: Observe the default folders – that is, `controllers`, `modules`, and so on – just as we did in *Chapter 2*, as a way for you to refresh your memory:

  - **Running the application**: Start the application using `npm run start:dev`. This will spin up the local server.

With the first step complete, let's dive deeper.

Designing your first RESTful endpoint

Let's embark on crafting our first RESTful endpoint. To keep our demonstration simple to follow and straightforward, we're going to build a basic user management API that features the basics of CRUD operations: creating a user (*POST*), retrieving users (*GET*), updating (*PUT*), and deleting a user (*DELETE*). But first, our initial task is to create a simple `GET` endpoint that will return a mocked array of users.

Here's the deal: we're going to set up everything manually this time. Why? Because it's essential to understand how to build modules from scratch and connect them to the root module. Sure, the **NestJS CLI** is super handy, but nothing beats the learning you get from doing things by hand. So, let's get started!

1. **Creating UsersModule**:

   - Inside your `src/` directory, create a new sub-directory named `users`.

   - Now, let's create our first file in this new directory: `users.module.ts`. This is where we'll define our `Users` module – the cornerstone of our user management system:

     ```
     import { Module } from '@nestjs/common';

     @Module({})
     export class UsersModule {}
     ```

   We start with a simple class decorated with `@Module`. This is our module's declaration.

2. **Connecting to the root module**:

   - Now, let's integrate this new module into the heart of our application. As of now, `UsersModule` is an isolated node from the application graph, so we need to import it into `AppModule` so that we can play with its components, such as its controller and defined HTTP operations.

   - In your `src/app.module.ts` file, add `UsersModule` to the imports array:

     ```
     // ... existing imports
     import { UsersModule } from './users/users.module';

     // ... existing code
     ```

```
imports: [UsersModule], // Add this line
// ... the rest of the code
```

With this, our `Users` module is now part of our application's ecosystem.

3. **Setting up the user entity**:

- In the `src/users/` directory of our NestJS project, we'll create a new sub-directory named `entities/`. In NestJS architecture, this directory is where we place our resource-related entity types. It's especially important when your application interacts with a database. This directory serves as the optimal location for storing things such as your resource schema or tables for relational databases.

- Now, within this newly created `entities/` folder, let's create a file named `users.entity.ts`. Here's the code you must include in that file:

```
// src/users/entities/users.entity.ts

export class User {
  id: number;
  name: string;
  email: string;
}
```

This class will define the structure of a `User` entity in our application, keeping it straightforward for now. Note that depending on which **object-relational mapping** (**ORM**) you're using for your database, this class can be annotated with the ORM's related decorators, such as `@Schema()` and its field, as well as decorators such as `@Prop()` and others, depending on your ORM. For our use case, since we aren't using any ORM, this class suits our needs.

4. **Creating UsersService**:

- Next, we need a service to handle our business logic. In `src/users/`, create a `users.service.ts` file.

- This service will manage our user data. In real use cases, this will be the place where you can put interactions with your database. For now, we'll use a simple array to mimic a database:

```
import { Injectable } from '@nestjs/common';
import { User } from './entities/users.entity';

@Injectable()
export class UsersService {
  private readonly users: User[] = [
    // Here are our mock users
    { id: 1, name: 'Tshimanga Mukendi', email:
      'tshim@myapp.com' },
```

```
    { id: 2, name: 'Kasereka Akim', email:
      'kase@myapp.com' },
  ];

  findAll(): User[] {
    return this.users;
  }
}
```

Let's see what we've done in this service file:

- We've created a class variable of the Users [] type with a mock array of users. In real-world examples consisting of database interactions, we should either use seeders to populate the array or only rely on data that already exists in the database to perform operations, instead of hard-coding users. But for demonstration purposes, this is perfect (for now).

- Then, we implemented the findAll() method, which only returns the user list we already have in the class.

- Note the @Injectable() decorator, marking this class as a provider.

5. **Implementing UsersController**:

- It's time to handle incoming **Hypertext Transfer Protocol** (**HTTP**) requests. To do so, create a users.controller.ts file in the src/users/ directory.

- This controller will direct our *GET* requests:

```
import { Controller, Get } from '@nestjs/common';
import { UsersService } from './users.service';

@Controller('users')
export class UsersController {
  constructor(
    private readonly usersService: UsersService
  ) {}

  @Get()
  findAll() {
    return this.usersService.findAll();
  }
}
```

Let's see what we've done in this controller file:

- We specify that it's a `users` controller, which means that all the requests under the `users/` endpoint will be handled here

- We implement a `@Get()` operation, with no additional parameter, that only uses the `findAll()` method we implemented earlier in the service file

- As an additional note, we have the constructor for the class, which injects `usersService` as a dependency

6. **Applying the finishing touches in UsersModule**:

    Let's ensure that our service and controller are recognized in the module

    - In `users.module.ts`, update the module definition:

    ```
    @Module({
      providers: [UsersService],
      controllers: [UsersController],
    })
    ```

    This connects our service and controller to the module.

    Adding the providers and controllers helps connect the service file to the module itself so that it can be injected into the controller class (via the `providers` array) and register the controller's operation to the module so that we can start listening to its implemented HTTP requests.

Hint

Something that may happen to you in certain scenarios while creating modules is that you'll end up omitting the providers or omitting the controller in the module definition. The first omission will give you the following error:

```
ERROR [ExceptionHandler] Nest can't resolve dependencies of
the UsersController (?).
```

```
Please make sure that the argument UsersService at index [0]
is available in the UsersModule context
```

For the second omission, NestJS will inform you that it doesn't recognize the users' route with the following response:

```
{"message":"Cannot GET /users","error":"Not
Found","statusCode":404}
```

In the module definition, ensure that both the controller and providers are specified to avoid running into one of these errors.

7. **Testing our endpoint**:

- Start your NestJS application with `yarn start:dev`.

- To test it, run the following `curl` command or use **Postman**:

```
$ curl -H 'content-type: application/json' <http://
localhost:3000/users>
```

You should now see your mock users as a response. Great job!

A note on the NestJS CLI

While we've done everything manually here, remember that the NestJS CLI can speed up this process in the future. It's perfect for quick development tasks, and you can learn more about it in the NestJS documentation (`https://docs.nestjs.com/cli/usages`). We've used some of these commands already in previous chapters, but don't hesitate to play with them to increase your productivity.

Congratulations on successfully setting up your first RESTful endpoint in our user management API! We've laid the groundwork with essential parts of the CRUD operations, connected our modules, and established a solid foundation with basic entities and services. This hands-on approach has given you a taste of NestJS's simplicity and power in building functional, scalable APIs.

But the journey doesn't end here – we've only scratched the surface of what NestJS can do. As we transition from these fundamentals, it's time to dive deeper and explore the more intricate, powerful features of NestJS. These advanced concepts will not only enhance the functionality and robustness of your API but also introduce best practices in modern API development.

Integrating advanced concepts into your API

We're about to elevate our user management API to new heights. NestJS offers a suite of advanced tools and features that can optimize performance, tighten security, and make our code more efficient and maintainable. Some of these concepts were taught theoretically in *Chapter 4*. If you feel like you need a recap, don't hesitate to read it over before we dive into the practical aspects.

We'll explore the following topics in this section:

- **Pipes** for input validation and data transformation, ensuring the integrity and correctness of the data our API handles

- **Guards** to secure our routes and manage who has access to what, implementing essential aspects of API security such as authentication and authorization

- **Middleware** for handling requests and implementing cross-cutting concerns such as logging and request validation

- **Interceptors** to transform and log responses, giving us a way to manage outgoing data and interactions efficiently

- **Custom providers** for advanced dependency injection, allowing for more dynamic and flexible code

These are just a handful of the features we'll cover here. Each will bring us closer to a robust, enterprise-level API. Let's embark on this journey and harness the full potential of NestJS, crafting an API that's not only functional but also secure, efficient, and scalable.

Pipes for validation and transformation

In the realm of API development, data validation is critical. It ensures that the incoming data adheres to the expected format and meets the criteria set by our application logic. In NestJS, **pipes** are the tools of choice for this task. They don't only validate but *can* also transform input data, making them incredibly versatile. For our user management API, we'll employ pipes to validate user data when creating and updating a user. Now, let's do some actual coding.

Before we get started with pipes, let's build our **data transfer object** (**DTO**). A DTO is an object that defines how the data will be sent over the network. We can use interfaces to describe it but NestJS recommends using classes since they're part of Javascript ES6 standards, meaning that they don't need to be compiled at runtime. Let's define the one we need for demonstration purposes:

1. **Defining user DTOs:**

   - First, we need to define the structure of the data we expect when creating or updating a user. This is where DTOs come in.

   - In the `src/users/dtos` directory (new), create two files called `create-user.dto.ts` and `update-user.dto.ts`:

     ```
     // src/users/dtos/create-user.dto.ts

     export class CreateUserDto {
       name: string;
       email: string;
     }

     // src/users/dtos/update-user.dto.ts

     // export class UpdateUserDto {
     //    name?: string;
     //    email?: string;
     //    id: number; // required to identify the user we
     //                // are updating
     // }
     ```

```
// a short form and the most used one

// you will need to install the package
import { PartialType } from '@nestjs/mapped-types';
import { CreateUserDto } from './create-user.dto';

export class UpdateUserDto extends
  PartialType(CreateUserDto)
{}
```

Here, `CreateUserDto` defines the required fields for creating a user, whereas `UpdateUserDto` uses optional fields since not all user details might change during an update. We're using `PartialType()` to generate the `UpdateUserDto` class, a utility function provided by NestJS that returns the original class passed as a parameter, with all the properties of the input type set to optional. The output will be the same as the commented line in the preceding code snippet.

2. **Implementing validation pipes**: Now that the DTOs are in place and we know exactly what our data should look like, let's implement our pipes.

   • **Applying validation pipes**:

       ◦ While NestJS's native pipes are used to validate and transform inputs, we'll first use `class-validator` and `class-transformer`, both of which are widely used and validated packages by the NestJS community that enforce validation rules in our DTOs.

       ◦ Install these packages with `yarn add class-validator class-transformer`.

   • **Enhancing DTOs with validators**:

       ◦ Add validation rules to the DTOs using decorators from the `class-validator` package:

```
// src/users/dtos/create-user.dto.ts

import { IsEmail, IsNotEmpty } from 'class-validator';

export class CreateUserDto {
  @IsNotEmpty()
  name: string;

  @IsEmail()
  email: string;
}
```

Here, we're using some of the built-in decorators from the `class-validator` package to specify how we need this data to come in from the client. Using the `@IsNotEmpty` decorator on the `name` property, we're setting a rule that's now preventing us from attempting to enter an empty string as a name for a user; the `@IsEmail` decorator also prevents us from building custom **regular expressions** (**regexes**) to handle the `email` field. With something as simple as this, we're sure that any invalid input data isn't hitting our database, keeping our data consistent.

- **Implementing the business logic to create and update a user**: Now, let's focus on developing the logic for creating and updating users in our `users.service.ts` file. If you haven't already, here are the methods we need to add:

```
// src/users/users.service.ts

// ... rest of the code
  createUser(user: CreateUserDto) {
    this.users.push({
      ...user,
      id: this.users.length + 1,
    });
  }

  updateUser(user: UpdateUserDto & { id: number }) {
    const index = this.users.findIndex(
      (u) => u.id === user.id);
    if (index === -1) {
      throw new Error('User not found');
    }

    this.users[index] = {
      name: user.name ?? this.users[index].name,
      email: user.email ?? this.users[index].email,
      id: this.users[index].id,
    };
  }
// .. remaining code
```

In the preceding code, we added two methods (`createUser` and `updateUser`) to `users.service.ts`. There are a few key points to note here:

- Currently, we're directly modifying the `users` array within the `service` class. Remember that in real-world applications, this operation would typically be asynchronous and interact with a database via ORMs. The service file is where such database interactions should be placed.

- The `updateUser` method expects an additional `id` parameter, which ideally should be received from the `path` parameter in the request, not the request body. In RESTful API design, the resource identifier (in this case, the user's ID) is best placed in the URL path rather than the request body. Note that `UpdateUserDto` doesn't include an ID field as it's meant for the payload, not resource identification. While there can be exceptions based on specific use cases, the standard practice is to put the ID in the path. If the ID is incorrect, we throw an error with a clear message while adhering to best practices in API error handling.

- It's crucial to handle errors effectively and provide clear feedback to the client. This is part of the best practices for building robust APIs. We did this here, throwing a clear error message if the user ID is incorrect.

By following these guidelines, we can ensure our user management API is not only functional but also aligns with established RESTful principles and practices. Now, let's move on to the controller.

- **Integrating pipes into controllers**:

  - Now, let's integrate these validation pipes into our controllers. To do so, we'll modify the `POST` and `PATCH` routes in `UsersController`:

```
// src/users/users.controller.ts

import {
  Body,
  Controller,
  Get,
  Param,
  ParseIntPipe,
  Patch,
  Post,
  ValidationPipe,
} from '@nestjs/common';

import { UsersService } from './users.service';
import { CreateUserDto } from './dto/create-user.dto';

@Controller('users')
export class UsersController {
  // ... existing code

  @Post()
  createUser(
    @Body(new ValidationPipe()) createUserDto:
    CreateUserDto
  ) {
```

```
    return this.usersService.createUser(
      createUserDto
    );
  }

    // without the PaseIntPipe, the id will be a
    // string => needs to be converted to a number
    // manually -- not recommended

  // @Patch(':id')
  // updateUser(@Body() updateUserDto: CreateUserDto,
  // @Param('id', ParseIntPipe) id: string) {

  // on this line, we are converting the id to a
  // number -- using the `+` sign
  // return this.usersService.updateUser({
  // ...updateUserDto, id: +id });
  // }

  // using the ParseIntPipe -- recommended
  @Patch(':id')
  updateUser(
    @Body(new ValidationPipe()) updateUserDto:
      CreateUserDto,
  @Param('id', ParseIntPipe) id: string,
  ) {
    return this.usersService.updateUser({
      ...updateUserDto,
      id
    });
  }

  // ... rest of the class methods
}
```

Here are some key things to take away regarding this code snippet:

- The @Post() method uses the @Body() decorator from the payload object and specifies in which format the payload is expected using CreateUserDto, which we created in our code.

- The object is then passed to the service file to be processed – in this case, to add the new user to the user array.

- In both methods, we pass the new `ValidationPipe()` parameter to the `@Body()` decorator. In doing so, we bind the pipe instance to the route handler's `@Body()` decorator so that our pipe is called to validate the user body. Omitting this binding may result in NestJS ignoring your rules and processing any data.

- The `@Patch()` method triggers more observations. First, we're expecting the user ID to be part of the path. This means that to update a user, we'll make a `PATCH` request to the `users/:id` endpoint.

- Secondly, since any route parameter comes as a string by default, our *database* expects a number. Hence, we need to transform the current input into a number. This is when the built-in `ParseIntPipe` pipe comes into play. By adding the pipe as a second parameter to the `@Param()` decorator, the given parameter gets turned into the desired format, and if the transformation fails, the pipe will trigger an exception. Nest has a set of built-in pipes for such operations that can be found in the official documentation: `https://docs.nestjs.com/pipes#built-in-pipes`.

With our pipes in place, let's play with our API once again and see them in action by testing it.

You can use any tool of choice to test the API out and see how NestJS responds to you.

> ⚒ **Quick takeaway**
>
> Try to create and update users with random data and see which responses you get – for example, bad email addresses, empty names, or anything that our API can't currently process. Write your findings down; they'll come in useful before we close this chapter.

Now that you know how to validate and transform users' inputs into the desired format while leveraging the use of pipes, let's learn how to protect our endpoints from being accessed by unknown or unauthorized sources.

By integrating validation pipes and DTOs, we've added a layer of data integrity and structure to our user management API. This approach not only makes our API more robust but also easier to maintain and understand. As we progress, we'll continue enhancing our API with more advanced NestJS features, ensuring it's not just functional but also resilient and secure. Now, let's talk about gatekeepers.

Guards for securing our routes

In NestJS, **guards** play a crucial role in determining whether a given request will be handled by the route handler or not. They're particularly essential in implementing authentication and authorization logic. In our user management API, we'll employ a custom guard to simulate a basic authentication process, giving you a hands-on understanding of how guards operate in a NestJS application.

Let's create a mock authentication guard for demonstration purposes:

1. **Conceptualizing the mock authentication guard**:

   - In a real-world scenario, guards often verify user credentials or tokens against a database or an authentication service. We'll simulate this process for learning purposes.

   - We'll create a guard that checks for a specific, hardcoded token in the request headers to mock user authentication.

2. **Building MockAuthGuard**:

   - Create a new directory called `src/auth` and within it, a file called `mock-auth.guard.ts`

   - This guard will inspect the request headers and allow access if a mock authentication token is present

   ```
   // src/auth/mock-auth.guard.ts

   import {
     CanActivate,
     ExecutionContext,
     Injectable }
   from '@nestjs/common';

   @Injectable()
   export class MockAuthGuard implements CanActivate {
     canActivate(context: ExecutionContext): boolean {
       const request =
         context.switchToHttp().getRequest();
       // Simple check for a mock token
       return request.headers['authorization'] ===
         'Bearer mock-token';
     }
   }
   ```

   In NestJS, remember that a guard should implement the `CanActivate` interface and be annotated with the `@Injectable()` decorator. In this example, we're checking for header authorization with a specific mock token value. We also have access to the execution context.

   Now, let's implement and apply the guard we just created so that we can test it.

3. **Integrating the guard into the application**:

   - Let's apply this guard so that we can protect certain routes in our user management API, specifically the routes that modify user data. In most use cases, those routes need special attention so that write operations (creates and updates) can't be done by anyone.

- Update `UsersController` so that it uses `MockAuthGuard` for the `POST`, `PATCH`, and `DELETE` routes (if you've implemented it already):

```
// src/users/users.controller.ts

// ... imports
import {
  MockAuthGuard
} from '../auth/mock-auth.guard';

@Controller('users')
export class UsersController {
  // ...other methods

  @Post()
  @UseGuards(MockAuthGuard)
  createUser(
    @Body(new ValidationPipe()) createUserDto:
    CreateUserDto
  ) {
    // Logic to create a user
  }

  @Patch(':id')
  @UseGuards(MockAuthGuard)
  updateUser(
    @Body(new ValidationPipe()) updateUserDto:
      CreateUserDto,
    @Param('id', ParseIntPipe) id: number,
  ) {
    // Logic to update a user
  }

  // the delete operation
}
```

Here, `@UseGuards(MockAuthGuard)` is used to secure our routes, ensuring that only requests with the correct mock token can access these endpoints.

Finally, test that your implementation was a success by putting the mock token in the Authorization header and following these few steps:

- To test the effectiveness of our guard, we can use **Postman** or a similar tool to send requests to our protected routes.

- Send requests with the Authorization header's Bearer mock-token and observe the API's behavior. The request should be successful.

- Then, send requests without the header or with an incorrect token. The API should reject these requests, demonstrating the guard's functionality.

Here are a few important takeaways:

- In real applications, guards would typically interact with more complex authentication mechanisms, such as validating JWTs or OAuth tokens, strategies, and more

- You can extend this concept by integrating a database for managing users and tokens and updating the guard so that it performs actual authentication checks

With that, we've successfully integrated a mock authentication guard into our user management API. This exercise has provided a practical understanding of how guards function in NestJS and their importance in securing APIs. As you progress in your NestJS journey, you'll find guards to be indispensable in building secure, production-ready applications. Now, let's move on to something else also very important to know about: middleware.

Middleware for request handling and logging

In NestJS, **middleware** functions similarly to middleware in other frameworks, such as Express.js. It sits between the request and the response, acting as a powerful tool for request processing, logging, and even request validation. For our user management API, a logging middleware can help us keep track of incoming requests, which is invaluable for debugging and monitoring.

Let's not wait any longer and create a request logging middleware for our API:

1. **Conceptualizing the logging middleware**:

    - The aim is to create middleware that logs details of each request (such as the HTTP method, path, and timestamp) to the console or a log file.

    - This middleware will be applied globally to all routes in our API.

    - We can also create scoped middleware, but for now, let's keep it simple. We'll have a lot more opportunities to explore them in the upcoming chapters.

2. **Implementing the logging middleware**:

    - Create a new file in the src/common/middleware directory (create the directory if it doesn't exist) named logging.middleware.ts.

- We'll define our logging middleware in this file:

```
// src/common/middleware/logging.middleware.ts

import {
  Injectable,
  NestMiddleware
} from '@nestjs/common';
import {
  Request,
  Response,
  NextFunction
} from 'express';

@Injectable()
export class LoggingMiddleware implements
  NestMiddleware
{
  use(req: Request, res: Response, next: NextFunction) {
    const { method, originalUrl } = req;
    const timestamp = new Date().toISOString();
    console.log(
      `[${timestamp}] ${method} ${originalUrl}`
    );
    next();
  }
}
```

Here, we log the timestamp, HTTP method, and URL of each request, then pass on the execution to another handler using the next() function. This can be another middleware in the stack or simply the route handler in the controller. In our case, we'll only have one middleware. However, in some scenarios, we may have more.

Now, let's apply the middleware we've just created globally.

3. **Integrating the middleware into the application**:

- To apply this middleware in the global context, we'll configure it in AppModule.

- Update AppModule so that it applies LoggingMiddleware globally:

```
// src/app.module.ts

import {
  Module,
```

```
  NestModule,
  MiddlewareConsumer
} from '@nestjs/common';
import {
  LoggingMiddleware
} from './common/middleware/logging.middleware';
import { UsersModule } from './users/users.module';

@Module({
  imports: [UsersModule],
  // ...other configurations
})
export class AppModule implements NestModule {
  configure(consumer: MiddlewareConsumer) {
    consumer
      .apply(LoggingMiddleware)
      .forRoutes('*'); // Apply for all routes
  }
}
```

Here, we're telling NestJS to use `LoggingMiddleware` for every route in the application. If we want this to only work for `user/` endpoints, the `forRoutes()` method's first parameter is the place for us, or inside `UserModule` while implementing the same interface `NestModule`.

To see the middleware that we just created in action, we need to do the following:

- Run the application and make various requests to our API endpoints.
- Observe the console or log file (depending on where we're logging the details). We should see logs for each request that's been made to the API, displaying the method, path, and timestamp.

Middleware, like the one we've just implemented, plays a crucial role in real-world applications. It can be used for more complex tasks such as authenticating API tokens, handling CORS, or even performing rate limiting. The flexibility of middleware in NestJS allows developers to implement a wide range of functionalities that can intercept and modify requests and responses as needed.

With the integration of our logging middleware, our user management API now has an additional layer of monitoring and debugging capabilities. This example serves as a foundation for you to build more sophisticated middleware according to your application's requirements.

Interceptors – transforming and logging API responses

In NestJS, **interceptors** serve two primary purposes: transforming the data that's returned from a route handler and extending the basic response behavior (such as logging). They are ideal for tasks such as wrapping response data in a specific format, adding additional headers, or logging response details for monitoring. So far, we've only been getting built-in responses from NestJS, but most of the time, we may need to be in control of what we're sending to the client. We can do this using interceptors – let's see how.

Let's create a response transformation and logging interceptor:

1. **Planning our interceptor**:

    -   We aim to create an interceptor that both logs the response details and wraps the response data in a standard format. This way, we can set up a clear contract between the server-side team and the client-side team.

    -   This format might include fields such as `success`, `data`, and `timestamp`.

2. **Implementing the interceptor**:

    -   In the `src/common/interceptors` directory (create it if it doesn't exist), add a new file named `response-logging.interceptor.ts`.

    -   Define the interceptor so that it logs response details and transforms the response structure:

    ```
    // src/common/interceptors/
    // responselogging.interceptor.ts

    import {
      CallHandler,
      ExecutionContext,
      Injectable,
      NestInterceptor,
    } from '@nestjs/common';
    import { map, Observable } from 'rxjs';

    @Injectable()
    export class ResponseLoggingInterceptor implements
      NestInterceptor
    {
      intercept(
        context: ExecutionContext, next: CallHandler):
        Observable<any>
      {
        const request =
          context.switchToHttp().getRequest();
        const start = Date.now();

        return next.handle().pipe(
          map((data) => {
    ```

```
          const executionTime = Date.now() - start;
          console.log(
            `Request to ${request.url} took
            ${executionTime}ms`
          );

          return {
            success: !(data instanceof Error) && data
              !== null,
            data: data,
            timestamp: new Date().toISOString(),
          };
        }),
      );
    }
  }
```

This code seems to handle a lot. Let's break it down:

- **Imports**:

  - `CallHandler`, `ExecutionContext`, `Injectable`, and `NestInterceptor`: These are imported from `@nestjs/common`. They're essential building blocks for creating an interceptor in NestJS.

  - `Map` and `Observable`: Imported from `rxjs`. `map`, like the well-known `Array.prototype.map` function, this operator applies a projection to each value and emits that projection in the output `Observable`. Note that `Observable` is a core concept in RxJS for handling asynchronous data streams. For more information about `rxjs`, I recommend spending some time reading the official documentation: `https://rxjs.dev/api/index/function/map`.

- **Interceptor declaration**:

  - `@Injectable()`: This decorator marks the class as a provider that can be managed by Nest's dependency injection system

  - The `ResponseLoggingInterceptor` class implements the `NestInterceptor` interface, indicating that this class is an interceptor

- **The intercept method**:

  - Every interceptor in NestJS must implement the `intercept` method. This method provides access to `ExecutionContext` and `CallHandler`.

- ExecutionContext: This provides details about the current request process. Here, it's used to extract the HTTP request object.

- CallHandler: This is used to handle the route handler method.

- **Request logging logic**:

  - The method starts by capturing the current timestamp (start) to measure execution time.

  - next.handle(): This triggers the next piece of middleware or route handler. After this function is called, the request proceeds to the next step in the pipeline (such as the actual route handler).

- **Response transformation and logging**:

  - The pipe method from RxJS and the map operator are used to transform the response data.

  - Inside map, we calculate executionTime by subtracting the start time from the current timestamp.

  - A log statement prints the URL of the request and how long it took to process.

  - The response is then transformed so that it includes a success flag, the original data, and a timestamp. This structure is returned to the client.

- **Observable return**:

  - The method returns Observable. This is required because NestJS supports both synchronous and asynchronous route handlers.

Now, let's apply the interceptor to our API.

- **Integrating the interceptor into the application**:

- Apply this interceptor globally or to specific routes as needed.

- For the global application, update AppModule:

```
// src/app.module.ts

import {
  Module,
  NestModule,
  MiddlewareConsumer
} from '@nestjs/common';
import { APP_INTERCEPTOR } from '@nestjs/core';
import {
  ResponseLoggingInterceptor
} from './common/interceptors/
response-logging.interceptor';
```

```
import { UsersModule } from './users/users.module';

@Module({
  imports: [UsersModule],
  providers: [
    AppService,
    {
      provide: APP_INTERCEPTOR,
      useClass: ResponseLoggingInterceptor,
    },
  ],
  // ...other configurations
})
export class AppModule {}
```

Here, the APP_INTERCEPTOR token is used to apply ResponseLoggingInterceptor globally.

Now, let's observe our interceptor in action:

- With the interceptor integrated, we can make requests to our API and observe the response format

- We should see the response data wrapped in the structure defined in the interceptor, along with console logs indicating the execution time for each request

While our interceptor is relatively simple, the concept can be expanded for more complex scenarios. In a real-world application, interceptors are often used for tasks such as adding pagination metadata, handling encryption and decryption, or even streaming large datasets.

With that, we've successfully integrated a response logging and transformation interceptor into our user management API. Interceptors are a powerful feature in NestJS that offers extensive possibilities to manipulate and extend the behavior of our API responses.

Custom providers – enhancing dependency injection

In NestJS, **custom providers** allow for more advanced scenarios beyond the standard class-based dependency injection. They can be particularly useful when integrating with third-party services, creating dynamic providers, or handling more complex dependency resolution scenarios. In the context of our user management API, imagine a situation where we need to integrate with an external service for user data retrieval.

Let's implement a custom provider for an external user data service:

1. **Conceptualizing the custom provider**:

    *   We aim to simulate an external service integration, such as fetching user data from an external API or database service

    *   This external service will be represented as a custom provider in our NestJS application

2. **Building the external service**:

    *   First, let's create a simple service that simulates external user data retrieval

    *   In the `src/external-services` directory (create this directory), add a file named `external-user-data.service.ts`:

    ```typescript
    // src/external-services/external-user-data.service.ts

    export class ExternalUserDataService {
      async fetchUsers(): Promise<any[]> {
        // Simulate an HTTP call to an external service
        return Promise.resolve([
          { id: 3,
            name: 'External User',
            email: 'external@example.com'
          }
        ]);
      }
    }
    ```

3. **Creating the custom provider**:

    *   Now, let's define a custom provider that uses this `ExternalUserDataService`

    *   We'll set up this custom provider in `UsersModule`:

    ```typescript
    // src/users/users.module.ts

    import { Module } from '@nestjs/common';
    import { UsersController } from './users.controller';
    import { UsersService } from './users.service';
    import {
      ExternalUserDataService
    } from '../external-services/
    external-user-data.service';
    ```

```
@Module({
  controllers: [UsersController],
  providers: [
    UsersService,
    {
      provide: 'EXTERNAL_USER_DATA_SERVICE',
      useClass: ExternalUserDataService,
    },
  ],
})
export class UsersModule {}
```

Here, we're providing a custom provider with the EXTERNAL_USER_DATA_SERVICE token, which uses ExternalUserDataService.

Next, let's understand how we'll be using the custom provider in the service.

4. **Integrating the custom provider into UsersService:**

    - We'll modify UsersService so that it can utilize this custom provider and fetch additional user data

    - Inject the custom provider into UsersService using the @Inject decorator:

    ```
    // src/users/users.service.ts

    import { Injectable, Inject } from '@nestjs/common';
    import { User } from './entities/users.entity';
    import {
      ExternalUserDataService
    } from '../external-services/
    external-user-data.service';

    @Injectable()
    export class UsersService {
      private readonly users: User[] = [
        /* ...existing users */
      ];

      constructor(
        @Inject('EXTERNAL_USER_DATA_SERVICE') private
        externalUserService: ExternalUserDataService
      ) {}
    ```

```
    async findAll(): Promise<User[]> {
      const externalUsers =
        await this.externalUserService.fetchUsers();
      return [...this.users, ...externalUsers];
    }

    // ...other methods
  }
```

In this service, we're now combining our locally stored users with those fetched from the external service.

Now, let's test and observe the custom provider integration:

- Run the application and make a request to the endpoint that triggers `findAll` in `UsersService`

- We should see a combined list of users, including those from the mock external service

Custom providers are a gateway to integrating complex external dependencies and services into your application. In real-world scenarios, this could include database connections, third-party APIs, or dynamically created services based on runtime parameters.

With the integration of a custom provider, our user management API now demonstrates an advanced aspect of dependency injection in NestJS. This enhancement not only showcases the flexibility of NestJS but also prepares you for scenarios where complex service integrations are required, making your application both scalable and modular.

In the following short section, we'll go over some of the best practices for REST APIs.

Reflecting on REST API best practices

Now, it's time to reflect on what we've done so far. While coding, we may have forgotten a couple of best practices we already know from previous chapters. So, let's go back and see where we didn't do well and appreciate things we did well:

1. **Consistent and resource-oriented URL design**:

    - **Best practice**: REST APIs should have clear, logical, and resource-oriented URLs. Each URL should consistently represent a specific resource or collection of resources.

    - **Implementation in our API**:

        - Our user management API uses RESTful routes such as `/users` to access the user collection and `/users/:id` for specific user operations

- Here's an example code snippet:

```
@Controller('users')
export class UsersController {
  @Get() findAll() { /*...*/ }
  @Get(':id') findOne(@Param('id') id: string) {
    /*...*/
  }
  // ...other methods
}
```

2. **Use of HTTP methods and status codes**:

- **Best practice**: Utilize HTTP methods (GET, POST, PUT, and DELETE) appropriately and respond with the correct HTTP status codes

- **Implementation in our API**:

  - We've used GET to fetch data, POST to create a new user, PUT for updating, and DELETE for removal

  - Appropriate status codes are used, such as 200 for successful operations, 201 for creation, and 404 for not found

Here's an example code snippet:

```
@Post()
createUser(@Body() createUserDto: CreateUserDto) {
  // Logic to create a user
  return {
    status: 'success', code: HttpStatus.CREATED
  };
}
```

3. **Effective error handling**:

- **Best practice**: Implement comprehensive error handling for clear and informative error responses

- **Implementation in our API**:

  - Use exception filters to catch and format errors consistently

  - Here's an example code snippet:

```
@Catch(HttpException)
export class HttpErrorFilter implements
  ExceptionFilter
{
```

```
catch(exception: HttpException, host: ArgumentsHost) {
   // Custom error formatting
}}
```

4. **Data validation and sanitization**:

   - **Best practice**: Validate incoming data to ensure it meets the API's expectations; sanitize data to prevent security vulnerabilities

   - **Implementation in our API**:

     - Use validation pipes to validate request data based on DTOs

     - Here's an example code snippet:

     ```
     @Post()
     @UsePipes(new ValidationPipe())
     createUser(@Body() createUserDto: CreateUserDto) {
        // User creation logic
     }
     ```

5. **Security best practices**:

   - **Best practice**: Implement security measures such as authentication, authorization, input validation, and rate limiting

   - Implementation in our API:

     - Use guards for route protection

     - Rate limiting and CSRF protection can be added as middleware

     - Here's an example code snippet showcasing the use of guards:

     ```
     @UseGuards(AuthGuard)
     @Delete(':id')
     deleteUser(@Param('id') id: number) {
        // Delete user logic
     }
     ```

Reflecting on these best practices, we can see how each contributes to making our user management API more robust, secure, efficient, and user-friendly. While our implementation covers the fundamentals, real-world applications might require more in-depth adaptations of these practices. This reflection serves as a foundation for building high-quality, professional REST APIs with NestJS.

As we wrap up our exploration of creating a basic RESTful endpoint in our user management API, we've laid a solid foundation. We've implemented crucial operations effectively – from fetching and creating users to updating and deleting them – all while ensuring best practices in API design. Our journey has taken us through the nuances of NestJS, demonstrating its power and elegance in crafting efficient, scalable, and maintainable APIs.

But as any seasoned developer knows, an API is never static. It evolves to meet new requirements, integrate additional features, and improve user experiences. This brings us to an essential aspect of API development: versioning. How do we adapt and expand our API without disrupting the existing ecosystem? We'll delve into this in the next section.

Versioning your API

In the dynamic world of software development, change is the only constant. As our user management API grows to accommodate new features and enhancements, it's crucial to manage these changes in a way that minimizes disruption for end users. This is where API versioning comes into play. **Versioning** is the practice of updating the API while maintaining multiple versions simultaneously, ensuring backward compatibility and a smooth transition for users.

In this section, we'll explore the following aspects:

- **Why versioning matters**: We'll understand the importance of versioning in maintaining and evolving an API
- **Strategies for versioning**: We'll evaluate different versioning approaches and learn how to select the most suitable one for our API
- **Implementing version 2**: We'll introduce pagination in our findAll method and add a new address field to our User entity, marking the rollout of our API's second version

Through this process, we'll learn how to keep our API flexible and robust so that it's capable of evolving without breaking the contracts with existing clients.

Context for v2

Before we jump into the technical details of implementing version 2, let's set the context. *Version 2 of our user management API* will not only enhance existing functionalities but also introduce new features. We aim to add pagination to the findAll method, significantly improving data handling efficiency, especially for large user sets. Additionally, we'll enrich our user data model by including an address field, offering more comprehensive user profiles. These enhancements reflect common real-world requirements, making our API more versatile and user-centric.

In the following sections, we'll guide you through each step of these enhancements, demonstrating how to gracefully evolve your API with NestJS while keeping it organized and maintainable.

Introduction to API versioning concepts

In the world of API development, versioning is an indispensable technique. It refers to the practice of managing changes and updates to your API without disrupting the service for existing users. Let's explore why versioning is crucial and the common strategies that are employed.

Here's why versioning is so important for RESTful APIs:

- **Backward compatibility**: When you update an API, you risk breaking compatibility with clients using older versions. Versioning allows you to introduce new features or make changes without affecting existing users.

- **Evolving APIs over time**: It provides a structured approach to evolve an API, accommodating new business requirements, technology changes, or user feedback.

- **Maintaining multiple versions**: In some scenarios, it's necessary to maintain multiple versions of an API simultaneously while catering to different sets of users or clients.

To make it work, a couple of well-known strategies can be used:

- **URL path versioning**: This involves including the version number in the API's path (for example, /v1/users). It's straightforward and easily understood, making it a popular choice.

- **Header versioning**: Version information is included in the header of the HTTP request. This approach keeps the URL clean but can be less intuitive.

- **Parameter versioning**: The version number is sent as a query parameter in the URL. This method is easy to implement but can clutter the API's query parameters.

For our user management API, we'll adopt the URL path versioning strategy due to its simplicity and clarity.

Setting up the version 2 infrastructure

Now that we understand the importance and methods of versioning, let's set up the infrastructure for version 2 of our user management API.

First, we need to enable the URI versioning type by applying the following update in the main.ts file:

```
// main.ts file

import { VersioningType } from '@nestjs/common';
// ... remaining imports

// ... remaining code
```

```
app.enableVersioning({
  type: VersioningType.URI,
  // prefix: 'v',
    // defaultVersion: '1',
});
```

Here, we enabled versioning on the application. Additionally, we set URI-based versioning for our application.

By default, NestJS prefixes with the letter *v* and lets you specify a default version for your application.

A version can be applied to a whole controller but can also be applied to a specific route. In our case, we only need to have version 2 on the `findAll` handler.

But what about the input field? Well, there are also strategies for managing new input fields, though they may vary depending on the nature of the database. This may consist of running migrations – or seeders, in our sample use case. We'll only make it optional, and specify both *version 1* and *version 2* so that we can retrieve the field.

Enough talking – let's do some actual coding:

- Since we've already enabled versioning for our API, let's add the `address` field to the `users/entities/users.entity.ts` file, as well as in the DTO file, using the following code:

```
// users/entities/users.entity.ts
// v2 field
address?: string;


// users/dto/create-user.dto.ts
// v2 field
@IsNotEmpty()
@IsOptional()
address?: string;
```

Here, we're updating the content of two files. In the first one (`user.entity.ts`), we simply added a new field address, which is optional. We did almost the same in the second one (`users/dto/createUser.dto.ts`), using class-validator's decorators to make sure the `address` field isn't required and that it's not empty when sent.

- Now, in the `users.service.ts` file, make the following changes:

```
// ... everything remains similar

// add these two users to our mock array
// v2 mocks
    {
        id: 3,
```

```
        name: 'Ushindi Joseph',
        email: 'ushindi@myapp.com',
        address: '1234, Kinshasa, DRC',
      },
      {
        id: 4,
        name: 'Kabeya Jean',
        email: 'kabeya@myapp.com',
        address: '1234, Goma, DRC',
      },

  // implement the findAllV2
  // findall v2 -- with pagination
    findAllV2(page = 1, limit = 10) {
      const start = (page - 1) * limit;
      const end = page * limit;

      return {
        data: this.users.slice(start, end),
        meta: {
          page,
          limit,
          total: this.users.length,
        },
      };
    }

  // ... the rest of the class methods
```

As you can see, we've added a new function that can take page and limit as parameters, with default number values that set the type to number for both. In this case, the method returns an object containing data and metadata for the client to handle pagination.

- Now, let's do the remaining work in the controller file and update the current controller with the following changes:

```
// ... remaining controller class code

    @Version('1') // don't forget to import Version
                  // from @nestjs/common
  @Get()
  findAll() {
    console.log('version 1');
    return this.usersService.findAll();
  }
```

```
@Version('2')
@Get()
findAllV2() {
  return this.usersService.findAllV2();
}
```

With these updates, we're deciding to use the old version of the findAll route handler for *version 1* only and the new implementation with pagination for *version 2*. With the help of the @Version() decorator, upon hitting the API with a GET request at users/v1, we get the same behavior that was shown initially, while upon hitting the API with a GET request at users/v2 we get a paginated version.

Here's a challenge: what happens to the rest of the route handlers? How do we handle them? Since we haven't specified with which version they work, by default, they will be handled by defaultVersion, which is defined in the bootstrap() function. We can go ahead and add the following option to the options parameter of the app.enableVersioning() method, as follows:

```
// ... the rest of the code remains the same
    app.enableVersioning({
    type: VersioningType.URI,
    defaultVersion: '1',
  })
```

This may seem to be solving our issue since all the existing routes will be prefixed with a v1 and handled by the application.

Another challenge: what happens to existing clients consuming the API without the versioning in mind or even in a plan? We need to make sure that all the old implementations still function as they did previously and that the resources will still be available. While every business requirement may be different, let's make our trade-off:

- All the requests without versioning in their paths will be intercepted and turned into v1 requests, meaning that if we make a GET request at users/, we need to make sure we query users/v1 instead.

- All the requests with valid versioning aren't changed, meaning that requests with either v1 or v2 in their paths are processed as they're received.

- For all the requests with the wrong version, haven't been implemented yet, or are in an invalid format, we query their corresponding v2 instead, meaning that a GET request at users/v555 or users/v404x will be treated as users/v2 instead.

How could we achieve this? Wait a second – we have a solution: the middleware. Remember that our middleware can intercept requests and update them based on several criteria? This is an additional example of when they can be very useful. To achieve this business requirement, let's create a new middleware in `common/middleware/version-management.middleware.ts` and paste the following content:

```typescript
import {
  Injectable,
  NestMiddleware
} from '@nestjs/common';
import { NextFunction, Request, Response } from 'express';

@Injectable()
export class VersionManagementMiddleware implements
  NestMiddleware
{
  use(req: Request, res: Response, next: NextFunction) {
    // Extract the first segment of the path
    const firstPathSegment = req.originalUrl
      .split('/')[1]
      ?.toString()
      ?.toLowerCase();

    // Check if the first segment is a version
    if (!firstPathSegment.startsWith('v')) {
      // If not, prepend 'v1' to the path
      req.url= '/v1' + req.url;
    } else if (!['v1', 'v2'].includes(firstPathSegment)) {
      // If an invalid version is detected, set to the
      // latest version ('v2' in this case)
      req.originalUrl =
        req.originalUrl.replace(firstPathSegment, 'v2');
    }

    next();
  }
}
```

Here, we just accomplished what we described in the trade-offs. After making the right transformation on the `originalUrl` property of the request, we proceed to the route handler with the `next()` function.

Now, we need to apply this middleware globally so that every previous route can benefit from it. In the `app.module.ts` file, add the newly created middleware, as follows:

```
configure(consumer: MiddlewareConsumer) {
    // needs to be imported
    consumer
      .apply(
        LoggingMiddleware,
        VersionManagementMiddleware
      )
      .forRoutes('*'); // apply for all routes
}
// ... the rest of the file remains the same
```

As you can see, we've added the middleware to the `apply()` function. Remember that the order counts and middleware will be executed in the same order as they're being applied – that is, we'll log in immediately after the request is received before we apply versioning transformation and verification.

Well done! Let's test this out and make sure everything runs as expected by using the `yarn start:dev` command before we move on to another important aspect of scalable REST APIs.

Well done – this versioning capability is giving our application some magic powers. We're now aware of how we can scale our API, implement important changes for a specific version of the API, and still serve the end client in a resilient way. Now, let's talk about error handling.

Robust error handling in REST APIs

In the realm of RESTful API development, robust error handling is not just a luxury—it's a necessity. It's crucial for maintaining a reliable, user-friendly service. As we've been building our user management API, ensuring that any errors are handled gracefully will enhance the overall quality and reliability of the API. Let's dive into the strategies and implementations that constitute robust error handling in REST APIs.

Understanding error handling

In APIs, error handling involves detecting errors, responding with appropriate error messages and status codes, and, when possible, logging these errors for further analysis. Well-handled errors provide clarity to the client about what went wrong and what action they can take, if any. This fosters a trustful and transparent relationship between the API and its consumers.

Key aspects of robust error handling

Here are some of the key aspects of a robust error handling system you should consider when you're working on your next NestJS API:

- **Clear error messages**: Error messages should give a clear understanding of what went wrong. Avoid technical jargon that might be confusing or intimidating to the end user.

- **Appropriate status codes**: Use the correct HTTP status codes to indicate the nature of the error (4xx for client errors, 5xx for server errors, and so on).

- **Consistent error response structure**: Ensure that all errors return a consistent format, making it easier for clients to parse and handle them.

- **Logging and monitoring**: Implement logging to capture errors for monitoring and debugging purposes. This can help in quickly pinpointing issues and improving the API.

Implementing error handling in the user management API

Now, let's implement these best practices in our existing API to gain more practical context from theories:

- **Custom exception filters**:

  - NestJS allows the use of exception filters for custom error handling

  - Implement a custom exception filter that catches exceptions and formats them into a consistent JSON structure:

    ```
    import {
      ExceptionFilter,
      Catch, ArgumentsHost,
      HttpException
    } from '@nestjs/common';
    import { Response } from 'express';

    @Catch(HttpException)
    export class HttpErrorFilter implements
      ExceptionFilter
    {
      catch(exception: HttpException, host: ArgumentsHost)
      {
        const ctx = host.switchToHttp();
        const response = ctx.getResponse<Response>();
        const status = exception.getStatus();
        const errorResponse = exception.getResponse();
    ```

```
response.status(status).json({
  statusCode: status,
  message: errorResponse['message'] || null,
  timestamp: new Date().toISOString(),
  path: ctx.getRequest().url,
});
}
}
```

This filter captures all exceptions of the HTTPException type, returning a structured JSON response that includes the status code, message, timestamp, and path of the request.

- **Using interceptors for additional error handling**: Interceptors can also manage errors by adding extra layers of error handling or transforming error responses

- **Validation and business logic errors**:

  - Ensure that all user input is validated using pipes and that any validation errors return informative messages

  - For business logic errors (such as User not found or Email already exists), throw custom exceptions that can be caught and formatted by the exception filters

- **Testing error scenarios**:

  - Implement unit and integration tests to cover various error scenarios. Ensure that errors are being caught and handled as expected.

  - Test various API requests with invalid data and unauthorized access attempts, and simulate server errors to validate the error responses.

Best practices for client-friendly errors

Here are some best practices to consider:

- **Avoid exposing sensitive details**: Never send stack traces or any sensitive information back to the client in error messages

- **Rate limiting and handling abuse**: Implement rate limiting to prevent abuse and handle excessive requests gracefully, using appropriate HTTP status codes such as 429 Too Many Requests

- **Documentation**: Document common errors and their meanings in your API documentation to help clients understand how to handle them

Robust error handling is a critical component of a professional and reliable API. By implementing custom exception filters, appropriate error logging, and consistent error structures, we can significantly improve the resilience and usability of our user management API. Not only does this lead to a better developer experience for API consumers, but it also eases maintenance and troubleshooting for API developers. As our API evolves, maintaining a strong focus on error handling will ensure that it remains robust, user-friendly, and trustworthy.

Documenting your API

In the journey of API development, documentation isn't merely a finishing touch; it's an integral part of creating a successful, usable, and maintainable API. Now that we've developed our user management API, providing clear and comprehensive documentation is essential to ensure that it's easily understandable and usable by developers. Let's delve into the best practices and strategies for effectively documenting an API.

The importance of API documentation

Good documentation is crucial for any API. It serves as a guide, explaining how the API works, what it offers, and how to use it. This is especially important in collaborative environments and public APIs, where clear communication is key to the API's adoption and success.

Key components of effective API documentation

When documenting an API, there are some key components to keep in mind:

- **Overview of the API**: Start with a high-level overview of what the API does, its main features, and its potential use cases.

- **Authentication and authorization**: Clearly explain how clients should authenticate and authorize with your API. Include any keys or tokens they might need.

- **Endpoint descriptions**: Each endpoint should be thoroughly documented with its purpose, URI, required headers, request and response formats, and any query or path parameters.

- **Error codes and messages**: Document common error responses and what they mean to help users troubleshoot issues.

- **Examples and use cases**: Provide practical examples of requests and responses. Real-world scenarios or use cases can significantly enhance understanding.

Implementing documentation in the user management API

With a solid understanding of the importance of API documentation, we can now move on to implementing documentation for our user management API in NestJS. By leveraging automated documentation tools, we can generate comprehensive API documentation that stays up to date as our application evolves. NestJS provides excellent support for tools such as Swagger (OpenAPI) to generate and maintain API documentation with ease.

Adding Swagger annotations to DTOs and entities

To provide rich API documentation, it's crucial to add metadata to your DTOs and entities. NestJS offers the @ApiProperty decorator from the @nestjs/swagger package, which allows you to define and describe the properties of your DTOs and entities for Swagger. This enhances the clarity of your API documentation by explicitly defining each field, its type, and any relevant details.

Here's an example of how to use @ApiProperty with the user management API:

```
import { ApiProperty } from '@nestjs/swagger';
import {
  IsString,
  IsEmail,
  IsOptional
} from 'class-validator';

export class CreateUserDto {
  @ApiProperty({
    description: 'The name of the user',
    example: 'John Doe',
  })
  @IsString()
  name: string;

  @ApiProperty({
    description: 'The email address of the user',
    example: 'john.doe@example.com',
  })
  @IsEmail()
  email: string;

  @ApiProperty({
    description: 'The password for the user account',
    example: 'password123',
  })
  @IsString()
```

```
  password: string;

  @ApiProperty({
    description: 'Optional role of the user',
    example: 'admin',
    required: false,
  })
  @IsOptional()
  @IsString()
  role?: string;
}
```

In this example, the @ApiProperty decorator is used to document each property of the DTO, including descriptions and example values. This will be reflected in the generated Swagger documentation, making it easier for API consumers to understand the required and optional fields.

Setting up Swagger in the controller

In addition to documenting DTOs and entities, you can use Swagger decorators to enhance your controller documentation. NestJS provides decorators such as @ApiOperation, @ApiBearerAuth, and @ApiOkResponse so that you can document the purpose and behavior of each endpoint.

Here's an example of how to document a controller method in the user management API:

```
import {
  Controller,
  Get,
  Post,
  Body,
  Param
} from '@nestjs/common';
import {
  ApiTags,
  ApiOperation,
  ApiBearerAuth,
  ApiOkResponse
} from '@nestjs/swagger';
import { CreateUserDto } from './dto/create-user.dto';
import { UserService } from './user.service';
import { UserEntity } from './entities/user.entity';

@ApiTags('Users')
@Controller('users')
```

```
export class UserController {
  constructor(private readonly userService: UserService) {}

  @ApiOperation({ summary: 'Create a new user' })
  @ApiOkResponse({
    description: 'The user has been successfully created.',
    type: UserEntity,
  })
  @Post()
  async create(@Body() createUserDto: CreateUserDto):
    Promise<UserEntity>
  {
    return this.userService.create(createUserDto);
  }

  @ApiOperation({ summary: 'Retrieve a user by ID' })
  @ApiOkResponse({
    description: 'The user has been successfully
      retrieved.',
    type: UserEntity,
  })
  @Get(':id')
  async findOne(@Param('id') id: string):
    Promise<UserEntity>
  {
    return this.userService.findOne(id);
  }
}
```

In this controller, the `@ApiOperation` decorator provides a summary of the endpoint's functionality, while `@ApiOkResponse` specifies the expected response type and description. The Swagger documentation for these endpoints will automatically include this information.

Generating Swagger documentation

Once you've annotated your DTOs, entities, and controllers, you can set up Swagger in your NestJS application so that it automatically generates and serves the API documentation. Use `SwaggerModule` in your `main.ts` file to configure and expose the documentation:

```
import {
  SwaggerModule,
  DocumentBuilder
} from '@nestjs/swagger';
import { NestFactory } from '@nestjs/core';
```

```
import { AppModule } from './app.module';

async function bootstrap() {
  const app = await NestFactory.create(AppModule);

  const config = new DocumentBuilder()
    .setTitle('User Management API')
    .setDescription('API for managing users')
    .setVersion('1.0')
    .build();
  const document =
    SwaggerModule.createDocument(app, config);
  SwaggerModule.setup('api', app, document);

  await app.listen(3000);
}
bootstrap();
```

In this configuration, the `SwaggerModule.setup` method is used to serve the Swagger UI at the `/api` route, which will display your API documentation based on the annotations provided throughout your application.

Keeping documentation up to date

As your API evolves, it's essential to ensure that your Swagger documentation remains accurate and up to date. You can achieve this by doing the following things:

- **Maintaining DTOs and entities**: Ensure that all DTOs and entities are properly annotated with `@ApiProperty`

- **Versioning**: Indicate version-specific changes in your API documentation if you implement versioning

- **Testing**: Regularly review the generated Swagger documentation to confirm it reflects the current state of the API

By following these practices, you can ensure that your API documentation isn't only accurate but also helpful for developers using your API.

Example – complete user management API Swagger documentation

Here's an example of how the complete Swagger documentation for the user management API might look:

- **API overview**: Lists all available endpoints with summaries and descriptions
- **DTO definitions**: Displays the structure of each DTO, including required and optional fields
- **Response formats**: Documents the expected structure of responses, including example data
- **Error handling**: Provides details on error codes and potential issues users may encounter
- **Versioning**: If applicable, the documentation will include different API versions and their respective changes

By using Swagger in conjunction with `@ApiProperty` and controller annotations, you provide developers with an intuitive and detailed reference for interacting with your API.

Best practices for maintaining API documentation

The following are some best practices for API documentation:

- **Keep documentation up to date**: Always update the documentation in tandem with changes in the API. Outdated documentation can lead to confusion and misuse of the API.
- **User feedback**: Encourage and incorporate feedback from users to improve the documentation. Their insights can reveal what aspects are unclear or missing.
- **Accessibility and readability**: Make the documentation easily accessible and ensure it's written in clear, straightforward language.

Well-documented APIs are as important as well-designed APIs. They empower developers to use the API correctly and efficiently, reducing learning curves and potential frustrations. In our user management API, effective documentation acts as a roadmap, guiding users through the API's capabilities and usage. As we continue to evolve and improve our API, keeping the documentation clear, comprehensive, and up to date will remain a top priority, ensuring it remains a valuable resource for all its users.

The code source for this chapter's sample project can be found in this book's GitHub repository: `https://github.com/PacktPublishing/Scalable-Application-Development-with-NestJS/tree/main/ch05`. Feel free to fork it and compare it to your own version or use it as a boilerplate for your future REST APIs.

Summary

In this chapter, we did a deep dive into crafting a functional REST API while tackling key aspects from basic setup to advanced features. We began by exploring REST principles and quickly transitioned to hands-on development, setting up routes, handling authentication, and embedding error-handling mechanisms. Then, our journey advanced to API versioning, where we integrated features such as pagination and new user attributes seamlessly, ensuring backward compatibility. Something essential to our development was the emphasis on robust error handling and effective documentation. We did this by utilizing NestJS's powerful tools to enhance API reliability and usability.

With these foundational skills in place, *Chapter 6* awaits us with an exciting shift in focus. *Unleashing the Power of GraphQL and the Apollo Federation Architecture in NestJS* promises to expand our horizons into the realm of GraphQL, offering a new perspective on API development. We'll explore the intricacies of GraphQL's query language, set up a GraphQL server using Apollo Federation, and delve into advanced features, setting the stage for building more dynamic, efficient, and scalable web applications.

6

Unleashing the Power of GraphQL and the Apollo Federation Architecture in NestJS

Welcome to this transformative journey into the world of GraphQL with NestJS! Having delved into the essentials of NestJS and REST API development in the previous chapters, we're now poised to elevate our skills to the next level. *Chapter 6* is dedicated to unraveling the dynamic and powerful features of GraphQL, an advanced query language for APIs, and exploring how it integrates seamlessly with NestJS. This chapter will also introduce you to Apollo Federation, setting the stage for building scalable, microservice-based architectures.

Are you ready to dive deep into the realm of modern API development? Here's the exciting path we'll travel together in this chapter:

- Understanding GraphQL fundamentals in NestJS
- Building and optimizing a GraphQL API with NestJS
- Real-time data with GraphQL subscriptions
- Securing GraphQL – authentication and authorization
- Introduction to Apollo Federation

As you journey through this chapter, I encourage you to code along and put these concepts into practice. Each section includes hands-on exercises designed to reinforce your learning and enhance your skills. By the end of this chapter, you'll not only have a deep understanding of GraphQL and Apollo Federation but also practical experience in crafting efficient and scalable APIs with NestJS.

So, let's embark on this exciting adventure and unlock the full potential of GraphQL and Apollo Federation in our web development projects!

Technical requirements

The code files for the chapter can be found at `https://github.com/PacktPublishing/Scalable-Application-Development-with-NestJS`

Understanding GraphQL fundamentals in NestJS

In this chapter, we'll embark on a journey to understand GraphQL, a revolutionary query language that has redefined the way we think about APIs. Unlike traditional REST APIs, GraphQL offers a more flexible and efficient approach to handling data requests and responses. Let's unravel the core concepts of GraphQL and explore how NestJS enhances these features, guiding you to build more flexible and efficient APIs.

What is GraphQL?

GraphQL, developed by Facebook in 2015, is a query language for APIs that enables clients to request only the data they need, providing a more efficient and flexible alternative to traditional RESTful APIs. With GraphQL, clients can specify the exact shape and structure of the data they require from the server, reducing over-fetching and under-fetching issues, something that's common in RESTful architectures. It allows developers to define a schema that describes the data available in the API, after which clients can query this schema to fetch precisely the data they need, improving performance and developer productivity. Additionally, GraphQL supports real-time data updates through subscriptions, making it suitable for modern web and mobile applications, no matter the database or the technology used to build your application.

Here are the key features of GraphQL:

- **Efficient data retrieval**: Unlike REST, where you often over-fetch or under-fetch data, GraphQL allows clients to request exactly what they need – nothing more, nothing less. This precision significantly reduces network traffic and improves performance.

- **Single endpoint**: GraphQL APIs have a single endpoint, simplifying the API structure. This single point of entry contrasts with the multiple endpoints in REST APIs.

- **Strongly typed**: GraphQL APIs are strongly typed. This means each operation is defined by a type system and executed with predictability.

- **Real-time data with subscriptions**: GraphQL supports real-time data updates through subscriptions, making it ideal for applications that require real-time feedback.

GraphQL and NestJS – a perfect match

NestJS provides first-class support for GraphQL, making it a breeze to set up and use within your application. It leverages the power of TypeScript and integrates seamlessly with the GraphQL module.

Setting up GraphQL in NestJS

When working on any NestJS project, you can add GraphQL support. Follow these steps to do so:

1. To start using GraphQL, you need to install the required packages:

   ```
   $ npm install @nestjs/graphql graphql-tools graphql apollo-
   server-express
   ```

2. NestJS allows you to create a dedicated module for GraphQL. This module can configure the GraphQL server:

   ```
   // graphql.module.ts
   import { Module } from '@nestjs/common';
   import { GraphQLModule } from '@nestjs/graphql';

   @Module({
     imports: [
       GraphQLModule.forRoot({
         autoSchemaFile: true,
       }),
     ],
   })
   export class GraphqlModule {}
   ```

In this setup, `autoSchemaFile: true` tells NestJS to automatically generate the schema based on your TypeScript definitions. This approach is called **code-first**, and we'll explore it in more detail shortly.

Advantages of using GraphQL with NestJS

Building GraphQL APIs with NestJS has several advantages:

- **Type safety with TypeScript**: NestJS's TypeScript support enhances the development experience with GraphQL by providing type safety and reducing runtime errors.

- **Modular structure**: NestJS's modular structure complements GraphQL's approach. You can organize your resolvers and types within dedicated modules, maintaining a clean and scalable code base.

- **Integration with existing features**: GraphQL, when used in NestJS, can seamlessly integrate with other features such as guards, filters, and interceptors, offering a rich development experience.

- **Powerful tooling**: With tools such as Apollo Federation, you can build scalable and efficient GraphQL services, something we'll explore in detail in the following sections.

Understanding GraphQL's fundamentals sets the stage for building more efficient, flexible, and scalable APIs. Its integration with NestJS not only enhances these capabilities but also provides a familiar and powerful environment for developers. As we move forward, we'll delve deeper into building a GraphQL API with NestJS, leveraging these fundamentals to create an API that is not only powerful but also a joy to use.

Big companies using GraphQL in production

At the time of writing, it's common to encounter companies using GraphQL in production. Let's look at some of the most famous ones:

- **Meta**: Previously known as Facebook, Meta is the company that created GraphQL. After facing too many challenges related to over-fetching and under-fetching resources, they decided to move from RESTful APIs to GraphQL. Later on, around 2015, they open sourced it and opened it to global adoption.

- **Netflix**: Around 2018, Netflix engineers decided to use GraphQL and improved their video content delivery, resulting in fewer bandwidth bottlenecks.

- **Zalando**: Zalando's engineering team moved from a RESTful API design to a **unified backend for frontend** (**UBFF**) solution, exposing a single entry point to consume on their client applications (mobile applications and websites).

There are many other success stories out there with the adoption of GraphQL APIs becoming more and more popular, including those from Samsung, LinkedIn, and many more.

Building and optimizing a GraphQL API with NestJS

As we venture deeper into the world of GraphQL, we arrive at a pivotal moment in our journey: building and optimizing a GraphQL API using NestJS. This chapter is where theory meets practice, and we'll apply our newfound knowledge of GraphQL to construct a real-world application. Our focus will be on developing the same user management system we built in *Chapter 5* with REST APIs, but this time, we'll harness the power of GraphQL to enhance its capabilities and efficiency.

Contextualizing our application

First, we'll rebuild our user management system, a cornerstone project that includes basic features such as creating, retrieving, updating, and deleting user information. However, with GraphQL, we'll approach these tasks with more finesse and flexibility. The goal is to demonstrate how GraphQL can transform the way we handle data operations, offering a more streamlined, client-centric approach compared to traditional RESTful methods.

Two approaches to GraphQL with NestJS

NestJS's versatility with GraphQL allows us to explore two distinct approaches to building our API:

- **Code-first approach**: With this approach, we'll focus on using TypeScript classes and decorators to define the GraphQL schema. NestJS will automatically generate the schema based on our code, allowing us to work with familiar concepts and patterns. This approach is particularly beneficial for those who prefer to work with strongly typed languages and enjoy the benefits of immediate feedback and validation that come with it.

- **Schema-first approach**: Alternatively, we'll explore the schema-first approach, where we'll start by writing the GraphQL **schema definition language** (**SDL**). This method is often favored for its straightforwardness and the ease of defining the schema upfront. It's particularly useful when the schema is agreed upon beforehand or when we're working in teams, where the schema serves as a contract.

The beauty of this chapter lies in the parallel construction of the same user management system using both approaches. This dual perspective will not only deepen your understanding of GraphQL in NestJS but also equip you with the insights to choose the approach that best suits your project's needs.

In the next section, we'll build our API using the code-first approach.

Code-first approach

Let's build a user management application, as we did in *Chapter 5*, but using the code-first approach.

First, let's create a new NestJS project by running the following command in the terminal:

```
$ nest new user-management-graphql
```

This command will generate a new project named user-management-graphql.

> **Tip**
> ✂ Take a moment to explore the structure of the generated project again.

As you can see, the project's structure looks like a REST API project with controller files for handling HTTP requests.

Since we're building a GraphQL API here, our first challenge will be to transform this project into a GraphQL one. To do so, we must follow some simple steps. At this point, don't forget to create a branch called code-first or something similar so that you can implement the schema-first approach later:

1. Install all the required packages using the following command:

```
$ yarn add @nestjs/graphql @apollo/server @nestjs/apollo graphql
apollo-server-express apollo-server-core
```

2. In the `app.module.ts` file, change the empty `imports` array so that it looks like this:

```
// app/app.module.ts

imports: [
  GraphQLModule.forRoot<ApolloDriverConfig>({
    driver: ApolloDriver,
    autoSchemaFile: join(process.cwd(),
      'src/schema.gql'),
    playground: false,
    plugins: [
      ApolloServerPluginLandingPageLocalDefault()
    ],
  }),
],
```

Here, `GraphQLModule` has been imported from `@nestjs/graphql`, `ApolloDriver` and `ApolloDriverConfig` from `@nestjs/apollo`, and `ApolloServerPluginLandingPageLocalDefault` from `@apollo/server/plugin/landingPage/default`.

We've added a couple of other properties to GraphQLModule:

- By setting the `autoSchemaFile` property to `join(process.cwd(), 'src/schema.gql')`, we can use the code-first approach instead of the schema-first approach. This way, NestJS will automatically generate our schemas based on our model classes. We've chosen to store the schema file in the `src/schema.gql` location, but you can also let NestJS determine the location by simply setting `autoSchemaFile` to `true`.

- We set `playground` to `false` so that we can use Apollo Sandbox instead of `graphql-playground` as a GraphQL IDE for local development.

- We defined `plugins` as `ApolloServerPluginLandingPageLocalDefault` based on the `playground` value. If it's set to `true`, we don't necessarily need to add it so that it's part of our plugins.

3. Now, let's rename the `app.controller.ts` file to `app.resolver.ts` and enter the following code:

```
// app/app.resolver.ts

import { Query, Resolver } from '@nestjs/graphql';
import { AppService } from './app.service';

@Resolver()
export class AppResolver {
  constructor(
```

```
      private readonly appService: AppService
    ) {}

    @Query(() => String)
    getHello(): string {
      return this.appService.getHello();
    }
  }
```

There are a few differences in this code compared to the code we looked at previously:

- The `@Controller` decorator has been changed to `@Resolver`

- The `@Get` decorator has been set to `@Query(() => String)`

Everything else remains the same.

4. Let's get back to our `app.module.ts` file and fix the imports by doing the following:

    - Change the import of the controller. We should no longer have one but have a resolver instead.

    - Remove the `AppController` controller from the `controllers` array.

    - Add `AppResolver` to the `providers` array alongside `AppService`.

Our file should now look like this:

```
import { Module } from '@nestjs/common';
import { AppResolver } from './app.resolver';
import { AppService } from './app.service';
import { GraphQLModule } from '@nestjs/graphql';
import {
  ApolloDriver,
  ApolloDriverConfig
} from '@nestjs/apollo';
import { join } from 'path';
import {
  ApolloServerPluginLandingPageLocalDefault
} from '@apollo/server/plugin/landingPage/default';

@Module({
  imports: [
    GraphQLModule.forRoot<ApolloDriverConfig>({
      driver: ApolloDriver,
      autoSchemaFile: join(process.cwd(),
        'src/schema.gql'),
      playground: false,
      plugins: [
```

```
        ApolloServerPluginLandingPageLocalDefault()
      ],
    }),
  ],
  controllers: [],
  providers: [AppService, AppResolver],
})
export class AppModule {}
```

With that, we've transformed our initial REST API into a GraphQL one in just a few steps.

Let's run the application once again and confirm that our API is now a GraphQL API:

```
$ yarn start:dev
```

You should see the following output:

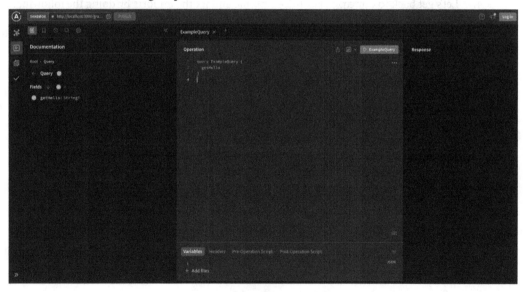

Figure 6.1: GraphQL playground

Well done – you've made your first GraphQL API run with NestJS! It's quite impressive how we moved from a REST API to a GraphQL one so quickly. This is all thanks to the framework we're using.

Now, let's have a look at what's been generated for us as the schema for the project so far. To do so, open the file you created under `src/schema.gql`; note that we've generated some code. This is how the code-first approach works – we don't need to worry about the schema for the project; all we need to do is focus our energy on writing code, specifying correct types, and writing our mutations and queries. NestJS will generate the schema for us.

> ⚒ **Try this**
>
> Play around with the playground and make some requests to see how the API responds.

At this stage, we can build our user module and add some features to it. Note that we'll be using the Nest CLI more often now since it increases productivity. Let's follow these simple steps together:

1. The first step is to generate the `users` resource. We can do this using the Nest CLI, like so:

    ```
    $ nest g resource users
    # > GraphQL (code first)
    # ? Would you like to generate CRUD entry points? (Y/n) y
    ```

    This command will prompt you to choose the transport layer you're using. Make sure you choose the code first. After, you'll be asked whether you want it to generate a CRUD entry for you; simply accept.

    By doing this, the `users` folder will be created with all the required files in it, such as those for our resolvers, services, and DTOs.

> ⚒ **Try this**
>
> Take a look at the generated code base and note down any differences compared to the REST API we built.

    Now, let's use this as a starting point so that we can build our user management application.

2. Let's shape the generated module so that our application works the way we want it to. First, update the `entities/user.entity.ts` file with the following content:

    ```ts
    // users/entities/user.entity.ts

    import {
      ObjectType,
      Field,
      Int
    } from '@nestjs/graphql';

    @ObjectType()
    export class User {
      @Field(() => Int, {
        description: 'the unique id of a user'
      })
      id: number;

      @Field(() => String, {
        description: 'the name of a user'
    ```

```
  })
  name: string;

  @Field(() => String, {
    description: 'the email of a user'
  })
  email: string;
}
```

This is the same entity we used in our REST API – the only difference is the decorators we added to the definition. All of this helps NestJS to construct the schema file. We're using the `@Field()` decorator to specify that the class property is a GraphQL field – in other words, that decorator isn't necessary for REST APIs.

3. Now, let's have a look at our service file. We need to use the same mocking strategy we used previously since we're not interacting with real data from a database yet. Let's update the existing code:

```
import { Injectable } from '@nestjs/common';
import {
  CreateUserInput
} from './dto/create-user.input';
import {
  UpdateUserInput
} from './dto/update-user.input';
import { User } from './entities/user.entity';

@Injectable()
export class UsersService {
  private readonly users: User[] = [
    {
      id: 1,
      name: 'Tshimanga Mukendi',
      email: 'tshim@myapp.com',
    },
    {
      id: 2,
      name: 'Kasereka Akim',
      email: 'kase@myapp.com',
    },
    {
      id: 3,
      name: 'Ushindi Joseph',
      email: 'ushindi@myapp.com',
    },
```

```
      {
        id: 4,
        name: 'Kabeya Jean',
        email: 'kabeya@myapp.com',
      },
    ];

    create(createUserInput: CreateUserInput) {
      this.users.push(createUserInput);
      return createUserInput;
    }

    findAll() {
      return this.users;
    }

    findOne(id: number) {
      return this.users.find((user) => user.id === id);
    }

    update(id: number, updateUserInput: UpdateUserInput)
    {
      const user = this.users.find(
        (user) => user.id === id
      );
      if (!user) {
        return null;
      }

      Object.assign(user, updateUserInput);
      return user;
    }

    remove(id: number) {
      const userIndex = this.users.findIndex(
        (user) => user.id === id
      );
      if (userIndex >= 0) {
        this.users.splice(userIndex, 1);
      }
    }
  }
}
```

In this file, we updated the CRUD operations so that they match our user management application's context. Note that we're using the `CreateUserInput` and `UpdateUserInput` DTOs. Upon performing our writing operation, you may receive some errors in the code via TypeScript.

> **Hands on exercise**
>
> ⚒ Update the `dtos/*` files so that all TypeScripts errors are removed.

Since all the parameters in the service file were the same, we don't need to touch our resolver file for now – they'll still work as expected.

Let's test this out by running the server again.

4. After adding these new entities, mutations, and queries, you'll notice that the `schema.gql` file has evolved. Here's its new content:

```
# ------------------------------------------------------------
# THIS FILE WAS AUTOMATICALLY GENERATED (DO NOT MODIFY)
# ------------------------------------------------------------

type User {
  """the unique id of a user"""
  id: Int!

  """the name of a user"""
  name: String!

  """the email of a user"""
  email: String!
}

type Query {
  getHello: String!
  users: [User!]!
  user(id: Int!): User!
}

type Mutation {
  createUser(createUserInput: CreateUserInput!): User!
  updateUser(updateUserInput: UpdateUserInput!): User!
  removeUser(id: Int!): User!
}

input CreateUserInput {
  """ unique id for a user """
```

```
    id: Int!

    """name of a user"""
    name: String!

    """ email of a user """
    email: String!
}

input UpdateUserInput {
    id: Int!

    """ name of a user ""
    name: String

    """ email of a user """
    email: String
}
```

In an ideal scenario, this file will never be touched and will continue evolving as we add more modules.

Congratulations – you've built a GraphQL API using the code-first approach! Now, let's do the same using the schema-first approach so that we can see the differences.

Schema-first approach

In this section, we'll explore the schema-first approach so that we can build our user management application in GraphQL with NestJS. This approach involves defining the GraphQL schema upfront and then implementing the corresponding resolvers. It's particularly useful when the API's structure is predetermined or when you're working collaboratively on API design.

Setting up for the schema-first approach

Let's set up our project for the schema-first approach by following these simple steps:

1. To differentiate from the code-first approach, create a new branch – say, schema-first – in your project.

2. Start by creating a `.graphql` file so that you can define your schema. For our user management application, we'll define the schema in `src/user.graphql`:

```
# src/user.graphql

type User {
  id: ID!
  name: String!
  email: String!
}

type Query {
  users: [User!]!
  user(id: ID!): User
}

type Mutation {
  createUser(
    name: String!,
    email: String!
  ): User!
  updateUser(
    id: ID!,
    name: String,
    email: String
  ): User
  deleteUser(
    id: ID!
  ): Boolean
}
```

This schema outlines the structure of the `User` type, along with the queries and mutations we'll be supporting.

3. Next, ensure that the required GraphQL packages have been installed:

```
$ npm install @nestjs/graphql graphql-tools graphql apollo-
server-express
```

4. Now, configure `GraphQLModule` in `app.module.ts` so that it uses your schema file:

```
// app.module.ts

import { GraphQLModule } from '@nestjs/graphql';

@Module({
```

```
  imports: [
    GraphQLModule.forRoot({
      typePaths: ['./**/*.graphql'],
    }),
  ],
  // other configurations
})
export class AppModule {}
```

In the preceding code snippet, `typePaths` points to the location of your `.graphql` files.

Building the users module

Follow these steps to build the `users` module:

1. Use the Nest CLI to generate the `users` module and its service file:

    ```
    $ nest generate module users
    $ nest generate service users
    ```

2. At this stage, we need to create some resolvers:

    - In the `users` module, create a resolver file (`users.resolver.ts`) so that you can implement the logic for queries and mutations defined in the schema.

    - In the newly created resolver file, paste the following code:

    ```
    // users/users.resolver.ts

    import {
      Query,
      Resolver,
      Args,
      Mutation
    } from '@nestjs/graphql';
    import { UsersService } from './users.service';
    import { User } from './entities/user.entity';

    @Resolver('User')
    export class UsersResolver {
      constructor(
        private readonly usersService: UsersService
      ) {}

      @Query('users')
      async getUsers(): Promise<User[]> {
    ```

```
    return this.usersService.findAll();
  }

  @Mutation('createUser')
  async addUser(
    @Args('name') name: string,
    @Args('email') email: string
  ): Promise<User> {
    return this.usersService.create({ name, email });
  }

  // Additional resolvers for updateUser and
  // deleteUser
}
```

Here, we implemented the `UserResolver` class using the `@Resolver()` decorator. In the resolver file, we have one query and one mutation. These are very basic since they're for demonstration purposes and consist of the `getUsers` and `addUsers` operations.

3. Note that `UsersService` will contain the business logic for handling user data, similar to the RESTful API we built earlier. You can simply reuse the one we built while following the code-first approach. You can simply reuse the one we built while following the code-first approach. The same applies for DTO and entity files.

4. In the UsersModule's providers' array, let's add the UsersResolver class so we can query the logic within the resolver

```
@Module({
  providers: [UsersService, UsersResolver],
})
export class UsersModule {}
```

5. Now, you need to test your GraphQL API while following the schema-first approach:

   I.   Run your application and use a GraphQL playground to test your queries and mutations:

   $ npm run start:dev

   II.   Ensure that the API behaves as expected, creating, fetching, updating, and deleting user data.

By following the schema-first approach, you've experienced a different methodology for building a GraphQL API in NestJS. This approach emphasizes upfront design and can be particularly beneficial in scenarios where the API contract needs to be agreed upon before it's implemented. Both the code-first and schema-first approaches have their merits, and how you choose one over the other depends on your project requirements and personal or team preferences.

In the next section, we'll learn about GraphQL subscriptions and how NestJS supports this feature, allowing developers to build real-time applications. Let's not waste any time and jump into it!

Learning about GraphQL subscriptions

Welcome to the intriguing world of GraphQL subscriptions in NestJS, where we'll elevate our applications to real-time interactivity. This section is designed to unravel the complexities of GraphQL subscriptions and help us integrate them seamlessly into our NestJS-based user management system. As we progress, you'll discover how these subscriptions enhance the application's responsiveness and user experience, making it more dynamic and engaging.

Subscriptions in GraphQL are a game-changer in the API landscape, offering a new dimension to data interaction. Unlike traditional request-response models, subscriptions maintain a persistent connection, allowing your server to push updates to clients as events occur. This capability is crucial for features such as live notifications, real-time data feeds, and collaborative environments, where immediate updates are essential.

Let's embark on this journey and explore how NestJS facilitates the implementation of GraphQL subscriptions, enabling us to build more interactive and efficient web applications. By integrating real-time updates, we aim to add a layer of immediacy and engagement to the user management system, enriching the overall user experience.

Implementing and testing subscriptions in NestJS

Integrating GraphQL subscriptions into our existing user management application brings an exciting layer of real-time functionality. Using the code-first approach in NestJS, we'll enhance our application so that it notifies clients instantly about changes, such as new user registrations or updates to existing users. Let's dive into the practical steps to achieve this, ensuring that we maintain the engaging and informative style we've established.

To introduce subscriptions, we need to modify our GraphQL types. In the code-first approach, this means updating our TypeScript classes so that they define new subscription fields.

Defining subscription types

In your existing user GraphQL type file (`user.entity.ts`), add the necessary subscription fields. These fields represent the events that clients can subscribe to:

```
// user.entity.ts

import { ObjectType, Field, ID } from '@nestjs/graphql';

@ObjectType()
export class UserType {
```

```
  @Field(() => ID)
  id: string;

  @Field()
  username: string;

  @Field()
  email: string;
}


@ObjectType()
export class UserSubscriptionType {
  @Field(() => UserType)
  userAdded: UserType;

  @Field(() => UserType)
  userUpdated: UserType;
}
```

Here, `UserSubscriptionType` includes two fields – `userAdded` and `userUpdated` – both of which we'll use in our subscription resolvers.

Implementing the subscription resolvers

At this point, we need subscription resolvers in our resolver file. To ensure everything we already have remains the same, here's how we can add a `Subscription` feature to our `users.resolver.ts` file:

1. In `UsersResolver`, implement methods to handle subscriptions. NestJS allows us to use the `@Subscription()` decorator for this purpose:

```
// users.resolver.ts
import { PubSub } from 'graphql-subscriptions';

const pubSub = new PubSub();

@Resolver(() => User)
export class UsersResolver {
  // ... the rest of the code

  // Subscriptions
  @Subscription(() => User, {
    name: 'userCreated',
  })
```

```
    userCreated() {
      return pubSub.asyncIterator('userCreated');
    }

    @Subscription(() => User, {
      name: 'userUpdated',
    })
    userUpdated() {
      return pubSub.asyncIterator('userUpdated');
    }
  }
```

2. We are using the PubSub class from the graphql-subscription package to create a new pubSub instance that helps us listen to events like the userCreated or the userUpdated

Publishing events

With the listeners in place, we now need to publish them at some points in our resolvers. To publish events, we can use the publish method from the pubSub instance right after the user creation and the user update.

To do so, let's modify both createUser and updateUser methods in the resolver class with the following lines:

```
// users.resolver.ts

@Mutation((() => User)
updateUser(@Args('updateUserInput') updateUserInput:
  UpdateUserInput
{
  const updatedUser = this.usersService.update(
    updateUserInput.id,
      updateUserInput,
  );
  pubSub.publish('userUpdated', { userUpdated: updatedUser });
  return this.usersService.update(updateUserInput.id,
    updateUserInput);
}

@Mutation((() => User)
createUser(@Args('createUserInput') createUserInput:
  CreateUserInput)
{
  const newUser = this.usersService.create(createUserInput);
  pubSub.publish('userCreated', { userCreated: newUser });
```

```
    return newUser;
  }
```

In the code above, we updated the createUser and the updateUser methods so we can also publish events, note that the name placed as the first parameter of the publish() method is the same as the one we used in the listeners, otherwise, the event won't be handled properly.

Note that the auto generated schema.gql file now contains a new Subscription type with the newly created subscriptions.

Testing subscriptions in action

To test the subscriptions, use a GraphQL client such as Apollo Client or a tool such as GraphQL Playground. Then, subscribe to userAdded and userUpdated to see real-time updates when a user is added or updated in the system:

```
subscription {
  userAdded {
    id
    username
    email
  }
  userUpdated {
    id
    username
    email
  }
}
```

Finally, execute the subscription and perform user addition or update actions. You should see the subscription's response update in real time.

Finally, in the playground, create a new user using the payload, and make sure you can see the code event listened anytime you create or update a user, as shown in Figure 6.2 below:

Figure 6.2: GraphQL subscription in action

Note that the subscription call sends the information about the timestamp and contains a data field with the corresponding object type. If any error occurs, you will get a null data with an error field explaining what happened.

By integrating GraphQL subscriptions, our user management system gains an impressive real-time communication feature, enhancing user experience and interactivity. This implementation showcases the flexibility and power of NestJS with GraphQL, allowing us to build sophisticated, modern web applications. As you experiment with these features, you'll appreciate the depth and possibilities that GraphQL subscriptions bring to your projects.

In the next section, we'll talk about how you can secure your GraphQL API so that you can avoid building zombies for your clients.

Securing GraphQL – authentication and authorization

Securing a GraphQL API, particularly in a NestJS environment, requires a nuanced approach compared to traditional REST APIs. While the fundamental principles of authentication and authorization remain the same, the implementation details can differ due to the nature of GraphQL's single endpoint and complex query structures. Let's delve into the intricacies of securing a GraphQL API, highlighting the differences from REST APIs and exploring mechanisms to handle authentication and authorization effectively.

Understanding the differences

We're now familiar with the authentication and authorization mechanisms that are available for REST APIs. However, building secure GraphQL APIs can be a little bit different. Here are some of the key differences you need to keep an eye on:

- **Single endpoint challenge**: Unlike REST APIs, which typically have multiple endpoints corresponding to different resources, a GraphQL API generally exposes a single endpoint. This means authentication and authorization logic can't be based on URLs or HTTP methods and needs to be more granular and context-aware.

- **Complex query structures**: GraphQL queries can be nested and multifaceted, fetching data from multiple resources in a single request. Therefore, securing a GraphQL API requires a more dynamic approach to authentication and authorization that considers the specific data fields and types requested.

Authentication in GraphQL

Authentication works almost the same as it does with REST APIs. Here are some well-known and popular authentication mechanisms you may opt for:

- **Token-based authentication**:
- Similar to REST, token-based authentication (such as JWT) is a common approach in GraphQL. Clients send an authentication token, usually in the HTTP header, with each request.
- In NestJS, you can use middleware or guards to intercept incoming requests and validate authentication tokens.
- **Contextual authentication**:
- NestJS allows you to inject the user context into your GraphQL resolvers. This context includes the authenticated user's information, which you can use to implement fine-grained access control.
  - When setting up the GraphQL module, ensure that the context includes user authentication details:

```typescript
// app.module.ts

GraphQLModule.forRoot({
  context: ({ req }) => ({ user: req.user }),
  // other configurations...
});
```

Authorization in GraphQL

Here are some of the popular authorization mechanisms you may wish to use in your future applications:

- **Field-level authorization**:
- Given the nature of GraphQL queries, authorization might need to be enforced at the field level, not just the operation level
- Use custom decorators or directive-based approaches in NestJS to protect individual fields based on user roles or permissions

- **Resolver-level authorization**:
- For operations that are more straightforward, such as mutations, you can implement authorization logic at the resolver level using guards
- NestJS guards can inspect the user context and decide whether a request should be processed or denied, similar to REST API controllers

- **Handling complex queries**:
- Complex queries that involve multiple resources pose a unique challenge. Implement a mechanism that analyzes the query structure and applies authorization logic accordingly.
- Consider using tools such as GraphQL Shield, which provides a middleware layer for your GraphQL API and allows you to set permission rules based on the query's structure.

All the best practices we learned about in *Chapter 5* are still valid here, including rate limiting and validation.

Securing a GraphQL API in NestJS requires a comprehensive and flexible approach that adapts to the unique characteristics of GraphQL. By focusing on context-aware authentication, granular authorization, and field-level security, you can ensure that your GraphQL API is not only powerful and efficient but also secure and resilient. As GraphQL continues to evolve, staying updated on best practices and emerging security strategies will be crucial for maintaining robust and secure applications.

In the next section, we'll introduce a very important concept known as Apollo Federation. We'll use this when we start building real use cases regarding GraphQL microservices later in this book.

Introduction to Apollo Federation

Apollo Federation is designed to build a single, coherent GraphQL API from multiple services, a concept that's especially beneficial in a microservices architecture. Its implementation in NestJS harnesses the power of both GraphQL and Apollo to create a robust, scalable, and efficient GraphQL API.

Federation in microservices architecture

As we delve into the realm of GraphQL and its implementations, one groundbreaking concept stands out for its ability to redefine how we build and scale our GraphQL APIs: Apollo Federation. In this introduction, we'll explore the fundamental principles of Apollo Federation, understand its purpose, and how it revolutionizes the way we approach GraphQL in a microservices architecture.

What is Apollo Federation?

Apollo Federation is an architecture for building a distributed graph across multiple services. Developed by Apollo, a leader in GraphQL technology, Federation allows you to compose multiple, separate GraphQL services into a single data graph. This approach provides several advantages over the traditional monolithic GraphQL server.

The core principles of Apollo Federation

Here are the core principles of Apollo Federation:

- **Decomposition of monolithic APIs**: Federation enables you to break down a monolithic GraphQL API into smaller, more manageable microservices. Each microservice can define its own GraphQL schema, focusing on a specific domain or functionality.

- **Single data graph**: Despite the decomposition process, Apollo Federation allows these separate schemas to be combined into a single, unified GraphQL API. From the client's perspective, it interacts with a single GraphQL endpoint, regardless of how many services contribute to the graph.

- **Ease of extension**: Adding new features or services to a federated architecture doesn't require changes to be made to the existing services. New services can be developed and deployed independently, enhancing the scalability and flexibility of the application.

The purpose of Apollo Federation

The primary goal of Apollo Federation is to tackle the challenges associated with building a complex, scalable GraphQL API in a microservices architecture:

- **Managing complexity**: As GraphQL APIs grow, managing them as a single, monolithic code base can become unwieldy. Federation allows for a more manageable approach by dividing the API into smaller, domain-driven microservices.

- **Scalability**: Federation promotes scalability. Teams can work on different services independently, deploy updates without affecting the entire graph, and scale services individually based on demand.

- **Improved performance**: By allowing clients to fetch data from a single, unified graph, Federation optimizes the number of requests and data over-fetching, which is a common issue in microservices-based architectures.

How Apollo Federation works

Apollo Federation relies on a set of specifications and tools:

- **Federated schemas**: Services define their portion of the graph using the standard GraphQL **Schema Definition Language (SDL)**, along with Federation-specific directives such as `@key`, `@extends`, and `@external`.

- **Apollo Gateway**: This is a special service that acts as the entry point for clients. It composes the individual schemas from federated services into a single schema and routes queries to the appropriate services.

- **Subgraph services**: These are the individual services that make up the federated graph. Each subgraph service is responsible for a specific part of the data graph and can be developed and deployed independently.

Apollo Federation is a transformative approach to building GraphQL APIs in a microservices architecture. It provides an elegant solution to the complexities and challenges of scaling and maintaining large-scale GraphQL implementations. As we progress through the following chapters, we'll dive deeper into the intricacies of Apollo Federation, exploring how to build federated schemas and manage dependencies in a distributed GraphQL environment. This journey will equip you with the knowledge and skills required to leverage the full potential of Apollo Federation in your GraphQL projects.

Summary

As we conclude *Chapter 6*, we reflect on a journey that has taken us deep into the world of GraphQL, revealing its capabilities, intricacies, and how it seamlessly integrates with NestJS for building sophisticated APIs.

We began by demystifying GraphQL, understanding its fundamental principles, and how it offers a more efficient and flexible approach to data retrieval compared to traditional REST APIs. Emphasizing its single endpoint structure and complex query capabilities, we explored how GraphQL revolutionizes data fetching and manipulation.

Our practical journey commenced with building and optimizing a GraphQL API in NestJS, adopting both the code-first and schema-first approaches. We showcased how to define GraphQL schemas, set up resolvers, and implement CRUD operations, highlighting NestJS's versatility and strength in GraphQL API development.

Delving into GraphQL subscriptions, we added real-time data functionalities to our user management system. This section illuminated how subscriptions work under the hood, using WebSockets to maintain a persistent connection and push updates from the server to the client, enhancing the interactivity and responsiveness of applications.

Securing our GraphQL API was our next focus. Here, we tackled the unique challenges posed by GraphQL's single endpoint and complex queries, discussing strategies for implementing robust authentication and authorization mechanisms. This ensured our API was not only powerful but also secure and resilient.

Introduction to Apollo Federation marked a pivotal point in our exploration. In this section, we learned how Apollo Federation allows monolithic GraphQL APIs to be decomposed into a federated architecture, enabling scalability and flexibility. We covered how to set up federated services and Apollo Gateway in NestJS, illustrating how multiple services can contribute to a unified GraphQL schema.

Throughout this chapter, we emphasized best practices, performance considerations, and security measures that are essential for building efficient and secure GraphQL APIs. From optimizing WebSockets connections to handling large volumes of real-time data and ensuring secure subscriptions, we covered a broad spectrum of considerations that are crucial for any GraphQL developer.

In the following two chapters, we'll learn about testing in general and its purpose in modern application development. So, get ready – we'll be ensuring our APIs are scalable and resilient by testing them.

Part 3:
Testing and Debugging APIs in NestJS

This part introduces testing with NestJS and Jest. It guides you on testing the APIs that were built in Part 2.

This part includes the following chapters:

- *Chapter 7, Testing and Debugging REST APIs in NestJS*
- *Chapter 8, Testing and Debugging GraphQL APIs in NestJS*

7

Testing and Debugging REST APIs in NestJS

Welcome to *Chapter 7*. This chapter delves into the crucial aspects of ensuring your APIs are not just functional, but also robust and error-free. **Testing** and **debugging** are indispensable stages in the development life cycle, providing a safety net against unexpected behavior and ensuring that your application behaves as intended under various circumstances. Through this chapter, you will gain practical experience and insights into the methodologies and tools that make testing and debugging in NestJS not just necessary but also manageable and efficient.

By focusing on the REST API we developed in *Chapter 5*, we will revisit the user management system, applying rigorous testing strategies to each component. You'll learn how to write and execute both unit and integration tests, ensuring each part of your API is thoroughly verified. Furthermore, we'll explore effective debugging techniques to identify and resolve issues within your REST APIs quickly. This hands-on approach not only solidifies your understanding of NestJS's testing capabilities but also reinforces best practices in API development.

Testing isn't just about finding bugs; it's a proactive approach to software quality assurance. By the end of this chapter, you'll be well-equipped to implement a robust testing framework for your NestJS applications, enhancing reliability and trust in your APIs.

In this chapter, we're going to cover the following main topics:

- Understanding the importance of testing
- Unit testing in NestJS
- Integration testing in NestJS
- Testing guards, interceptors, and middleware
- Debugging REST APIs

By mastering these areas, you will be able to ensure the functionality and reliability of your APIs, as well as adopt a workflow that prioritizes quality and efficiency from the very start of the development process.

Technical requirements

Since this is a practical chapter, make sure you have the required setup before we proceed. The most important things to have set up are as follows:

- Node.js, NestJS, and Nest-CLI installed on your computer
- User management application from *Chapter 5* set up and running

The code files for the chapter can be found at `https://github.com/PacktPublishing/Scalable-Application-Development-with-NestJS`

Understanding the importance of testing

Imagine building a beautiful birdhouse, adorned with intricate details. In normal temperature and climate circumstances, everything looks perfect, and you feel proud of yourself. The birdhouse, which was built in the summertime, seems to satisfy your needs. If you haven't tested its resistance against wind and rain, the first storm could send it crashing down, leaving your feathered friends exposed and your efforts wasted.

The same principle applies to building software, especially intricate systems such as NestJS REST APIs. Testing isn't a luxury; it's the sturdy foundation that ensures your API functions gracefully under diverse conditions, protecting your users and your reputation.

The painful cost of skipping tests

Many developers know the sting of skipping tests, only to encounter bugs in production environments. Imagine these scenarios:

- A critical login function malfunctions, preventing users from accessing your application. Frustration mounts, support tickets pile up, and you struggle to fix the issue, potentially impacting business operations.
- A security vulnerability goes unnoticed, exposing sensitive user data to attackers. The consequences can be immense, leading to financial losses, reputational damage, and even legal repercussions.
- Simple code changes trigger unexpected behavior, breaking previously working functionalities. Debugging turns into a time-consuming nightmare, slowing down development progress.

These are just a few examples of the real-world costs associated with neglecting testing. Testing serves as a proactive shield, catching issues early in the development cycle, and saving you time, money, and headaches down the line.

The powers of testing in NestJS

Fortunately, NestJS embraces testing and empowers you with built-in tools and libraries. Here's how testing unlocks your development superpower:

- **Early bug detection**: Unit and integration tests act as sentries, identifying issues within individual components and their interactions. You fix problems before they manifest in production, preventing user-facing disasters.

- **Improved code quality**: Writing tests force you to think critically about your code's structure and logic. This leads to cleaner, more maintainable code that's easier to understand and modify.

- **Increased confidence**: A robust test suite provides peace of mind. When changes are made, you can confidently deploy knowing your API's core functionalities remain intact.

- **Faster development cycles**: Automated tests allow for rapid feedback loops, enabling you to experiment and iterate quickly without fearing regressions.

- **Stronger foundations for agile and continuous delivery**: By integrating testing into your development process, you ensure continuous quality throughout the delivery pipeline.

Think of testing not as a burden, but as an investment in building a resilient and reliable API. It's the silent guardian that allows you to scale with confidence, knowing your creation can weather any storm.

In the upcoming sections, we will talk about different techniques we can use when testing a REST API built in NestJS, ensuring we can scale our application confidently and everything can be caught up before attempting to go live.

Unit testing in NestJS

Unit testing is a process of testing the smallest parts of a system that handle a certain business logic in the app and that can be isolated from the system itself.

It's crucial to understand that having a clear separation of concern is key for better unit testing. A function that handles user creation, sends emails, and updates session management at the same time can give a developer a hard time when it comes to testing it, since it's hard to isolate it from the system. That's because it handles multiple logics at the same time.

We talked about the modular design of NestJS applications in prior chapters and we built our base REST API following it, so we can isolate our application blocks and test them.

In the philosophy of NestJS, all the business logic should be handled in the service files. In most cases, unit testing the service file is enough to cover the app's unit testing.

Now that we know what unit testing is, let's apply it to our existing REST API.

Identifying units in the existing application

Before diving deep into testing, we will identify which pieces of logic can be tested separately. Since the REST API is a simple user management system, we currently have the following units in the app:

- **Get all users to feature without pagination**: For version *1* of the API, we have a feature that allows us to get all the users. This logic can be tested by itself since it only fetches users and returns value so the controller can send a proper API response.

- **Get all users with pagination**: We added this feature for version *2*; it can also be tested as a unit.

- **Create a user**: With a `CreateUserDto` object, we should be able to check that the user creation works as expected.

- **Update a user**: With a `UpdateUserDto` object, we should be able to update a user.

These are the units of business logic that we will test. Feel free to add more, such as deleting a user, as a take-home exercise.

Writing unit tests for the users' service

With the logic unit identified, we can implement unit testing and make sure all tests pass.

> **Important note**
>
> In real-life applications, unit testing may involve more than just testing units of code. When the app is interacting with a database, techniques such as mocking the database can be required. For now, we will simply test these functions without any actual database interaction.

Now let's write our unit tests following these simple steps:

1. Create a `users.service.specs.ts` file, then paste the following content:

```
// users.service.spec.ts

import { Test, TestingModule } from '@nestjs/testing';
import { UsersService } from './users.service';

describe('UsersService', () => {
  let service: UsersService;

  beforeEach(async () => {
    const module: TestingModule = await Test
      .createTestingModule({
        providers: [UsersService],
    })
```

```
        .compile();

      service = module.get<UsersService>(UsersService);
    });

    it('should be defined', () => {
      expect(service).toBeDefined();
    });
  });
```

By default, the preceding code is the one we get when we generate a resource using the Nest CLI.

Let's take a closer look at the preceding code snippet:

- **Test module setup**: The `Test.createTestingModule` method creates a module specifically for testing. This module mimics the setup you would have in your application, but it's tailored for testing purposes. By providing the `UsersService` in the `providers` array, you're making an instance of `UsersService` available for **Dependency Injection (DI)**, just like in the actual application module. If the `UsersModule` had more than one dependency, they should be added the same way we added the `UsersService` earlier.

- **Hook**: We are using the `beforeEach` hook to create a fresh new testing module any time before a new test case.

- **Service instantiation**: After compiling the module, the service instance is retrieved using `module.get<UsersService>(UsersService)`. This method fetches the `UsersService` instance from the NestJS DI container, ensuring that the service, along with its dependencies (if it had any), is properly instantiated according to the configuration defined in the testing module.

- **Defined expectation**: The `'should be defined'` test case checks that the service instance is successfully created and is not undefined. This is a basic sanity check ensuring that the service is correctly instantiated and can be used for further testing. It's a starting point for more detailed tests that would verify the service's functionality.

This is a very basic test file and as you can see, all the features we intended to test aren't tested yet.

2. Now, let's add more tests for our service file by starting with the creation of a user. In the `users.service.spec.ts` file, add the following test case:

```
    // create a const of the user we will create
    const newUser: CreateUserDto = {
      name: 'Kitoko Mwana',
      email: 'kitoko@test.com',
      address: '1234, Lubumbashi, DRC',
    };
```

```
// then add one more test case to make sure our
// service logic works
it('should create a new user', () => {
  const user = service.createUser(newUser);
  expect(user).toBeDefined();
  expect(user.name).toBe(newUser.name);
  expect(user.email).toBe(newUser.email);
  expect(user.id).toBe(5); // new user id
});
```

When testing an API, we usually need to operate with data we already know. In this case, the newUser object is shaped from the CreateUserDto and we know all its properties.

Then we call the createUser method from our service and verify that it works as expected. We check that the name has been saved as it should. We also check that email and id have been added successfully. Knowing that our initial mock user array has four users, the create user action here will normally increment and make it five, with our last added user being the fifth one.

3. Now, let's check the test pass using the $ yarn test command. Check the output and make sure it looks like *Figure 7.1* below:

```
$ jest
PASS  src/app.controller.spec.ts
PASS  src/users/users.service.spec.ts

Test Suites: 2 passed, 2 total
Tests:       3 passed, 3 total
Snapshots:   0 total
Time:        1.19 s, estimated 2 s
Ran all test suites.
✨  Done in 1.72s.
```

Figure 7.1: Unit test output

Figure 7.1 shows that we have two test suites – normally equal to the number of test files we have – and three tests within those two files. From what we can see, all of them pass.

Testing unit blocks of an application is about verifying assumptions we already know, as well as edge cases. For example, when we get users, in the first version of the API, we only return an array of users without pagination. In the second version, we have a pagination feature. What happens if we try to get a user's list on a page that doesn't exist? For example, what happens if we send a query with page = 100 while the database only has four users? To ensure our application sends correct information, let's write tests related to both findAll users' v1 and v2 features, with the following code:

```
it('should return an array of users', async () => {
  const users = await service.findAll();
  expect(users.length).toBeGreaterThan(0);
```

```
    expect(users[0].name).toBeDefined();
    expect(users[0].email).toBe('tshim@myapp.com');
    expect(users[1].address).not.toBeDefined();
  });

  // findall v2
  it('should return an array of users with pagination', ()
  => {
    const users = service.findAllV2(1, 2);
    expect(users.data.length).toBe(2);
    expect(users.data[0].name).toBeDefined();
    expect(users.meta).not.toBeNull();
    expect(users.meta.page).toBe(1);
    expect(users.meta.limit).toBe(2);
    expect(users.meta.total).toBe(4);

    // bad request with a wrong page number
    const users2 = service.findAllV2(100, 2);
    expect(users2.data.length).toBe(0); // no data
    expect(users2.meta).not.toBeNull(); // still return
                                        // meta
  });
```

In the preceding test cases, we are checking that the mocked users list has a length greater than 0, that the first user has an email we already know, that the user at index 1 doesn't have an `address` field (v1 user), and so on.

The second test case is about testing the v2 feature. We make sure it returns a `meta` object and test for a bad request when a client asks for a page that doesn't exist.

Well, now, what happens when we have exceptions to be triggered from a service file? Remember that in our service file, we throw an error when a user tries to update a user with a bad ID.

Here is the code, as a reminder:

```
// users.service.ts
// update user feature
updateUser(user: UpdateUserDto & { id: number }) {
  const index = this.users.findIndex(
    (u) => u.id === user.id
  );
  if (index === -1) {
    throw new Error('User not found');
  }
}
```

```
this.users[index] = {
  name: user.name ?? this.users[index].name,
  email: user.email ?? this.users[index].email,
  id: this.users[index].id,
};


return this.users[index];
```

The code snippet above is updating the user's information based on its id, and when the user with the specified id doesn't exist yet, we throw an error.

Testing this behavior can be a little bit tricky. Since we are aware that this is going to happen, we need to catch this exception in the test file or the test will fail. A technique often used is to add a try catch block in the code and verify that the error object exists with the right message.

Here is how you can test it:

```
// users.service.spec.ts
it('should update a user', () => {
  const user = service.updateUser({
    name: 'Tshimanga MUKENDI John',
    id: 1
  });
  expect(user).toBeDefined();
  expect(user.name).toBe(
    'Tshimanga MUKENDI John'
  ); // name has been updated
  expect(user.email).toBe(
    'tshim@myapp.com'
  ); // email remains the same

  try {
    // should throw an error if user is not found
    service.updateUser({
      name: 'Tshimanga MUKENDI John',
      id: 100
    });
  } catch (error) {
    expect(error).toBeDefined();
    expect(error.message).toBe('User not found');
  }
});
```

Perfect, this looks good. After testing normal behavior, we have added a `try catch` block so that we can assert that the error exists, and it's returning a correct error message.

Well done! We have covered a good amount of tests. As a take-home exercise, try to add a `deleteUser` feature and its corresponding test cases.

Now, let's run the tests once again and verify that everything behaves as expected. *Figure 7.2* illustrates what should be the output after running `$ yarn test` one more time:

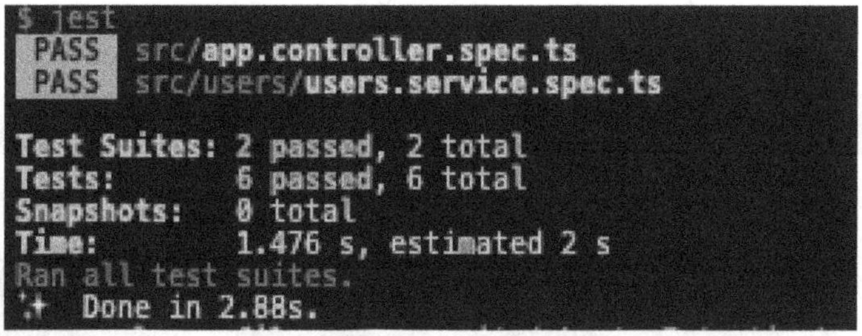

Figure 7.2: Unit test user service

Now, how do I confidently say that the tests I wrote are enough in the context of my application? When your code base grows, it may be challenging to remember everything that must be tested or whether it has been. We need to find a mechanism that will help us assert whether the tests cover most of our functions, blocks, statements, and so on. To do so, we need to measure the test coverage.

Test coverage

NestJS is very powerful. It has test coverage supported by default and includes every TypeScript and JavaScript file we have in the working directory.

Before starting to measure the actual coverage, let's specify which files need to be considered while reporting the test coverage. Files such as `.dto`, `.entity`, `constants`, and so on are not relevant to be considered unless we have some complex logic within them.

For now, let's go into the `package.json` file. Under the `jest` property, let's update the `collectCoverageFrom` array with the following:

```
{
"collectCoverageFrom": [
              "**/*.(t|j)s",
              "!main.(t|j)s",
              "!**/*.module.(t|j)s",
              "!**/*.dto.(t|j)s",
              "!**/*.entity.(t|j)s",
              "!**/*.args.(t|j)s",
              "!**/*.types.(t|j)s",
```

```
            "!**/node_modules/**"
        ],
}
// everything else remains the same
```

With this setup, we inform Jest to only collect coverage from `.js` or `.ts` files that do not follow patterns indicated in the preceding list with a negation.

To get the coverage, run $ `yarn test:cov`. The output should look like *Figure 7.3*:

```
$ jest --coverage
PASS  src/users/users.service.spec.ts
PASS  src/app.controller.spec.ts
```

File	% Stmts	% Branch	% Funcs	% Lines	Uncovered Line #s
All files	35.29	33.33	47.36	33.82	
src	100	100	100	100	
app.controller.ts	100	100	100	100	
app.service.ts	100	100	100	100	
src/auth	0	100	0	0	
mock-auth.guard.ts	0	100	0	0	1-8
src/common/interceptors	0	0	0	0	
response-logging.interceptor.ts	0	0	0	0	1-20
src/common/middleware	0	0	0	0	
logging.middleware.ts	0	100	0	0	1-18
version-management.middleware.ts	0	0	0	0	1-37
src/users	50	57.14	54.54	48.27	
users.controller.ts	0	100	0	0	1-54
users.service.ts	100	57.14	100	100	39,69

Figure 7.3: Test coverage report after adding some unit tests

As we can see, the `user.service` file is almost fully tested, but our controller is barely tested. This is normal since we only tested the units in the service file. However, what can we do to make sure our controllers, middleware, guards, and so on are covered by tests?

The answer is adding integration tests. Remember that our controllers are responsible for handling incoming HTTP requests and sending appropriate responses to the client. This is exactly what will be done by integration tests.

The question we will ask ourselves here will be: *when a user performs a certain HTTP request, what should the server send back as a response?* To answer this question, let's jump into the next section and explore integration tests in NestJS.

Integration testing in NestJS

In the realm of software development, particularly within the robust framework of NestJS, integration testing emerges as a cornerstone practice. It's indispensable for ensuring that the various components of your application not only function correctly on their own but also interact seamlessly.

This form of testing transcends the confines of unit testing, embarking on a mission to validate the harmony between services, modules, and external integrations. It's about painting a comprehensive picture of your application's behavior in scenarios that mirror real-world usage.

As we pivot from the theoretical underpinnings of integration testing toward its practical applications, it's crucial to lay the groundwork properly. The preparation phase is not just about selecting the right tools; it's about creating an environment that accurately simulates the production setup, allowing for the meticulous examination of how different parts of your application coalesce.

Preparation for integration testing

To embark on integration testing with NestJS, particularly for our user management application, it's essential to first lay down a solid foundation. This process begins with setting up a testing environment that not only supports but also enhances our ability to simulate real-world scenarios accurately. NestJS, which is renowned for its comprehensive suite of testing utilities, provides us with Jest for assertions and supertests for HTTP request simulations, creating an ideal starting point for our integration tests.

For those diving into an existing NestJS project, you'll find a boilerplate **End-to-End (e2e)** test file located under the test/ directory, named app.e2e-spec.ts. This file is a testament to the framework's readiness for integration testing, offering a predefined structure that we can extend and adapt to our specific testing needs.

Here is what NestJS gives us initially:

```
// Initial test/app.e2e-spec.ts content
import { Test, TestingModule } from '@nestjs/testing';
import { INestApplication } from '@nestjs/common';
import * as request from 'supertest';
import { AppModule } from './../src/app.module';

describe('AppController (e2e)', () => {
  let app: INestApplication;

  beforeEach(async () => {
    const moduleFixture: TestingModule = await Test
      .createTestingModule({
        imports: [AppModule],
      }).compile();

    app = moduleFixture.createNestApplication();
    await app.init();
  });
```

```
it('/ (GET)', () => {
  return request(app.getHttpServer())
    .get('/')
    .expect(200)
    .expect('Hello World!');
});
});
```

While this code is still correct for the boilerplate project, running this test with yarn test:e2e might yield a failure, especially if your application – like ours – has implemented versioning support.

While understanding that we have updated the way our API sends responses to the server, it is vital to remember that we have a response-logging.interceptor that intercepts all the requests and sends a response with the following shape:

```
// response-logging.inerceptor.js
return {
  success: !(data instanceof Error) && data !== null,
  data: data,
  timestamp: new Date().toISOString(),
};
```

The test environment needs to be aware of this interceptor and configured to handle versions correctly.

To align our testing environment with the application's current state — particularly the versioning feature— modifications to the boilerplate e2e test setup are required. This involves configuring the AppModule within our e2e tests to recognize and route versioned requests appropriately.

Here's how you can adapt the initial setup to accommodate versioning:

```
beforeEach(async () => {
  const moduleFixture: TestingModule = await Test
    .createTestingModule({
      imports: [AppModule],
    }).compile();

  app = moduleFixture.createNestApplication();
  app.enableVersioning({
    type: VersioningType.URI,
  });
  await app.init();
});
```

By invoking `app.enableVersioning()` and specifying the versioning type, we ensure our integration tests consider the versioning strategy implemented in our application. This adjustment bridges the gap between our test environment and the application's actual behavior, setting the stage for more nuanced and accurate integration testing.

However, this is not enough. Therefore, let's now update our assumptions. We know the shape of the response that will always come from the server. Update the / (GET) test case with the following code:

```
it('/ (GET)', () => {
  return request(app.getHttpServer())
    .get('/v1')
    .expect(200)
    .expect((res) => {
      expect(res.body.success).toBe(true);
      expect(res.body.data).toBe('Hello World!');
      expect(res.body.timestamp).toBeDefined();
    });
});
```

In the preceding code, we test assumptions that the type of the response we are getting is no longer a string but an object with appropriate fields in it: the `success` of type Boolean, the `data` object, and the `timestamp`.

With these preparations in place, we're now poised to dive deeper into the intricacies of integration testing. Our user management application, equipped with a properly configured testing environment, is ready to undergo a series of tests designed to validate its integrated functionalities comprehensively. This readiness marks a significant milestone in our journey toward ensuring the reliability and robustness of our NestJS application through meticulous integration testing.

Before moving forward, run the `test:e2e` command once again and make sure that we don't get any errors.

Overview of the user management application

In the journey of ensuring that our user management system built with NestJS is robust and behaves as expected under various scenarios, integration testing plays a pivotal role. It's here that we simulate real-world interactions with our API, diving deep into how our endpoints respond to different requests. Let's roll up our sleeves and get into the practical steps of testing our user management system's HTTP endpoints.

When organizing tests in NestJS, adhering to a consistent structure is key for maintainability and readability. For our users' module, the integration tests reside in `test/users/users.e2e-spec.ts`. This convention helps in identifying test files immediately and aligns with the modular architecture of NestJS applications.

Preparing the test environment

Before we start crafting our tests, ensure the testing environment is set up correctly. In the `test/users/users.e2e-spec.ts` file, we begin by importing necessary modules and setting up the Nest application context to include versioning, which is crucial for accurately simulating our API's behavior.

Here is how:

```
import { Test, TestingModule } from '@nestjs/testing';
import {
  INestApplication,
  VersioningType
} from '@nestjs/common';
import * as request from 'supertest';
import { AppModule } from '../../src/app.module';

describe('User Management (e2e)', () => {
  let app: INestApplication;

  beforeEach(async () => {
    const moduleFixture: TestingModule = await Test
      .createTestingModule({
        imports: [AppModule],
      }).compile();

    app = moduleFixture.createNestApplication();
    app.enableVersioning({
      type: VersioningType.URI,
          defaultVersion: '1',
    });
    await app.init();
  });

  afterEach(async () => {
    await app.close();
  });

  // Test cases will be added here
});
```

In the code snippet provided, we've set up our user e2e test file by configuring it with the correct `AppModule` — specifically, a testing module rather than the actual application module. We've also introduced an `afterEach` hook. This step is crucial as it ensures the application shuts down after each test case, preventing e2e tests from interfering with each other's results or behavior. This practice is important because it guarantees that each module is tested in isolation, a necessity given the unpredictable order in which tests might run.

Simulating HTTP requests and asserting responses

Our focus will be on key operations within our user management system: creating users, retrieving user lists (with and without pagination), and updating user information. Through these tests, we aim to cover a comprehensive range of scenarios that our API is expected to handle.

Testing the POST /v1/users endpoint

This test simulates creating a new user, ensuring the operation is successful and the response includes the expected user details:

```
it('POST /v1/users - should create a new user',
async () => {
  const response = await request(app.getHttpServer())
    .post('/v1/users')
    .send({
      name: 'Justin Dusenge',
      email: 'justin@example.com'
    })
    .expect(201);
  expect(response.body).toHaveProperty('data');
  expect(response.body.data.name)
    .toEqual('Justin Dusenge');
  expect(response.body.data.email)
    .toEqual('justin@example.com');
});
```

While this test looks correct, when we run the `test:e2e` command again, we get a failure response that looks like *Figure 7.4*:

```
● User Module (e2e) › POST /v1/users — should create a new user

  expected 201 "Created", got 403 "Forbidden"

    28 |          .post('/v1/users')
    29 |          .send({ name: 'Justin Dusenge', email: 'justin@example.com' })
  > 30 |          .expect(201);

    31 |      expect(response.body).toHaveProperty('id');
    32 |      expect(response.body.name).toEqual('Justin Dusenge');
    33 |      expect(response.body.email).toEqual('justin@example.com');

    at Object.<anonymous> (users/users.e2e-spec.ts:30:8)

    at Test._assertStatus (../node_modules/supertest/lib/test.js:252:14)
    at ../node_modules/supertest/lib/test.js:308:13
    at Test._assertFunction (../node_modules/supertest/lib/test.js:285:13)
    at Test.assert (../node_modules/supertest/lib/test.js:164:23)
```

Figure 7.4: Error after running yarn test:e2e with the added create user test case

Hmm, it looks like we are not allowed to perform this operation; we're unauthorized at this time. Do you have any idea why? Let me tell you – remember that we have an `AuthGuard` we mocked that looks like the following code snippet:

```
@Injectable()
export class MockAuthGuard implements CanActivate {
  canActivate(context: ExecutionContext): boolean {
    const request = context.switchToHttp().getRequest();
    // Simple check for a mock token
    return request.headers['authorization'] ===
      'Bearer mock-token';
  }
}
```

This guard is only a mock, without proper logic, and it expects an authorization Bearer token with the `mock-token` string as value.

To simulate a header in the test file, we need to set it before performing the request. We add the following line of code:

```
const response = await request(app.getHttpServer())
  .post('/v1/users')
  // add the mock token to the request object as a header
  .set('Authorization', 'Bearer mock-token')
  .send({
    name: 'Justin Dusenge',
```

```
      email: 'justin@example.com'
  })
  .expect(201);
```

The preceding code snippet looks almost like what we had before, with a slight difference: adding the `Authorization` header to the request object.

Now let's update the create user test case with a full set of expectations with the following code snippet:

```
it('POST /v1/users - should create a new user', async ()
=> {
  const response = await request(app.getHttpServer())
    .post('/v1/users')
    // add the mock token to the request object as a
    // header
    .set('Authorization', 'Bearer mock-token')
    .send({
      name: 'Justin Dusenge',
      email: 'justin@example.com' })
    .expect(201);
  const { data, success, timestamp } = response.body;

  expect(data).toHaveProperty('id');
  expect(data.name).toEqual('Justin Dusenge');
  expect(data.email).toEqual('justin@example.com');

  expect(success).toBe(true);

  expect(timestamp).toBeDefined();
});
```

With these expectations added, let's test our project once again, you can specify the file you want to test by adding the name of the file at the end of the command. In this case, you can use `yarn test:e2e users.e2e-spec.ts` and see that the tests pass now.

Well done! You have been able to test the user creation scenario. Now, let's move forward with the `get users` ones.

Testing the GET /v1/users and /v2/users endpoints

These tests verify our application's ability to return the correct user data, with version 2 incorporating pagination logic.

> ⚒ **Hands-on exercise**
>
> Since these tests are particularly simple to test, try it yourself before seeing the result that follows.

Here, we have the complete code that tests the `get users` feature:

```
it('GET /v1/users - should retrieve all users',
async () => {
  const response = await request(app.getHttpServer())
    .get('/v1/users')
    .expect(200);
  const { data, success, timestamp } = response.body;

  expect(Array.isArray(data)).toBeTruthy();
  expect(data[0]).toHaveProperty('name');

  expect(success).toBe(true);

  expect(timestamp).toBeDefined();

  // negative test
  // version 1 does not have address
  expect(data[0]).not.toHaveProperty('address');
  // version 1 does not have pagination
  expect(data).not.toHaveProperty('meta');
});

it('GET /v2/users - should retrieve paginated users',
async () => {
  const response = await request(app.getHttpServer())
    .get('/v2/users?page=1&limit=2')
    .expect(200);

  const { data, success } = response.body;
  expect(data.data.length).toBeGreaterThan(2);
  expect(data).toHaveProperty('meta');
  expect(data.meta).toHaveProperty('total');
```

```
    // the default limit is 10 and the default page is 1
    expect(data.meta.limit).toBe(10);
    expect(data.meta.page).toBe(1);

    expect(success).toBe(true);
  });
```

You can add as many assumptions as you need, just make sure thats running the test once again gives you a successful result.

The preceding test cases test different assumptions depending on the version we are getting the users. These assumptions include expecting the `meta` field in the data object on the v2 request, expecting the right default `page`, `limit`, and `total` fields on the `meta`, and so on.

⚒ Hands-on exercise

Add more tests and make sure you test all the possible remaining use cases, as well as the user update and deletion features. You can always find a solution in the attached book resources or on the book's GitHub repository at: `https://github.com/PacktPublishing/Scalable-Application-Development-with-NestJS/tree/main/ch07`

By meticulously constructing these tests, we not only validate individual endpoint behaviors but also gain confidence in the integrated functionality of our user management system. This series of tests encapsulates a broad spectrum of operations, laying a solid foundation upon which further tests can be built to encompass additional features and scenarios as our application evolves.

Testing controller files

In the journey of crafting robust and reliable REST APIs with NestJS, testing plays a pivotal role. While e2e tests provide a broad safety net, ensuring that your application behaves correctly as a whole, there's a critical layer of testing that focuses more narrowly on the interaction between incoming requests and your controllers: testing controller files directly. This approach is particularly beneficial for verifying the behavior of your controllers in isolation, ensuring they properly handle requests and delegate business logic to the services.

Why test controllers separately?

Controllers are the entry point to your application's business logic. They interpret user inputs and determine which service methods to invoke. While e2e tests validate the system, controller tests allow you to do the following:

- **Isolate controller logic**: Verify that controllers are correctly parsing requests, applying validation, and calling the appropriate service methods

- **Mock dependencies**: By mocking service calls, you can test controllers without relying on the actual implementation of services, focusing solely on the controller's handling of requests and responses
- **Ensure correct HTTP responses**: Confirm that for each API endpoint, your controller responds with the correct status codes, headers, and body

Preparing for controller testing

Given our user management system developed in *Chapter 5*, let's focus on testing the `UsersController`. The controller includes methods such as `findAll()`, `createUser()`, and `updateUser()`, each corresponding to different HTTP endpoints.

For these tests, we'll use Jest alongside NestJS's testing utilities to mock the `UsersService` dependencies, allowing us to simulate different business logic outcomes and verify the controller's responses.

First, ensure your testing environment is properly set up to include NestJS's `Test` module, which allows for easy mocking and testing of controllers.

Example – testing the createUser endpoint

Let's test the `createUser` method in our `UsersController`. This method is responsible for creating a new user, requiring proper authorization and body validation:

```
describe('UsersController', () => {
  let usersController: UsersController;
  let mockUsersService: Partial<UsersService>;

beforeEach(async () => {
    // Mock the UsersService methods used by the
    // UsersController
    mockUsersService = {
      createUser: jest.fn((dto) => ({
        ...dto, id: Date.now()
      })),
      // Add other methods as necessary
    };

    const module: TestingModule = await Test
    .createTestingModule({
      controllers: [UsersController],
      providers: [
        {
          provide: UsersService,
          useValue: mockUsersService,
```

```
      },
    ],
  }).compile();

  usersController = module.get<UsersController>(
    UsersController
  );
});

it('should call UsersService to create a user', () => {
  const createUserDto: CreateUserDto = {
    name: 'John Doe',
    email: 'john@example.com',
  };

  const user = usersController.createUser(createUserDto);

  expect(
    mockUsersService.createUser
  ).toHaveBeenCalledWith(
    createUserDto
  );

  expect(user).toEqual({
    ...createUserDto,
    id: expect.any(Number),
  });

  expect(user.id).toBeDefined();
});
});
```

In the preceding test, we focus on ensuring that the createUser method in our controller correctly invokes the createUser method of our mocked UsersService with the expected DTO. This test validates that the controller is correctly delegating the creation logic to the service layer.

To have access to the service methods, we have mocked the createUser method using Jest's fn function, giving it the expected behavior and returning an object similar to what the real function returns.

> **Hands-on exercise – expanding controller tests**
>
> Following the example provided, extend your testing to cover other controller methods such as `findAll()` and `updateUser()`. Consider scenarios such as verifying that `findAll()` correctly retrieves all users without needing authorization or testing `updateUser()` to ensure it requires authorization and correctly passes the DTO and ID to the service layer.
>
> Remember to mock the service methods and assert that the controller calls them with the correct parameters. Additionally, verify that your controller methods return the expected HTTP responses, aligning with the RESTful standards established for your API. Verify your solution with the code in the GitHub repository.

By methodically testing your controllers, you're ensuring that each part of your application correctly interprets user requests and orchestrates the flow of data through your services. This layer of testing is crucial for identifying and fixing issues early in the development process, leading to more reliable and maintainable code.

As you become more comfortable with testing controllers, you'll find it an invaluable practice in your development workflow, complementing your e2e tests and providing a deeper understanding of how your application handles incoming requests.

This is not enough; some parts of our projects are not yet tested. By running the `test:cov` command, you will notice that files such as guards, middleware, and interceptors are not covered yet. Let's address this in the following section.

Testing guards, interceptors, and middleware

In the complex ecosystem of a NestJS application, components such as guards, interceptors, and middleware play pivotal roles in managing security, data transformation, request/response handling, and operational logging.

These elements are the unsung heroes that work behind the scenes to ensure the application operates securely, efficiently, and reliably. Testing these components individually is as crucial as testing your services or controllers. It ensures that each piece of your application not only performs its intended function in isolation but also interacts seamlessly within the broader application context.

Guards, for instance, are your first line of defense, determining whether a particular request should be processed or denied. Interceptors offer a powerful way to manipulate requests and responses, enabling logging, transformation, or even wrapping of return values. Middleware provides a mechanism to inspect and modify requests and responses, or to execute any code before your controller actions are called. Given their critical roles, any oversight in their behavior can lead to security vulnerabilities, data inconsistencies, or unexpected application behavior.

In this section, we will embark on a journey to rigorously test these components, ensuring they uphold the application's security, integrity, and performance standards. We will test the following:

- The `MockAuthGuard` simulates authentication by checking for a specific mock token in the request headers. Testing this guard will ensure our mock security mechanism behaves as expected.

- The `ResponseLoggingInterceptor` logs the request details and execution time, and modifies the response structure. Testing this interceptor ensures that our logging logic is correct and that it correctly transforms the response data.

- The `VersionManagementMiddleware` handles API versioning by modifying the request URL based on the version specified. Testing this middleware confirms that it correctly interprets and modifies request paths to route to the appropriate version of an endpoint.

- The `LoggingMiddleware` logs each incoming request's details. Testing this middleware ensures that our application can accurately log request information for monitoring or debugging purposes.

By focusing on these components, we aim to solidify the foundation of our application, ensuring every request is properly authenticated, logged, and routed, and every response is accurately transformed and logged. This meticulous approach to testing guards, interceptors, and middleware not only enhances the reliability and security of our application but also exemplifies a commitment to comprehensive quality assurance.

Testing MockAuthguard

The `MockAuthGuard` is a pivotal part of your application's security, conditionally granting access to various parts of your application based on the presence and validity of an authorization token. Testing this guard ensures that your authentication logic is solid, preventing unauthorized access and safeguarding sensitive operations. While this is only a mocked guard, a real guard testing will look very similar.

Step 1 – setting up the test environment

First, you need to create a test file for your guard, for example, `auth/mock-auth.guard.spec.ts`. Within this file, you'll simulate different request contexts to test the guard's behavior.

Step 2 – writing test cases

Your test cases should cover scenarios where access should be allowed (correct token) and denied (incorrect or no token). This involves mocking the `ExecutionContext` to simulate different request headers.

Here's a detailed breakdown of how you might implement these tests:

```
import { Test } from '@nestjs/testing';
import { MockAuthGuard } from './mock-auth.guard';
```

```
// to implement
import {
  createMockExecutionContext
} from '../common/helpers/mock-execution-context.helper';

describe('MockAuthGuard', () => {
  let guard: MockAuthGuard;

  beforeEach(async () => {
    const module = await Test.createTestingModule({
      providers: [MockAuthGuard],
    }).compile();

    guard = module.get<MockAuthGuard>(MockAuthGuard);
  });

  it('should allow access with correct token', () => {
    const context = createMockExecutionContext(
      'Bearer mock-token'
    );
    expect(guard.canActivate(context)).toBe(true);
  });

  it('should deny access with incorrect token', () => {
    const context = createMockExecutionContext(
      'Bearer incorrect-token'
    );
    expect(guard.canActivate(context)).toBe(false);
  });

  it('should deny access without token', () => {
    const context = createMockExecutionContext('');
    expect(guard.canActivate(context)).toBe(false);
  });
});
```

In the preceding code snippet, let's understand the key components:

- **Test module setup**: By using `Test.createTestingModule`, you create a NestJS testing module that mimics your application's module, allowing you to test the guard in an isolated environment.

- **Mocking** ExecutionContext: The createMockExecutionContext function simulates different request scenarios by manipulating the request headers. This function returns an object that mimics the structure of ExecutionContext, allowing you to test how the guard reacts to various tokens. We need to create this helper function so the test file can function without errors (*step 3* section).

- **Assert guard behavior**: Each test case uses expect assertions to check whether the guard correctly grants or denies access based on the token provided in the request headers.

Step 3 – implement createMockExecutionContext

Now, create a new file at src/common/helper/mock-execution-context.helper.ts with the following code:

```
import { ExecutionContext } from '@nestjs/common';
export function createMockExecutionContext(token: string):
ExecutionContext {
  return {
    switchToHttp: () => ({
      getRequest: () => ({
        headers: {
          authorization: token,
        },
      }),
    }),
  } as ExecutionContext;
}
```

In this helper function, we mock what looks like an execution context with the fields we need to have explored by the guard file. In this case, that's the authorization field.

With all in place, let's test our guard file with the yarn test mock-auth.guard.spec.ts command and note that everything looks good.

Testing the MockAuthGuard provides confidence in your application's authentication mechanism, ensuring that only authorized requests proceed to protected routes. This approach to testing guards can be extended to other guards in your application, ensuring comprehensive coverage and security.

Next, let's work on the interceptor test cases.

Testing the response interceptor

The ResponseLoggingInterceptor is designed to log request details and modify the response structure sent back to the client. Testing this interceptor involves verifying that it correctly logs request details and formats responses as expected.

Step 1 – setting up the test environment

Create a test file named `response-logging.interceptor.spec.ts`. This file will contain your tests for the interceptor, focusing on its ability to modify the response and perform logging.

Step 2 – writing test cases

To effectively test the interceptor, you need to simulate the interceptor's execution context and verify its behavior.

Here's an example of how you could approach this:

```
import {
  CallHandler,
  ExecutionContext
} from '@nestjs/common';
import { Test } from '@nestjs/testing';
import { Observable, of } from 'rxjs';
import {
  ResponseLoggingInterceptor
} from './response-logging.interceptor';

describe('ResponseLoggingInterceptor', () => {
  let interceptor: ResponseLoggingInterceptor;

  beforeEach(async () => {
    const module = await Test.createTestingModule({
      providers: [ResponseLoggingInterceptor],
    }).compile();

    interceptor = module.get<ResponseLoggingInterceptor>(
      ResponseLoggingInterceptor
    );
  });

  it('should log and format the response', done => {
    const mockExecutionContext: ExecutionContext =
      createMockExecutionContext();
    const callHandler: CallHandler = {
      // Simulate a handler returning an observable with
      // data
      handle: () => of({ data: 'test' }),
    };
```

```
    interceptor.intercept(mockExecutionContext,
    callHandler).subscribe(response => {
      expect(response).toHaveProperty('success', true);
      expect(response).toHaveProperty('data',
        { data: 'test' });
      expect(response).toHaveProperty('timestamp');
      done();
    });
  });
});
```

In the preceding code snippet, here are the key components:

- **Test module setup**: Like testing guards, you create a NestJS testing module that includes the interceptor. This isolated environment allows for focused testing.

- **Simulating** `CallHandler` **and** `ExecutionContext`: The test simulates the `CallHandler` and `ExecutionContext` objects. `CallHandler` is mocked to return an observable, mimicking a controller's response. `ExecutionContext` can be mocked to provide necessary request details. However, in this specific test, its details are not as crucial.

- Verifying interceptor logic: The test subscribes to the `Observable` returned by the interceptor's intercept method. It then asserts that the interceptor adds the success and timestamp properties to the response, ensuring the interceptor formats responses correctly.

Now, execute your tests once again to ensure the interceptor behaves as expected. Verify that it logs request details and modifies the response structure appropriately.

Testing `ResponseLoggingInterceptor` ensures that your application's response structure is consistently formatted and that request processing times are logged correctly. This pattern can be applied to other interceptors within your application, guaranteeing that your custom response manipulation logic works flawlessly.

Now, let's test our middleware.

Testing middleware

Middleware in NestJS plays a crucial role in processing requests before they reach the route handlers. Testing these middleware ensures that it behaves as expected, such as modifying request objects, managing authentication, or logging requests. For our user management system, we'll focus on testing two specific pieces of middleware: `VersionManagementMiddleware` and `LoggingMiddleware`.

Testing VersionManagementMiddleware

VersionManagementMiddleware dynamically adjusts the request URL based on the API version. It's essential to test it to ensure that requests are correctly routed to the appropriate version of our API.

Setting up the test environment

For testing middleware, you typically simulate the middleware's execution within a request's life cycle. Here's how you can set up a test for VersionManagementMiddleware:

```
import {
  VersionManagementMiddleware
} from './version-management.middleware';

describe('VersionManagementMiddleware', () => {
  let middleware: VersionManagementMiddleware;

  beforeEach(() => {
    middleware = new VersionManagementMiddleware();
  });

  it('should prepend /v1 to requests without a version',
  () => {
    const req: any = {
      originalUrl: '/users',
    };
    const res: any = {};
    const next = jest.fn();

    middleware.use(req, res, next);

    expect(req.originalUrl).toBe('/v1/users');
    expect(next).toHaveBeenCalled();
  });

  it('should correct invalid version to the latest
  supported version', () => {
    const req: any = {
      originalUrl: '/v3/users',
    };
    const res: any = {};
    const next = jest.fn();
```

```
    middleware.use(req, res, next);

    expect(req.originalUrl).toBe('/v2/users');
    expect(next).toHaveBeenCalled();
  });
});
```

Here are the key components of the preceding code snippet:

- **Middleware instantiation**: Instantiate the middleware directly since it doesn't rely on DI for its functionality

- **Request simulation**: Simulate request objects (`req`) to test how the middleware modifies the `originalUrl` based on versioning rules

- **Next function mocking**: Mock the next callback to verify that it gets called, indicating that the middleware successfully processes the request and passes control to the next middleware or route handler

Now, let's see how we can test the other middleware we have in the project: `LogginMiddleware`.

Testing LoggingMiddleware

`LoggingMiddleware` logs details about incoming requests. Testing this middleware verifies that it correctly logs information without interfering with the request processing.

Here is how we can write tests for it:

```
import { LoggingMiddleware } from './logging.middleware';

describe('LoggingMiddleware', () => {
  let middleware: LoggingMiddleware;

  beforeEach(() => {
    middleware = new LoggingMiddleware();
  });

  it('should log request details', () => {
    console.log = jest.fn(); // Mock console.log

    const req: any = {
      method: 'GET',
      originalUrl: '/users',
    };
    const res: any = {};
    const next = jest.fn();
```

```
    middleware.use(req, res, next);

    expect(console.log).toHaveBeenCalledWith(
      expect.stringContaining('GET /users')
    );
    expect(next).toHaveBeenCalled();
  });
});
```

In the preceding code snippet, here are the key components:

- **Console mocking**: Mock `console.log` to verify that the middleware logs the expected request details

- **Verification**: Ensure that the next function is called, indicating that the logging does not halt the request life cycle

Testing middleware in NestJS is about ensuring they correctly modify request/response objects and perform expected side effects, such as logging. By simulating requests and using mocks for functions such as next, you can validate middleware behavior effectively. These tests help maintain the reliability of your application's request processing pipeline, which is crucial for both functionality and security.

All right, we have tested almost every important piece of code in our project. Now, let's introduce a very important concept, which is debugging a NestJS project,s in the next section.

Debugging REST APIs

Debugging is an integral part of the development process, especially when working with complex systems like REST APIs in NestJS. A well-thought-out debugging strategy not only helps in quickly identifying the root causes of issues but also ensures that the APIs remain reliable and performant. In this section, we'll explore various techniques and tools that can significantly enhance your debugging efficiency.

Understanding the issue

The first step in debugging is to accurately understand the problem. This involves gathering as much information as possible about the issue, including error messages, request logs, and the conditions under which the issue occurs. NestJS provides built-in support for logging that can be leveraged to capture detailed information about each request and its outcome.

While NestJS has its logging mechanism, you might find it beneficial to implement custom logging for more detailed insights, especially for capturing request and response bodies.

Here's a simple example of how to set up a custom logger in NestJS:

```
import {
  Injectable,
  NestMiddleware
} from '@nestjs/common';
import { Request, Response } from 'express';

@Injectable()
export class LoggingMiddleware implements NestMiddleware {
  use(req: Request, res: Response, next: Function) {
    console.log(`Incoming Request:
    ${req.method} ${req.url}`, {
      body: req.body,
    });

    res.on('finish', () => {
      console.log(`Outgoing Response: ${res.statusCode}`, {
        response: res,
      });
    });

    next();
  }
}
```

In the preceding middleware, we log the details of incoming requests and outgoing responses, providing visibility into the data flowing through the API.

Now let's see the different debugging strategies the framework gives us in the following sections.

Leveraging debugging tools

Several tools can aid in debugging NestJS applications:

- **NestJS CLI**: The NestJS CLI offers commands such as nest info to give you an overview of the NestJS environment, which can be useful for ensuring that all dependencies are correctly installed and up to date.

- **Visual Studio Code Debugger**: VS Code's built-in debugger is incredibly powerful for debugging Node.js applications, including NestJS projects. By setting breakpoints and inspecting variables at runtime, you can gain deep insights into the application's behavior.

- **Postman and Insomnia**: These API development environments are invaluable for manually testing API endpoints and observing their responses. They can simulate different request types, headers, and bodies, making it easier to replicate and diagnose issues.

This is not the only way we can debug our NestJS application. In the next section, let's learn about a native alternative NestJS gives us: using environment variables.

Enhancing debugging with environment variables

Setting the NEST_DEBUG environment variable to true is a simple yet powerful way to unlock additional logging capabilities within your NestJS application. This can provide more granular details about the application's execution, especially regarding the module resolution, middleware configuration, and request handling processes.

To enable this, adjust your npm start script as follows:

```
"scripts": {
  "start:debug": "NEST_DEBUG=true node dist/main"
}
```

Running your application with npm run start:debug or including NEST_DEBUG=true in your environment variables file (.env) can illuminate issues that might not be evident through standard logging, especially during the application startup phase.

Leveraging NestJS DevTools for a streamlined development experience

The @nestjs/devtools-integration package introduces an integration layer for using NestJS with popular development tools, enhancing the debugging process. This package facilitates a more interactive debugging experience, allowing developers to inspect the application's structure, dependencies, and runtime operations in real time. However, accessing the DevTool dashboard requires a payment fee with seven days of free trial.

Installing and configuring it is straightforward. Follow the steps given here:

1. Run the following command:

    ```
    yarn add @nestjs/devtools-integration
    ```

2. Then, integrate the DevtoolModule into your application by adding the following import in the AppModule:

    ```
    @Module({
      imports: [
        DevtoolsModule.register({
          http: process.env.NODE_ENV !== 'production',
        }),
        UsersModule,
      ],
    // the rest remains the same
    ```

This setup ensures that the DevTools are only activated in a development environment, preserving performance in production. Once enabled, you'll have access to a suite of debugging features directly within your IDE or a web interface, depending on the development tool you're using.

The DevTool dashboard looks like *Figure 7.5*. This shows a simplified representation of what the DevTool dashboard offers, omitting features such as measuring the app's performance, inspecting modules, and more:

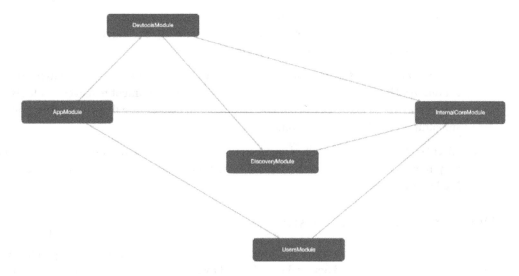

Figure 7.5: Application graph from the nest devTool

Playing around with the dashboard will give you some NestJS super-power, so don't hesitate to take some time to do so. In the next sections, let's see what debugging really looks like in real-world development scenarios.

Real-world debugging scenario revisited

Considering these additional tools, let's revisit the debugging of the /api/users endpoint. After enabling NEST_DEBUG and integrating the NestJS DevTools, we can re-examine the application's behavior when the endpoint is accessed. The additional logging might reveal misconfigurations in module imports or DIs that were not apparent before.

Simultaneously, the DevTools interface can provide a visual representation of the application's structure, highlighting any anomalies in service dependencies or middleware applications.

By combining the granular insights from NEST_DEBUG and the visual overview provided by @nestjs/devtools-integration, we can pinpoint the issue more quickly and accurately. For instance, if the error is related to a service not being properly injected into a controller, these tools can help identify the missing link in the dependency chain, guiding us to a swift resolution.

Common pitfalls and how to address them

Here are a few common pitfalls you need to consider that you may face in the future:

- **Unhandled promise rejections**: These can lead to silent failures in your application. Always ensure that promises are correctly handled with `try-catch` blocks or by `chaining .catch()` methods.

- **DI issues**: A common issue in NestJS applications is incorrectly configured DI, leading to errors such as **Nest can't resolve dependencies**. Reviewing the module imports and provider configurations usually helps resolve these issues.

- **Environment-specific bugs**: Sometimes, bugs only appear under specific environmental conditions. Utilizing Docker containers or consistent environment management tools such as `dotenv` for managing environment variables can help ensure that your application runs smoothly across different environments.

- **Circular dependency**: We talked about circular dependency in the past. One rule we should keep in mind here is to avoid having more than one export per file and leverage the use of **Madge** anytime it happens.

Debugging in action – a step-by-step example

To demonstrate the debugging process, consider a scenario where a particular endpoint, `/api/users`, returns a **500 Internal Server Error**. The following steps outline a systematic approach to resolving the issue:

- **Review logs**: Check the application logs for any error messages related to the request

- **Isolate the issue**: Use Postman or Insomnia to replicate the request and observe the response

- **Identify the faulty component**: By setting breakpoints in the VS Code debugger around the endpoint's handler and related services, identify where the application fails

- **Address the root cause**: Once identified, make the necessary corrections, whether it be fixing a logic error, handling a missing case in a service method, or correcting a data model issue

- **Test and verify**: After applying the fix, retest the endpoint to ensure the issue is resolved and no new issues have been introduced

Debugging is as much an art as it is a science. By combining a clear understanding of the issue with the right tools and a methodical approach, you can efficiently resolve problems in your NestJS REST APIs, enhancing their reliability and performance.

Remember, the goal is not just to fix the immediate issue but to understand its cause and apply that knowledge to prevent similar issues in the future. Nest's DevTool is a very powerful tool you should definitely try, especially if you are working on a very big project where debugging can become tricky.

This approach to debugging, centered around understanding, tooling, and methodical problem-solving, complements the testing strategies discussed earlier in the chapter. Together, they form a comprehensive strategy for developing, testing, and maintaining robust NestJS applications.

Summary

As we wrap up *Chapter 7*, we reflect on the critical journey of fortifying our APIs, ensuring they are not only operational but also robust and fault tolerant. This chapter equipped us with the necessary tools and insights to elevate our testing and debugging practices, which are foundational elements for crafting high-quality NestJS applications.

Our exploration commenced with an in-depth exploration of the significance of testing. We underscored how testing transcends mere bug detection, serving as a cornerstone for software quality assurance and reliability. Through practical applications of our user management system, we delved into unit and integration testing methodologies, demonstrating how each plays a pivotal role in validating our application's components and their interactions.

The journey into debugging unveiled strategies and tools integral to identifying and resolving issues within our REST APIs. We emphasized the importance of a methodical approach to debugging, leveraging NestJS's robust features, including environment variables and development tools, to diagnose and fix problems efficiently.

By revisiting the user management system developed in *Chapter 5*, we applied rigorous testing strategies, ensuring a comprehensive verification process. This hands-on approach not only solidified our grasp of NestJS's testing capabilities but also highlighted the framework's adaptability and efficiency in fostering best practices in API development.

In synthesizing these elements, we laid a foundation that prioritizes quality and efficiency from the development process' outset. The methodologies and tools discussed in this chapter are not merely theoretical concepts but practical resources that will enhance the reliability and trustworthiness of your NestJS applications.

Looking ahead, the skills and knowledge acquired in this chapter will be invaluable assets as we continue to evolve and scale our applications. The emphasis on testing and debugging underscores a proactive approach to software development, ensuring that our APIs can withstand the complexities and demands of modern digital ecosystems.

As we conclude this chapter, let's carry forward the principles of meticulous testing and diligent debugging. These practices are not just tasks to be checked off but are integral to the life cycle of robust, scalable, and reliable software development. Armed with these capabilities, the next chapter will guide us on testing our GraphQL API we built in *Chapter 6*.

Get This Book's PDF Version and Exclusive Extras

UNLOCK NOW

Scan the QR code (or go to packtpub.com/unlock). Search for this book by name, confirm the edition, and then follow the steps on the page.

Note: Keep your invoice handly. Purchase made directly from packt don't require one.

8

Testing and Debugging GraphQL APIs in NestJS

Welcome to *Chapter 8*, where we're diving deep into the world of GraphQL APIs with NestJS. If you thought testing and debugging REST APIs was fun, wait until you get a load of what GraphQL brings to the table. We're talking about a whole new playground of testing strategies and debugging techniques that are as unique as GraphQL itself. This isn't just about making sure things work; it's about unlocking the full power of GraphQL to create APIs that are not just error-free but downright bulletproof.

Remember the GraphQL version of the user management system we built back in *Chapter 6*? Well, it's about to get a whole lot more interesting as we gear up to apply some serious GraphQL testing magic to it. From the nitty-gritty of unit testing GraphQL resolvers to the thrill of **end-to-end (E2E)** testing, we've got a lot to cover. Let's not forget the detective work of debugging, where we'll arm you with the tools and tricks to sniff out and solve those pesky issues that keep you up at night.

But here's the thing: testing and debugging aren't just items on a checklist. They're the secret sauce to building applications that stand the test of time, applications that are not just functional but truly exceptional and easy to scale. So, by the end of this chapter, you'll be equipped with the knowledge and skills to ensure your applications are reliable, performant, and secure.

Ready to embark on this adventure? Here's what's on our agenda:

- Unit testing for GraphQL resolvers
- E2E testing in GraphQL
- Debugging GraphQL APIs

By the time we're done, you'll be well prepared to tackle GraphQL API development head-on, armed with best practices that will take your projects to the next level. Let's get started and turn those GraphQL challenges into triumphs!

Technical requirements

The code files for the chapter can be found at `https://github.com/PacktPublishing/Scalable-Application-Development-with-NestJS`

Unit testing for GraphQL resolvers

Unit testing GraphQL resolvers in NestJS is about verifying that each resolver behaves as expected, independent of the others. In a code-first approach, where the schema is generated based on TypeScript decorators, testing becomes crucial to ensure that the schema accurately represents the underlying business logic encapsulated within these resolvers.

For our demonstration, we'll be extending the user management system developed in *Chapter 6*, focusing on the resolvers within our code-first GraphQL API. This approach allows us to validate the logic of fetching, creating, updating, and deleting users, ensuring that our GraphQL API is robust and behaves predictably under various conditions.

Setting up for testing

Before we dive into writing tests, let's set up our testing environment. Assuming you've followed along from *Chapter 6*, you should have a user management system with resolvers ready for testing. If not, I encourage you to check out the code-first branch on our GitHub's GraphQL repository as a starting point.

The initial setup for testing GraphQL resolvers involves creating test files for each resolver. In NestJS, these are typically located alongside your resolver files and named using the `.spec.ts` suffix. For `UsersResolver`, the test file would be `users.resolver.spec.ts`.

With the test file generated by the Nest CLI, try to execute the test file and make sure everything works without any errors.

Writing unit tests for resolvers

The cornerstone of unit testing in NestJS is the `@nestjs/testing` module, which provides utilities for creating a test environment that simulates your application's runtime. Here's a basic structure for a test suite that tests `UsersResolver`:

```
import { Test, TestingModule } from '@nestjs/testing';
import { UsersResolver } from './users.resolver';
import { UsersService } from './users.service';

describe('UsersResolver', () => {
  let resolver: UsersResolver;
```

```
beforeEach(async () => {
  const module: TestingModule = await Test
    .createTestingModule({
      providers: [UsersResolver, UsersService],
  }).compile();

  resolver = module.get<UsersResolver>(UsersResolver);
});

it('should be defined', () => {
  expect(resolver).toBeDefined();
});

// Additional tests will go here
});
```

This setup ensures that our resolver is properly instantiated with all its dependencies and ready for testing. It's a foundational step that verifies our testing infrastructure is correctly configured before proceeding with more specific tests.

In the next section, let's learn about the mocking strategy and how it can be applied to a module's dependencies.

Mocking dependencies

Since resolvers often depend on services for data fetching and manipulation, we need to mock these dependencies to isolate our tests. Mocking allows us to simulate the behavior of these services without requiring an actual database connection or external API call; you are already familiar with the mocking strategy since we have done almost the same in the previous chapter for controllers.

Here's how you could mock UsersService for our tests:

```
providers: [
  UsersResolver,
  {
    provide: UsersService,
    useValue: {
      findAll: jest.fn(() => [
        // Mocked user data
      ]),
      // Additional mocked functions
    },
  },
],
```

By providing a mock implementation for `UsersService`, we can control the return values and simulate various scenarios for our resolver tests.

Since we know the shape of the returned object from our service files, mocking is easy.

Now, let's test the resolver logic in the following section.

Testing resolver logic

With our testing setup and mocks in place, we can now write tests that validate the behavior of our resolvers. For instance, to test the `findAll` resolver, we could write a test case like this:

```
it('should return an array of users', async () => {
  const users = await resolver.findAll();
  expect(users).toBeInstanceOf(Array);
  expect(users).toHaveLength(mockedUsers.length);
});
```

This test ensures that our `findAll` resolver returns an array of users, matching the expected number of mocked users.

With all in place, here is what the resolver testing file should look like:

```
// users.resolver.spec.ts
import { Test, TestingModule } from '@nestjs/testing';
import { UsersResolver } from './users.resolver';
import { UsersService } from './users.service';
import { CreateUserInput } from './dto/create-user.input';

describe('UsersResolver', () => {
  let resolver: UsersResolver;
  let mockUsersService: Partial<UsersService>;

  beforeEach(async () => {
    mockUsersService = {
      create: jest.fn((dto: CreateUserInput) => ({
        id: Date.now(), ...dto
      })),
      // other methods
    };

    const module: TestingModule = await Test
      .createTestingModule({
        providers: [
          UsersResolver,
```

```
            {
                provide: UsersService,
                useValue: mockUsersService,
            },
        ],
    }).compile();

    resolver = module.get<UsersResolver>(UsersResolver);
});

it('should be defined', () => {
    expect(resolver).toBeDefined();
});

it('should create a user', () => {
    const dto: CreateUserInput = {
        name: 'Test User',
        email: 'test@test.com',
    };
    expect(resolver.createUser(dto)).toEqual({
        id: expect.any(Number),
        ...dto,
    });
    expect(mockUsersService.create)
        .toHaveBeenCalledWith(dto);
});
});
```

In the given code snippet, we have put everything together and tested the user creation. Note that almost everything is similar to what we had on the REST API, in fact, the resolver function, once mocked, behaves exactly the same as the controller ones.

> **Hands-on exercise**
>
> Now that you know how to test a resolver and controller functions, complete this file with other test cases and make sure edge cases are also tested.

Unit testing GraphQL resolvers in NestJS is an essential practice for ensuring the reliability and correctness of your GraphQL API. By following the steps outlined, from setting up your testing environment to mocking dependencies and writing specific test cases, you can build a solid foundation for your GraphQL applications.

Well done; we have tested our resolver files and learned about mocking strategies. In the next section, we will get benefits from implementing E2E tests in our application, making it even more robust.

E2E testing in GraphQL

We have only tested blocks of codes separately, but we haven't tested the nest decorators, such as @Query or @Mutation. In this section, let's do so.

Let's see how we can test the GetHello query, one of the operations we have in our resolver file, as it is the simplest one.

By default, Nest installs the supertest package for us; this package will help us simulate HTTP requests.

As you already know, all the GraphQL requests (mutations and queries) are just POST requests to the entry point of the app, which is /graphql. Having that in mind will help us focus on testing our GraphQL as a single endpoint REST API.

The next question would be this: Which body object and query param headers do I use to simulate a GraphQL API?

From a client app (we use this point of view as our E2E test will simulate clients' requests), *Figure 8.1* shows what we send as a payload to that entry point.

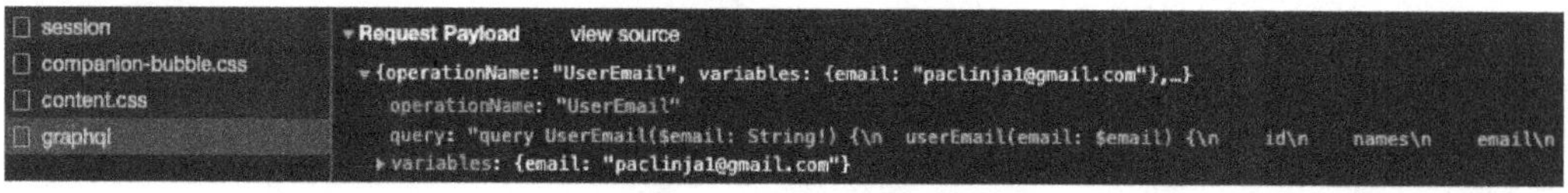

Figure 8.1 – GraphQL requests

As you can see here, our GraphQL query is sent as a string in the query of the http request, and we are sending variables using the variables property. To simulate this, let's create helper files that will hold these parameters for us.

Under src/common/helpers/graphql.helper.ts, add this content:

```
export const GRAPHQL_ENDPOINT = '/graphql';
export const HELLO_WORLD = 'Hello World!';


export const GET_HELLO_OPERATION_NAME = 'Query';

export const GET_HELLO = `query Query {
  getHello
}`;
```

As you can see, the GET_HELLO string will contain the GraphQL operation as a string, just like what we have in our Apollo playground.

Update the existing `app.e2e-spec.ts` file with the following code:

```
// test/app.e2e-spec.ts

import { Test, TestingModule } from '@nestjs/testing';
import { INestApplication } from '@nestjs/common';
import * as request from 'supertest';
import { AppModule } from '../src/app.module';
import {
  GET_HELLO,
  GET_HELLO_OPERATION_NAME,
  GRAPHQL_ENDPOINT,
  HELLO_WORLD,
} from '../src/common/helpers/graphql.helper';

jest.setTimeout(70000);

describe('AppResolver (e2e)', () => {
  let app: INestApplication;

  beforeEach(async () => {
    const moduleFixture: TestingModule = await Test
      .createTestingModule({
        imports: [AppModule],
      }).compile();

    app = moduleFixture.createNestApplication();
    await app.init();
  });

  afterEach(async () => {
    await app.close();
  });

  it('should get a hello world', () => {
    return request(app.getHttpServer())
      .post(GRAPHQL_ENDPOINT)
      .send({
        operationName: GET_HELLO_OPERATION_NAME,
        query: GET_HELLO,
      })
      .expect(200)
      .expect((res) => {
        expect(res.body.data.getHello).toBe(HELLO_WORLD);
```

```
    });
  });
});
```

In the preceding code snippet, we have done the following:

- We have set up a timeout to `70000 ms`. Sometimes, you can experience timeout especially because we have made integration tests, which can be an addition of more than one method executed together, and when we have async operations in our test files that interact with a mocked database.

- We have used request methods from `supertest` to simulate HTTP requests; don't hesitate to read more about `supertest` (`https://github.com/ladjs/supertest`), a very popular NodeJS server. With `supertest`, you can simulate a `post`, `get`, `put`, `patch` request, just like we did on the rest API. Here, we will only use `post` (to simulate a post request) with its callbacks, such as `send()`, `expect()`, and so on.

Now, let's see how we can test a user's creation. First, let's add helpers with operation names, variables, mutations, and so on.

For context, don't forget the `createUser` mutation looks like the following:

```
@Mutation(() => User)
  createUser(@Args('createUserInput') createUserInput:
  CreateUserInput) {
    return this.usersService.create(createUserInput);
  }
```

The preceding mutation is expecting an input named `createUserInput` in the query. The query string we need to provide has to take this into consideration; let's work on it.

Under the `common/helpers/create-user.helper.ts` file, just paste this:

```
// common/helpers/create-user.helper.ts
import * as Chance from 'chance';
const chance = new Chance();


export const CREATE_USER_OPERATION_NAME = 'CreateUser';


export const CREATE_USER_MUTATION = `mutation
CreateUser($createUserInput: CreateUserInput!) {
  createUser(createUserInput: $createUserInput) {
    id
    email
    name
  }
```

```
}`;

export const generateCreateUserVariables = () => {
  return {
    createUserInput: {
      name: chance.name(),
      email: chance.email(),
    },
  };
};
```

In the preceding code snippet, we have done the following:

- We have created all the pieces that are required to send requests, such as variables, GraphQL operations, and so on.

- We have used chance, a library that helps us create fake data. Here, we needed a name and an email, and instead of hardcoded values, chance will generate for us random ones.

- CREATE_USER_MUTATION is written just like a client app would query our API in the future, specifying what we need to have in the response, being one of the key characteristics of GraphQL APIs.

Now, let's create a file for testing the user resolvers E2E, under the test folder. Let's add the users/ users.e2e-spec.ts file and paste the following code there:

```
// test/users/users.e2e-spec.ts

import { Test, TestingModule } from '@nestjs/testing';
import { INestApplication } from '@nestjs/common';
import * as request from 'supertest';

import { AppModule } from '../../src/app.module';

import {
  GRAPHQL_ENDPOINT
} from '../../src/common/helpers/graphql.helper';
import {
  CREATE_USER_MUTATION,
  CREATE_USER_OPERATION_NAME,
  generateCreateUserVariables,
} from '../../src/common/helpers/create-user.helper';

import {
  User
```

```
} from '../../src/users/entities/user.entity';

jest.setTimeout(70000);

describe('User resolver (e2e)', () => {
  let app: INestApplication;
  let user: User;

  beforeEach(async () => {
    const moduleFixture: TestingModule = await Test
      .createTestingModule({
        imports: [AppModule],
      }).compile();

    app = moduleFixture.createNestApplication();
    await app.init();
  });

  afterEach(async () => {
    await app.close();
  });

  it('Should create an user with user mutation', () => {
    const createUserInput =
      generateCreateUserVariables().createUserInput;
    return request(app.getHttpServer())
      .post(GRAPHQL_ENDPOINT)
      .send({
        operationName: CREATE_USER_OPERATION_NAME,
        query: CREATE_USER_MUTATION,
        variables: { createUserInput },
      })
      .expect(200)
      .expect((res) => {
        expect(res.body.data.createUser).toBeDefined();
        user = res.body.data.createUser;
        expect(user.id).toBeDefined();
        expect(user.name).toBe(createUserInput.name);
        expect(user.email).toBe(createUserInput.email);
      });
  });
});
```

Looks similar to what we had before, right?

We are expecting to receive a `200` status, and the response we get will have a `body.data` object with the payload of the response.

Now, let's run our E2E tests:

```
# run end-to-end tests
$ yarn test:e2e
```

If you were following, you will be able to get something similar to *Figure 8.2*:

Figure 8.2 – E2E test results

> **Hands-on exercise**
>
> Now, try to replicate the same process by creating E2E tests for the `updateUser`, `removeUser`, and `getUser` features.

Buckle up! We've just nailed the unit testing of our services and resolvers and even added some slick E2E tests.

We hope you are getting real superpowers when it comes to manipulating GraphQL APIs. Now, it's time to debug in the upcoming section.

Debugging GraphQL APIs

Debugging GraphQL APIs can be challenging due to the complexity involved in query execution, schema definitions, and resolver logic. The challenge becomes even more pronounced in a project such as ours, which uses the code-first approach to generate the schema. With a schema automatically generated from the code, issues can arise from mismatched types, invalid queries, or resolver misconfigurations. Unlike REST APIs, which rely on distinct endpoints, GraphQL's single endpoint structure adds another layer of complexity, making it harder to identify the root cause of an issue.

In this section, we'll explore how to debug GraphQL APIs efficiently within the context of our project. We'll cover tools and practices tailored to the code-first approach, ensuring that schema, queries, and mutations work as expected.

Understanding debugging challenges for GraphQL APIs

Debugging GraphQL APIs presents distinct challenges compared to traditional REST APIs. In GraphQL, the schema ties everything together—queries, mutations, and types. In the code-first approach, where the schema is generated from TypeScript decorators, any issue in the code can propagate to the GraphQL layer, leading to runtime errors that are often tricky to trace back to their source.

For instance, consider the following code-first generated schema for our project:

```
#
type User {
  id: Int!
  name: String!
  email: String!
}
type Query {
  users: [User!]!
  user(id: Int!): User!
}
type Mutation {
  createUser(createUserInput: CreateUserInput!): User!
  updateUser(updateUserInput: UpdateUserInput!): User!
  removeUser(id: Int!): User!
}
input CreateUserInput {
  name: String!
  email: String!
}
input UpdateUserInput {
  id: Int!
  name: String
  email: String
}
```

Debugging challenges can stem from the following:

- **Resolver misconfigurations**: Resolvers must match the schema and handle the data correctly. For example, a bug in the `user(id: Int!)` resolver might return the wrong user or fail if the resolver logic is incorrect.

- **Input validation failures**: GraphQL can fail when executing mutations such as `createUser` if input validation isn't handled properly.

- **Schema synchronization issues**: Since the schema is auto-generated, there can be inconsistencies between the TypeScript code and the final GraphQL schema. For example, missing required fields or incorrect data types in the TypeScript code will propagate to the schema and cause issues during execution.

These issues can be hard to catch with typical debugging techniques, making using specialized tools and best practices critical. By leveraging the right tools and understanding the inner workings of the GraphQL execution pipeline, you can reduce the time spent identifying and resolving these issues.

Leveraging debugging with built-in NestJS tools

NestJS includes a built-in `Logger` service that can log critical information at different levels (`log`, `error`, `warn`, `debug`, `verbose`). By default, the logger is enabled and logs during application bootstrapping, as well as in cases such as displaying caught exceptions. This built-in logging system helps monitor and debug different parts of your GraphQL API.

Here's an example of using the `Logger` service in a GraphQL resolver:

```
import { Resolver, Query, Args } from '@nestjs/graphql';
import { Logger } from '@nestjs/common';
import { UserService } from './user.service';
import { User } from './user.entity';

@Resolver(() => User)
export class UserResolver {
  private readonly logger = new Logger(UserResolver.name);

  constructor(private readonly userService: UserService) {}

  @Query(() => User)
  async user(@Args('id') id: number): Promise<User> {
    this.logger.debug(`Fetching user with id: ${id}`);
    const user = await this.userService.findOne(id);

    if (!user) {
      this.logger.warn(`User with id ${id} not found`);
      throw new Error(`User with id ${id} not found`);
    }

    this.logger.log(
      `User fetched successfully: ${JSON.stringify(user)}`
```

```
    );
    return user;
  }
}
```

In the preceding code snippet, the `Logger` service is instantiated for the `UserResolver` class. The `logger.debug()` method is used to log the ID of the user being fetched, `logger.warn()` issues a warning if the user is not found, and `logger.log()` provides general logging when a user is successfully fetched. This demonstrates how logging levels can help track various stages of a request's life cycle.

To globally configure logging across your entire NestJS application, you can specify the log levels during the application's bootstrap process in the `main.ts` file:

```
async function bootstrap() {
  const app = await NestFactory.create(AppModule, {
    logger: ['log', 'warn', 'debug'], // Selecting specific
                                      // log levels
  });
  await app.listen(3000);
}
bootstrap();
```

In the preceding code snippet, only `log`, `warn`, and `debug` logs will be captured globally. You can also disable logging entirely by setting `logger: false`.

Inspecting requests and responses with middleware

NestJS supports custom middleware that allows you to intercept and log HTTP requests and responses, providing deeper insights into the behavior of your GraphQL API. Middleware can be especially valuable for monitoring and debugging network-level operations.

Here's an example of a piece of middleware that logs every incoming GraphQL request:

```
import {
  Injectable,
  NestMiddleware,
  Logger
} from '@nestjs/common';
import { Request, Response, NextFunction } from 'express';

@Injectable()
export class LoggingMiddleware implements NestMiddleware {
  private readonly logger =
    new Logger(LoggingMiddleware.name);
```

```
use(req: Request, res: Response, next: NextFunction) {
  this.logger.log(
    `Incoming Request: ${req.method} ${req.url}`
  );
  next();
  }
}
```

In the preceding code snippet, `LoggingMiddleware` logs each incoming HTTP request using `logger.log()`. The `req` object captures details about the request (such as the method and URL), while `next()` passes control to the next middleware or controller in the pipeline. This piece of middleware helps track every GraphQL query, mutation, or subscription, giving you insight into which operations are being executed.

To use this middleware, you need to apply it to your application by registering it in the `main.ts` file or your module's middleware configuration.

Using exception filters for enhanced error handling

Exception filters in NestJS offer a structured way to catch and handle errors across your application, including in GraphQL resolvers. These filters can capture and log error details, making it easier to identify and resolve issues.

Here's an example of an exception filter that logs detailed error information:

```
import {
  ExceptionFilter,
  Catch,
  ArgumentsHost,
  Logger
} from '@nestjs/common';
import { GqlArgumentsHost } from '@nestjs/graphql';
import { GraphQLError } from 'graphql';

@Catch(GraphQLError)
export class GraphQLExceptionFilter implements
ExceptionFilter {
  private readonly logger =
    new Logger(GraphQLExceptionFilter.name);

  catch(exception: GraphQLError, host: ArgumentsHost) {
    const gqlHost = GqlArgumentsHost.create(host);
    this.logger.error(
```

```
      `Error in GraphQL resolver: ${exception.message}`,
      exception.stack
   );
   return exception;
  }
}
```

In the preceding example, `GraphQLExceptionFilter` is an exception filter that captures `GraphQLError` exceptions. It logs the error message and stack trace using `logger.error()`. By logging these errors, you gain valuable information about resolver issues or GraphQL execution problems, making it easier to debug the system. This filter can be applied to your GraphQL module to ensure that all exceptions are logged effectively.

By using NestJS's built-in debugging tools, such as the `Logger` service, environment variables for debug mode, middleware for request inspection, and exception filters for error handling, you can streamline the debugging process for your GraphQL APIs. These tools offer deep insights into the inner workings of your application, from query execution to resolver issues, providing you with the visibility needed to diagnose and resolve errors efficiently.

Apollo Server debugging tools

Apollo Server, commonly used with NestJS for GraphQL, provides several debugging tools that can help you better understand the performance and execution of your GraphQL API. One of the standout features of Apollo is its robust plugin system, which enables developers to track the performance of individual field resolutions and format errors in a way that offers more insights into potential issues.

Field-level logging with Apollo plugins

Apollo allows you to add custom logging and performance tracking at a more granular level using plugins. You can log the performance of specific fields, which is especially helpful when troubleshooting slow queries or tracking down inefficient resolvers.

Here's an example of how to create a custom plugin that logs the execution time of every field resolver in your schema:

```
import {
  ApolloServerPlugin
} from 'apollo-server-plugin-base';

export const fieldLoggingPlugin: ApolloServerPlugin = {
  requestDidStart() {
    return {
      didResolveField(field) {
        const start = Date.now();
        return () => {
```

```
            const duration = Date.now() - start;
            console.log(
              `Resolved ${field.name} in ${duration}ms`
            );
          };
        },
      };
    },
  };
```

In the preceding code snippet, `fieldLoggingPlugin` hooks into the life cycle of a GraphQL request. Specifically, the `didResolveField` function is invoked every time a field resolver is executed. The start time is recorded, and after the resolver finishes, the time taken to resolve the field is logged. This allows you to measure the performance of specific resolvers and identify bottlenecks in your API.

Error formatting in Apollo

Apollo also provides robust error-handling mechanisms, including custom error formatting. By formatting GraphQL errors, you can include additional context in error responses that will assist in debugging, particularly in production environments.

Here's how to customize the error format in Apollo:

```
import { ApolloError } from 'apollo-server-express';

const server = new ApolloServer({
  typeDefs,
  resolvers,
  formatError: (err) => {
    if (err instanceof ApolloError) {
      return err;
    }
    return {
      message: err.message,
      code: err.extensions?.code ||
        'INTERNAL_SERVER_ERROR',
      stack: process.env.NODE_ENV === 'development'
        ? err.stack
        : null,
    };
  },
});
```

In the preceding code snippet, the `formatError` function allows you to control the structure of the error response sent to clients. If an error is an instance of `ApolloError`, it is returned as is. For other errors, additional fields such as a custom error code and stack trace (only in development mode) are included. This gives you better visibility into the source of errors, while also ensuring sensitive information, such as stack traces, is hidden in production.

Using requestDidStart for query tracing

Apollo provides a `requestDidStart` life cycle hook that is useful for tracing the entire life cycle of a GraphQL request. You can use this hook to monitor when a query starts and ends, which helps track down slow or failed requests, as shown in the following example:

```
const server = new ApolloServer({
  typeDefs,
  resolvers,
  plugins: [
    {
      requestDidStart() {
        console.log('Query started');
        return {
          willSendResponse() {
            console.log('Query finished');
          },
        };
      },
    },
  ],
});
```

In the preceding code snippet, `requestDidStart` logs a message when a query starts and `willSendResponse` logs another message when the query finishes. This simple implementation allows you to trace the execution of requests and pinpoint where issues might arise.

To make these debugging strategies more practical, let's explore some real-world scenarios where these tools can be used to resolve common issues in a production API. Here are some examples:

- **Slow query resolution**: Imagine you're running a production GraphQL API and you receive reports that a specific query is much slower than expected. By using Apollo's field-level logging, you can isolate the issue to a specific field.

  Steps to diagnose and resolve:

  I.   **Enable field-level logging**: Use `fieldLoggingPlugin` described earlier to track the execution time of each field.

  II.   **Monitor slow fields**: Once the logging is enabled, monitor the logs to find the field that takes the longest to resolve.

III.   **Optimize resolver logic**: After identifying the slow field, review and optimize its resolver logic. The issue could be an inefficient database query or excessive data fetching.

IV.   **Test improvements**: After making optimizations, monitor the logs again to ensure that the query performance has improved.

- **Debugging third-party GraphQL services integration**: In another scenario, you might be integrating a third-party GraphQL service into your API and are facing errors related to that service's responses.

    Steps to diagnose and resolve:

    I.   **Use Apollo error formatting**: Format the errors as demonstrated earlier to include as much detail as possible, especially for third-party services.

    II.   **Enable verbose logging**: If the issue persists, enable verbose logging using the `DEBUG=nestjs*` environment variable to capture detailed information about how the request is being handled internally.

    III.   **Check response payloads**: Inspect the request and response payloads using middleware to ensure that the correct data is being sent and received.

    IV.   **Collaborate with the third-party service**: If you identify issues related to the third-party service, use the logs and error messages to communicate more effectively with their support team.

The strategies provided will guide your debugging journey, but we should always be aware that situations may differ a lot depending on the context of the application you are building. However, some best practices will make your life easy; let's explore some in the next section.

Best practices for debugging GraphQL APIs in production

When debugging GraphQL APIs in production, it's important to follow best practices to ensure smooth operations without compromising performance or security. Here are some strategies you can implement to improve your debugging process.

Structured logging

Implement structured logging to capture critical information without overwhelming the system with verbose logs. Tools such as Winston or Pino can help structure your logs for better searchability and analysis:

```
import * as winston from 'winston';
import { WinstonModule } from 'nest-winston';

@Module({
  imports: [
```

```
  WinstonModule.forRoot({
    transports: [
      new winston.transports.Console({
        format: winston.format.combine(
          winston.format.timestamp(),
          winston.format.json()
        ),
      }),
    ],
  }),
  ],
})
export class AppModule {}
```

In this example, Winston is configured as the logging library in NestJS. The logs are formatted with timestamps and output in JSON format, which can be easily parsed by monitoring tools.

Monitoring and performance tracking

Use monitoring tools, such as Apollo Studio or Grafana, to visualize performance metrics and track potential bottlenecks in real time. These tools can provide insights into query performance, request success rates, and error occurrences.

Handling high-scale production environments

When scaling GraphQL APIs in production, follow these additional practices:

- **Implement rate limiting**: To prevent overloading your system, consider rate-limiting requests at the GraphQL endpoint

- **Error handling**: Use Apollo's custom error formatting to ensure consistent and informative error responses

- **Monitor for memory leaks**: Use tools such as **PM2** or **Node.js heap snapshots** to monitor memory usage and prevent memory leaks

- **Use caching**: Caching results at the resolver or data-fetching level can significantly improve performance, especially for frequently requested data

By incorporating these tools and best practices, you'll be better equipped to handle common issues that arise in production GraphQL APIs. From field-level logging to structured error handling, these debugging techniques offer the insight and control you need to maintain a high-performance, reliable API.

Summary

As we conclude *Chapter 8*, we've built upon the foundation laid in the previous chapter to adapt our testing and debugging strategies specifically for GraphQL within the NestJS ecosystem. This focused exploration into GraphQL's unique testing needs underscores the importance of specialized approaches to ensure our APIs are both effective and resilient.

In this chapter, we honed in on unit testing GraphQL resolvers, emphasizing the critical role of isolating and testing the functionalities that power our GraphQL APIs. By demonstrating how to effectively mock dependencies and simulate scenarios, we've provided the tools needed to ensure our resolvers operate as intended under various conditions.

Our journey through the E2E testing of GraphQL APIs has reinforced the value of testing our applications as integrated wholes, ensuring that every layer, from the resolver down to the database, works in harmony. This comprehensive testing strategy is key to delivering GraphQL APIs that are robust and ready for production.

Through a pragmatic approach to debugging, we've uncovered methods to efficiently identify and solve issues specific to GraphQL, enhancing the stability and reliability of our APIs. This practical knowledge equips us to tackle the complexities of GraphQL development with confidence.

By revisiting the user management system with a focus on GraphQL, we applied what we learned in a real-world context, solidifying our understanding of NestJS's capabilities for GraphQL API development. This hands-on experience not only reinforces our learning but also prepares us to apply these strategies in our projects.

Looking forward, the methodologies and insights gained from this chapter will be instrumental as we continue to develop and refine our GraphQL APIs. Embracing the principles of rigorous testing and effective debugging will ensure our APIs are not only functional but also dependable and efficient. Armed with these skills, we're better prepared to navigate the challenges of modern API development, making the most of NestJS and GraphQL.

Part 4:
Scaling with Microservices and NestJS

This part introduces microservices using *NestJS*, their necessity, architectural styles, and their implementation in *NestJS*.

This part includes the following chapters:

9

Deep Dive into Microservices: Concepts and Architectural Styles

Welcome to *Chapter 9*. Embarking on this chapter is like setting sail on a voyage across the vast ocean of microservices – yes, vast – navigating through the waves of concepts, benefits, and challenges, as well as the rich tapestry of architectural styles that make microservices not just a buzzword but a transformative approach to building scalable, resilient, and flexible applications.

Microservices architecture has reshaped how we think about software development, breaking down complex applications into manageable, loosely coupled services. This chapter will serve as your compass, guiding you through the essentials of microservices, from understanding their core principles to exploring the architectural landscapes that define this approach. We'll uncover the myriad benefits that microservices bring to the table, alongside the hurdles you might encounter along the way.

However, we won't stop there. As we delve deeper, we'll explore the architectural styles that underpin microservices, shedding light on patterns such as **Event-Driven Architecture** (**EDA**) and Database per Service, as well as the pivotal role of API Gateways. These concepts are not just theoretical musings; they are practical blueprints that will help you architect systems that are built to evolve and withstand the demands of modern digital ecosystems.

Here's a sneak peek at the journey ahead:

- Understanding microservices

- Benefits and challenges of microservices

- Microservices architectural styles

This chapter is more than a lesson; it's an invitation to rethink how you design and build software. By the end, you'll not only grasp the essence of microservices but also be equipped to apply these concepts and architectures in creating systems that are robust, scalable, and ready to meet the future head-on.

Let's set forth on this enlightening journey together, unraveling the mysteries of microservices and emerging with a new perspective on building software in the era of distributed computing.

Technical requirements

The code files for the chapter can be found at `https://github.com/PacktPublishing/Scalable-Application-Development-with-NestJS`

Understanding microservices

Microservices architecture has emerged as a revolutionary approach to designing and developing software applications. Unlike traditional monolithic architectures, where a single code base encompasses the entire application, microservices architecture decomposes an application into smaller, independent services. Each service focuses on a specific business capability and operates independently of other services, communicating through well-defined APIs.

What are microservices?

Microservices architecture is an architectural style that structures an application as a collection of multiple independent services. It represents a modular approach to building software systems, where an application is composed of loosely coupled (the opposite of tightly coupled), independently deployable services. These services are organized around specific business functions and interact with each other through APIs. Each microservice is responsible for a single task, enabling teams to develop, deploy, and scale components independently.

Here are the key characteristics of a microservice architecture:

- **Decomposition**: Breaking down an application into smaller, manageable services based on business capabilities

- **Independence**: Each microservice operates independently, with its own database and code base

- **Scalability**: Services can be scaled independently based on demand, optimizing resource utilization

- **Flexibility**: Polyglot architecture allows each service to be implemented using the most suitable programming language and technology stack, each service being treated as a black box from the outside

- **Resilience**: Failure in one service does not affect the entire system, ensuring fault isolation and resilience

Figure 9.1 represents an example of a microservice architecture, where each service is managed by a separate team, owning their deployment pipelines, and loosely coupled. This means that a change in the orders service for example doesn't require a change in any other service.

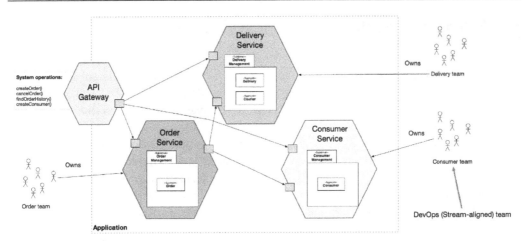

Figure 9.1: An example of a microservices architecture – credit: `microservices.io`

With a clear understanding of what a microservices architecture is, let's move on to exploring the possible benefits of considering it for your future applications.

Benefits of microservices architecture

When the application becomes messy and hard to debug, engineering teams may decide to move to an architecture design so the application can be well maintained without a lot of refactoring. Here are some important benefits of the microservices architecture you may get:

- **Improved agility**: Microservices enable teams to develop, test, and deploy services independently, accelerating the delivery of new features and updates

- **Enhanced scalability**: Services can be scaled horizontally to handle increased load, ensuring optimal performance and responsiveness

- **Fault isolation**: When designed properly, a failure in one service does not propagate to other services, minimizing the impact of errors and improving the resilience of your system

- **Technology diversity**: Microservices allow teams to choose the most suitable technology stack for each service, fostering innovation and flexibility

- **Easier maintenance**: Smaller code bases and well-defined boundaries simplify maintenance and troubleshooting, leading to more efficient development cycles

Microservices architecture offers a scalable, resilient, and flexible approach to software development. By decomposing complex systems into smaller, independently deployable services, organizations can achieve greater agility and maintainability. Understanding the fundamental principles and benefits of microservices architecture is essential for embracing this transformative approach to building modern software applications.

Microservices architectural styles

In the context of microservices architecture, where flexibility, scalability, and reliability are dominant, the choice of architectural styles will be instrumental in the structuring and functioning of distributed systems. Architectural styles are like torchbearers, laying down the framework for how different microservices are to collaborate within the wider ecosystem. Microservices architecture, which represents a unique style with a decentralized system and independently deployable services, is not the only option available as there are various subtleties and variations within this style. Every architectural style has its principles, patterns, and trade-offs that play a large role in the decision-making process regarding service boundaries, data management, communication methods, and so on. Through mastery and use of different architectural styles, developers will be able to construct microservices-based systems uniquely to their immediate needs and strike a balance in terms of flexibility, performance, and maintainability.

Key microservices architectural styles

In the landscape of microservices architecture, several pivotal architectural styles have emerged, each offering distinctive approaches to designing and implementing distributed systems. Understanding these architectural styles is crucial for architects and developers aiming to build scalable, resilient, and maintainable microservices-based applications. Let's delve into some of the most prominent architectural styles.

EDA

Event-oriented architecture evolves around generation, detection, consumption, and hitting events' reactions. In this scenario, services become event-driven and communicate asynchronously through events, whereby these factors imply meaningful occurrences or state transitions within the system. They are usually published to a message broker or event bus, and it enables several services to receive and react to those events according to their requirements. EDA involves data decoupling between services, facilitating the services to react upon events independently without the need to wait for a downstream service. This kind of style is best suited for cases where real-time updates, scalability, and flexibility are considered first. This scenario is most often applied to Internet of Things applications and financial systems, as well as social media platforms.

EDA offers numerous benefits, but it also presents certain challenges and forces that architects and developers must contend with. Here are some challenges to consider:

- **Eventual consistency**: Properly establishing consistency among microservices stands as one of the toughest challenges in distributed systems where events might take different routes or can be inconsistently processed with latencies or in a wrong order. The gap between vision and actualization could have been bridged through very surveyed and simultaneous instruments.

- **Complex event flows**: The larger the number of events and microservices, the more you need to handle the event flows, which get more complex. Getting to the bottom of what happens in the gloomy maze of the system is a herculean task, and so it is hard for us to spot and remove problems.

- **Message reliability**: Messages' reliability in an event-driven ecosystem can be difficult to guarantee, especially when the architecture becomes complex. To ensure that messages are delivered exactly once, in the correct order, and only after all related data has been processed accurately, a robust messaging infrastructure and effective error-handling mechanisms are essential.

On the other hand, here are some forces the architecture represents. These may lead to opting for it:

- **Scalability**: EDA inherently supports scalability by decoupling services and allowing them to react independently to events. However, ensuring that the system scales gracefully as the event load increases requires careful design and consideration of factors such as message throughput and partitioning strategies.

- **Resilience**: EDA encourages fault isolation and resilience by design. Microservices can continue to operate independently even if other services experience failures or downtime. Implementing circuit breakers, retry mechanisms, and fallback strategies further enhances system resilience.

- **Complexity management**: Managing the complexity introduced by EDAs requires disciplined design practices and tooling support. Using event-driven design patterns, such as event sourcing and CQRS, can help simplify complex event flows and improve system maintainability.

Figure 9.2 illustrates how EDA can work within a system, showing how a service can publish an event (for example, `orderCreatedEvent`) that can be consumed by any service that subscribed to that event through an event broker (such as Kafka or RabbitMQ), then become a consumer (`orderDeliveredEvent`).

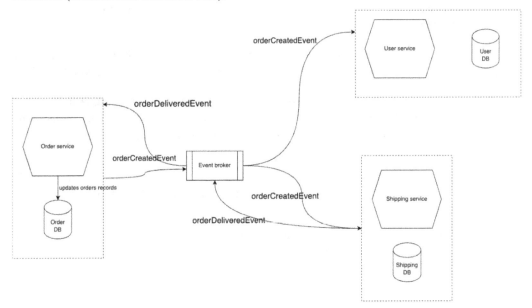

Figure 9.2: EDA illustration

Database per service

Database per service entails allocating a dedicated database to each microservice. Unlike traditional monolithic architectures, where multiple components share a single database, this approach ensures that each microservice possesses exclusive access to its data store. This setup offers numerous advantages, including enhanced autonomy, scalability, and fault isolation. Each service can opt for the most suitable database technology based on its specific requirements, optimizing data storage and retrieval performance. However, managing multiple databases introduces challenges related to data consistency, synchronization, and cross-service transactions, necessitating careful consideration.

Implementing a database per service architecture introduces several challenges and forces that architects and developers must address. Here are some challenges:

- **Data consistency**: Ensuring consistency across multiple databases can be challenging, especially in scenarios where data updates need to be propagated across services. Maintaining data consistency without relying on distributed transactions requires implementing alternative strategies such as eventual consistency, compensation transactions, or distributed locking mechanisms.

- **Data synchronization**: Keeping data synchronized across distributed databases requires robust synchronization mechanisms. Changes made to one database must be propagated to other relevant databases in a timely and efficient manner to maintain data integrity and coherence.

- **Cross-service transactions**: Coordinating transactions that span multiple microservices becomes more complex when each service has its dedicated database. Implementing cross-service transactions without resorting to distributed transactions necessitates careful design and the adoption of patterns such as saga orchestration or event-driven consistency.

Despite these challenges, the database-per-service architecture offers significant benefits that make it a popular choice for building scalable microservices. Let's have a look at the strengths of this architecture:

- **Autonomy**: Database per service promotes service autonomy by allowing each microservice to manage its data independently. This autonomy enables services to evolve and scale independently without being tightly coupled to other services' data models or schemas.

- **Scalability**: By decoupling databases from each other, the database-per-service architecture supports horizontal scalability. Each service can scale its database independently based on its workload and performance requirements, enabling elastic scaling of individual components without affecting the entire system.

- **Fault isolation**: Isolating databases per service enhances fault tolerance and resilience. A failure in one service's database is less likely to impact other services, limiting the blast radius of failures and enabling graceful degradation of functionality.

Addressing these challenges while leveraging the forces inherent in the database per service architecture enables architects and developers to design resilient, scalable, and maintainable microservices-based systems. Implementing effective data consistency, synchronization, and transaction management strategies is essential to realizing the full benefits of this architectural approach.

Figure 9.2 shows how this can be implemented such that every service is responsible for its data integrity and consistency. We can then combine this with the EDA to trigger some events after saving data from a publisher service so consumer service can also update their data accordingly.

API Gateway

The API Gateway pattern is an architecture style in which one service – called API Gateway – serves as a unified entry point for client requests, seamlessly routing them to the appropriate microservices. It functions as a facade for the microservices architecture, abstracting complexities such as service discovery, load balancing, and authentication from clients. The API Gateway undertakes various functions, including request routing, protocol translation, rate limiting, caching, and enforcement of authentication/authorization policies. By consolidating these responsibilities, the API Gateway simplifies client interaction with the microservices ecosystem, bolstering security and enhancing overall system performance.

However, this style introduces the potential for a single point of failure and additional overhead in managing and scaling the gateway component.

Implementing the API Gateway architecture introduces several challenges and forces that architects and developers must navigate. Here are its challenges:

- **Single point of failure**: The API Gateway serves as a central entry point for client requests, making it a potential single point of failure. Any issues or downtime with the gateway can disrupt client access to the entire microservices ecosystem. Implementing redundancy, failover mechanisms, and load-balancing strategies is crucial to mitigate this risk and ensure high availability.

- **Scalability**: As the gateway handles all client requests, it may become a bottleneck under high loads, impacting overall system scalability. Scaling the API Gateway horizontally to handle increased traffic requires careful consideration of load distribution, session management, and data consistency across gateway instances.

- **Complexity**: Managing and maintaining an API Gateway introduces additional complexity to the system architecture. Configuration, routing rules, authentication policies, and rate-limiting settings must be carefully configured and maintained to ensure consistent behavior and security across all client interactions.

- **Security**: The API Gateway becomes a critical security enforcement point, responsible for enforcing authentication, authorization, and rate-limiting policies. Ensuring robust security measures, such as HTTPS encryption, API key management, OAuth integration, and protection against common security threats such as **Cross-Site Request Forgery (CSRF)** and **Cross-Site Scripting (XSS)** is essential to safeguarding the microservices ecosystem.

After discussing the challenges, let's now explore the strengths of the API Gateway architecture:

- **Simplified client interaction**: The API Gateway abstracts complexities such as service discovery, load balancing, and authentication/authorization from clients, providing a unified and simplified interface for client applications. Clients interact with the gateway without needing to be aware of the underlying microservices architecture, streamlining development and integration efforts.

- **Centralized management**: Centralizing common functionalities such as routing, caching, and security enforcement in the API Gateway simplifies management and administration tasks. Changes to routing rules, security policies, or service configurations can be applied uniformly across all client requests, reducing maintenance overhead and ensuring consistency.

- **Improved performance**: By caching responses, optimizing request routing, and offloading common tasks from microservices, the API Gateway can enhance overall system performance. Caching frequently accessed data at the gateway reduces the load on backend services, improves response times, and minimizes latency for client requests.

Addressing these challenges while leveraging the forces inherent in the API Gateway architecture enables architects and developers to design scalable, secure, and efficient microservices-based systems. Balancing the benefits of centralized management and simplified client interaction with the challenges of scalability, complexity, and potential single points of failure is essential for the successful implementation and operation of the API Gateway pattern.

Figure 9.3 illustrates a microservice architecture where an API Gateway sits between the client and the microservices handling requests.

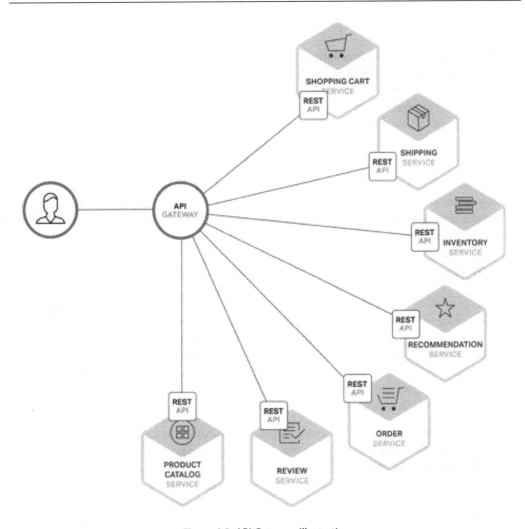

Figure 9.3: API Gateway illustration

Command-Query Responsibility Segregation (CQRS)

Command-Query Responsibility Segregation (**CQRS**) involves segregating the read and write operations of a system into distinct paths. In this architecture, commands are utilized to modify the system's state, while queries are employed to retrieve data from it. By decoupling these functionalities, CQRS enables independent optimization of read and write operations, leading to improved scalability, performance, and flexibility. It finds applications in scenarios where the read and write workloads significantly differ, such as complex reporting, analytics, and high-throughput transactional systems. However, implementing CQRS introduces complexities concerning data synchronization, consistency, and eventual consistency models, necessitating careful deliberation.

Saga pattern

The Saga pattern is a distributed transactional pattern employed to maintain data consistency across multiple microservices. It achieves this by decomposing long-lived transactions into a series of smaller, local transactions, each associated with a compensating action to reverse its effects if needed. Sagas coordinate the execution of these local transactions through choreographed or orchestrated steps, ensuring eventual consistency without relying on distributed transactions. This pattern proves invaluable in scenarios where distributed transactions are impractical or undesirable, such as e-commerce order processing, inventory management, and workflow orchestration.

It's also common to combine the Saga pattern with the EDA to build resilient applications and maintain data integrity. Mechanisms such as data transactions and rollbacks come often into play when one service is unavailable, and an unexpected failure happens to maintain data consistent overall in the services' databases.

API composition

API composition entails aggregating data from multiple microservices to fulfill client requests. Instead of exposing fine-grained APIs for each microservice, API composition endpoints amalgamate data from various services into a single response. This approach minimizes the number of client-server round trips and mitigates the over- or under-fetching of data, resulting in enhanced performance and efficiency. API composition can be achieved through diverse techniques, including server-side, client-side, and gateway-based composition. Nonetheless, it necessitates meticulous consideration of data consistency, versioning, and service dependencies to evade tight coupling and sustain scalability.

By comprehending and leveraging these fundamental architectural styles, architects and developers can craft microservices-based systems that are adaptable, resilient, and scalable to evolving business needs. Each style presents a distinct set of principles, patterns, and trade-offs, empowering teams to architect solutions tailored to their specific requirements and constraints. As we delve deeper into the microservices realm, let's explore how these architectural styles converge to shape the future of distributed systems. Moreover, it's important to note that architects often combine elements from different architectural styles to leverage the strengths of each while mitigating the weaknesses of others. This hybrid approach allows for the creation of complex applications that harness the forces of various architectural paradigms to achieve optimal performance, scalability, and maintainability.

Best practices and considerations

As we conclude our exploration of microservices architectural styles, it's essential to highlight some best practices and considerations for designing and implementing microservices-based systems effectively:

- **Modularity and boundaries**: Embrace the principle of modularity by defining clear boundaries between microservices. Each service should have a single responsibility and encapsulate a specific business capability. This approach fosters autonomy, flexibility, and ease of maintenance.

- **Communication protocols**: Select appropriate communication protocols for inter-service communication based on your application's requirements. While RESTful APIs are widely adopted, consider alternatives such as messaging protocols (e.g., MQTT and AMQP) for EDAs or gRPC for efficient RPC-based communication.

- **Fault tolerance and resilience**: Design microservices with fault tolerance and resilience in mind. Implement retry mechanisms, circuit breakers, and graceful degradation strategies to handle failures gracefully and prevent cascading failures across the system.

- **Monitoring and observability**: Establish robust monitoring and observability mechanisms to gain insights into the health, performance, and behavior of microservices. Use tools such as Prometheus, Grafana, and distributed tracing systems to monitor service metrics, logs, and traces in real time.

- **Security and access control**: Prioritize security by implementing authentication, authorization, and encryption mechanisms to protect sensitive data and prevent unauthorized access. Employ security best practices such as least privilege access, secure communication channels, and regular security audits.

- **Testing and quality assurance**: Invest in comprehensive testing strategies, including unit tests, integration tests, and end-to-end tests, to validate the functionality, performance, and reliability of microservices. Embrace test automation and continuous integration practices to ensure consistent quality throughout the development life cycle.

- **Scalability and elasticity**: Design microservices for scalability and elasticity to accommodate varying workload demands. Utilize container orchestration platforms such as Kubernetes to dynamically scale and manage microservice instances based on traffic patterns and resource utilization.

- **Documentation and collaboration**: Document architectural decisions, APIs, and service contracts comprehensively to facilitate collaboration among development teams and stakeholders. Maintain up-to-date documentation and conduct regular knowledge-sharing sessions to ensure alignment and understanding across the organization.

By adhering to these best practices and considerations, organizations can navigate the complexities of microservices architecture more effectively and build robust, scalable, and maintainable systems that align with business objectives and requirements. As you embark on your microservices journey, remember that continuous learning, adaptation, and refinement are key to success in this ever-evolving landscape.

Summary

As we conclude *Chapter 9*, we've journeyed through the fundamental aspects of microservices architecture, gaining a comprehensive understanding of its principles and architectural styles.

Beginning with an exploration of microservices' core concepts, we uncovered their pivotal role in modern software development, emphasizing modularity, scalability, and autonomy. Delving deeper, we examined the benefits and challenges inherent in microservices, acknowledging the trade-offs associated with decentralized systems.

Our exploration extended to the key architectural styles of microservices, including EDA, database per service, and API Gateway. Each style offers unique principles and patterns, empowering architects and developers to design systems tailored to specific requirements and constraints, as we learned in this chapter.

It's clear that microservices architecture is not a one-size-fits-all solution. Instead, success lies in strategically combining architectural styles to leverage their strengths while mitigating weaknesses. Armed with this understanding, we're poised to architect resilient, scalable, and adaptable microservices-based systems that meet the evolving needs of modern applications. In the next chapter, we will put these theoretical foundations into practice, building an actual microservices application.

10
Building Scalable Microservices with NestJS

Welcome to *Chapter 10*, where we will transition from the theoretical aspects learned in the previous chapter into practice. We will build a robust microservices application using a mono repo to leverage the way NestJS gracefully handles microservices architectures.

NestJS offers a wide range of possibilities when it comes to building microservices; we will explore them with a handful of examples and real-life challenges you may face when designing your scalable application.

In this chapter, we will also learn how to build inter-services operations using various communication transport layers, all applied to practical use cases developers struggle with when dealing with data integrity in microservices architectures.

Here is what we'll be covering in this chapter:

- Defining and implementing microservices in NestJS
- Exploring the microservices package in NestJS
- Inter-service communication and data management in NestJS
- Best practices for building microservices with NestJS
- Troubleshooting and debugging microservices

To proceed with the chapter, make sure you prepare your local environment as we gear up for an interactive coding session. By the end of this chapter, you'll not only understand how to implement microservices using NestJS but also be armed to overcome common pitfalls.

Ready to put theory into practice? Let's start coding!

Technical requirements

The code files for the chapter can be found at `https://github.com/PacktPublishing/Scalable-Application-Development-with-NestJS`

Defining and implementing microservices in NestJS

Building on the NestJS foundations we've established in earlier chapters, in this section, we will focus on defining and implementing microservices within our existing NestJS environment. By transitioning from a monolithic architecture to a microservices-oriented architecture, we'll harness NestJS' robust capabilities for managing complex, scalable systems.

We'll explore how NestJS supports microservices architectures through its modular approach and built-in features that facilitate service independence and inter-service communication. The transition from a monolithic architecture to a microservices-oriented one is vital for developers aiming to create systems that are scalable, easier to maintain, and capable of evolving over time.

Throughout this section, we'll delve into the practical steps required to restructure your NestJS applications into microservices.

Let's enhance your NestJS applications by advancing from monolithic designs to dynamic, distributed microservice systems.

Setting up a new project

We will start by creating a new NestJS project using the following command:

```
$ nest new microservices-sample
```

You can use any other name of your choice. This command will generate a new NestJS project, ready to be transitioned to a microservices one.

In NestJS, a microservice is an application that uses a different layer than HTTP.

The next step will be installing the necessary packages using the following command:

```
$ yarn add @nestjs/microservices
```

Now, our project is ready to become a microservice.

Setting up a new microservice project

To transform the newly created application into a microservice one, we simply need to update the `main.ts` file with the following code:

```
import { NestFactory } from '@nestjs/core';
import { AppModule } from './app.module';
import {
  MicroserviceOptions,
  Transport
} from '@nestjs/microservices';

async function bootstrap() {
  const app = await
    NestFactory.createMicroservice<MicroserviceOptions>(
      AppModule,
      {
        transport: Transport.TCP,
      },
    );
  await app.listen();
}
bootstrap();
```

The preceding code snippet looks almost the same as the one generated by Nest-CLI. However, one can clearly notice a few differences:

- The app is now created with the `createMicroservice()` method from the `NestFactory` instance type instead of the `create()` method.

- The app is no longer an `INestApplication` instance but an `INestMicroservice` instance.

- The app's `listen` function no longer takes a `PORT` as a parameter.

- We are using the TCP transport layer (which is different from HTTP, and in a NestJS context, the app is now a microservice). The `Transport` enum has multiple options. Depending on the application's use case, we can use `REDIS`, `KAFKA`, `NATS`, `RabbitMQ`, and so on. For demonstration purposes, in this chapter, we will use the default one, which is **Transmission Control Protocol** (**TCP**).

NestJS also supports hybrid applications. Hybrid applications, in the context of NestJS are applications that listen for requests from two or more sources; this can combine an HTTP server with one or more microservices listeners.

As we saw with the preceding code, the `createMicroservice()` method returns an instance that doesn't allow us to set up an HTTP server (it doesn't support the port parameter). So, we need another method for hybrid applications.

We can create a hybrid application in NestJS by updating the `main.ts` file with the following code:

```
const app = await NestFactory.create(AppModule);
const microservice =
  app.connectMicroservice<MicroserviceOptions>({
    transport: Transport.TCP,
  });

await app.startAllMicroservices();
await app.listen(3001);
```

The `app.listen(3001)` method starts an HTTP server at the specified port and allows your application to listen for both HTTP and TCP requests, making it a hybrid NestJS application.

Well done! With these simple changes, we have a microservice application, thanks to NestJS. Before we move forward with further implementations, let's talk about the `@nestjs/microservices` package in the next section.

Overview of the microservices package in NestJS

With your NestJS project now configured to operate as a microservice using TCP, it's essential to understand the capabilities and features provided by the `@nestjs/microservices` package. This package is the backbone of microservices architecture in NestJS, facilitating robust options for communication and configuration that can scale with the complexities of your application.

Introduction to @nestjs/microservices

The `@nestjs/microservices` module is designed to integrate seamlessly with the core NestJS framework, enabling the development of lightweight, highly scalable microservice applications. It supports a variety of transport layers such as TCP, Redis, NATS, MQTT, RabbitMQ, and Kafka, which means that your NestJS microservices can communicate over different channels, depending on the specific requirements and constraints of your application.

Key features and advantages

The `@nestjs/microservices` package offers several key features that are critical for developing resilient microservices:

- **Transport independence**: The ability to abstract away the details of the underlying transport layer allows developers to switch between different communication strategies with minimal changes to the application code

- **Message and event handling**: It provides decorators and helpers to handle incoming messages and events effectively depending on the pattern used, enabling clear and concise setup for message routes and handlers

- **Resilient communication**: Built-in strategies for dealing with service outages, such as retries and back-off mechanisms, ensure that your services remain robust under failure conditions

- **Integration with other modules**: @nestjs/microservices is designed to work harmoniously with other NestJS modules, ensuring that aspects such as security and configuration are consistently managed across your services

Having discovered the core concepts and benefits of the @nestjs/microservices module, let's now dive into a practical example to see how this module can be used to implement communication between microservices.

Implementing a simple communication example

Let's implement a basic example to illustrate how a NestJS microservice can send and receive messages. Suppose that we have a service that needs to process user data asynchronously:

```
import { Controller } from '@nestjs/common';
import {
  MessagePattern,
  Payload
} from '@nestjs/microservices';

@Controller()
export class UserDataProcessor {
  @MessagePattern({ cmd: 'process_user_data'})
  async processUserData(@Payload() data: any) {
    // Logic to process user data
    console.log('Processing user data:', data);
  }
}
```

In this example, @MessagePattern decorates the processUserData method to listen for messages with the { cmd: 'process_user_data' } pattern. Whenever a message with this topic is received, the method is triggered with the message payload.

The @nestjs/microservices package extends the powerful, scalable architecture of NestJS into the realm of microservices, providing tools and techniques that are essential for modern backend systems. Understanding and utilizing this package will empower you to build efficient, maintainable, and robust microservices.

By mastering these tools, you are well-equipped to handle various challenges that arise in distributed systems, ensuring that your applications can scale and evolve alongside your business needs.

In the next section, we will delve deeper into setting up inter-service communication patterns and managing data consistency across services to further enhance your microservices architecture.

Inter-service communication and data integrity in NestJS

Now that we understand how NestJS supports the microservices architecture, let's see how microservices communicate with one another. Before we proceed, we need to transform our current structure into a mono repo one. Note that depending on the application's requirements, you may need to have multiple repositories. We will keep things simple for now and use a mono repo structure.

To do this transition – from the standard mode to a mono repo structure – we can use the power of the `nest-cli` and generate multiple applications easily. We need to have a unique API gateway project, which will expose the entry point to our clients, and two more services, for example, the order service and the inventory service. Feel free to use any example that resonates better with you.

To generate those services, use the following command at the root of the project:

```
$ nest generate app order
# then
$ nest generate app inventory
```

Running these commands will update your project structure to something like *Figure 10.1*:

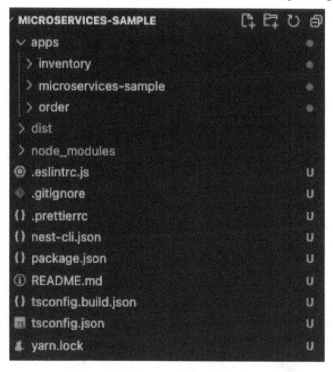

Figure 10.1: Mono repo apps structure

From our new structure, you may have noticed a few changes:

- We now have an `apps/` folder in the project's root.

- The existing project is now located under `/apps/original-application-name`, where `original-application-name` is `microservices-sample` in my case.

- In the `package.json` file, we can see that a few commands have been updated. For example, now the `start:prod` command looks like this: `"start:prod": "node dist/apps/microservices-sample/main"`. This means that the `microservices-sample` project will be treated as our entry point, or in common words, our API gateway.

- The `nest-cli.json` file has been updated to the following:

```
{
  "$schema":
    "<https://json.schemastore.org/nest-cli>",
  "collection": "@nestjs/schematics",
  "sourceRoot": "apps/microservices-sample/src",
  "compilerOptions": {
    "deleteOutDir": true,
    "webpack": true,
    "tsConfigPath":
      "apps/microservices-sample/tsconfig.app.json"
  },
  "monorepo": true,
  "root": "apps/microservices-sample",
  "projects": {
    "microservices-sample": {
      "type": "application",
      "root": "apps/microservices-sample",
      "entryFile": "main",
      "sourceRoot": "apps/microservices-sample/src",
      "compilerOptions": {
        "tsConfigPath": "apps/microservices-sample/
          tsconfig.app.json"
      }
    },
    "order": {
      "type": "application",
      "root": "apps/order",
      "entryFile": "main",
      "sourceRoot": "apps/order/src",
      "compilerOptions": {
        "tsConfigPath": "apps/order/tsconfig.app.json"
```

```
        }
      },
      "inventory": {
        "type": "application",
        "root": "apps/inventory",
        "entryFile": "main",
        "sourceRoot": "apps/inventory/src",
        "compilerOptions": {
          "tsConfigPath":
            "apps/inventory/tsconfig.app.json"
        }
      }
    }
  }
```

In the preceding configuration file, you can see that our project now recognizes three different projects, with the main source root being set to our API gateway app, and both microservices being of the application type.

Well done! You have a mono repo ready to be cooked.

Depending on the application's requirement, we may need to expose additional ports for each microservice. Those will be considered as **hybrid applications** since they will communicate using both HTTP and another communication layer (TCP, Kafka, etc.).

Our project is ready, so let's discuss a little bit about what we will be building now.

Key features of the application

While trying to keep things simple for now, here is the list of the most important features we will build in this project:

- When someone places an order, we send a POST request to the order service with the payload that contains information about the order such as the user that wants to buy, the product, and the total price for the order.

- When the order service receives the request, it initiates an order creation – even though we don't have any database implemented here, think of it as a database transaction initiated – which emits an event with the order_created topic that will be consumed by the inventory service.

- When the inventory service receives the order_created event, it checks whether there are sufficient products in the inventory. If yes, it updates the inventory level and the status of the order via another event of the order_processed topic; if not, it rejects the order creation via an event of the same order_processed topic with a different payload that will be handled by the order service to update the status of the order accordingly.

Note that this is a very simplified version of an **order management system**: the goal is to demonstrate how two applications can communicate in NNestJS.

With the context in place, let's build our microservices.

The order service

With our mono repo set up, and our understanding of the scope of the project solidified, let's now work on the order service.

Here are the most important technical requirements for our order service:

1. The order service will listen to incoming HTTP requests to create a new order, that is, a POST request at the /orders endpoint.

2. Then, it will emit an event when the order has been created to be handled by the inventory service.

3. Then, it will listen to events coming from the inventory service, and update the order's status accordingly. For example, if the inventory level for the product in the order isn't enough to fulfill the order request, the inventory will send an order_processed event to the order service. Then the order service will update the order's status from PENDING to CANCELLED.

The fact that our order service can listen to both HTTP and TCP requests makes it a hybrid application, in the context of NestJS.

This sounds minimalist for now but will demonstrate how two microservices applications can communicate and interchange information. Next, let's build our order service according to our technical requirements.

Building the order service logic

Inside our order application, let's replace the generated code from the main.ts file with the following content:

```
// apps/order/src/main.ts
import { NestFactory } from '@nestjs/core';
import { OrderModule } from './order.module';

async function bootstrap() {
  const app = await NestFactory.create(OrderModule);
  // to connect to the microservices linked to the order
  // service
  app.startAllMicroservices();
  await app.listen(3001);
}
bootstrap();
```

In the preceding code, we have updated the initial code so our order service can start all the microservices linked to it, waiting for incoming events or emitting new events to those services. In our sample, we simply expect events coming from the inventory service while being able to also send events to it. We are also listening to incoming HTTP requests to port 3001.

Shaping the data

Next, we need to shape our data. While staying minimalistic, let's create an apps/order/entities/ order.entity.ts file and paste the following content:

```
export enum OrderStatus {
  PENDING = 'Pending',
  COMPLETED = 'Completed',
  CANCELLED = 'Cancelled',
}

export class Order {
  id: string;
  name: string;
  product: string;
  price: number;
  status: OrderStatus;
  quantity: number;
}
```

For now, let's export two entities from the same file. We will improve the architecture later, following some very good practices.

Note that in the Order class in the preceding code, we have fields such as product, but in real-life scenarios, instead of a string, this could be another entity. Alternatively, you can create a user entity and establish a relationship between the user and orders. For now, let's keep things straightforward. We have case studies in the upcoming chapters where we will build real applications and consider all the architecture constraints – no worries :).

Registering the Inventory service

Now, let's register the Inventory service in the OrderModule so we can set up a contract between our services with the following code snippet:

```
@Module({
  imports: [
    ClientsModule.register([
      {
        name: 'INVENTORY_SERVICE',
        transport: Transport.TCP,
```

```
      options: {
        port: 8002,
      },
    },
  ]),
],
controllers: [OrderController],
providers: [OrderService],
})
export class OrderModule {}
```

With `ClientsModule` and `Transport` being imported from our good friend, `@nestjs/microservices`, we simply informed the `OrderModule` that we may be sending and receiving TCP events from a module called `INVENTORY_SERVICE` using port `8002`. No need to make sure that the port is alive, it's a **MAYBE** contract. If the service is out of service, that's not the order service's problem, but we know that we should be able to communicate with the inventory service from this configuration.

Next, let's implement the business logic in the order creation process.

Implementing the business logic to order creation

In the `order/order.service.ts` file, add the following `createOrder` method. Make sure to create and import the `CreateOrderInput` **Data Transfer Object (DTO)** under `order/dto/create-order.dto.ts`:

```
// order/order.service.ts
constructor(
  @Inject('INVENTORY_SERVICE') private inventoryClient:
  ClientProxy,
) {}
// in memory storage - for demo purposes
private orders: Order[] = [];

  createOrder(createOrderInput: CreateOrderInput): Order {
  const order = {
    ...createOrderInput,
    id: `${this.orders.length + 1}`,
    status: OrderStatus.PENDING,
  };
  this.orders.push(order);
  console.log('Order created:', order, this.orders);
  // emit event to the inventory service
  this.inventoryClient.emit('order_created', order);
  return order;
}
```

```
// order/dto/create-order.dto.ts
export class CreateOrderInput {
  name: string;
  product: string;
  price: number;
}
```

In the preceding code snippet, we implement the `createOrder` method in the `order.service` file, which does the following:

- **Injects the inventory service client**: The constructor uses dependency injection to bring in the inventory client proxy, which is used for communicating with the inventory service, using the token `INVENTORY_SERVICE`.

- **Maintains an in-memory order list**: A simple array of named orders is used to store order data in memory for demonstration purposes.

- **Generates a new order**: The `createOrder` method takes an instance of `CreateOrderInput`, generates a new order ID based on the current number of orders, and assigns an initial status of `PENDING`.

- **Stores the order**: The newly created order is added to the orders array, simulating storage.

- **Logs the order creation**: For visibility during testing and debugging, it prints the created order and the entire order list to the console.

- **Communicates with the inventory service**: The `emit()` method on the inventory client is used to send an `order_created` event to the inventory service, passing the newly created order as the payload. In NNestJS, the `emit()` method returns a hot Observable, which means listeners don't have to subscribe to the stream to receive that event. This is how services communicate and share data with each other in a decoupled manner.

The `CreateOrderInput` DTO, defined in `order/dto/create-order.dto.ts`, serves as a structured template for incoming order data, ensuring that each order has a `name`, `product`, and `price`.

This setup demonstrates the foundational aspects of inter-service communication, allowing you to decouple services while ensuring they remain coordinated in processing business logic, especially when scaling independently.

Adding a Controller method

To complete the process and all the order services to receive and treat this request, let's add a `Controller` method with the `@POST()` decorator and specify a path to this operation. In the `order/order.controller.ts` file, add the following method:

```
// order/order.service.ts
  @Post('create-order')
  createOrder(@Body() createOrderInput: CreateOrderInput):
  Order {
    return this.orderService.createOrder(createOrderInput);
  }
```

This method simply listens to incoming `POST` requests at the create-order endpoint and calls the dedicated service we talked about earlier.

Is this enough? Well, if we're only talking about the order service order creation operation, then yes.

Running the order service

When the order is placed, the order service takes the incoming request and informs the inventory service that an order has been placed. The event can either be received or not, that's no longer the order service's business; this means that we can scale this service without worrying about the other ones that are linked to it – that's the magic of microservices.

Let's try things out by running the order service with the following command:

```
$ yarn start:dev order
```

This will only start the order service and start listening to HTTP requests at port 3001, according to our configuration in the `main.ts` file.

Send a sample request that initiates an order creation using curl (or any other GUI platform such as Postman) with the following command:

```
$ curl -H 'Content-Type: application/json' \
    -d '{
          "name": "Joseph Diakese",
          "product": "Laptop",
          "price": 2000,
          "quantity": 10,
    }' \
    -X POST \
    <http://localhost:3001/create-order>
```

This command will perform a POST request at the specified URL. The -H option contains the headers of the request, the -d option the body, and -X the verb. It will initiate an order creation without any trouble, without questioning the receiver of that event.

Looking at the terminal, *Figure 10.2* shows how it should look, printing the newly created order and the updated list in the in-memory database we created, just as intended by the service file:

```
webpack 5.90.1 compiled successfully in 185 ms
Type-checking in progress...
[Nest] 41572  - 05/06/2024, 3:21:53 AM     LOG [NestFactory] Starting Nest application...
[Nest] 41572  - 05/06/2024, 3:21:53 AM     LOG [InstanceLoader] ClientsModule dependencies initia
lized +6ms
[Nest] 41572  - 05/06/2024, 3:21:53 AM     LOG [InstanceLoader] OrderModule dependencies initiali
zed +0ms
[Nest] 41572  - 05/06/2024, 3:21:53 AM     LOG [RoutesResolver] OrderController {/}: +8ms
[Nest] 41572  - 05/06/2024, 3:21:53 AM     LOG [RouterExplorer] Mapped {/, GET} route +1ms
[Nest] 41572  - 05/06/2024, 3:21:53 AM     LOG [RouterExplorer] Mapped {/create-order, POST} rout
e +0ms
[Nest] 41572  - 05/06/2024, 3:21:53 AM     LOG [NestApplication] Nest application successfully st
arted +1ms
[Nest] 41572  - 05/06/2024, 3:21:53 AM     LOG [NestMicroservice] Nest microservice successfully
started +6ms
No errors found.
Order created: {
  name: 'Joseph Diakese',
  product: 'Laptop',
  price: 2000,
  quantity: 5,
  id: '1',
  status: 'Pending'
} [
  {
    name: 'Joseph Diakese',
    product: 'Laptop',
    price: 2000,
    quantity: 5,
    id: '1',
    status: 'Pending'
  }
]
```

Figure 10.2: Order service – output when initiating an order creation

Well done! We just submitted an order creation operation. However, our job has only just begun. What if while processing the order, we don't have enough products in stock? How do we confirm to the user that their order has been completed when we have enough products in stock, or canceled due to many probable issues? For example, maybe the inventory service is not available now, maybe we are out of stock for that specific product, and so on. This is where the inventory service shows up. Let's work on it.

Building the inventory service logic

The inventory service's responsibility is simple for now, listening to incoming order_created events coming from the order service. Then, depending on the inventory level of the specified product, it sends back another event with the order_processed pattern with a payload that indicates whether the inventory level was enough.

This means we don't need a hybrid application here, at least for now. Let's start by updating the `inventory/main.ts` file with the following code:

```
// inventory/main.ts

import { NestFactory } from '@nestjs/core';
import { InventoryModule } from './inventory.module';
import {
  MicroserviceOptions,
  Transport
} from '@nestjs/microservices';

async function bootstrap() {
  const app = await
    NestFactory.createMicroservice<MicroserviceOptions>(
      InventoryModule,
      {
        transport: Transport.TCP,
        options: {
          port: 8002,
          host: 'localhost',
        },
      },
    );
  await app.listen();
}
bootstrap();
```

With the preceding code snippet, we configured a microservice using a TCP transport and communicating at port 8002, the host being `localhost`, since we are not planning to go live for now. Note that the second parameter of the `createMicroservice()` method looks almost the same as the options with what we registered the inventory service in the `OrderModule`; if the port and the transport mismatch here, the event will never be received or sent from one service to another because contracts are not same.

Next, we need to test whether the event sent from the order service is being received here.

Testing whether the event is being received

For that, let's create an event handler with the `order_created` topic in the `inventory/inventory.controller.ts` file, adding the following `handleOrderCreated` method:

```
// inventory/inventory.controller.ts

  @EventPattern('order_created')
  async handleOrderCreated(data: any) {
```

```
    console.log('Order created:', data);
}
```

The preceding method, decorated with the `@EventPattern`, will be called anytime an `order_created` event is emitted from one of the producers. We don't really care about the source. We simply need to react upon the event reception, and since the `emit()` function called in the order service returns a hot Observable, there is no need to subscribe to this topic, as seen previously.

So, keeping the order service up, in another terminal, let's start the inventory service with the following command:

```
$ yarn start:dev inventory
```

Now, let's initiate the same HTTP request from the order service using curl and see what happens in both terminals.

In the order service terminal, things are pretty much the same, but in the inventory service, notice that we have the order payload printed, as if the inventory service is acknowledging that it has received our request.

This is very good. Now we need to implement the business logic that will handle this event in the inventory service. However, first, let's clean the project a little bit because this is getting a little bit messy.

> **Let's grab a coffee**
>
> Before we proceed, take some time to go through the whole process once again and make sure it's clear. The next steps will be the same, with the producer becoming the consumer this time.

Cleaning the project

For now, we hard-coded a lot of values. Imagine writing `order_creted` mistakenly instead of `order_created` in one of those services, or having a `3003` port registered in the `OrderModule` and `3002` set up in the inventory service. It will be impossible for our services to communicate, and as the application grows, more operations and constants are added, and things can quickly get out of hand.

Some values, such as service ports or service names, can be added as environment variables and have different values depending on the environment. However, for application instances or most used pieces of code, another solution is needed. Remember the **Don't Repeat Yourself** (**DRY**) principle.

This is where creating libraries becomes important. In NestJS, when you have a mono repo, you can generate a library using `$ nest generate lib library-name`. This will update the `nest-cli.json` and `package.json` files and then create a new project under the `libs/library-name` folder.

Libraries are also important when some business logic, constants, or functions can be used in multiple places in the application.

In more sophisticated scenarios, when you have a poly repo architecture, these libraries can be published as npm packages and imported into any repo that needs them.

So, let's generate our first module and call it `constants` using the following command:

```
$ nest generate lib constants
# accept the default configuration
```

This command will do the following:

- Create a new project under `libs/constants`.

- Update the `nest-cli.json`, adding the following properties:

```
"constants": {
  "type": "library",
  "root": "libs/constants",
  "entryFile": "index",
  "sourceRoot": "libs/constants/src",
  "compilerOptions": {
    "tsConfigPath":
      "libs/constants/tsconfig.lib.json"
  }
}
```

Note that the `type` property is set to `library` while the others as set to `application`.

- Update the `package.json` file, adding the following property:

```
"moduleNameMapper": {
  "^@app/constants(|/.*)$":
    "<rootDir>/libs/constants/src/$1"
}
```

Now, remove all the generated files under `libs/constants/src` except the `index.ts` file, which is needed to export all the library's instances.

Now, in the `constants` folder, let's add a new file (`constants.events.ts`) and paste the following code:

```
// libs/constants/src/constants.events.ts

export const EVENTS = {
  ORDER_CREATED: 'order_created',
  ORDER_UPDATED: 'order_updated',
};
```

```
// update the constants/src/index.ts file

export * from './events';
```

In the preceding code, we have simply exported the EVENT object with the needed properties, then exported it from the index file.

Now, replace the hard-coded event pattern from the order and the inventory service, importing the pattern from @app/constants instead.

Back to the project with a note. Whenever we start hard-coding strings, or copy-paste a block of code, it may be time to migrate it in a library.

Now, let's handle the order creation in the inventory service.

Handling order creation in the inventory service

First, we should implement the business logic, updating the inventory.service.ts file with the following code:

```
import { EVENTS } from '@app/constants';
import {
  Inventory,
  Order,
  OrderProcessPayload
} from '@app/shared';
import { Inject, Injectable } from '@nestjs/common';
import { ClientProxy } from '@nestjs/microservices';

@Injectable()
export class InventoryService {
  constructor(@Inject('ORDER_SERVICE') private orderClient:
    ClientProxy) {}

  // in memory storage of inventory - for demo purposes
  private inventory: Inventory[] = [
    { id: 1, name: 'Laptop', quantity: 100 },
    { id: 2, name: 'Mouse', quantity: 50 },
    { id: 3, name: 'Keyboard', quantity: 75 },
  ];
```

```
handleOrderCreated(order: Order) {
  let success = false;
  let message = '';
  const item = this.inventory.find((i) => i.name ===
    order.product);

  if (item) {
    if (item.quantity < order.quantity) {
      message = 'Insufficient quantity in inventory';
    } else {
      item.quantity -= order.quantity;
      success = true;
      message = 'Order processed successfully';
    }
  } else {
    message = `Product ${order.product} not found in
      inventory`;
  }

  const payload: OrderProcessPayload = {
    success,
    message,
    orderId: order.id,
  };
  console.log('Order processed with the payload:',
    payload);
  // emit event to the order service
  return this.orderClient.emit(EVENTS.ORDER_PROCESSED,
    payload);
}

  // keep whatever we had before
}
```

As you can see in the preceding code snippet, this looks similar to what we did in the orders service file. We have an `orderClient` emitting events to be handled by the order service. We also have an in-memory database to store the inventory.

The `handleOrderCreated()` method expects an `Order` instance as a parameter to be passed from the event handler in the controller, instead of importing the `Order` entity from the order service, which is a separate application. It's preferable to create a new library called `shared` and export entities from `libs/shared/entities/*.entities.ts`.

The method also returns an Observable to be consumed by the order service. Wait a second; can the order service listen to the TCP request? Right now, it can't. We need to set up a TCP connection as well, but not in the same way as we did for the inventory service. Remember, our order service is supposed to be hybrid.

To set a TCP connection up, let's update the `order/main.ts` file, adding the following method call on the `INestApplication` instance:

```
// apps/order/main.ts

// configure the microservice to listen on port 3001 using
// the TCP transport layer
  app.connectMicroservice<MicroserviceOptions>({
    transport: Transport.TCP,
    options: {
      port: 8001,
      host: 'localhost',
    },
  });
```

According to the **Nest official documentation**, the `connectMicroservice()` method does the following:

> *"Connects microservice to the NestApplication instance. Transforms application to a hybrid instance."*

This means that adding this method in the `main.ts` file now makes the order service an actual hybrid application.

Registering the order service into the inventory service

Next, we need to register the order service into the inventory service the same way as we did in the order service. To do so, let's add the following code to the imports array of the `InventoryModule`:

```
// inventory/inventory.module.ts

    ClientsModule.register([
  {
    name: 'ORDER_SERVICE',
    transport: Transport.TCP,
    options: {
      port: 8001,
    },
  },
    },
  ]),
```

Note that the port is identical to what we set in the order service.

Let's replace the code in the inventory controller file with the following code so it consumes the business logic in its service file instead of a `console.log`:

```
@EventPattern(EVENTS.ORDER_CREATED)
  async handleOrderCreated(data: Order) {
    // change this line
    this.inventoryService.handleOrderCreated(data);
  }
```

Well done! We registered the order service in the inventory service and invoked the business logic from the controller file, which sends an event to the order client with the right payload according to the inventory level of a specific product.

From the moment the inventory service sends an event to the order service, it completes its part of the contract. Handling those events is an order service's responsibility. Let's simply manage it by adding an event handler in the `order.controller.ts` file as follows:

```
// order.controller.ts
  @EventPattern(EVENTS.ORDER_PROCESSED)
  async handleOrderProcessed(data: OrderProcessPayload) {
    this.orderService.handleOrderProcessed(data);
  }


// order.service.ts
  handleOrderProcessed(data: OrderProcessPayload) {
    const order = this.orders.find((o) => o.id ===
      data.orderId);
    if (order) {
      order.status = data.success
        ? OrderStatus.COMPLETED
        : OrderStatus.CANCELLED;
      console.log('Order status updated:',
        order, this.orders);
    } else {
      console.log('Order not found');
    }
  }
```

In the preceding code snippet, we implemented a listener so anytime an event of the EVENTS. ORDER_PROCESSED pattern from anywhere to the specified port in the `main.ts` file. It triggers a function call in the service file, which then updates the status of the order if it's found.

Well done! You have made it. We have now operations navigating through services like a queen on a chess board (limitlessly).

Running the order and inventory services

Let's test everything out once again, starting both services from different terminals using the following:

```
$ nest start:dev order
$ nest start:dev inventory
```

Figures 10.3 and *10.4* illustrate what you should see in both terminals when you make the same curl request if everything goes according to plan.

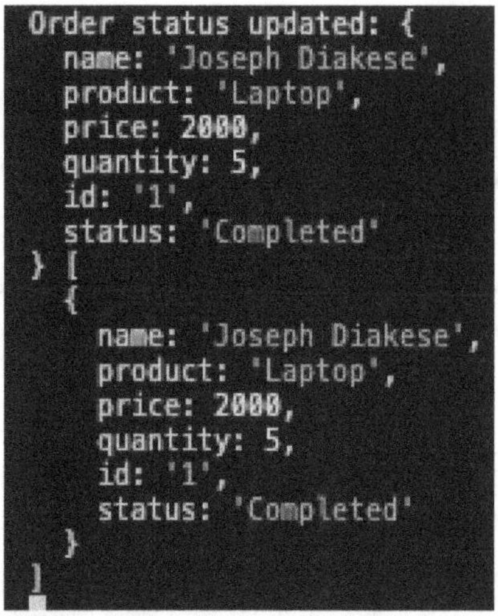

```
Order status updated: {
  name: 'Joseph Diakese',
  product: 'Laptop',
  price: 2000,
  quantity: 5,
  id: '1',
  status: 'Completed'
} [
  {
    name: 'Joseph Diakese',
    product: 'Laptop',
    price: 2000,
    quantity: 5,
    id: '1',
    status: 'Completed'
  }
]
```

Figure 10.3: Output from the orders service

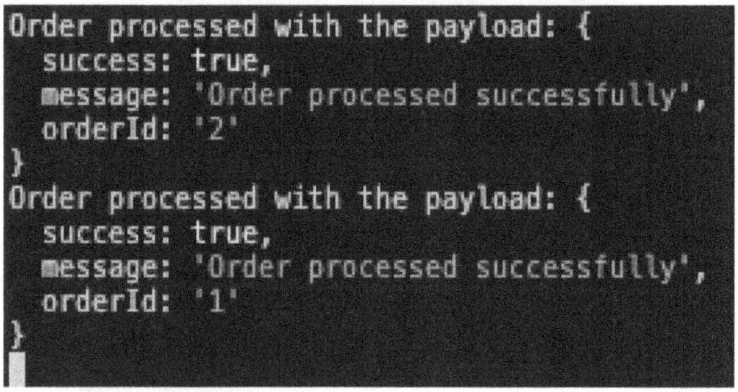

```
Order processed with the payload: {
  success: true,
  message: 'Order processed successfully',
  orderId: '2'
}
Order processed with the payload: {
  success: true,
  message: 'Order processed successfully',
  orderId: '1'
}
```

Figure 10.4: Output from the inventory service

Well done! This has been great so far.

Before we close this section, a question must be on your mind: what's the role of the API gateway then, if it never gets involved? I have got you, you are right, we have ignored it so far. Let's demonstrate how it can play a crucial role in our architecture in the following section.

API gateway, our gatekeeper

An API gateway is an essential part of the microservices architecture, acting as the single entry point for external clients to interact with the system. In this architecture, the API gateway offers a unified interface for various services and handles tasks such as request routing, composition, and protocol translation.

Key functions of an API gateway

In a microservices architecture, here are the key functions of an API gateway:

- **Centralized routing:** The API gateway directs incoming client requests to the appropriate microservice based on the URL, HTTP method, or other routing logic

- **Authentication and authorization:** It ensures that only authenticated and authorized requests reach the services, managing security centrally

- **Load balancing:** It distributes requests evenly across multiple instances of a service to enhance reliability and performance

- **Request transformation:** It modifies request and response formats to align with service-specific requirements, abstracting complexity from clients

- **Rate limiting and caching:** It protects against excessive load by limiting request rates and improves performance by caching responses

- **Service discovery:** It automatically discovers available service instances and routes traffic, accordingly enhancing flexibility and scalability

With an understanding of the critical functions an API gateway performs within a microservices architecture, we can now explore how to implement an API gateway in NestJS, bringing these concepts into practice.

Implementing an API Gateway in NestJS

Let's implement our API gateway by following these simple steps:

1. **Initial setup:** Begin by configuring the API gateway application as an entry point for client requests. Update the `main.ts` file of the API gateway app to set up basic HTTP functionality:

```
// apps/microservice-sample/src/main.ts

import { NestFactory } from '@nestjs/core';
import { AppModule } from './app.module';

async function bootstrap() {
  const app = await NestFactory.create(AppModule);
  await app.listen(3000);
}
bootstrap();
```

2. **Proxying requests to microservices**: Set up the gateway to proxy client requests to the appropriate microservice using HTTP or another transport layer. In this case, the order service listens on port 3001, and the inventory service listens on port 8002.

Next, you need to set up HTTP proxying in the gateway. There are multiple ways to handle this, such as using a reverse proxy module or manually forwarding requests to the appropriate services.

Using @nestjs/terminus

Reverse proxy middleware such as @nestjs/terminus can handle the proxying:

1. **Installing packages**: Install the required package with the following command:

```
$ yarn add @nestjs/terminus
```

2. **Setting up routes in app.module.ts**: Update the gateway's AppModule to include routes that forward requests to the order and inventory services:

```
// apps/api-gateway/src/app.module.ts

import { Module } from '@nestjs/common';
import { TerminusModule } from '@nestjs/terminus';
import { HttpModule } from '@nestjs/axios';

@Module({
  imports: [TerminusModule, HttpModule],
  controllers: [],
  providers: [],
})
export class AppModule {}
```

3. **Implementing a proxy controller**: Create a controller to handle forwarding requests. Here's a basic example:

```
// apps/api-gateway/src/proxy.controller.ts

import {
  Controller,
  Get,
  Post,
  Req,
  Res,
  HttpService
} from '@nestjs/common';
import { Request, Response } from 'express';
```

```
@Controller('orders')
export class ProxyController {
  constructor(private httpService: HttpService) {}

  @Post()
  async forwardToOrderService(@Req() req:
  Request, @Res() res: Response) {
    const { data } = await this.httpService.post(
      '<http://localhost:3001/orders>',
      req.body
    ).toPromise();
    res.json(data);
  }
}
```

4. **Adding a proxy controller to the module**: Register the controller in the module:

```
// apps/microservice-sample/src/app.module.ts

import { Module } from '@nestjs/common';
import { ProxyController } from './proxy.controller';

@Module({
  imports: [TerminusModule, HttpModule],
  controllers: [ProxyController],
  providers: [],
})
export class AppModule {}
```

5. **Handling authentication and authorization**: Integrate middleware or modules to manage user authentication centrally in the gateway. The gateway verifies the client's credentials and ensures secure access to underlying services.

6. **Advanced configuration**: Implement rate limiting, response caching, and other advanced features using available NestJS modules or third-party libraries.

7. **Service discovery and load balancing**: Consider implementing dynamic routing and load balancing by integrating service discovery with a tool such as Consul or Eureka.

In a microservices architecture, the API gateway serves as the cohesive entry point for client interactions, acting as the gatekeeper to the internal network of services. By centralizing routing, security, and request processing, it simplifies client interactions while enabling service scalability and independence. With NestJS, setting up a robust API gateway ensures your microservices architecture remains modular, scalable, and secure.

> **Hands-on exercise**
>
> As we are closing this long section, take some time to transform the inventory service into a hybrid application so it can also listen to HTTP calls such as a POST at the `add-product` endpoint, to add products to the inventory.

In the next section, let's discuss service discovery and its importance in microservices architecture.

Service discovery with Consul in NestJS

Service discovery is a crucial aspect of microservices architecture. It enables services to dynamically register themselves and discover other services in a distributed environment. In this section, we will integrate Consul (`https://www.consul.io/`), a widely used service discovery and configuration tool, with our NestJS application.

What is Consul?

Consul is a service mesh solution that provides several features, including the following:

- **Service discovery**: Services can register themselves with Consul, which acts as a directory for all running services
- **Health checking**: Consul can actively monitor the health of services and only route traffic to healthy instances
- **Key-value store**: Consul provides a distributed key-value store for configuration and coordination

With Consul, microservices no longer need to hard-code the IP addresses or ports of other services. Instead, they query Consul to discover services dynamically, ensuring greater flexibility and scalability.

Let's implement the service discovery by following these simple steps.

Step 1 – Installing the Consul client for Node.js

To interact with Consul in a NestJS application, we need to install the official Consul Node.js client:

```
$ yarn add consul
```

Step 2 – Creating the Consul Service in NestJS

To integrate `Consul` into our NestJS microservices, we'll create a `ConsulService` responsible for registering the service on startup and deregistering it upon shutdown. This service will be reusable across microservices and provide necessary discovery methods:

```
// consul.service.ts
import {
  Injectable,
```

```
  OnModuleInit,
  OnModuleDestroy
} from '@nestjs/common';
import * as Consul from 'consul';

@Injectable()
export class ConsulService implements OnModuleInit,
OnModuleDestroy {
  private consul: Consul.Consul;
  private serviceId: string;

  constructor() {
    // Initialize Consul client
    this.consul = new Consul({
      host: 'localhost', // Change to your Consul server
                         // address
      port: 8500, // Default port for Consul
    });
    this.serviceId = 'inventory-service'; // Unique ID for
                                          // the service
  }

  // Register the service in Consul when the module
  // initializes
  async onModuleInit() {
    const serviceName = 'inventory-service';
    const serviceHost = 'localhost'; // Change to your
                                     // service's hostname
    const servicePort = 8002; // Change to your service's
                              // port

    try {
      await this.consul.agent.service.register({
        id: this.serviceId,
        name: serviceName,
        address: serviceHost,
        port: servicePort,
        check: {
          http:
            `http://${serviceHost}:${servicePort}/health`,
          interval: '10s', // Health check every 10 seconds
          timeout: '5s', // Timeout for the health check
        },
```

```
      });
      console.log(`${serviceName} registered with Consul`);
    } catch (error) {
      console.error(
        'Error registering service with Consul:', error
      );
    }
  }

  // Deregister the service in Consul when the module is
  // destroyed
  async onModuleDestroy() {
    try {
      await this.consul.agent.service
        .deregister(this.serviceId);
      console.log(
        `${this.serviceId} deregistered from Consul`
      );
    } catch (error) {
      console.error(
        'Error deregistering service from Consul:', error
      );
    }
  }

  // Discover other services using Consul
  async discoverService(serviceName: string) {
    try {
      const services = await this.consul.catalog
        .service.nodes(serviceName);
      return services;
    } catch (error) {
      console.error(
        'Error discovering service with Consul:', error
      );
      return null;
    }
  }
}
```

Here are some things to note about the preceding code:

- onModuleInit: When the InventoryService module starts, it registers itself with Consul. It provides the service name, address, and port, along with a health check endpoint.

- `onModuleDestroy`: When the module is destroyed (e.g., on shutdown), it deregisters the service from Consul.

- `discoverService`: This method allows us to query Consul for other services by their name. This will be particularly useful for making service-to-service calls without hardcoding addresses.

Step 3 – Adding health checks for the service

Consul uses health checks to ensure the availability of services. We can create a simple health check route in our `InventoryService`:

```
// inventory.controller.ts
import { Controller, Get } from '@nestjs/common';

@Controller('health')
export class HealthController {
  @Get()
  checkHealth() {
    return { status: 'UP' }; // Indicate the service is
                             // healthy
  }
}
```

This endpoint will respond with an HTTP 200 status and a simple JSON message to indicate that the service is healthy.

Step 4 – Registering the ConsulService in the module

Now, we need to register the ConsulService in the `InventoryModule` so it starts and stops correctly:

```
// inventory.module.ts
import { Module } from '@nestjs/common';
import {
  ConsulService
} from './consul.service'; // Import the Consul service

@Module({
  providers: [ConsulService],
  exports: [ConsulService], // Export if other modules need
                           // it
})
export class InventoryModule {}
```

Step 5 – Discovering other services

In microservices architecture, it's common for one service to communicate with others. Instead of hardcoding the address of the `OrderService`, we can query Consul for the correct instance.

Here is an example of how we can discover the `OrderService` from the inventory service:

```typescript
@Injectable()
export class InventoryService {
  // Inject the Consul service
  constructor(
    private readonly consulService: ConsulService,
  ) {}

  async processOrder() {
    // Discover the Order service
    const services = await this.consulService
      .discoverService('order-service');

    if (services && services.length > 0) {
      const orderService = services[0]; // Choose one
                                        // instance of the
                                        // order service
      const orderUrl =
        `http://${orderService.ServiceAddress}:
        ${orderService.ServicePort}`;
      console.log('Order service URL:', orderUrl);

      // Use the discovered URL to make a request to the
      // order service
      // e.g., using HttpService to place an order
    } else {
      console.error('Order service not found');
    }
  }
}
```

Here, instead of hardcoding the address for `OrderService`, the `InventoryService` queries Consul for available instances of the `OrderService` and retrieves its address dynamically.

By integrating Consul into our microservices, we enable dynamic service discovery, improving the flexibility and scalability of our architecture. Now, each service can independently register itself and discover others, making the system more robust and adaptable to changes in service instances or network conditions.

Best practices for building microservices with NestJS

Building microservices is complex, but following best practices can significantly improve the system's scalability, reliability, and maintainability. Here are some best practices specific to NestJS microservices.

Structure and modularization

Consider the following best practice when structuring your microservices:

- **Modular design**: Organize your services into modules for easier maintenance and testing. Each module should have a single responsibility, making it easy to identify and manage dependencies.

- **Separation of concerns**: Ensure each microservice focuses on a specific business capability to keep the boundaries between services clear.

Configuration management

In terms of configuration, the following best practice may be useful:

- **Environment variables**: Use the `@nestjs/config` package to manage environment-specific configurations. Avoid hardcoding values to ensure easy deployment across environments.

- **Centralized configuration**: For shared configurations across multiple services, consider using centralized configuration management tools.

Inter-service communication

When it's time to communicate between microservices, consider the following best practices:

- **Asynchronous messaging**: Prefer event-driven communication (using Kafka, RabbitMQ, or other messaging systems) for loosely coupled services. This enhances fault tolerance and scalability.

- **HTTP communication**: For synchronous communication, leverage NestJS's built-in HTTP client features and proxy support to simplify communication.

Resilience and error handling

To make sure the architecture is resilient and is handling errors gracefully, consider the following best practices:

- **Circuit breaker pattern**: Implement circuit breakers to prevent cascading failures across services

- **Retries and timeouts**: Use retries and timeouts for idempotent operations to handle transient errors effectively

Data management

When dealing with a large dataset (which is probably the reason why you migrate to a microservice architecture), consider the following practices:

- **Saga pattern**: For distributed transactions, implement the Saga pattern to maintain data consistency across services

- **Event sourcing**: Use event sourcing to maintain the state of data changes and to ensure reliable state synchronization

Logging and monitoring

For a better logging system, consider the following best practices:

- **Centralized logging**: Use centralized logging to monitor distributed services, making it easier to trace issues

- **Metrics and health checks**: Implement health checks and metrics using packages such as `@nestjs/terminus` to monitor service health and performance

Testing and CI/CD

The following practices help you build a robust architecture:

- **Unit and integration tests**: Write unit tests for individual components and integration tests for service interactions

- **Continuous Integration and Deployment (CI/CD)**: Set up CI/CD pipelines to automatically build, test, and deploy services on each commit

API Gateway and security

For security concerns, make sure you consider adding the following components:

- **API Gateway**: Use an API gateway to centralize external access to services and implement cross-cutting concerns such as authentication and rate limiting

- **Authentication and authorization**: Implement security best practices to protect services from unauthorized access

By adhering to these best practices for building microservices with NestJS, you can create a system that is not only scalable and reliable but also easy to maintain and evolve over time. From modular design to effective configuration management and robust error handling, these strategies will help you build resilient microservices that can adapt to changing business needs.

With these best practices in mind, the next section will guide you through common challenges you might face while developing microservices and offer troubleshooting and debugging techniques to overcome them.

Troubleshooting and debugging microservices

Microservices architectures often involve complex distributed systems, making troubleshooting and debugging crucial. Here are strategies and tools specific to NestJS microservices that can help.

Centralized logging

For a centralized logging system, consider the following practices:

- **Implement structured logging**: Use structured logging to make logs easier to parse. Integrate libraries such as `winston` or `bunyan` to structure log data.

- **Log aggregation**: Aggregate logs using tools such as ELK Stack (Elasticsearch, Logstash, and Kibana) or centralized logging platforms to get a unified view of your system.

Tracing and monitoring

For a better monitoring, consider adding the following components:

- **Distributed tracing**: Integrate tracing tools such as OpenTelemetry or Jaeger to visualize request flows across microservices, helping identify bottlenecks and failures

- **Metric monitoring**: Use monitoring tools such as Prometheus and Grafana to track critical metrics such as latency, error rates, and throughput

Service health and resilience

To make sure you can assess the health of your system, consider adding the following capabilities to your system:

- **Health checks**: Implement health checks using `@nestjs/terminus` to monitor the availability of services and dependencies

- **Circuit breakers and retry logic**: Use tools such as `@nestjs/microservices` or `@nestjs/bull` to implement circuit breakers and retry logic for managing service failures

Debugging techniques

Below are some of the most common techniques for a better debugging:

- **Local debugging**: Use tools such as the Nest CLI's `start:debug` command and VSCode's debugger to step through code locally
- **Remote debugging**: Enable remote debugging by configuring your NestJS application with the appropriate flags to attach debuggers to running services

Version control and rollback

For a better version control, make sure to consider the following techniques:

- **Versioning services**: Maintain version control for each microservice independently to track changes and their impact
- **Canary deployments and rollbacks**: Implement canary deployments to gradually roll out changes and roll back in case of issues

Dependency management

For a better dependency management, consider the following best practices:

- **Keep dependencies updated**: Regularly update dependencies to avoid security vulnerabilities and benefit from the latest features and bug fixes
- **Dependency analysis**: Use tools such as **npm audit** to analyze your dependencies for known vulnerabilities

Service isolation and testing

For a better testing in a microservices architecture, the following practices can save your day:

- **Service stubs and mocks**: Use stubs and mocks to isolate services for testing, making it easier to identify the root causes of failures
- **Integration Testing**: Develop comprehensive integration tests that simulate service interactions in a controlled environment

Documentation and knowledge sharing

Consider the following practices for a better maintainability:

- **Document service contracts**: Clearly document API contracts and event patterns to help developers understand service interactions

- **Knowledge sharing**: Share troubleshooting guides and postmortem analyses to foster a culture of continuous improvement

By understanding and implementing these troubleshooting and debugging strategies, you can effectively navigate the complexities of microservices architecture, especially when using NestJS. From centralized logging to distributed tracing and health checks, these techniques help maintain the reliability and performance of your microservices. Whether you're debugging locally or remotely, managing dependencies, or rolling out updates, these best practices ensure your services remain resilient and responsive.

Summary

This chapter offered a comprehensive guide to building robust microservices with NestJS, transitioning from monolithic to scalable architectures. We started by defining and implementing microservices, highlighting the strengths of NestJS's modular design that facilitates inter-service communication and data management. We then created a mono repo structure that hosts multiple services, enabling them to harness the full potential of NestJS's microservices architecture.

Moving on, we focused on inter-service communication, demonstrating how services can interact through both synchronous HTTP requests and asynchronous event-driven patterns. Using practical examples such as an order management system, we learned to set up event handlers, define DTOs, and implement event patterns for seamless interaction between services.

Furthermore, we explored best practices for building microservices with NestJS, emphasizing modularization, environment-specific configuration management, and resilience through circuit breakers and retries. We learned the importance of a centralized API gateway that routes external traffic to the appropriate services, handles authentication, and ensures secure and efficient communication.

Finally, we explored strategies for troubleshooting and debugging microservices, focusing on structured logging, distributed tracing, and performance monitoring to ensure the system's reliability and maintainability. We learned the importance of techniques such as centralized logging, health checks, and circuit breakers to enhance resilience and provide early detection of failures.

In the next chapter, we will learn how to test a microservices architecture in NestJS, so stay tuned.

Get This Book's PDF Version and Exclusive Extras

Scan the QR code (or go to `packtpub.com/unlock`). Search for this book by name, confirm the edition, and then follow the steps on the page.

Note: Keep your invoice handly. Purchase made directly from packt don't require one.

11

Testing and Debugging Microservices in NestJS

Welcome to *Chapter 11*, where we'll transition from the practical building blocks of microservices architecture in NestJS into the critical aspects of testing. With the project setup in *Chapter 10*, this chapter will focus on enhancing the reliability and performance of your microservices through comprehensive testing.

While everything learned in *Chapters 7* and *8* about testing a NestJS application will remain applicable here, NestJS offers a versatile platform for microservices development and testing, and this chapter will delve into writing tests for inter-service operations and ensuring data integrity. We'll tackle real-world scenarios, building on the examples introduced in previous chapters to demonstrate the importance of testing and debugging in scalable microservices architectures.

In this chapter, here is what we will explore together:

- Unit testing for microservices
- Integration testing for microservices
- Debugging common issues and solutions in microservices testing
- Best practices for testing and debugging microservices

The project from *Chapter 10* should be ready now as we delve into testing it. By the end of this chapter, you'll be equipped with the skills to write unit and integration tests, troubleshoot issues, and implement best practices for testing and debugging NestJS microservices.

Ready to enhance your microservices testing and debugging skills? Let's begin!

Technical requirements

For this chapter, ensure you have your local environment ready by following the steps in *Chapter 3*. You should also have the project built in *Chapter 10* ready to avoid facing any issues when reading this one. `https://github.com/PacktPublishing/Scalable-Application-Development-with-NestJS`.

Unit testing for microservices

In this section, we'll focus on testing microservice-specific functionalities in NestJS, with particular attention to inter-service operations rather than the basic unit testing of APIs. If you need a refresher on the fundamentals of unit testing, please refer to *Chapters 7* and *8*. Here, we assume you're already familiar with those basic concepts and are now diving deeper into testing for microservices.

Unit testing microservices involves testing individual units of functionality in isolation, including inter-service communication, which is a defining aspect of microservice architecture. In NestJS, microservices often communicate via events or messages passed through a message broker or a client proxy. This means we need to focus on mocking external services and ensuring the inter-service calls are properly handled and tested in isolation.

Let's get started by testing the order creation flow.

Testing createOrder in the order service

For unit testing, similarly to what we did in *Chapters 7* and *8*, we focus on testing every single piece of logic contained in service files (which contain the business logic of the application).

Since we are writing tests for the project built in the previous chapter, take the following example from the `OrderService` class (this code can be found in *Chapter 10*'s folder in the book's GitHub repository: (`https://github.com/PacktPublishing/Scalable-Application-Development-with-NestJS/tree/main/ch10`), where an order is created and an event is emitted to the `InventoryService`:

```
// order.service.ts
createOrder(createOrderInput: CreateOrderInput): Order {
  const order = {
    ...createOrderInput,
    id: `${this.orders.length + 1}`,
    status: OrderStatus.PENDING,
  };
  this.orders.push(order);
  console.log('Order created:', order, this.orders);
  // emit event to the inventory service
  this.inventoryClient.emit(EVENTS.ORDER_CREATED, order);
```

```
    return order;
}
```

Here, the createOrder method does two things:

1. It creates and stores an order.

2. It emits an ORDER_CREATED event to the inventory service.

For unit testing this method, you need to do the following:

1. Ensure the order is created and stored correctly.

2. Ensure the event is emitted to the inventory service.

Since this method depends on ClientProxy (for emitting events), we will mock this dependency to isolate the functionality.

To be able to test the createOrder method, we need to follow the following steps:

1. **Mocking dependencies**: We will mock ClientProxy to simulate the inter-service communication without actually sending the event.

2. **Testing the logic**: We will test whether the order is properly created and stored.

3. **Verifying event emission**: We will verify that the ORDER_CREATED event is emitted with the correct payload.

We will use Jest as our testing framework, as it's fully compatible with NestJS creating .spec.ts files.

In the apps/order/src/ directory, create an order.service.spec.ts file and paste the following code:

```
// add necessary imports
describe('OrderService', () => {
  let orderService: OrderService;
  let inventoryClient: ClientProxy;
  beforeEach(async () => {
    const module: TestingModule = await Test
    .createTestingModule({
      providers: [
        OrderService,
        {
          provide: 'INVENTORY_SERVICE',
          useValue: { emit: jest.fn() }, // Mocking
                                         // ClientProxy's
                                         // emit function
        },
      ],
```

```
    }).compile();
    orderService = module.get<OrderService>(OrderService);
    inventoryClient =
      module.get<ClientProxy>('INVENTORY_SERVICE');
  });
  it('should create an order and emit an event to the
inventory service', () => {
    const createOrderInput: CreateOrderInput = {
      product: 'Laptop',
      quantity: 2,
      userId: 'user123',
    };

    // Call the createOrder method
    const result =
      orderService.createOrder(createOrderInput);

    // Assertions
    expect(result).toEqual({
      ...createOrderInput,
      id: '1',
      status: OrderStatus.PENDING,
    });

    // Ensure the order was added to the orders array
    expect(orderService['orders'].length).toBe(1);

    // Verify that the emit function was called with the
    // correct event and payload
    expect(inventoryClient.emit).toHaveBeenCalledWith(
      EVENTS.ORDER_CREATED,
      {
        ...createOrderInput,
        id: '1',
        status: OrderStatus.PENDING,
      }
    );
  });
});
```

In the preceding code, here are the main components:

- **Mocking inter-service communication**: We mock `ClientProxy` (which is responsible for communicating with `InventoryService`) using Jest's `jest.fn()` to ensure that the `emit` method is called correctly without actually making the network call.

- **Isolating logic**: Since the goal of unit testing is to test the functionality in isolation, we ensure that only the `OrderService` logic is being tested, without real interactions with `InventoryService`

- **Assertions**: We check that the order creation logic is correct, and we also verify that the event was emitted with the right payload

Similarly, other inter-service operations in microservices can be tested by mocking the communication layer, such as the following:

- Testing the `handleOrderProcessed` method, which updates an order based on the result from `InventoryService`

- Testing failure scenarios, such as when `InventoryService` is down or responds with an error

Unit testing microservices involves mocking dependencies to ensure each service works as expected in isolation. In the case of NestJS, inter-service communication often happens through events or messages, so we mock those communication layers to verify that services interact correctly. By following this pattern, you can thoroughly test each microservice component and be confident in your microservice architecture's reliability.

For a more detailed explanation of basic unit testing practices, please refer to *Chapters 7* and *8*. Here, we are focusing solely on microservices-specific testing strategies.

Next, we will explore integration testing, where we move beyond isolated unit tests to test how services work together in a microservices architecture.

Integration testing for microservices

Now that we've covered unit testing, let's move on to integration testing—a critical step in ensuring that microservices work together as expected in a real-world environment. While unit testing focuses on testing individual service logic in isolation, integration testing verifies that different services can communicate, share data, and perform coordinated tasks effectively.

In microservice architecture, services often interact via message queues, HTTP requests, or event-driven mechanisms. Therefore, integration testing goes beyond just testing the logic of individual services; it ensures the reliability of inter-service communication.

We'll use the example of `OrderService` and `InventoryService` from the project to demonstrate how integration testing is done in a microservices setup. Since these services interact through event emission (for example, when an order is created in `OrderService`, an event is sent to `InventoryService` to process the order), our integration tests will focus on ensuring these interactions work as intended.

When writing integration tests for microservices, you'll generally need to do the following:

- **Run services together**: Start the services so they can communicate with each other.

- **Use actual communication protocols**: Instead of mocking the inter-service calls as you would in unit testing, real message brokers (e.g., RabbitMQ, Kafka) or transport layers (e.g., `Transmission Control Protocol (TCP)`, HTTP) will be used. In our example project, remember we were using TCP, but the principle is pretty much the same.

- **Test real data flow**: Ensure the services send and receive data properly through these communication channels.

In our example, we will focus on testing the following flow:

1. When an order is created in `OrderService`, an event is emitted to `InventoryService`.

2. `InventoryService` handles the event, processes the order, and emits an event back to `OrderService` with the result (success or failure).

3. `OrderService` updates the order status based on the result from the `InventoryService`.

Integration testing for order creation and inventory update

In this example, we'll test how `OrderService` interacts with `InventoryService`. This includes creating an order, sending an event to `InventoryService`, and ensuring that the order is updated accordingly.

Testing setup and initialization

In this sub-section, we will set up the NestJS application, establish microservice communication over TCP, and initialize the test environment using Jest. To begin, in the `apps/microservices-sample/test/app.e2e-spec.ts` file (our API gateway project), paste the following code:

```
// add all the necessary imports
describe('Order and Inventory Services Integration Test',
() => {
  let app: INestApplication;
  let orderClient: ClientProxy;
  let inventoryClient: ClientProxy;

  beforeAll(async () => {
```

```
    const module: TestingModule =
      await Test.createTestingModule
    ({
      imports: [
        OrderModule,
        InventoryModule,
        ClientsModule.register([
          {
            name: 'ORDER_SERVICE',
            transport: Transport.TCP,
            options: { port: 8001 },
          },
          {
            name: 'INVENTORY_SERVICE',
            transport: Transport.TCP,
            options: { port: 8002 },
          },
        ]),
      ],
    }).compile();

    app = module.createNestApplication();
    app.connectMicroservice({
      transport: Transport.TCP,
      options: { port: 8001 },
    });
    app.connectMicroservice({
      transport: Transport.TCP,
      options: { port: 8002 },
    });

    await app.startAllMicroservices();
    await app.init();

    orderClient = app.get<ClientProxy>('ORDER_SERVICE');
    inventoryClient =
      app.get<ClientProxy>('INVENTORY_SERVICE');
  });

  afterAll(async () => {
    await app.close();
  });
});
```

In the preceding code, we have the following components:

- **Creation of the module**: We use `Test.createTestingModule` to set up the test environment, importing both `OrderModule` and `InventoryModule`.

- **Microservice connections**: We connect the microservices over TCP. `OrderService` listens on port `8001`, and `InventoryService` on port `8002`.

- **Starting the application**: We use `startAllMicroservices()` to initialize the microservices and start communication.

Now, let's work on the actual testing.

Creating an order and testing response

Next, we simulate the creation of an order using `supertest` (we used `supertest` in *Chapter 7*, so make sure to have a look for a refresher) and verify that `OrderService` handles it properly:

```
import as request from 'supertest';
import { OrderStatus } from '@app/constants';

it('should create an order and update the inventory
accordingly', async () => {
  // Step 1: Create an order by making a POST request to
  // the Order Service
  const createOrderResponse = await request(
    app.getHttpServer()
  )
    .post('/orders')
    .send({
      product: 'Laptop',
      quantity: 2,
      userId: 'user123'
    })
    .expect(201);

  const order = createOrderResponse.body;
  expect(order.status).toBe(OrderStatus.PENDING);
});
```

In the preceding code, we use `supertest` to simulate a POST request to `OrderService` to create a new order. After the order is created, we verify that the order status is set to `PENDING`. This is the expected behavior.

Emitting events and testing inventory processing

After the order is created, we test the communication between `OrderService` and `InventoryService`. We will spy on the emit function of `InventoryService` to ensure it receives the order and processes it:

```
import { EVENTS } from '@app/constants';
it('should create an order and update the inventory
accordingly', async () => {
  // step 1 remains the same

  // ...

  // step 2: Verify that the Inventory Service processes
  // the order and emits a result
  const orderProcessedSpy = jest.spyOn(
    inventoryClient, 'emit'
  );

  // Emit event to simulate InventoryService processing the
  // order
  await inventoryClient.emit(EVENTS.ORDER_CREATED, order);

  // Simulate response from Inventory Service
  const inventoryProcessedPayload = {
    success: true,
    message: 'Order processed successfully',
    orderId: order.id,
  };

  // Ensure the order was processed
  expect(orderProcessedSpy)
    .toHaveBeenCalledWith(
      EVENTS.ORDER_PROCESSED,
      inventoryProcessedPayload
    );

  // next step below
}
```

In the preceding code, we use `jest.spyOn` to monitor when `InventoryService`'s emit method is called. This allows us to verify that the ORDER_CREATED event is correctly emitted. Then, we simulate the inventory processing by emitting the ORDER_CREATED event with the order payload. We finally confirm that `InventoryService` emits the ORDER_PROCESSED event with the correct payload.

Finally, to check that `OrderService` updates the order status to COMPLETED after receiving a response from `InventoryService`, we will add the following code in the `app.e2e-spec.ts` file:

```
// Step 3: Verify that the Order Service updates the
// order status to COMPLETED
const updatedOrder = await request(app.getHttpServer())
  .get(`/orders/${order.id}`)
  .expect(200);

expect(updatedOrder.body.status)
  .toBe(OrderStatus.COMPLETED);
```

In the preceding code, we send a GET request to retrieve the order by its ID. After processing, we verify that the order status has been updated from PENDING to COMPLETED.

Now, let's test everything running the yarn test:e2e command in the root of the project, and make sure the test run successfully as shown in Figure 11.1 below

```
PASS  apps/microservices-sample/test/app.e2e-spec.ts
  Order and Inventory Services Integration Test
    ✓ should create an order and update the inventory according
ly (18 ms)

Test Suites: 1 passed, 1 total
Tests:       1 passed, 1 total
Snapshots:   0 total
Time:        0.945 s, estimated 2 s
Ran all test suites.
```

Figure 11.1: integration tests in the API Gateway project

In this section, we demonstrated how to perform integration testing between `OrderService` and `InventoryService`. The test simulates real HTTP requests and inter-service communication via event emission, ensuring the entire order processing flow works as expected. This approach to integration testing ensures that both services operate correctly together in a distributed environment and that data flows smoothly between them.

By breaking down the test into smaller steps—initializing the application, simulating the creation of an order, verifying event emission, and confirming status updates—you can test microservice interactions effectively while keeping each test case clear and focused.

In the next section, let's focus on debugging.

Debugging common issues and solutions in microservices testing

When testing microservices, especially in a distributed environment, debugging can quickly become complex due to inter-service communication, asynchronous processes, and potential failures across multiple components that are difficult to trace. The good news is that NestJS provides powerful features and tools to help resolve these issues systematically and efficiently. In this section, we will walk through some common issues and present sophisticated techniques to debug them in a scalable way.

Issue 1 – microservices failing to connect

A common issue in microservices is connection failure between services. This can be caused by the following:

- Incorrect port configurations
- Unreachable network endpoints
- Mismatched service names

Let's simulate and troubleshoot this issue step by step.

To reproduce this issue, follow these steps:

1. Start your microservices ensuring they are configured to communicate over TCP.

2. Run your integration tests and check for connection errors, such as `ECONNREFUSED` or `ECONNRESET`.

3. You might simulate an incorrect port scenario in your code like this:

```
app.connectMicroservice({
  transport: Transport.TCP,
  options: { port: 8001 }, // Simulating an incorrect
                           // port
});
```

Here, we simulate a situation where the port configuration is incorrect, leading to connection issues between `OrderService` and `InventoryService`.

Whenever you encounter such a situation, we have a few possible ways to debug and fix it, as shown in the following list:

- **Check port configurations**:

  Ensure that the ports configured in your test match the actual ports of the running services. For example, verify the ports using the following command in your terminal:

  ```
  $ netstat -an | grep 8001
  ```

Alternatively, you can use `lsof` to check which ports are in use:

```
$ lsof -i :8001
```

This helps you ensure the services are not running on conflicting ports. Here's how you can correctly configure your microservice to avoid hardcoding ports:

```
app.connectMicroservice({
  transport: Transport.TCP,
  options: {
    port: process.env.ORDER_SERVICE_PORT || 8001
  }, // Avoid hardcoding ports
});
```

By using environment variables, you allow flexibility for different environments (local development, staging, production), making it easier to manage port conflicts.

- **Verify service names and ports**:

  If you've registered services with specific names (e.g., ORDER_SERVICE, INVENTORY_SERVICE), ensure that these names are consistent across both the test environment and the actual microservice setup. Inconsistent naming can cause microservices to fail during service discovery.

  To verify, you can add debug logs to confirm that services are starting with the correct names and ports:

```
console.log(
  'Order Service running on port',
  process.env.ORDER_SERVICE_PORT || 8001
);
console.log(
  'Inventory Service running on port',
  process.env.INVENTORY_SERVICE_PORT || 8002
);
```

In large-scale, distributed applications, hardcoding ports can lead to issues in environments, such as CI/CD pipelines or containerized systems, where ports might need to be dynamically allocated. The best practice is to use environment variables to manage service configurations, including ports.

Here, we have an example of how to do so:

```
// app.module.ts
@Module({
  imports: [
    ClientsModule.register([
      {
        name: 'ORDER_SERVICE',
        transport: Transport.TCP,
        options: {
```

```
          port: process.env.ORDER_SERVICE_PORT || 8001
        }, // Flexible port assignment
      },
      {
        name: 'INVENTORY_SERVICE',
        transport: Transport.TCP,
        options: {
          port: process.env.INVENTORY_SERVICE_PORT || 8002
        }, // Flexible port assignment
      },
    ]),
  ],
})
export class AppModule {}
```

In the preceding code snippet, the `AppModule` class is decorated with the `@Module()` decorator, which is a fundamental building block in NestJS for organizing and grouping related components. Inside the module, we are importing `ClientsModule` and registering two microservices: `ORDER_SERVICE` and `INVENTORY_SERVICE`.

Both services use the `Transport.TCP` transport layer for inter-service communication. Instead of hardcoding the port numbers, we are using environment variables (`process.env.ORDER_SERVICE_PORT` and `process.env.INVENTORY_SERVICE_PORT`) to dynamically assign ports. If the environment variables are not set, default ports (`8001` for `ORDER_SERVICE` and `8002` for `INVENTORY_SERVICE`) are used.

This approach ensures flexibility and scalability, allowing the microservices to run in different environments (development, staging, production) without requiring hardcoded values, which can cause issues such as port conflicts. By leveraging environment variables, the application is better suited for containerized or CI/CD environments, where port assignments can vary dynamically.

Issue 2 – unreliable event emission between microservices

Microservices often communicate through events, but event emissions may fail due to network issues, configuration errors, or service discovery problems. This can result in events not being delivered or processed.

Here are the steps to reproduce the issue:

1. Simulate an event emission failure by introducing a deliberate configuration error or stopping the receiving service.

2. Emit an event from `OrderService` to `InventoryService` and observe the failure in processing:

```
// apps/inventory/inventory.service.ts
// ...
orderClient.emit(
  EVENTS.ORDER_CREATED,
  Order
);  // Simulate event emission
```

In this case, the `ORDER_CREATED` event might not be received by `InventoryService` due to communication failure.

To gracefully handle this scenario, here are the simple steps that can be followed:

I.   **Check service registration:**

Ensure that both services are correctly registered and reachable. Use `nestjs-devtools` or logs to verify that the services are registered properly, and emitting/receiving events as expected.

```
console.log(
  'Emitting ORDER_CREATED event for Order ID:',
  order.id
);
```

II.   **Enable retry mechanism:**

Configure a retry mechanism for event emission in case of transient failures. NestJS provides an easy way to implement retries for event-based communication:

```
ClientsModule.register([
  {
    name: 'ORDER_SERVICE',
    transport: Transport.TCP,
    options: {
      port: process.env.ORDER_SERVICE_PORT || 8001,
      retryAttempts: 5, // Retry 5 times before
                        // failing
      retryDelay: 3000, // Delay of 3 seconds between
                        // retries
    },
  },
]);
```

Retries are particularly useful for mitigating temporary network outages or service startup delays.

III.   **Use Dead Letter Queues (DLQs):**

To handle failed event emissions in production systems, consider setting up a DLQ where undeliverable messages are routed for further investigation. This helps avoid data loss and allows for post-mortem analysis of failed events.

Issue 3 – inconsistent data between microservices

In microservices architectures, data inconsistency can arise if one service updates its state but another service fails to do so (e.g., if `OrderService` updates an order but `InventoryService` doesn't adjust inventory).

Follow these steps to reproduce this scenario:

1. Simulate a failure in `InventoryService` after an order is successfully created but before the inventory update occurs. You can do this by manually throwing an exception or returning an error in `InventoryService` after `OrderService` completes its transaction. For example, within the `updateInventory` method, introduce a conditional block like the following code:

```
updateInventory(productId: number, quantity: number):
void {
  if (productId === 123) {
    throw new Error(
      'Simulated inventory update failure'
    );
  }
  // Proceed with inventory update logic
}
```

2. As a result, the data in `OrderService` and `InventoryService` becomes inconsistent.

To debug this scenario, follow these steps:

1. **Use distributed transactions:**

While distributed transactions can be complex, a good alternative in a microservices architecture is using sagas or transactional outbox patterns to ensure consistency across services. NestJS has excellent support for implementing sagas using the `@nestjs/cqrs` module.

Here is an example of a saga pattern implementation that can help avoid the precedent scenario:

```
// Saga example in OrderService
@Injectable()
export class OrderSaga {
  @Saga()
  orderCreated = (
```

```
      events$: Observable<OrderCreatedEvent>
    ): Observable<void> => {
      return events$.pipe(
        switchMap((event) => {
          // Handle transaction across services (Order
          // and Inventory)
          return of(
            inventoryService.updateInventory(
              event.orderId
            )
          );
        }),
        catchError(err => {
          console.error(
            'Error updating inventory:', err
          );
          return EMPTY;
        })
      );
    }
  }
```

In the preceding code snippet, we use the saga pattern to handle distributed transactions across multiple services, such as `OrderService` and `InventoryService`. This pattern is particularly useful for managing long-running or multi-step processes. We have the following components:

- `Observable<OrderCreatedEvent>`: The `orderCreated` method listens to events related to an order being created. The `events$` stream represents an observable that emits events when an order is successfully created.

- `switchMap`: Once an order is created, the `switchMap` operator switches the execution to the `inventoryService.updateInventory` method, which updates the inventory for the corresponding `orderId`. This helps manage the transactional flow between `OrderService` and `InventoryService`.

- `Error Handling (catchError)`: If the `inventoryService.updateInventory` operation fails, the error is caught using the `catchError` operator, which logs the error (`Error updating inventory:`) and returns an empty observable (`EMPTY`) from RxJS. This prevents the entire process from crashing and allows the system to either retry or apply compensating actions, depending on your broader system design.

This pattern ensures that even if `InventoryService` fails during the update, the system can gracefully handle the failure, either by retrying or taking alternative measures. It avoids the issue where a failure in one service (`Inventory`) causes the entire operation (`Order`) to fail.

2. **Use eventual consistency and outbox patterns**:

   To ensure eventual consistency, use the outbox pattern, where events are stored in a database table (the "outbox") and processed asynchronously. This ensures that even if the inventory update fails, the event is retried until successful:

   ```
   // Outbox pattern implementation
   await this.outboxService.saveEvent(
     EVENTS.ORDER_CREATED,
     { orderId: order.id }
   );
   ```

   In the preceding code snippet, the `saveEvent` method stores an `ORDER_CREATED` event in the outbox table, which allows the event to be processed asynchronously. This ensures that if a service such as `InventoryService` fails, the event remains in the outbox for retry until successfully processed, guaranteeing eventual consistency across services by retrying failed operations without losing important data.

   With this pattern, your services can recover from transient failures without risking inconsistent data states.

Issue 4 – slow performance in inter-service communication

Performance bottlenecks in microservices can arise from slow network communication or inefficient message handling between services.

Here is the way to reproduce this issue:

1. Simulate high traffic by creating a large number of orders in `OrderService` and sending them to `InventoryService` for processing. To simulate high traffic, you can create a stress test by generating a large number of orders in `OrderService` and sending them to `InventoryService` for processing. This will help identify bottlenecks in inter-service communication.

2. Here's an example of how to simulate high traffic in your service:

   ```
   // Simulate high traffic by creating multiple orders
   for (let i = 0; i < 1000; i++) {
     await this.orderService.createOrder(
       { productId: i, quantity: 1 }
     );
   }
   ```

   In the preceding code snippet, a loop is used to create 1000 orders asynchronously. Each order is processed by `OrderService`, which sends the relevant messages to `InventoryService`. This method helps simulate high traffic and can highlight potential performance issues, such as network latency or bottlenecks in message handling between services.

3. Observe delays in processing and potential service overload.

Follow these steps to debug it:

1. **Use message batching**:

    Instead of processing events one by one, implement message batching where multiple events are processed in a single request. This reduces the number of network calls and improves overall throughput.

    ```
    // Batch processing in InventoryService
    inventoryClient.emit(
      EVENTS.ORDER_BATCH_CREATED,
      ordersBatch
    );  // Emit batch instead of single order
    ```

    The preceding code emits a batch of events, which reduces the load instead of emitting events one after another.

2. **Use asynchronous communication**:

    Ensure that long-running tasks are offloaded to background workers or queues. You can use NestJS queues (via @nestjs/bull for example) to handle heavy background processing.

    The following example shows how you can use Bull in the order queue:

    ```
    // Example of queueing with Bull
    @Processor('order_queue')
    export class OrderProcessor {
      @Process('process_order')
      async handleOrder(job: Job<OrderData>) {
        // Process order asynchronously
      }
    }
    ```

    In the preceding code snippet, the OrderProcessor class listens to order_queue. When a job is added to the queue with the type process_order, the handleOrder method processes the order in the background. This ensures that long-running tasks don't block the main execution flow, improving overall system performance.

3. **Monitor with NestJS DevTools and profilers**:

    Use NestJS DevTools or integrated APM solutions, such as Jaeger or Zipkin, to monitor the performance of your services. These tools can provide insights into inter-service communication, response times, and bottlenecks:

    ```
    $ npm install --save @nestjs/terminus @nestjs/devtools
    ```

    You can then visualize real-time performance metrics and identify areas where communication delays are occurring. More details about the NestJS DevTools can be found here: https://docs.nestjs.com/devtools/overview.

By addressing these common microservice issues and implementing the suggested solutions, you should see improvements in both the reliability and scalability of your distributed systems. Of course, every microservices architecture is unique, and while we've covered a variety of techniques here, the debugging process is often an iterative one. As you test and refine your system, you may encounter other challenges, such as service timeout configurations, message loss, or security concerns in inter-service communication.

There are plenty of additional tools and techniques, such as distributed tracing with OpenTelemetry, load testing with tools such as Apache JMeter, or using more advanced orchestration strategies with Kubernetes, that can further enhance your microservices development and debugging processes. Feel free to explore these alternatives and adapt them to your architecture to ensure that your microservices operate smoothly in all environments.

Now that we've tackled some of the common debugging challenges, let's dive into the best practices for testing and debugging microservices, which will further solidify your microservices architecture for both current and future scaling needs.

Best practices for testing and debugging microservices

Testing and debugging microservices effectively can be challenging due to the distributed nature of its architecture. However, following certain best practices can streamline the process, make your services more reliable, and help you catch potential issues before they impact production. In this section, we'll focus on practical strategies using the sample code and concepts we've explored earlier.

Isolating microservices for unit testing

While integration testing across services is essential, unit testing each microservice independently ensures that individual services behave as expected. In microservice testing, isolation is crucial because each service should be tested without dependencies on other services.

You can achieve this by mocking or stubbing dependencies, such as database calls, external APIs, or other services. Here's an example of how to mock a dependency when unit testing `OrderService`:

```typescript
// order.service.spec.ts
import { Test, TestingModule } from '@nestjs/testing';
import { OrderService } from './order.service';
import {
  ClientsModule,
  Transport
} from '@nestjs/microservices';

describe('OrderService', () => {
  let service: OrderService;
```

```
beforeEach(async () => {
    const module: TestingModule = await Test
      .createTestingModule({
        providers: [OrderService],
        imports: [
          ClientsModule.register([
            {
                name: 'INVENTORY_SERVICE',
                transport: Transport.TCP,
                options: { port: 8002 },
                // Stubbed Inventory service
            },
          ]),
        ],
    }).compile();

    service = module.get<OrderService>(OrderService);
});

it('should create an order and emit an event',
    async () => {
      // Mock the Inventory service's response
      const order = { id: 1, items: ['item1', 'item2'] };
      const spy = jest.spyOn(service, 'createOrder');
      await service.createOrder(order);
      expect(spy).toHaveBeenCalledWith(order);
    });
});
```

In this code, we're testing OrderService and its ability to create an order and emit an event. The test uses ClientsModule to register a mock INVENTORY_SERVICE, simulating communication over TCP. The createOrder method is spied on using Jest to verify that it's called with the correct arguments.

Why it's important

Isolating services using mocks or stubs helps catch issues within a single service without relying on other services being available. This practice allows faster feedback during testing.

Using environment variables for configurations

We've already discussed the pitfalls of hardcoding values, such as ports, in your services in the *Debugging common issues and solutions in microservices testing* section. Using environment variables is a best practice that makes your microservices more configurable and easier to test across multiple environments (local, CI/CD, production).

Here's how you can set up microservices to use environment variables effectively:

```
// app.module.ts
@Module({
  imports: [
    ClientsModule.register([
      {
        name: 'ORDER_SERVICE',
        transport: Transport.TCP,
        options: {
          port: process.env.ORDER_SERVICE_PORT || 8001
        },  // Use environment variables
      },
    ]),
  ],
})
export class AppModule {}
```

In this code, we are defining `AppModule`, registering the `ORDER_SERVICE` microservice, and using `ClientsModule`. The transport is set to `TCP`, and the port is dynamically assigned using an environment variable (`ORDER_SERVICE_PORT`) with a default of `8001`. This setup allows flexibility in different environments.

> **Why it's important**
>
> Environment variables make your application more flexible. You can run the same service in different environments without needing to change the code, reducing the chance of configuration errors.

Leveraging integration testing for cross-service communication

In microservices, services often interact with one another. It's essential to ensure these interactions work as expected. Integration tests should verify that services can communicate, exchange data, and handle responses correctly.

Here's a simplified example of how to write an integration test that verifies communication between `OrderService` and `InventoryService`:

```
// order.integration.spec.ts
import { Test } from '@nestjs/testing';
import { OrderService } from './order.service';
import {
  ClientsModule,
  Transport
} from '@nestjs/microservices';

describe('OrderService Integration Test', () => {
  let service: OrderService;

  beforeAll(async () => {
    const module = await Test.createTestingModule({
      providers: [OrderService],
      imports: [
        ClientsModule.register([
          {
            name: 'INVENTORY_SERVICE',
            transport: Transport.TCP,
            options: { port:
              process.env.INVENTORY_SERVICE_PORT || 8002
            }, // Simulating Inventory service
          },
        ]),
      ],
    }).compile();

    service = module.get<OrderService>(OrderService);
  });

  it('should create an order and communicate with
  InventoryService', async () => {
    const order = { id: 1, items: ['item1', 'item2'] };
    await service.createOrder(order);
    // Verify that communication with InventoryService was
    // successful
  });
});
```

In this code, we are setting up an integration test for `OrderService` using NestJS' `TestingModule`. The `ClientsModule` registers the `INVENTORY_SERVICE` with a TCP transport layer, simulating the service by assigning a port via environment variables. The test ensures that when an order is created, it communicates properly with `InventoryService`.

> **Why it's important**
>
> Integration tests catch issues that unit tests might miss, such as communication failures between services or mismatches in data formats.

Enabling retry mechanisms for robustness

Microservices often communicate over unreliable networks, and therefore, transient failures can occur. It's crucial to build in retry mechanisms to handle temporary service outages or delays. NestJS makes it easy to configure retries. Look at the following code, for example:

```
ClientsModule.register([
  {
    name: 'ORDER_SERVICE',
    transport: Transport.TCP,
    options: {
      port: process.env.ORDER_SERVICE_PORT || 8001,
      retryAttempts: 5,   // Retry up to 5 times
      retryDelay: 3000,   // 3-second delay between retries
    },
  },
]);
```

In this code, the `OrderSaga` class handles the `orderCreated` event using the `@Saga()` decorator. The `orderCreated` saga listens for `OrderCreatedEvent` events and processes them using RxJS operators. When an order is created, it attempts to update the inventory through `inventoryService`. If an error occurs during the update, it is caught and logged, and the stream returns EMPTY to prevent further propagation of the error. This setup ensures smooth transaction handling across services.

> **Why it's important**
>
> Without retries, your microservices may fail when encountering temporary network issues. Retry mechanisms ensure your services are resilient and can recover from transient failures.

Using NestJS DevTools for real-time debugging

For real-time insight into your services during development, NestJS provides a powerful devtool that allows you to visualize and interact with your application. It helps in monitoring performance and debugging issues across microservices.

Run the following command in the project's root to install the necessary debugging tools:

```
$ npm install --save @nestjs/terminus @nestjs/devtools
```

After installation, you can easily monitor your service interactions, measure latencies, and identify bottlenecks.

> **Why it's important**
>
> Real-time monitoring tools such as NestJS DevTools give you immediate feedback on how your services are performing, making it easier to diagnose and resolve issues before they escalate.

Monitoring and tracing distributed systems

In a microservices architecture, it's crucial to track requests as they flow across different services. Tools such as Jaeger or Zipkin can help you trace requests and diagnose issues such as slow performance or service failures.

Integrating distributed tracing is relatively straightforward and helps you visualize how data moves between services. Here's how you might integrate a tracing system in a NestJS application.

In our project, we can set up Jaeger by installing all the required dependencies first, running the following command in the root of the project:

```
$ yarn add @opentelemetry/sdk-trace-base @opentelemetry/sdk-node @
opentelemetry/instrumentation-http @opentelemetry/instrumentation-
express @opentelemetry/instrumentation-nestjs-core @opentelemetry/
resources @opentelemetry/semantic-conventions
```

Next, we need to create a `tracing.ts` file in the root of the project with the following content:

```
import {
  ConsoleSpanExporter,
  SimpleSpanProcessor,
} from '@opentelemetry/sdk-trace-base';
import { NodeSDK } from '@opentelemetry/sdk-node';
import as process from 'process';
import {
  HttpInstrumentation
} from '@opentelemetry/instrumentation-http';
import {
  ExpressInstrumentation
} from '@opentelemetry/instrumentation-express';
import {
  NestInstrumentation
} from '@opentelemetry/instrumentation-nestjs-core';
```

```
import { Resource } from '@opentelemetry/resources';
import {
  SemanticResourceAttributes
} from '@opentelemetry/semantic-conventions';
const traceExporter = new ConsoleSpanExporter();
export const otel = (serviceName: string) => {
  const otelSDK = new NodeSDK({
    resource: new Resource({
      [SemanticResourceAttributes.SERVICE_NAME]:
        `${serviceName}-service`,
    }),
    spanProcessor: new SimpleSpanProcessor(traceExporter),
    instrumentations: [
      new HttpInstrumentation(),
      new ExpressInstrumentation(),
      new NestInstrumentation(),
    ],
  });
  // gracefully shut down the SDK on process exit
  process.on('SIGTERM', () => {
    otelSDK.shutdown()
      .then(() =>
        console.log(
          'SDK shut down successfully',
          serviceName
        ),
      (err) =>
        console.log(
          'Error shutting down SDK',
          Err
        ),
      )
      .finally(() => process.exit(0));
  });
  return otelSDK;
};
```

In the preceding code snippet, we configure distributed tracing using OpenTelemetry with Jaeger in a NestJS microservice, structured for a monorepo. Here's a simple breakdown:

- **Span Exporter:** We use `ConsoleSpanExporter()` to print trace data to the console, which is useful for testing and verifying setup. In production, you would replace this with an exporter that sends traces to Jaeger or another trace collection tool.

- **OpenTelemetry NodeSDK**: The `NodeSDK` setup initializes tracing by gathering all necessary configurations. Key aspects include the following:

- **Resource**: We define a `serviceName` for each service with `SemanticResourceAttributes.SERVICE_NAME`. For example, setting this to `order-service` helps identify the specific microservice in Jaeger, making it easier to track requests across the system.

- **Instrumentation**: Instrumentations are added to automatically capture trace data for HTTP, Express, and NestJS.

- HTTP tracks outgoing and incoming requests, essential for monitoring inter-service communication.

- Express captures middleware and route handling, which can be useful if you have custom Express logic.

- NestJS captures internal NestJS operations, allowing insight into controller-level interactions.

- **Graceful shutdown**: The SDK handles any pending traces before the application shuts down. When the service receives a termination signal (`SIGTERM`), it closes gracefully, ensuring that no trace data is lost.

- **Using the SDK**: Each microservice can call this tracing setup by passing a unique `serviceName` to `otel(serviceName)`. This allows consistent tracing across the monorepo's various services, making it straightforward to monitor and diagnose issues through the console or Jaeger's dashboard.

This setup enables detailed tracking of requests as they travel through the NestJS application, offering full visibility into bottlenecks or failures, with each service identifiable within a distributed tracing UI. For further visualization, configure your Jaeger endpoint (e.g., `OTEL_EXPORTER_JAEGER_ENDPOINT`) to route trace data to your tracing backend.

To see the tracing in action, update all the `main.ts` code, adding the following line in their bootstrap function, before any other code:

```
// apps/inventory/main.ts
  const otelStd = otel('inventory');
  await otelStd.start();
// apps/order/src/main.ts
  const otelStd = otel('order);
  await otelStd.start();
// apps/main/src/main.ts
  const otelStd = otel('main);
  await otelStd.start();
```

Now, let's start all three applications once again, running the following commands in different terminals to be able to see the tracing in action:

```
# to start the gateway
$ yarn start:dev
```

```
# to start the order service
$ yarn start:dev order
# to start the inventory service
$ yarn start:dev inventory
```

With all the microservices started, let's make a POST request at the create-order endpoint and watch the console. *Figure 11.1* shows what we get in the console, informing us about the request received and the services involved.

```
No errors found.
{
  resource: {
    attributes: {
      'service.name': 'main-service',
      'telemetry.sdk.language': 'nodejs',
      'telemetry.sdk.name': 'opentelemetry',
      'telemetry.sdk.version': '1.27.0',
      'process.pid': 76047,
      'process.executable.name': '/Users/paclinjanja/.nvm/versions/node/v20.9.0/bin/node',
      'process.executable.path': '/Users/paclinjanja/.nvm/versions/node/v20.9.0/bin/node',
      'process.command_args': [
        '/Users/paclinjanja/.nvm/versions/node/v20.9.0/bin/node',
        '-r',
        '/Users/paclinjanja/Documents/writing/microservices-sample-chapter10-11/node_modules/source-map-support/reg
ister.js',
        '/Users/paclinjanja/Documents/writing/microservices-sample-chapter10-11/dist/apps/order/main'
      ],
      'process.runtime.version': '20.9.0',
      'process.runtime.name': 'nodejs',
      'process.runtime.description': 'Node.js',
      'process.command': '/Users/paclinjanja/Documents/writing/microservices-sample-chapter10-11/dist/apps/order/ma
in',
      'process.owner': 'paclinjanja',
      'host.name': 'Admins-MacBook-Pro.local',
      'host.arch': 'arm64',
      'host.id': '3125B206-2C87-5217-B6F9-F4B7A3FC1BB7'
    }
  },
  instrumentationScope: {
    name: '@opentelemetry/instrumentation-express',
    version: '0.44.0',
    schemaUrl: undefined
  },
  traceId: '2cca4f8a5882bd6d42582c6c86be4138',
  parentId: '2b77f8f7c2c026a3',
  traceState: undefined,
  name: 'middleware - query',
  id: '6291ff4cc6974045',
  kind: 0,
  timestamp: 1730113363239000,
  duration: 469.25,
  attributes: {
    'http.route': '/',
    'express.name': 'query',
    'express.type': 'middleware'
  },
  status: { code: 0 },
  events: [],
  links: []
}
{
```

Figure 11.1: Tracing distributed transactions

While this can be helpful when debugging microservices, Jaeger gives us the ability to display the same information in a dashboard, and this may require further setup; more information can be found in the official documentation here: https://opentelemetry.io/docs/demo/collector-data-flow-dashboard/.

For more complex communication patterns, such as message brokers such as RabbitMQ or Kafka, these systems often come with their own native dashboards. These tools display message flows and inter-service communication, giving valuable insights into system interactions. However, for simplicity, we will keep our focus here on HTTP-based tracing with Jaeger.

> **Why it's important**
>
> Distributed tracing allows you to identify where bottlenecks or failures occur as requests move through your system. This is essential for debugging performance issues in a distributed microservice architecture.

Using sagas for distributed transactions

Inconsistent data between services can occur if one service updates its state, but another service fails to do so. Implementing a saga pattern ensures that operations across services either complete successfully or are rolled back.

Here's how you can implement a saga in NestJS to handle a distributed transaction:

```
@Injectable()
export class OrderSaga {
  @Saga()
  orderCreated = (events$: Observable<OrderCreatedEvent>):
  Observable<void> => {
    return events$.pipe(
      switchMap((event) => {
        // Handle transaction across services (Order and
        // Inventory)
        return of(inventoryService.updateInventory(
          event.orderId)
        );
      }),
      catchError(err => {
        console.error('Error updating inventory:', err);
        return EMPTY;
      })
    );
  }
}
```

In this code, the `OrderSaga` class handles events in a saga pattern to ensure consistent processing across services. The `orderCreated` method listens to a stream of `OrderCreatedEvent` events and, for each event, attempts to update the inventory via the `inventoryService.updateInventory()` method. If an error occurs during this process, it catches the error, logs it, and returns an empty observable to prevent further propagation. This ensures that inventory updates are managed transactionally, allowing retries or compensating actions in case of failures.

> **Why it's important**
>
> Sagas help ensure consistency across services, especially in failure scenarios. This prevents data mismatches and ensures that your microservices are resilient.

By following these best practices, you can ensure that your microservices are well tested, scalable, and resilient to the common challenges of distributed systems. Testing and debugging in microservices require a proactive approach, but with the right tools and techniques, you can confidently build and scale your services with NestJS.

Summary

In this chapter, we explored best practices for building scalable microservices with NestJS, focusing on effective testing and debugging techniques.

We began by identifying common issues that arise in microservice communication, such as connection failures, unreliable event emissions, and inconsistent data. We then walked through practical solutions to debug these issues using tools such as environment variables, retry mechanisms, and DLQs, ensuring more robust and resilient service communication.

Next, we discussed the importance of ensuring data consistency across distributed services, introducing patterns such as sagas and the transactional outbox to maintain consistency in the face of failures. These techniques are essential for handling inter-service communication in real-world applications.

We also addressed the challenges of performance bottlenecks in microservices by demonstrating ways to optimize inter-service communication using batching, asynchronous processing, and message queues to improve throughput under high-traffic scenarios.

We then explored advanced testing techniques for microservices, providing real-world examples of integration tests, mocking services, and ensuring services interact as expected. By integrating tools such as NestJS DevTools and implementing sophisticated retry mechanisms, we developed a scalable and testable microservices architecture.

Finally, we discovered some of the best practices when debugging a microservices application, which will later help you debug confidently in your NestJS journey.

In the three upcoming chapters, we will dive into case studies and work on real-life projects, allowing you to apply these principles in practical scenarios. Starting with a real-life REST API in the next chapter, these projects will help solidify your understanding and equip you with the skills to handle complex microservice architectures in production environments. Get ready to bring your NestJS expertise to life!

Get This Book's PDF Version and Exclusive Extras

Scan the QR code (or go to packtpub.com/unlock). Search for this book by name, confirm the edition, and then follow the steps on the page.

Note: Keep your invoice handly. Purchase made directly from packt don't require one.

Part 5:
Real-World Application Examples and Case Studies

This part leverages everything we have learned so far to put you in real-life scenarios; here, you will learn from real challenges and build applications just as you would in real-life scenarios.

This part includes the following chapters:

- *Chapter 12, Case Study 1 - E-commerce Application*
- *Chapter 13, Case Study 2 - Social Networking Platform*
- *Chapter 14, Case Study 3 - Enterprise Resource Planning System*

12

Case Study 1 - E-commerce Application

Feeling the confidence to build real-life applications at scale? This is the place where we will make good use of that confidence. Welcome to our first case study, where we will build an e-commerce application with NestJS.

In this chapter, we will take advantage of everything we already know about Rest API, testing, and putting the data modeling constraint in our route, so we can build an application very close to any e-commerce we use daily.

We will also take this opportunity to integrate real databases, instead of our in-memories databases, adding more practical challenges as we are building. We will do this so we can build real authentication and authorization mechanisms in our application, putting all the theoretical security considerations into a real-world-like scenario.

For this chapter, here is what we've got on our agenda:

- Understanding the requirements of an e-commerce application
- Designing the application architecture and data modeling
- Implementing REST APIs for products and orders
- User authentication and authorization in an e-commerce context

By the end of this chapter, you will solidify your understanding of Rest API and its real-world architecture considerations, authentication and authorization, and database integration, among more. Get your environment ready before we proceed as we will be using PostgreSQL in addition to other tools we have used so far.

Let's step into this case study to understand the context and requirements of the application we are building.

Technical requirements

The code files for the chapter can be found at `https://github.com/PacktPublishing/Scalable-Application-Development-with-NestJS`

Understanding the requirements of an e-commerce application

Before we dive into coding, it's crucial to understand the requirements of an e-commerce application. This understanding will guide every decision we make, from the architecture to the specifics of implementation. It will ensure that the application we build meets user needs and industry standards.

Identifying user needs

When it comes to an e-commerce application, user needs can be quite diverse and specific. However, certain requirements prevail across a wide demographic of users:

- **Ease of navigation**: Users should be able to easily navigate through the application. An intuitive and well-structured layout is key. For example, Amazon has a clear and simple navigation menu that makes it easy for users to find what they're looking for. While this is a very important user need, in our context of server-side application, our focus won't be much oriented on this side. A user interface framework such as that of AngularJS or Next.js would take this very seriously. However, as a server-side application, our API should make sure we send the client a shape of data that won't require too much manipulation before displaying information to users.

- **Product information**: Detailed and accurate product information is paramount. Users want to know exactly what they're buying. High-quality images, detailed descriptions, and real customer reviews are all important aspects of this. In the context of our API, we should make sure the product description describes the product in a less ambiguous way in the data validation phase of the product creation endpoint. Why not add constraints such as description length, then couple it to an **Artificial Intelligence** (**AI**) tool that will help us validate the description to make it even more engaging?

- **Search and filter options**: Users should be able to quickly find the product they're looking for. Effective search capabilities and various filter options are important. For instance, eBay allows users to filter search results by various criteria such as price, condition, and location. Our API should be strong enough for all these kinds of filtering of data; we have multiple options that we will explore later while building.

- **Security**: Users need to feel safe when making transactions. Secure payment gateways and clear privacy policies are necessary. This is where all the security considerations will be put into practice.

- **Customer service**: Prompt and effective customer service is a must. Users should be able to easily reach out for support and get quick responses to their queries. Many successful e-commerce platforms, such as Zappos, excel in providing top-notch customer service.

- **Easy checkout process**: A simple and smooth checkout process is essential to prevent cart abandonment. Users prefer a checkout process that is quick and simple, and that allows for various payment methods. This will be a key consideration in the architecture part, allowing users to easily proceed with their order from the cart to the ordering itself.

Understanding these user needs is the first step in creating an e-commerce application that is user-friendly and meets industry standards.

Defining functional requirements

Functional requirements define the fundamental actions that an application must perform to be successful. They are the services the system should provide, how the system should react to particular inputs, and how it should behave under specific conditions. They are central to a system's utility and effectiveness, outlining specific system behavior or functions.

Having identified the user needs, we now turn our attention to the functional requirements of our e-commerce application. It's important to note that in the context of NestJS, our focus will primarily be on the server-side aspects of these requirements. Here are some of the most important functional requirements:

- **Product management**: The application should provide a standard set of operations for managing products. This includes creating new products, reading product details, updating product information, and deleting products. These operations should be encapsulated in a well-structured API that can easily be integrated with a frontend framework.

- **Order management**: Similarly, the application should support a range of operations for managing orders. This includes creating new orders, updating order statuses, and deleting orders. The API should also support operations for managing the items within an order.

- **User management**: The application should provide operations for managing users. This includes creating new users, reading user details, updating user information, and deleting users. It should also provide operations for managing user authentication and authorization.

- **Payment management**: The application should provide operations for managing payments. This includes creating new payments, updating payment statuses, and deleting payments. The API should support a range of payment methods to meet the diverse needs of users.

Since we are becoming comfortable with our framework, these requirements will most likely be encapsulated in separate modules, or split one big module into a reasonable number of modules, and (if needed) add relevant modules to allow the scalability of our application.

In the following sections, we will delve into these requirements in more detail and discuss how they can be implemented using NestJS. Remember, these functional requirements are just a starting point. As we build the application, we will likely identify additional requirements that need to be addressed.

As we move forward, we will see how these functional requirements guide the development of our e-commerce application.

Setting performance requirements

Performance requirements are a type of **non-functional requirement**, which are critical to the overall functionality and user experience of our e-commerce application. Non-functional requirements are the criteria that judge the operation of a system, rather than specific behaviors, such as system performance, reliability, and maintainability. They are often designed to improve system performance, making the system more reliable, easier to use, and more efficient. In our e-commerce application, performance requirements might include fast page loading times, efficient database queries, and the ability to handle many simultaneous users. As we progress in our application design, we will consider these non-functional requirements to ensure our application not only meets its functional goals but also delivers a high-quality user experience.

In summary, understanding the requirements of an e-commerce application sets the groundwork for the entire development process. We've explored user needs, functional requirements, and performance requirements, all of which will influence the decisions we make as we design and implement our application. With a solid grasp of these requirements, we can now move forward to designing the application architecture, ensuring that our design decisions align with the identified needs and requirements, and ultimately, result in an effective, efficient, and user-friendly e-commerce platform.

Designing the application architecture and data modeling

In this section, we will be focusing on the design of our e-commerce application's architecture. Effective architecture is crucial for the successful operation of any application, and in this case, it will form the backbone of our e-commerce platform. We will be considering how to structure our application, how different components interact with each other, and how data flows within the system. Our design decisions will be guided by the requirements we have identified and the need for scalability, maintainability, and performance. This process is key to ensuring that our application is robust, efficient, and capable of delivering a seamless user experience.

By the conclusion of this section, we will have a clear set of specifications and behaviors for our API. This is a result of adopting the **documentation-first** approach, whereby we design the API flexibly before moving on to implementation. This contrasts with the **implementation-first** approach, whereby the design is heavily influenced by what has already been implemented. The documentation-first approach is increasingly preferred by engineers in recent years due to the greater flexibility it offers during the implementation phase.

Steps to design a REST API

When designing a REST API, we first need to identify the objects that will be presented to the client as resources. In a REST API context, a resource can be seen as an individual object or a collection of objects that the API can provide information about. It is a specific piece of data that can be accessed and manipulated via the API. A resource can be as simple as a single data entity or it can be a complex structure with multiple data fields. Examples of resources might include users, products, or orders in an e-commerce application. Each resource in a REST API is identified by a unique **Uniform Resource Identifier (URI)**.

In the context of an e-commerce application, here are some important resources to pay attention to:

- **Products**: These are the items available for purchase in the e-commerce application. Each product would typically have attributes such as name, description, price, image, specifications, and so on.

- **Users**: These are the people who use the application as customers, administrators, or staff. User data might include information such as name, email, password, shipping address, and so on.

- **Orders**: These represent the purchases made by users. An order would usually include details such as the products purchased, quantities, total price, customer details, and payment information.

- **Payments**: These are the transactions made by users to pay for their orders. Payment information could include the payment method used, amount paid, date and time of the transaction, and status of the payment.

- **Reviews**: These are evaluations or feedback provided by customers about the products they have purchased. Reviews might include a rating, a text commentary, and the name of the user who provided the review.

Creating resource URIs

Now that we have identified the object that our API will present to clients, we can jump to the second step, which is creating resource URIs. This step aims to create a list of endpoints that we will potentially have in our application, without specifying their HTTP methods. Each resource will have a specific set of URIs, as listed here:

```
# products

/products
/products/{id}
/products/{id}/orders
/products/{id}/orders/{orderId}
/products/{id}/reviews
/products/search
```

```
# users
/users
/users/{id}
/users/{id}/orders
/users/{id}/orders/{orderId}
/users/{id}/reviews
/users/search

# orders
/orders
/orders/{id}
/orders/{id}/reviews

# payments
/payments
/payments/{id}
/payments/{paymentMethod}/orders

# reviews
/reviews
/reviews/{id}
/reviews/search
```

In the interest of trying to keep things straightforward, we only have a list of URIs that will be implemented in our API here. We have, for example, the /products/{id}/orders endpoint that will give clients access to orders placed for a specific orderId (the id path parameter) or the / payments/{paymentMethod}/orders endpoint that will most probably list the orders placed for a specific payment method.

Representing resources

Now, the next step is to work on the resource presentation. We need to have a common contract between the server and the client on how data will be presented. In our API, we will use JSON format since it's a widely adopted format in the modern era, but another option could be using XML instead.

For our data representation, we will force our API to send to the client this unique format in JSON:

```
Class APIResponse {
    success: boolean,
    message: string,
    error?: HttpExcetion,
    data: any,
}
```

The preceding class sets the expectation of how the data will be presented to clients. Despite it being a typescript class, we are expecting a JSON object with the shape defined by the `APIResponse` class, and for `HttpException` to be imported from the `@nestjs/common` package. It can be replaced by any of its inherited exceptions, such as `BadRequestException`, `UnauthorizedException`, and so on.

Assigning HTTP methods

Now that we have defined the resource representation, we can assign HTTP methods to our list of endpoints. They're grouped into three categories: getters, setters, and mutators:

- **Setters**: The setters are all the operations that will help us to create a resource. In the Restful world, we usually define setters with the POST verb since we expect POST requests to SET data into our database. Here are the most important setters for our API:

```
# product
HTTP POST /products

# users
HTTP POST /users

# orders
HTTP POST /orders

# payments
HTTP POST /payments

# reviews
HTTP POST /reviews
```

These are all the setters we need to have in the application to persist (set) information in the database.

- **Getters**: After setting data persistently in our database, we need to be able to retrieve it from there. Here is where getters are important. Getting them is good, but getting them in a meaningful way is better. Based on the list of URIs we defined in the first step, here are the most important getters for our API:

```
# products
HTTP GET /products?page=1&limit=100
HTTP GET /products/{id}
HTTP GET /products/{id}/orders?page=1&limit=10
HTTP GET /prodcuts/{id}/orders/{oderId}
HTTP GET /products/{id}/reviews?page=1&limit=100
```

```
HTTP GET /products/search?page=1&limit=100&keyword=sample&min-
Price=100&maxPrice=1000&color =red,black&specs=ram:8Go,ram:16Go

# orders
HTTP GET /orders?page=1&limit=100
HTTP GET /orders/{id}
HTTP GET /orders/{id}/reviews?page=1&limit=100

# users
HTTP GET /users?page=1&limit=100
HTTP GET /users/{id}
HTTP GET /users/{id}/orders?page=1&limit=10
****HTTP GET /users/{id}/reviews?page=1&limit=100
HTTP GET /users/
search?page=1&limit=10&keyword=John&verified=true

# payments
HTTP GET /payments?page=1&limit=100
HTTP GET /payments/{id}
HTTP GET /payments/{paymentId}/orders?page=1&limit=100

# reviews
HTTP GET /reviews?page=1&limit=100
HTTP GET /reviews/{id}
HTTP GET /reviews/search?page=1&limit=100&keyword=Excel-
lent&startDate=1716794723000
```

Here, we have a long list of getters that we may need to use in our API. Note that some of them come with sample query such as like the page and limit for pagination purposes; the keyword on search endpoints; the minPrice, maxPrice, and specs queries on the search product; or the verified on the search user endpoint to enhance the filtering capability of our API.

- **Mutators**: Among mutators, we have operations that can update the state of a single record in our database, or even delete a single record from the database. To keep track of the database's record, software developers tend to prioritize the soft-delete approach, whereby data is not deleted completely from the database but "hidden" with a specific label or tag. Our API should be resilient enough to allow the soft-delete via PUT (or PATCH) operations, and a proper deletion operation via DELETE operations on soft-deleted records after a certain period of time if they are not needed anymore.

Here is the list of the mutators we may need in our API:

```
# products
HTTP PUT /products/{id}
HTTP DELETE /product/{id}

# users
HTTP PUT /users/{id}
HTTP DELETE /users/{id]

# orders
HTTP PUT /orders/{id}
HTTP DELETE /orders/{id}

# reviews
HTTP PUT /reviews/{id}
HTTP DELETE /reviews/{id}
```

With these mutators, it's important to note that our API doesn't allow us to mutate payment information. Once a payment has been processed, no one should be able to mutate it. On the other hand, reviews can be mutated for different reasons, such as by the author when they need to update any information, or by the system admin if the review violates the policies of our project. This can also lead to the deletion of a user's account.

Well done; we have designed our API's main operations. Putting it all together, we need to come up with an API specification that is readable for both machines and human developers who are going to work on the implementation, or human clients that are going to consume our API in the future. There are several tools that can help us write the API documentation, including GUI products such as Postman, Spotlight, or Mulesoft. However, for this use case, we will use a free tool: OpenAPI (previously known as the Swagger specification), which is simply a .yaml file that describes the different operations supported by your API. OpenAPI also gives you the ability to test your .yaml file, share it with your team, and simulate API actions on the SwaggerHub (https://swagger.io/) platform.

Writing APIs

Let's go ahead and, with all that we have discussed until now, write our API documentation. This will also help us define the schema in which body objects need to come to the server for validation purposes later in the implementation phase.

Log in to the SwaggerHub dashboard (or create a new account if needed) and click on **Create New |
Create New API button** in the left-top corner, as shown in *Figure 12.1*:

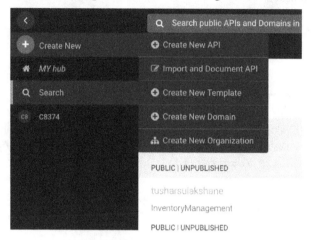

Figure 12.1: SwaggerHub dashboard control menu

You will be prompted to choose the template. Simply use the Simple API one, assign a name, and leave
the default options as they are (visibility and auto mock api), then click on the **Create API** button.

You will be redirected to a UI that looks like *Figure 12.2*:

Figure 12.2: SwaggerHub dashboard for the e-commerce API

You can copy and past the context in my public swagger hub specification for this project here:

```
https://app.swaggerhub.com/apis/pacyL2K19/e-commerce/1.0.0
```

The OpenAPI specification aims to be human and machine-readable documentation that provides a set of endpoints attached to their HTTP methods, as well as possible API responses.

For example, in the provided specification (follow the preceding link), we have the HTTP GET / products operation with a set of parameters and a successful response format attached to it. To learn more about the OpenAPI v3 specifications, check their official documentation at https:// swagger.io/docs/specification/about/.

Well done; we have our API design ready to be implemented. Note that designing it is not a one-time process. This file will be revisited in the future as the project evolves.

Now, for the implementation, let's write some code in the following section.

Implementing REST APIs for products and orders

Now that we have the design of our e-commerce application's architecture in place and have defined our API's main operations, it's time to turn our attention to the actual implementation of our REST APIs. In the following sections, we will be focusing on building the functional aspects of our e-commerce application – products, orders, and payments. This will involve coding our endpoints, setting up our database, and ensuring that our application runs smoothly. We will be using our previously defined API design as a guide for this implementation. Let's dive in and start building our e-commerce application.

Setting up the development environment

Though it's assumed that you are already familiar with setting up a NestJS project, it's worth mentioning that this process involves creating a new NestJS application using the Nest CLI, installing necessary dependencies, and setting up the main server file. We will be using TypeScript as our primary programming language, and we will follow a modular structure for our code. This will provide us with a clean and organized code base, making it easier to manage and scale our e-commerce application. In the following section, we will discuss in detail setting up and configuring our database using PostgreSQL.

Now, go ahead and create a new NestJS project with the following command:

```
$ nest new e-commerce-app
```

I am using the name e-commerce-app in the command to generate the project, but feel free to use the one you like most. This will generate a new NestJS project – the one we are already familiar with. Now let's work on setting up our database.

Database setup and configuration

To set up our PostgreSQL database, we first need to download and install PostgreSQL. It can be downloaded for free from the official PostgreSQL website (https://www.postgresql.org/ download/). During the installation process, you'll be asked to set a password for the PostgreSQL superuser (postgres), which you should remember as it will be needed later.

Once installed, we can create our database. For this, we need to open the pgAdmin (https://www.pgadmin.org/) tool that was installed with PostgreSQL. This tool provides a graphical interface to manage PostgreSQL databases.

In pgAdmin, expand the **Servers** section in the left sidebar, then **PostgreSQL**. Here, you'll be asked for the password you set during the installation. After entering the password, expand the **Databases** section and right-click on it. Select **Create | Database....** A new window will open where you can enter the name of your new database, for example, ecommerce_db. Click on the **Save** button to create the database.

Now that our database has been created, we are ready to connect it with our NestJS application. We'll use the TypeORM module (https://typeorm.io/) for this, which is a powerful ORM module that can work with several types of databases, including PostgreSQL.

First, we need to install the necessary dependencies in our project. In the terminal, navigate to the root folder of our NestJS project and run the following command:

```
$ yarn add @nestjs/typeorm typeorm pg
```

This will install the @nestjs/typeorm module, which is a NestJS module that integrates the TypeORM library itself, and pg, which is a PostgreSQL client for Node.js.

Now, we can set up the TypeORM module in our application. We'll do this in the app.module.ts file. Here, we'll import the TypeOrmModule class and add it to the imports array of our module. We'll use the forRoot() method of TypeOrmModule to configure it. We'll pass an object to forRoot with the following properties:

- type: The type of our database; in this case, it's postgres
- host: The host of our database; usually, it's localhost for development purposes.
- port: The port of our database; by default, it's 5432
- username: The username to connect to our database; by default, it's postgres
- password: The password to connect to our database; it's the password you set during the installation of PostgreSQL
- database: The name of our database; it's the name we gave to our database when we created it in pgAdmin
- entities: An array with the paths to our entities; entities in TypeORM are JavaScript classes that map to tables in our database
- synchronize: A Boolean value that indicates whether the database should be auto-created on every application launch; during the development, it's useful to set it to true

Following the preceding guide, the `app.module.ts` file should look like the following code:

```
import { Module } from '@nestjs/common';
import { AppController } from './app.controller';
import { AppService } from './app.service';
import { TypeOrmModule } from '@nestjs/typeorm';

@Module({
  imports: [
    TypeOrmModule.forRoot({
      type: 'postgres',
      host: 'localhost',
      port: 5432,
      username: 'postgres',
      password: 'your_password',
      database: 'ecommerce_db',
      entities: [],
      synchronize: true,
    }),
  ],
  controllers: [AppController],
  providers: [AppService],
})
export class AppModule {}
```

Start the server once again in dev mode and make sure it starts without any issues.

Try this out

While this minimalist database works perfectly fine for now, there is room to improve it by leveraging the power of NestJS's `ConfigModule` class following these simple steps:

1. Install the `@nestjs/config` package using Yarn.

2. Import the `ConfigModule` class and set it to global in the `AppModule` class's imports array.

3. Instead of using `TypeOrmModule`'s `forRoot()` method, use `forRootAsync()`, which will allow you to inject environment variables asynchronously.

4. Inject the `ConfigService` class isn `forRootAsync`'s `inject` property.

5. Replace hard-coded values with their equivalents in the `.env` file that you will have to create; for example, instead of hard-coding the password, you can do something such as setting the password to `configService.get<string>('POSTGRES_PASSWORD')` or however you decide to name it in your `.env` file.

6. Test the app once again and make sure the app starts successfully

The full code is available in this chapter's GitHub repository (`https://github.com/PacktPublishing/Scalable-Application-Development-with-NestJS/tree/main/ch12`). You can have a look if you are facing issues following the preceding steps.

With this, our database is ready and connected with our application, and we can start implementing the database operations in our API endpoints.

Implementing the product API endpoints

We have our design ready; we have the database set up; now, it's time to implement the core logic on different modules.

To ensure that the project structure keeps reflecting the data model we defined in the first section, our modules will be defined around the business models we already talked about, which are products, users, orders, payments, and reviews.

Creating the product module

First, let's generate the products resource using the Nest CLI, running the following command at the root of the project - make sure to select the REST API (first option) when prompted:

```
$ nest generate resource products
```

The preceding script will generate the products resource files and update the `app.module.ts` file to import the newly created module: `ProductsModule`. We already mastered the process of creating them by hand. However, to gain productivity, it's always recommended to leverage the use of the CLI.

Creating the Product entity

Next, we'll define the `Product` entity. In the generated `product/entities/product.entity.ts` file, paste the following content:

```
// src/products/entities/product.entity.ts
import {
  Column,
  Entity,
  PrimaryGeneratedColumn
} from 'typeorm';

@Entity('products')
export class Product {
  @PrimaryGeneratedColumn('uuid')
  id: string;
```

```
@Column('text')
name: string;

@Column('text')
description: string;

@Column('decimal', { default: 0.0 })
price: number;

@Column('text', { default: 'no-image.png' })
image: string;

@Column('simple-json', {
  default: {},
  comment: "a key-value pair that represents the
           product's specs",
})
specs: Record<string, string>;

@Column({
  type: 'timestamp',
  default: () => 'CURRENT_TIMESTAMP'
})
createdAt: Date;
}
```

The preceding code snippet is an entity definition for the product table in our database. Since we are no longer using an in-memory database, this table will be stored in the database we created in the preceding section thanks to TypeORM's specific decorators such as the `@Entity()` and `@Column()` decorators. The first one indicates that this is an actual database table (in the context of SQL databases). It accepts two optional parameters, the first one being the table name – when not specified, TypeORM will use the name of the entity class name in lowercase letters – and the second one being an `options` object that can be used to fill properties such as comments, database name (if using a different database than the default one), and so on. The second decorator – `@Column()` – indicates that this field is a column in the parent table. This decorator also takes two optional parameters; the first one enforces the type of data to be stored in that column. If it is not indicated, Postgres will assign a type based on the type associated with the field in the class. The second one is also an options object, that can add multiple properties to the column, such as the following:

- There's the `nullable` Boolean property that tells the database whether the field can be null or not. By default, when it is not set, the `nullable` property is set to `false`.

- The `default` property indicates the `default` value to set for this field, in case of an omission when it is being set in the database.

- Depending on the type of the column, additional properties such as `precision` – for decimal fields – can be added. For example, for our price column, we can do something like the following:

```
@Column('decimal', { precision: 5, default: 0 }) price: number
```

Note that each entity *must* have a primary column (for SQL-based databases) or an `ObjectId` (for noSQL-based databases) decorated with a specific decorator. In our case, we are using the `@PrimaryGeneratedColumn()` decorator, which is of the `number` type by default. Since we passed the `uuid` parameter, our primary column will be a **Universal Unique Identifier** (**UUID**) string. You can learn about `uuid` parameters and why they are preferred as primary identifiers at `https://www.techtarget.com/searchapparchitecture/definition/UUID-Universal-Unique-Identifier`.

Now, using a GUI tool such as pgAdmin (`https://www.pgadmin.org/`) for database visualization, check that you have the products table with its appropriate columns. Your table should look like *Figure 12.3*:

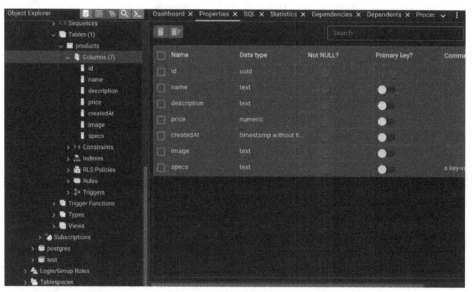

Figure 12.3: pgAdmin showing the newly created table

Note that this table is not complete as we will need to add a relationship between product and other resources such as orders or reviews. This will be discussed in the upcoming sections.

Product service

In the `products/products.service.ts` file, we have the generated **Create, Read, Update, and Delete** (**CRUD**) operations that the Nest CLI created for us. Let's improve them.

Feel free to delete any irrelevant code that you may find in there, and let's proceed step by step.

First, let's implement the product creation, as decided in the architectural and design phase. This can only be made by connected users with the admin role. To keep the implementation smooth, we will ignore this constraint for now and focus on the business logic. The last section will focus on protecting our endpoints, as well as senforcing authorizations and authentication mechanisms; don't worry about it for now.

To be able to create a new product, we need the product name, description, price, and image URL that obeys the following business and user requirements:

- The description field must be meaningful enough to help users understand what the product is. We should first consider the length of the description and set it to a minimum of 25 characters for now, then add an AI tool in the validation pipeline to make sure we are not adding long descriptions that don't mean anything. To add the AI tool, we can use some of the available free or paid AI tools. For demonstration purposes, we will use Gemini here for its short learning curve and its reputation in the industry.

- The name field should not be long. We should allow client applications to display the name in a mobile-first approach. A name that can easily fit the user's screen is preferable. Here, we will adopt a 5-to-25-characters constraint, but this can vary depending on the targeted clients.

- The price should be greater than zero.

- The image URL, if present, should be a valid URL.

- The product specs should be an object of key-values pairs following the `<spec_name>:<spec_value>` format. For example, a valid product specs array could take the form of `specs:{'color':'red', 'size:XL'}`.

Our input validator should be robust enough to check all this before persisting data in the database.

In the generated service file, locate the `create` function – feel free to remove the rest of the code. You will see something like the following:

```
// src/products/products.service.ts
@Injectable()
export class ProductsService {
  constructor(
    @InjectRepository(Product)
    private productsRepository: Repository<Product>,
  ) {}

  create(createProductDto: CreateProductDto) {
    console.log('see dto', createProductDto);
  }
}
```

Note that I simply printed the `createProductDto` object. We don't want to persist data at this point. The validation happens in the `CreateProductDto` class located at `src/products/dto/create-product.dto.ts`. Let's now complete some validation. Replace the generated empty class with the following code (make sure you install the required packages for this step using the `$ yarn add class-validator class-transformer` command):

```
// src/products/dto/create-product.dto.ts
import {
  IsDecimal,
  IsObject,
  IsString,
  IsUrl,
  Length,
  Validate,
} from 'class-validator';
import {
  ProductDescription
} from '../custom-validators/ProductDescription';
import {
  ProductSpecs
} from '../custom-validators/ProductSpecs';

export class CreateProductDto {
  @IsString({
    message: 'name must be a string',
  })
  @Length(5, 25, {
    message: 'name must be between 5 and 25 characters',
  })
  name: string;

  @IsString({
    message: 'description must be a string',
  })
  @Length(25, 255, {
    message: 'description must be between 25 and 255
             characters',
  })
  @Validate(ProductDescription)
  description: string;
```

```
@IsDecimal(
    {
      decimal_digits: '2',
    },
    {
      message: 'price must be a decimal number',
    },
  )
  price: number;

  @IsObject({
    message: 'specs must be a valid object',
  })
  specs: Record<string, string>;

  @IsString({
    message: 'image must be a string',
  })
  @IsUrl(
    {
      require_protocol: true,
    },
    {
      message: 'image must be a valid URL',
    },
  )
  image: string;
}
```

In the preceding code snippet, we designed what our createproduct input should look like. While this is basic validation, it's a good starting point. We are validating aspects such as the length of tests (product description and product name), the presence of a correct URL (in the image field), or the presence of an array entry on the specs field.

Based on our product requirements, this is not the end of the validation pipeline. We need to do two more things to complete it:

- Validate the product's specs field to make sure the input follows the correct format
- Validate the product description according to our users' requirements

Let's start with the easiest one: validating the format of the specs field. To achieve this, the `class-validator` package allows us to create custom providers out of the box, enforcing our rules. Let's create a folder under the `products` module named `custom-validators`. In the newly created folder, let's create a `ProductSpecs.ts` file and paste the following code:

```
// src/products/custom-validators/ProductSpecs.ts
import {
  ValidatorConstraint,
  ValidatorConstraintInterface,
} from 'class-validator';

@ValidatorConstraint({
  name: 'ProductSpecs',
  async: false
})
export class ProductSpecs
  implements ValidatorConstraintInterface
{
  accepetedSpecs = [
    'ram', 'processor', 'ssd', 'hdd', 'brand', 'model',
    'color', 'weight', 'dimensions', 'material',
    'capacity', 'power', 'voltage', 'warranty',
    'condition', 'chip', 'year', 'other_features',
    // we can support more specs as the application grows
  ];

  validate(specs: Record<string, string>) {
    const keys = Object.keys(specs);
    if (keys.length === 0) return true; // no specs
                                        // provided

    return keys.every(
      (key) => this.accepetedSpecs.includes(key) &&
      specs[key].trim() !== '',
    );
  }

  defaultMessage() {
    return 'Product specs must be a valid object with
            supported specs';
  }
}
```

In the preceding code snippet, we have created the `ProductSpecs` class that implements the `ValidatorConstraintInterface` interface, which obliges us to implement at least one method. That would be the `validate()` method, decorated with the `@ValidatorConstraint` decorator, which allows us to set a name for our custom decorator. In this case, we are validating the format of the `specs` object, which was passed as a parameter in the `validate` method implementation. Then we apply some checks on the object such as verifying that if the specs' items don't follow the desired format, we return `false`, and otherwise, we return `true`. We have hard-coded the `acceptedSpecs` parameter in an array for now that supports a set of specs such as the RAM, SSD, warranty, and so on. As the scope of our e-commerce app evolves, so will the array. Instead of having a hard-coded set of specs, we can later decide to create a dedicated table to store custom specs. However, for now, let's keep things simple – with your permission, of course :).

This validation is synchronous. In most scenarios, we need to validate in a synchronous way, but as we will see shortly, sometimes, asynchronous validation is a must. The implementation will be a little bit different.

Note that we also implemented the `defaultMessage()` method that allows us to set a default message in case we call this custom validator without an error message.

To consume this custom validator, we will have to add this constraint to the specs fields as the following code snippet:

```
// add this import
import {
  // everything else we had
  Validate,
} from 'class-validator';
import {
  ProductSpecs
} from '../custom-validators/ProductSpecs'; // the newly
                                            // created class

export class CreateProductDto {
    // everything else remains the same

    @IsObject({
    message: 'specs must be a valid object',
  })
    @Validate(ProductSpecs) // we added this line
    specs: Record<string, string>;
}
```

In the preceding code updates, we added the `ProductSpecs` constraint to our specs field. Now, the `IsArray()` decorator itself is not enough; the specs must follow our custom rules. We use the class-validator's `@Validate()` decorator to inject our rules. If this is not clear, I encourage you to take some time to check out the documentation about custom validators at `https://github.com/typestack/class-validator?tab=readme-ov-file#custom-validation-classes`.

We will test everything out in a few minutes. However, before testing everything out, let's implement our second custom validator, the `ProductDescription`. To proceed with this step, I suggest that you get your API key from Gemini AI studio at `https://ai.google.dev/gemini-api/docs/api-key`. Follow the steps in Google's tutorial and save your key in your `.env` file; let's name it `GEMINI_API_KEY`. You can use any other AI model, such as GPT-3.5 or 4. The idea here is to add a custom asynchronous validator thanks to the AI.

We need to do the following:

- Clearly define the prompt input to give to the AI model. Remember that these tools can be misleading, especially if the prompts itself is not clear.

- Clearly define which output we expect to get from the prompt. Defining the format will help us give customizable feedback to clients.

- It's important to also figure out how to send the feedback we get from the AI model as a response to our clients instead of a hard-coded default message, as we did in the previous example.

Let's now implement this logic. Create a new file under the `custom-validators` folder and name it `ProductDescription.ts`, then paste the following code:

```
// src/products/custom-validators/ProductDescription.ts
import {
  ValidatorConstraint,
  ValidatorConstraintInterface,
} from 'class-validator';
import { GoogleGenerativeAI } from '@google/generative-ai';
import * as dotenv from 'dotenv';

@ValidatorConstraint({
  name: 'ProductDescription',
  async: true
})
export class ProductDescription
  implements ValidatorConstraintInterface
{
  message: string = '';
```

```
async validate(description: string) {
  dotenv.config();
  const genAI = new
    GoogleGenerativeAI(process.env.GEMINI_API_KEY);
  const model = genAI.getGenerativeModel({
    model: 'gemini-1.5-pro',
  });
  const prompt = `Given the description provided below,
    check if it means something to a user perspective and
    that it doesn't contain any offensive content or
    vague informations
    \\n \\n the description: "${description}"
    \\n if you think the description is
    valid, please return "valid" otherwise type "invalid"
    + the reason why you think it's invalid
    \\n the response should be sent in a human-readable
    format, since it will be used to send feedback to the
    client`;

  const result = await model.generateContent(prompt);
  const response = result.response;
  const isValid =
    !response.text().toLowerCase().includes('invalid');

  if (!isValid) this.message = response.text();
  return isValid;
}

defaultMessage() {
  return this.message;
}
}
```

As you can see in the preceding code, we should make sure we install the required package with a $ yarn add @google/generative-ai command. The implementation looks almost the same as the ProductSpecs class except for the fact that now, we have an asynchronous validator (we set the async property to true in the ValidatorConstraint decorator). Therefore, the validate() method now makes an asynchronous API call to the GenAI API.

The prompt clearly asks the model to check the provided description and check whether the information provided is not misleading or doesn't contain offensive expressions. It expects that the model returns *valid* or *invalid*, plus details of why if the description is invalid. We then declared a class variable called message to allow us to paste the feedback from the AI model as an error message to send to the client instead of a hard-coded value.

Well done; make sure you consume this validator the same way we did for the `ProductSpecs` class before we test things out.

Now, it's time to test our validation. Remember that in the service file, we simply printed the incoming `createProductDto` object. However, we will never reach this line if the input is not valid because the validation happens at the controller level.

To make things work, don't forget to add the following line in the `main.ts` file, just to make sure the `GlobalPipe` instance type is applied to our product controller and any other controller we may have in the future:

```typescript
// main.ts
import { NestFactory } from '@nestjs/core';
import { AppModule } from './app.module';
import { ValidationPipe } from '@nestjs/common';

async function bootstrap() {
  const app = await NestFactory.create(AppModule);
  // <- add this line
  app.useGlobalPipes(new ValidationPipe());
  await app.listen(3000);
}
bootstrap();
```

Now, let's start the project in development mode once again and test it out with valid input to begin. Here is my input, which you can use to test on your side as well:

```json
{
  "name": "Macbook Pro M3",
  "description": "This product is a Macbook pro with an M3 chip, 16Go
of Ram and 1To of SSD, no scratches on it. We also offer 3 months
guarantee for this product.",
  "price": "1999.99",
  "image": "<https://www.apple.com/newsroom/images/2023/09/apple-
unveils-iphone-15-pro-and-iphone-15-pro-max/article/Apple-iPhone-15-
Pro-lineup-hero-230912_Full-Bleed-Image.jpg.large.jpg>",
  "specs": {
    "ram":"16Go",
    "ssd":"1To",
    "chip":"M3",
    "condition":"like new",
    "brand":"Apple",
    "model":"Macbook Pro",
```

```
      "color":"grey",
      "year":"2023"
   }
}
```

When it is given the preceding input, the AI tool doesn't complain and validates the product description. I can see the log in my terminal, a sign that it made it to the service file, and the input is ready to be persisted in the database.

Let's try doing something wrong and seeing how our validators respond. Let's use the following input:

```
{
   "name": "Macbook Pro M3",
   "description": "This product is a Macbook pro with an M3 Pro Ultra
Max chip, 32To of Ram and 100To of SSD, no scratches on it. We
also offer 3 months guarantee for this product. We also give you a
possibility to upgrade to newer models in the future",
   "price": "1999.99",
   "image": "<https://www.apple.com/newsroom/images/2023/09/apple-
unveils-iphone-15-pro-and-iphone-15-pro-max/article/Apple-iPhone-15-
Pro-lineup-hero-230912_Full-Bleed-Image.jpg.large.jpg>",
   "specs": {
      "something":"16Go",
      "ssd":"1To",
      "chip":"M3",
      "condition":"like new",
      "this_is_an_incorrect_spec":"Apple",
      "model":"Macbook Pro",
      "color":"grey",
      "year":"2023"
   }
}
```

As we can all agree, as of now, M3 Pro Ultra Max is not a valid Apple chip. 32 To of RAM and 100 To of SSD seems misleading and doesn't exist. Let's see the response we get. *Figure 12.4* shows what I get in my Postman client app:

```
"message": [
    "Invalid - The description contains unrealistic specifications for a Macbook Pro.
        \n\nHere's why:\n\n* **M3 Pro Ultra Max chip:**  While Apple has \"M3 Pro\" and
        \"M3 Max\" chips, there's no \"Ultra Max\" designation.\n* **32TB of RAM:**
        This amount of RAM is unheard of in consumer laptops. Even high-end
        workstations don't offer this much RAM. \n* **100TB of SSD:** Similar to the
        RAM, this storage capacity is extremely high and unlikely for a Macbook Pro.
        \n\n**Feedback to the Client:**\n\nThe product description for the Macbook Pro
        raises red flags due to the unrealistic specifications listed.  The RAM and SSD
        capacities are far beyond what's currently available, and the \"M3 Pro Ultra
        Max\" chip doesn't exist.  It's crucial to ensure product descriptions are
        accurate to avoid misleading potential buyers. Please review and correct the
        specifications to reflect the actual product. \n",
    "Product specs must be a valid array of strings"
],
"error": "Bad Request",
"statusCode": 400
```

Figure 12.4: Validation error

We are getting the output we were expecting. Our AI tool has been able to identify misleading information and reject the input. Additionally, the specs array doesn't follow the desired format. For example, the `"this_is_an_incorrect_spec":"Apple"` element is incorrect, so everything works as expected.

You can also try to add some buzzwords, or offensive content, in the description and see how the AI model reacts. Feel free to play with Gemini and test its accuracy.

> **Your turn**
>
> While this is a solid starting point, there is still room for improvement. Imagine a scenario where the description mentions *24 Go RAM* but in the product specs, it says *8 Go*. Alternatively, imagine a client describing the product as *cheaper than a phone charger* when the price field says *$2,000*. Both examples include information that is clearly misleading. In the current implementation, we only take the description itself as input, but it could be interesting to see how the AI model reacts when we parse more than one input to verify the description coupled with product details such as the specs, price, and so on. Update the product description custom validator so the AI tool can validate the description coupled with the product's details. You can find the solution in the chapter's GitHub repository.

To complete the work on the order service, we need to only persist valid data in our product table. We just saw that only valid input makes it to the service file, which is the preferred behavior.

Before starting to interact with the database via the `ProductEntity` class, we need to let TypeORM know about its existence. Remember, in the TypeORM configuration, we had this array:

```
// app.module.ts
// ...
TypeOrmModule.forRoot({
    entities: [],
    // ...
})
// ...
```

As of now, the `entities` array is empty. We need to specify which entities we have in the whole system by providing a list of entities in the `entities` array. TypeOrm gives us the ability to put `Entity` classes in the array, or directory paths to load from (using the glob pattern, which you can learn about at `https://developers.tetrascience.com/docs/common-glob-pattern`).

In our case, since we are following a naming convention forcing us to name all the entities in the format of `<module_name>.entity.ts`, we can update our entities array as follows:

```
// app.module.ts
// ...
        entities: ['/**/*.entity{.ts,.js}'],
        // we could list entities one by one using
        // entities: [ProductEntity],
// ...
```

It's important to note that once the TypeOrm module has been configured in the `AppModule` class using either `forRoot()` or `forRootAsync()`, it gives us access to a `DataSource` object containing all the information about the TypeOrm configuration, including everywhere in the project we can inject an instance of the `DataSource` class without any need to import it. This is worth knowing as we will need to have access to the entity class in the service class via the `dataSource` object.

Let's now update `ProductService`'s create method using the following code:

```
// src/products/products.service.ts
import { Injectable } from '@nestjs/common';
import {
  CreateProductDto
} from './dto/create-product.dto';
import { InjectRepository } from '@nestjs/typeorm';
import { Product } from './entities/product.entity';
import { Repository } from 'typeorm';
```

```
@Injectable()
export class ProductsService {
  constructor(
    @InjectRepository(Product)
    private productRepository: Repository<Product>,
  ) {}

  async create(createProductDto: CreateProductDto) {
    const product =
      this.productRepository.create(createProductDto);
    await this.productRepository.save(product);

    return {
      message: 'Product created successfully',
      product,
    };
  }
}
```

In the preceding code snippet, compared to the previous version, we have made a few changes:

- We injected the `productRepository` of the `Repository<Product>` type using the `@InjectRepository()` decorator. Note that TypeOrm supports the repository pattern where data access business logic is stored in a `Repository`. You can learn more about the pattern in one of my past articles at `https://www.freecodecamp.org/news/design-pattern-for-modern-backend-development-and-use-cases/#repository-pattern`.

- We turned the `create` function into an async operation since we are now doing an asynchronous call within it instead of a void `console.log`.

- Using the `Repository` instance, we are saving the `createProductDto` object by following two steps. The first one creates a product object based on the entity schema we have. It ignores fields that are not present in the schema and attaches a generated ID (uuid) to the product. The second saves the information in the database. Note that if the ID existed already, it will simply update the existing record in the database, but in the context of our creation, this doesn't have any chance of happening due to the uniqueness of the uuid mechanism.

- Then we return an object with a message to display to the client and the product we just saved. I admit, this is far from being perfect, since we have planned to return an object in the **APIResponse** format, which we will work on a bit later. For now, let's allow ourselves to be imperfect as the development phase continues.

Before we dive into testing our **createproduct** operation, let's do one more thing. We need to specify to the `ProductModule` class which repository to use in the current scope (the product module's scope). To achieve this, we simply need to add an import in the `ProductModule` class as follows:

```
// products/products.module.ts
@Module({
    // <- this line
    imports: [TypeOrmModule.forFeature([Product])],
    // ...
)}
export class ProductsModule {}
```

By doing so, we are telling the `ProductModule` module which repository we need for this scope. NestJS does this to avoid having to load all the repositories present in the project, which would impact the app's performance.

We are all set. Let's test this process once again, starting the project in dev mode using `$ yarn start:dev`. Your app should start without any errors.

Let's use the correct input we used earlier to test validators and see the response we get in Postman. *Figure 12.5* shows the output I get from my Postman client app:

```
"message": "Product created successfully",
"product": {
    "name": "Macbook Pro M3",
    "description": "This product is a Macbook pro with an M3 chip, 16Go of Ram and 1To of
        SSD, no scratches on it. We also offer 3 months guarantee for this product.",
    "price": "1999.99",
    "image": "https://www.apple.com/newsroom/images/2023/09/
        apple-unveils-iphone-15-pro-and-iphone-15-pro-max/article/
        Apple-iPhone-15-Pro-lineup-hero-230912_Full-Bleed-Image.jpg.large.jpg",
    "specs": {
        "ram": "16Go",
        "ssd": "1To",
        "chip": "M3",
        "condition": "like new",
        "brand": "Apple",
        "model": "Macbook Pro",
        "color": "grey",
        "year": "2023"
    },
    "id": "043ba968-ea49-487e-a8c0-3cf8a8ffca19",
    "createdAt": "2024-06-01T17:08:24.814Z"
}
```

Figure 12.5: API response with valid product body

As *Figure 12.6* suggests, the database accepted my changes, and it has persisted data in the database. You should be able to get a similar result in your local environment if instructions have been followed.

We may need to verify that the product has been persisted though. To do so, let's work on our product getters.

The goal here is to do the following:

- Get a paginated list of products via the HTTP GET /products endpoint
- Get a single product with its ID via the HTTP GET /products/{id} endpoint

To achieve these goals, let's add two more functions in our service files as the following code snippet suggests:

```
// ... the rest of the code remains the sam
  async getProducts(page = 1, limit = 10) {
    const products = await this.productRepository.find({
      skip: (page - 1) * limit,
      take: limit,
    });

    return {
      products,
    };
  }
  async getProductById(id: string) {
    const product = await this.productRepository.findOne({
      where: { id },
    });

    return {
      product,
    };
  }
// ...
```

In the preceding code snippet, we have added two more methods. The first one searches for a list of paginated products, with default values (page = 1 and limit = 10) and returns an array of products. The second one, given a product's ID, returns the product.

> **Your turn**
>
> We need to consume these two methods, creating their corresponding handlers in the controller class. Those ones should be easy. If you need a refresher on how to implement those handlers, you can always check out the repository. This goes doubly if you are getting unexpected behavior.

With the handlers in place, try things out once again. *Figures 12.6* and *12.7* show what you should get from your local Postman client for the two newly implemented endpoints:

```
1  {
2      "products": [
3          {
4              "id": "043ba968-ea49-487e-a8c0-3cf8a8ffca19",
5              "name": "Macbook Pro M3",
6              "description": "This product is a Macbook pro with an M3 chip, 16Go of Ram and
                   1To of SSD, no scratches on it. We also offer 3 months guarantee for this
                   product.",
7              "price": "1999.99",
8              "image": "https://www.apple.com/newsroom/images/2023/09/
                   apple-unveils-iphone-15-pro-and-iphone-15-pro-max/article/
                   Apple-iPhone-15-Pro-lineup-hero-230912_Full-Bleed-Image.jpg.large.jpg",
9              "specs": {
10                 "ram": "16Go",
11                 "ssd": "1To",
12                 "chip": "M3",
13                 "condition": "like new",
14                 "brand": "Apple",
15                 "model": "Macbook Pro",
16                 "color": "grey",
17                 "year": "2023"
18             },
19             "createdAt": "2024-06-01T17:08:24.814Z"
20         }
21     ]
22 }
```

Figure 12.6: Output for the /products endpoint

```
1  {
2      "product": {
3          "id": "043ba968-ea49-487e-a8c0-3cf8a8ffca19",
4          "name": "Macbook Pro M3",
5          "description": "This product is a Macbook pro with an M3 chip, 16Go of Ram and 1To
               of SSD, no scratches on it. We also offer 3 months guarantee for this product.
               ",
6          "price": "1999.99",
7          "image": "https://www.apple.com/newsroom/images/2023/09/
               apple-unveils-iphone-15-pro-and-iphone-15-pro-max/article/
               Apple-iPhone-15-Pro-lineup-hero-230912_Full-Bleed-Image.jpg.large.jpg",
8          "specs": {
9              "ram": "16Go",
10             "ssd": "1To",
11             "chip": "M3",
12             "condition": "like new",
13             "brand": "Apple",
14             "model": "Macbook Pro",
15             "color": "grey",
16             "year": "2023"
17         },
18         "createdAt": "2024-06-01T17:08:24.814Z"
19     }
20 }
```

Figure 12.7: Output for the /product/{id} endpoint

Well done, we have achieved a great milestone. The product service seems to reply perfectly. However, as mentioned earlier, we still have a lot of room for improvement, which will be discussed very soon as we implement the orders' endpoints in the next section.

Bring a coffee

We have explored a lot of new concepts and a lot of refreshers on our code base. That's worth a coffee 😃. Take some time to play with the API once again, making sure all the concepts are mastered, as we will need them very soon.

Implementing the Order API endpoints

To implement the Order API endpoints, we'll follow a similar structure to our Product API. First, let's create a new resource and name it `orders` with the following command:

```
$ nest generate resource orders
```

The preceding command will generate a new folder under the `src/` directory, with the well-known Nest CLI files.

Now, let's work on the `orders` entity in the following section.

The order entity

The entity file can be found in the generated `src/orders/entities/` folder. Let's customize it following our application's requirements.

Before diving deeper, we need to remind ourselves that the product entity actually doesn't have any relationship. We need to link the product entity to this newly created `OrderEntity` class in order to have a more functional model. No worries if it sounds like too much; let's break it down into small and simple steps:

1. **Update the Order entity**: In the generated `Entity` class, paste the following content:

   ```
   // src/orrders/entities/order.entity.ts
   import {
     Product
   } from 'src/products/entities/product.entity';
   import {
     Column,
     Entity,
     ManyToOne,
     PrimaryGeneratedColumn
   } from 'typeorm';
   ```

```
export enum OrderStatus {
  PENDING = 'PENDING',
  APPROVED = 'APPROVED',
  DECLINED = 'DECLINED', // by the merchant or payment
                         // gateway
  CANCELLED = 'CANCELLED', // by the customer
}

@Entity('orders')
export class Order {
  @PrimaryGeneratedColumn('uuid')
  id: string;

  @Column()
  quantity: number;

  // @ManyToOne(() => User, (user) => user.orders)
  // customer: User;

  @Column({ default: OrderStatus.PENDING })
  status: OrderStatus;

  @Column(
    'decimal', { precision: 5, scale: 2, default: 0 }
  )
  totalPrice: number;

  @ManyToOne(
    () => Product,
    (product) => product.orders
  )
  product: Product;

  @Column(
    { type: 'timestamp',
    default: () => 'CURRENT_TIMESTAMP' }
  )
  createdAt: Date;
}
```

As you can see in the preceding code snippet, we have normal decorators we already know about (`@Column()`, `@PrimaryGeneratedColumn()`, and `@Entity()`). In addition, we have `@ManyToOne()`, which helps us define the relationship between two entities in TypeORM.

With this relationship, we are linking *one* product field *to many* orders. Note that it takes two parameters. The first one is a function that returns the type to that field (in this case, the type is `Product`), and the second one indicates where to locate these orders in the product entity. We have decided to use the `product.orders` field. This second parameter is not required for a `ONE-TO-MANY` field, but since we have declared it, we need to update the product entity, so it also has an orders field, which doesn't exist as of now.

Also, note that we have a commented relationship between orders and users which is the `customer` field. For now, since we don't have the `user` entity, let's keep it commented out.

We also have `OrderStatus`, which is an enum object of the different statuses an order can have. The default value is the `PENDING` state.

The other thing to note before going forward and updating the `product` entity is that this will create a generated field in the order table, called `<relation_name>Id`. Using this example, we will have an additional column in the orders table called `productId`, which is a foreign key from the product table. Now let's go ahead and update the product entity.

2. **Update the product entity**: To reflect what we just told the order entity (that the product entity has a field called orders), we need to actually add that field in the product entity class, as in the following code snippet:

    ```
    // ... everything else remains same
      @OneToMany(() => Order, (order) => order.product)
      orders: Order[];
    // ...
    ```

    On this hand, we have created an `orders` field annotated with the `@OneToMany()` decorator instead. This tells the product entity that we may have many orders coming from the `Order` entity linked to one product. It's important to note that any `@OneToMany()` field needs a `@ManyToOne()` field on the other side. However, the opposite is not true, which means that if we didn't declare this field, it could be totally fine. We simply had to update the corresponding one in the order entity to the following:

    ```
    @ManyToOne(() => Product) // <- without the
                              // product.orders reference
      product: Product;
    ```

    In our case, since we have operations such as GET HTTP `/product/{d}/orders`, for a better separation of concerns, it's better to have an `orders` field we can filter with.

Well done, this is a good starting point. Now start the app once again and see the generated table with pgAdmin. Make sure we have a foreign key, `productId`, without which it will be impossible to proceed.

Now that the order entity looks good, let's work on the service fil, and create simple operations such as the `create` and `get` orders.

Create business logic, the order service file

The Nest CLI generated a service file for us. Let's use it and update its current content following these steps:

- First, we need to update the constructor so we can inject both the `productRepository` instance and the `orderRepository` instance with the following code snippet:

```
// order.entity.ts
// the constructor
  constructor(
    @InjectRepository(Order)
    private orderRepository: Repository<Order>,

    @InjectRepository(Product)
    private productRepository: Repository<Product>,
  ) {}
```

With these injections in place, we have the ability to access them anywhere in the class. Let's consume them, implementing the create order service method.

- We then need to update the generated `CreateOrderDto` class. The current version is an empty class, so let's update it with the following content:

```
// src/orders/dto/create-order-dto.ts
import {
  IsDecimal,
  IsPositive,
  IsString,
  IsUUID
} from 'class-validator';
export class CreateOrderDto {
  @IsString({
    message: 'customerId must be a string'
  })
  // @IsUUID('all', { message: 'customerId must be a
  // valid UUID' })
  customerId: string;

  @IsString({ message: 'productId must be a string' })
  @IsUUID(
    'all',
    { message: 'productId must be a valid UUID' }
  )
  productId: string;
```

```
@IsPositive({
  message: 'quantity must be a positive number'
})
quantity: number;

@IsDecimal(
  {
    decimal_digits: '2'
  },
  {
    message: 'totalPrice must be a decimal number'
  },
)
totalPrice: number;
}
```

This is a simple validation file. Note how I commented out the customerId validation. Since we don't have valid UUID for customers, we can use plan texts to simulate the request for now.

- Then, let's go back to the implementation of the create order method. We will need both repositories to make sure that the product exists, thanks to the product repository, before saving the order object in the database, thanks to the order repository. The create order method will look like the following code:

```
// orders.service.ts > the create method
async create(createOrderDto: CreateOrderDto) {
  try {
    const {
      productId, quantity, totalPrice
    } = createOrderDto;

    const product =
      await this.productRepository.findOne
    ({
      where: {
        id: productId,
      },
    });

    if (!product) {
      return {
        message: 'Product not found!',
      };
    }
```

```
        const order = this.orderRepository.create({
          product,
          quantity,
          totalPrice,
        });

        await this.orderRepository.save(order);

        return {
          message: 'Order created successfully',
          order,
        };
      } catch (error) {
      return {
        message: 'An error occurred!',
        error,
      };
    }
  }
}
```

In the preceding implementation, we first check whether the product exists before creating the order. We then put everything in a try … catch block just in case something happened during the execution code, such as if the database is unavailable for any reason. We then send the response to the client, depending on the way the request goes (in the try or the catch block).

Well done. Before testing things out, let's implement some getters.

- Let's implement the `orders` getters the same way we implemented the product ones. For this, we will need two more methods. In the `service` file, add the following code:

```
async getOrders(page = 1, limit = 10) {
    const orders = await this.orderRepository.find({
      skip: (page - 1) * limit,
      take: limit,
      relations: [
        'product',
        // 'customer', <-- Uncomment this line after
        // creating the User entity
      ],
    });

    return {
      orders,
    };
}
```

```
async getOrderById(id: string) {
  const order = await this.orderRepository.findOne({
    where: { id },
    relations: [
      'product',
      // 'customer', <-- Uncomment this line after
      // creating the User entity
    ],
  });

  return {
    order,
  };
}
```

The first one is getOrders, which returns a paginated list of orders. Then, with the relations parameter in the find() method's options, we ask the method to get the corresponding product to each order for us. Note that this will send back all the product fields. You can pick the ones you think are the most relevant to the client using the select option, as in the following code:

```
// select product's fields you need to send
  const orders =
    await this.orderRepository.find
  ({
    skip: (page - 1) * limit,
    take: limit,
    relations: [
      'product',
      // 'customer', <-- Uncomment this line after
      // creating the User entity
    ],
    select: {
      product: {
        name: true,
        price: true,
        image: true,
      },
    },
  });
```

By specifying these fields, you will only get products with the fields you want. This can reduce the request's bandwidth.

Since we are using both `productRepository` and `orderRepository`, we need to tell `OrderModule` that we will need these entity features, as we did for `productModule`. Let's update `OrderModule` with the following content:

```
// order.module.ts
@Module({
  imports: [TypeOrmModule.forFeature([Order, Product])],
  controllers: [OrdersController],
  providers: [OrdersService],
})
export class OrdersModule {}
```

This will actually make the corresponding repository available everywhere in the registered `OrdersModule` module's providers.

We are getting closer. Let's now work on consuming those service files in the `OrderController` file before we can test everything out.

Order controller

In the generated `orders.controller.ts` file, let's implement the service file we created in the preceding section.

We need a `@Post()` controller to create an order and a `@Get()` controller to get one or multiple orders. Let's go ahead and replace the generated code with the following:

```
// src/orders/orders.controller.ts
import {
  Controller,
  Post, Body,
  Get,
  Param,
  Query
} from '@nestjs/common';
import { OrdersService } from './orders.service';
import { CreateOrderDto } from './dto/create-order.dto';

@Controller('orders')
export class OrdersController {
  constructor(
    private readonly ordersService: OrdersService
  ) {}
```

```
@Post()
create(@Body() createOrderDto: CreateOrderDto) {
  return this.ordersService.create(createOrderDto);
}

@Get()
getOrders(
  @Query('page') page: number,
  @Query('limit') limit: number
) {
  return this.ordersService.getOrders(page, limit);
}

@Get(':id')
getOrderById(@Param('id') id: string) {
  return this.ordersService.getOrderById(id);
}
}
```

This looks almost the same as what we did for products, right? This is good; our `order` module is ready to be tested.

Make sure you start the server in dev mode once again, then use the following body object to test the `create product` API call:

```
{
    "productId": "043ba968-ea49-487e-a8c0-3cf8a8ffca19",
    "customerId": "fake-customer-id",
    "quantity": 4,
    "totalPrice": "124.53"
}
```

Note that we are using a fake customer ID for now (we commented out the validation for this field), but sending a request using any client application should work.

To verify that we have persisted successfully the order in the database, test both HTTP GET /orders and HTTP GET /orders/{id} and make sure we get the expected results.

Well done, we have an order service that's working very well. However, notice how we have some repetitive types, such as the parameter we pass in the paginated requests. Also, the response we are sending to the client is not uniform. When we were designing, we decided to use a unique object shape to send data back to clients. This will create trust between client and server such that no matter what updates we may implement in the future, it will reflect the exact same shape. This will prevent the client from crashing anytime we make updates on the server side. Let's work on it in the next section.

Common logic and interceptors

This section will help us identify what current common and shared logic we have in the application, as well as what potential future shared logics we may have. Then, we will focus on how we should structure them in the project. This will introduce us to what we already know: interceptors.

Common module

For our shared logic, let's put it in `CommonModule`. Create a new module using the Nest CLI using `$ nest generate module common`. This command will generate a new module and link it to the `AppModule` class.

Currently, when we send a paginated response to the client, we simply send the array of orders or products, which is good but not great. In most cases, the client needs to have access to more information, such as the total number of pages (so a frontend client can decide how many pages to show in its pagination component), the current page, and the current limit. Remember that our app uses default values for limit and pages.

Since this logic will be repeated across multiple modules, let's create a `PaginationService` class under the common module by following these steps:

1. In the `src/common/pagination/pagination.service.ts` file, paste the following content:

    ```
    import { Injectable } from '@nestjs/common';
    @Injectable()
    export class PaginationService {
      getPaginationMeta(
        page: number,
        limit: number,
        totalItems: number
      )
      {
        const totalPages = Math.ceil(totalItems / limit);
        return {
          page,
          limit,
          totalPages,
        };
      }
    }
    ```

    In the preceding code, we calculate the total number of pages based on the limit and the total number of items we have provided.

2. Now, we need to export this service from the common module to make it available outside of its scope. To do so, we need to update the generated `CommonModule` module with the following code:

```
import { Module } from '@nestjs/common';
import {
  PaginationService
} from './pagination/pagination.service';

@Module({
  providers: [PaginationService],
  exports: [PaginationService],
})
export class CommonModule {}
```

Here, we simply export the PaginationService class and declare it as a provider so it can be injected into another module's service file.

3. Next, we need to import it from the `Order` and `Product` modules before using it in their respective service files. Here is what we need to do:

```
// orders.module.ts
@Module({
  imports: [
    TypeOrmModule.forFeature([Order, Product]),
    CommonModule
  ],
  controllers: [OrdersController],
  providers: [OrdersService, PaginationService],
})
export class OrdersModule {}

// orders.service.ts
  constructor(
    @InjectRepository(Order)
    private orderRepository: Repository<Order>,

    @InjectRepository(Product)
    private productRepository: Repository<Product>,

    private readonly paginationService:
      PaginationService,
  ) {}
```

Here, we imported the CommonModule class in the OrderModule module, then added the PaginationService class as a provider. This allowed us to inject its instance into the order service and ensure it was ready to be consumed there. Do the same for the product service, before the last step.

4.   Finally, we consume it, updating the object we return. Instead of returning an array of orders, let's return an object with an `orders` array, plus a meta object returned by the pagination service, as the following code suggests:

```
// ... the rest remains the same
    const totalItems =
      await this.orderRepository.count();
    const meta =
      this.paginationService.getPaginationMeta
      (
        page,
        limit,
        totalItems,
      );

    return {
      orders,
      meta,
    };
```

Now that we have a different object returned, let's go back to our client Postman app, test the get orders endpoint once again, and notice that we have a meta object now returned.

This looks nice but we can improve it further. Let's formalize the response we send to the client in the next section.

API response interceptor

The goal now is to always return a response in a unique shape no matter what happens. We need our response to always be in the same shape as the `APIResponse` class we defined in the architectural discussion.

To achieve this goal, let's follow these steps:

1.   Create an `APIResponse` class. First things first, let's define what the response should look like. In the `src/common/types/APIResponse.ts` file (this needs to be created first), paste the following content:

```
export class APIResponse {
  success: boolean;
  data: any;
```

```
  error: any;
  message: string | string[];
}
```

As you can see in the preceding class, we are defining how we need our response to look. This will be a contract between our server and our potential clients. In the documentation we worked on, it's already specified to clients that they are going to receive responses in that shape. Let's accomplish that desire now.

2. Create an `APIResponseInterceptor` class. Now, let's create our interceptor file, located under `common/interceptors/api-response-interceptor.ts`, and paste the following content:

```typescript
// src/common/interceptors/api-response-interceptor.ts
import {
  CallHandler,
  ExecutionContext,
  Injectable,
  NestInterceptor,
} from '@nestjs/common';
import { Observable, map } from 'rxjs';
import { APIResponse } from '../types/APIResponse';

@Injectable()
export class APIResponseInterceptor
  implements NestInterceptor
{
  intercept(
    context: ExecutionContext,
    handler: CallHandler<any>,
  ): Observable<any> | Promise<Observable<any>> {
    return handler.handle().pipe(
      map((data): APIResponse => {
        const message =
          data && data.message
            ? data.message :
            'Request successful';
        if (data?.message) delete data.message;
        const data_ = data instanceof Error ? null :
          data?.data ? data.data : data;
        const success = !(data instanceof Error)
          && data_ !== null;

        return {
          success,
```

```
            data: data_,
            error: data instanceof Error ? data : null,
            message,
        };
    }),
  );
  }
}
```

In the preceding code, we implemented the `NestInterceptor` interceptor's method, which aims to intercept the request before it gets to the route handler, and the response right after the handler. The handler we implemented is such a basic one that we simply need to update the response to return at the very end of it, putting the desired field in the response, such as the message, error, data, and so on. We also removed the message field from the objects that already have one and returned it as part of the response object instead.

3. Now, since we need this interceptor to intercept all the incoming responses, let's update the `main.ts` file by adding the following line:

```
// ... the rest remains the same
app.useGlobalInterceptors(
  new APIResponseInterceptor()); // <- add this line
```

Note that you can have a scoped interceptor. Let's say that we want it to only intercept `Product` requests; to do so, we can update the module, adding the following decorator:

```
@Controller('products')
@UseInterceptors(new APIResponseInterceptor())
export class ProductsController {}
```

Try this out

With our interceptor implemented, try to perform some API requests and see the behavior. Are you getting the expected response? If not, make sure to review the preceding steps.

When playing with the API, you may have noticed something. We sometimes get Nest's built-in responses, for example, when the validation fails, or when we have an internal server error. The reason is that the request is not reaching the route handler, and our interceptor is not informed about the response until we get there. This is not our expected behavior, right?

We can use RxJS's `catchError()` operator on the observable we had and return a proper response. Fortunately, NestJS provides an elegant way of handling these by implementing custom exception filters. Let's implement one for us in the following section.

Exception filters

The goal here is to intercept any exception raised at the API level and still send back the same shape of data in the response (following our `APIResponse` class).

To accomplish this, let's create another file located at `common/exception-filters/http-exception.filter.ts` with the following content:

```
import {
  ArgumentsHost,
  Catch,
  ExceptionFilter,
  HttpException,
} from '@nestjs/common';
import { Response } from 'express';
import { APIResponse } from '../types/APIResponse';


@Catch(HttpException)
export class HttpExceptionFilter implements ExceptionFilter
{
  catch(exception: HttpException, host: ArgumentsHost) {
    const ctx = host.switchToHttp();
    const response = ctx.getResponse<Response>();
    const status = exception.getStatus();

    const errorMessage = exception.getResponse()['message']
      ? exception.getResponse()['message']
      : exception.message || 'Internal server error';

    const error: any =
      exception.getResponse() ||
        exception.getResponse()['error'];

    delete error['message'];

    const body: APIResponse = {
      success: false,
      message: errorMessage,
      data: null,
      error,
    };

    response.status(status).json(body);
  }
}
```

Here, we have used the @Catch() decorator with the HttpException class as a parameter. This tells our exception to only look up to HttpException (and its children) and injects the metadata required in this class, such as the execution context.

Then, we implemented the catch() method with some logic inside. The logic has access to the context and the host (injected by the @Catch() decorator) and with some manipulation, we are able to update the response's body without changing its status.

This will catch any HttpException exception, and instead of getting the built-in response, we will get the response we are expecting.

To apply this filter globally, we can follow the same techniques as we did for the interceptor, adding this line in the main.ts file:

```
app.useGlobalFilters(new HttpExceptionFilter());
```

This will apply the filter on every controller and route handler we have in the project.

Let's test things out by sending a bad object to the product creation. Here, I will simply add a some_ spec spec in the specs object – which is incorrect. *Figure 12.8* shows what I got as a response from the Postman client.

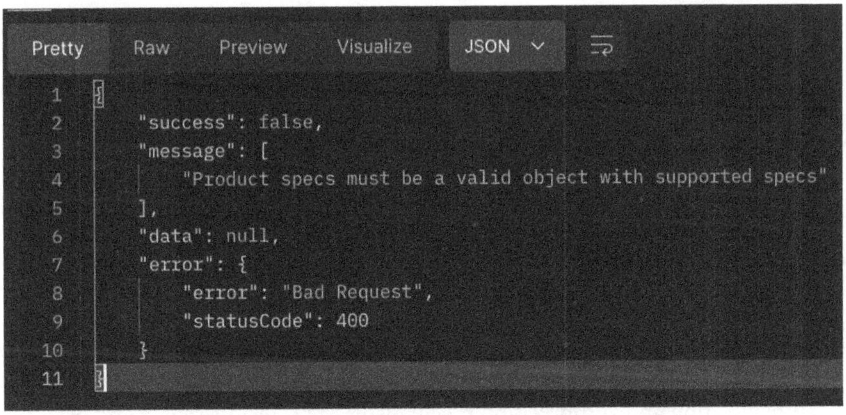

```
Pretty    Raw    Preview    Visualize    JSON  ⌄    ⇄

1    {
2        "success": false,
3        "message": [
4            "Product specs must be a valid object with supported specs"
5        ],
6        "data": null,
7        "error": {
8            "error": "Bad Request",
9            "statusCode": 400
10       }
11   }
```

Figure 12.8: Response handled by the exception filter

As you can see in this figure, the response is no longer the built-in one, but our APIResponse instance.

Well done, we are getting there. Before we move on with the authentication and authorization, let's look at an exercise.

> **Some challenges for you**
>
> In the same way as we did for the `Order` and `Product` services, let's implement the basic logic for the `Review` service, following the same path. You can always go back to the repository and see the implementation. First, we recommend that you try this yourself. Remember, practice makes perfect :).

Moving forward, it's time to protect our endpoint from unauthorized clients. Those clients will be users, such as admins, customers, merchants, or developers dabbling with our APIs. In the next section, let's build the authorization and authentication layers of our system.

User authentication and authorization in an e-commerce context

In an e-commerce application, user authentication and authorization are critical for several reasons.

Here is a list of a few examples of the importance of implementing authentication and authorization in your API. Some of these reasons are already familiar to us since we already explored the topic in *Chapters 5* and *6*:

- **Security**: Authentication ensures that only registered users can access certain features of the application, such as placing orders or viewing order histories. Authorization ensures that users can only access resources they are permitted to access, preventing unauthorized actions.

- **User experience**: Proper authentication and authorization mechanisms improve the user experience by allowing users to manage their accounts, view personalized content, and perform secure transactions.

- **Data integrity**: By restricting access to sensitive operations and data, these mechanisms help maintain the integrity of user data, preventing unauthorized modifications or data breaches.

- **Compliance**: Many regulations and standards, such as **General Data Protection Regulation (GDPR)** and **Payment Card Industry Data Security Standards** (**PCI DSS**), require robust authentication and authorization mechanisms to protect user data and privacy.

We have everything to gain from implementing authentication and authorization in our system. Plus, since we haven't worked on the user module, it's time to do so now.

We will implement user authentication and authorization using **JSON Web Tokens** (**JWT**) for secure, stateless authentication.

Setting up the User module

First, we need to create the `User` module, service, and controller. Using the Nest CLI, let's generate the user resource with the following command:

```
$ nest generate resource users
```

This command will generate boilerplate files for us under `src/users`, as usual.

Creating the User entity

Update the generated `entity` file to the following code:

```
import { Order } from 'src/orders/entities/order.entity';
import {
  Column,
  Entity,
  OneToMany,
  PrimaryGeneratedColumn
} from 'typeorm';

export enum UserRole {
  ADMIN = 'admin',
  USER = 'user',
  MERCHANT = 'merchant',
}

@Entity()
export class User {
  @PrimaryGeneratedColumn('uuid')
  id: string;

  @Column({ unique: true })
  email: string;

  @Column({ unique: true })
  username: string;

  @Column()
  password: string;

  @OneToMany(() => Order, (order) => order.customer)
  orders: Order[];
```

```
// @OneToMany(() => Review, (review) => review.user)
// reviews: Review[];

@Column({
  type: 'enum',
  enum: UserRole,
  default: UserRole.USER
})
role: UserRole;

@Column({
  type: 'timestamp',
  default: () => 'CURRENT_TIMESTAMP'
})
createdAt: Date;
}
```

The preceding file is a normal entity file with columns and a OneToMany relationship to the Order service (one user can have multiple orders). The rest of the content is very similar to what we already know. Since we have a OneToMany relationship in the user model, we *must* create an associated @ManyToOne() in the order entity. However, remember that we already have it. Just make sure that you uncomment this line and update the import in the order.entity.ts file:

```
// orders/entities/order.entity.ts
  @ManyToOne(() => User, (user) => user.orders)
  customer: User;
```

Well done, our entity is ready. Before we move on, remember that we need to register it in the UserModule module's context so we can have access to its repository.

> **Try this**
>
> Register the UserEntity class in the UserModule using the TypeOrmModule class so we can have access to its repository. You can always check out the feat/auth branch to see the result.

Now, let's work on the business logic.

Implementing the service file

We need to implement the core features of the users module. For this, let's ignore the security and hashing password; we will work on those later. Instead of storing a hashed password, we will be storing a constant string, let's say hashedPassword. This is fine for now, as we will improve it on the way.

Now, in the `users/users.service.ts` file, paste the following content:

```
// src/users/users.service.ts
@Injectable()
export class UsersService {
  constructor(
    @InjectRepository(User)
    private readonly userRepository: Repository<User>,
  ) {}

  async create(user: CreateUserDto) {
    try {
      const newUser = this.userRepository.create(user);
      await this.userRepository.save(newUser);

      return newUser;
    } catch (error) {
      throw new Error(error);
    }
  }

  async getUserById(id: string) {
    return await this.userRepository.findOne({
      where: { id },
      relations: ['orders'],
    });
  }

  async getUserByUsername(username: string) {
    return await this.userRepository.findOne({
      where: { username },
      relations: ['orders'],
    });
  }
}
```

In the preceding code snippet, we have a service file with some interaction with the database through the `userRepository` instance. We have one write operation, which creates a new user, and a few read-only operations. Feel free to add more, for example, the `findAll()` method with a paginated response.

With the service file ready, let's work on the route handler that is going to consume these business logic blocks.

Route handlers and the controller file

Each service method should ideally be associated with its route handler; while working on the controller file, we will focus on consuming methods we already have in the service file. However, before we do so, let's create a DTO file.

We need to validate the input we are getting from the client on both signup and login requests. In the auto-generated users/dto/create-user.dto.ts file, paste the following content:

```
// src/users/dto/create-user.dto.ts
import {
  IsEmail,
  IsString,
  IsStrongPassword,
  Length
} from 'class-validator';

export class CreateUserDto {
  @IsString()
  username: string;

  @IsString()
  @Length(8, 20)
  @IsStrongPassword(
    {
      minLength: 8,
      minLowercase: 1,
      minUppercase: 1,
      minNumbers: 1,
      minSymbols: 1,
    },
    {
      message:
        'password should contain at least one lowercase
        letter, one uppercase letter, one number, and one
        symbol',
    },
  )
  password: string;

  @IsEmail()
  email: string;
}
```

The preceding file tells the client which shape of data we are expecting and sets constraints. For the `password` field, for example, we tell clients that we need at least an eight-character password with at least one lowercase letter, one uppercase letter, one symbol and, one number via the class-validator's `@IsStrongPassword()` decorator.

Having the DTO file ready, let's now focus on the controller file and paste the following content:

```
// src/users/user.controller.ts
import {
  Controller,
  Get,
  Post,
  Body,
  Param
} from '@nestjs/common';
import { UsersService } from './users.service';
import { CreateUserDto } from './dto/create-user.dto';
import { LoginUserDto } from './dto/login-user.dto';

@Controller('users')
export class UsersController {
  constructor(
    private readonly usersService: UsersService
  ) {}

  @Post('create')
  create(@Body() createUserDto: CreateUserDto) {
    return this.usersService.create(createUserDto);
  }

  @Get(':id')
  findOne(@Param('id') id: string) {
    return this.usersService.getUserById(id);
  }

  @Get('username/:username')
  findOneByUsername(@Param('username') username: string) {
    return this.usersService.getUserByUsername(username);
  }
}
```

In the preceding controller file, we have created a few route handlers. Each one of them is associated with a service method. The signup and login methods being POST requests, we added the required `@Body()` object in its expected DTO.

Well done, now it's time to test the flow. From any client (such as the Postman client app), let's perform these actions and see what we get as responses after starting the server in dev mode once again.

For example, using the following payload, *Figure 12.9* shows what I get from Postman as a response from the server:

```
{
    "username": "tester1",
    "password": "newPassword123!",
    "email": "tester1@email.com"
}
```

The preceding snippet is the payload for testing. Here is the response:

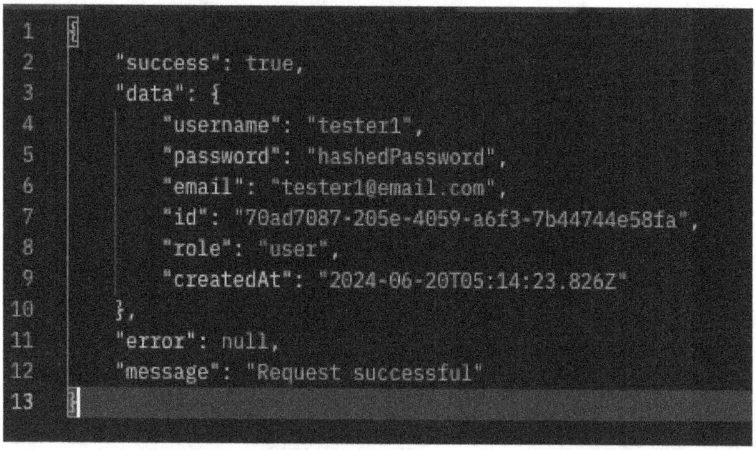

```
1   {
2       "success": true,
3       "data": {
4           "username": "tester1",
5           "password": "hashedPassword",
6           "email": "tester1@email.com",
7           "id": "70ad7087-205e-4059-a6f3-7b44744e58fa",
8           "role": "user",
9           "createdAt": "2024-06-20T05:14:23.826Z"
10      },
11      "error": null,
12      "message": "Request successful"
13  }
```

Figure 12.9: Signup request with valid data

When I try to create the same username twice, since it's supposed to be unique, *Figure 12.10* shows the response I get:

```
"success": false,
"data": null,
"error": {
    "query": "INSERT INTO \"user\"(\"id\", \"email\", \"username\", \"password\", \"role\", \"createdAt\") VALUES (DEFAULT, $1, $2, $3, DEFAULT,
        DEFAULT) RETURNING \"id\", \"role\", \"createdAt\"",
    "parameters": [
        "tester@email.com",
        "tester123",
        "hashedPassword"
    ],
    "driverError": {
        "length": 237,
        "name": "error",
        "severity": "ERROR",
        "code": "23505",
        "detail": "Key (email)=(tester@email.com) already exists.",
        "schema": "public",
        "table": "user",
        "constraint": "UQ_e12875dfb3b1d92d7d7c5377e22",
        "file": "nbtinsert.c",
        "line": "671",
        "routine": "_bt_check_unique"
    },
    "length": 237,
    "severity": "ERROR",
    "code": "23505",
    "detail": "Key (email)=(tester@email.com) already exists.",
    "schema": "public",
    "table": "user",
    "constraint": "UQ_e12875dfb3b1d92d7d7c5377e22",
    "file": "nbtinsert.c",
    "line": "671",
    "routine": "_bt_check_unique"
},
"message": "duplicate key value violates unique constraint \"UQ_e12875dfb3b1d92d7d7c5377e22\""
```

Figure 12.10: Server response for an attempt to duplicate a username

When the data doesn't fit the constraints we set in our DTOs, such as a weak password, *Figure 12.11* shows what we get from the server:

```
1
2      "success": false,
3      "message": [
4          "password should contain at least one lowercase letter, one uppercase letter, one number, and one
              symbol"
5      ],
6      "data": null,
7      "error": {
8          "error": "Bad Request",
9          "statusCode": 400
10     }
11
```

Figure 12.11: Wrong request body on signup

Note how we always get the same shape of data, be it for successful requests or failed ones. This means that our interceptor and exception handlers are still doing a great job, and therefore marks another win.

We have our user module, but we still have a little work to do on it: hashing the password and creating a proper login/signup flow. These are very important aspects when dealing with people's secret data. We should never know users' passwords and if the system is hacked, attackers should never have access to users' secret data. While more robust authentication mechanisms are emerging, it's still common to see users using a single password or pattern on all the platforms they use daily. Therefore, our system shouldn't be the point of failure. As you may have noticed, we ignored the password we got from the request to use a hard-coded value, well, until now. Let's protect our users, and make sure that we hurry up...

Authentication module

While it's common to use the user module to handle authentication and authorization, the logic behind it can become so complex that maintaining it alongside the user module can become a nightmare. It's always preferable to handle it in a separate module so it can be scaled and maintained separately, or even moved into a new microservice if you decide to do so in the future, keeping the users and authentication modules loosely coupled and avoiding a single point of failure in our system.

To get started, let's generate a new auth module and service. Instead of generating the whole module with controllers we won't need, let's use the following commands:

```
# generate the module
$ nest generate module auth
# generate the service file
$ nest generate service auth
```

These commands will create a new module folder called `auth`, register the new module in the `AppModule`, and register the `Service` file as a provider in the `AuthModule` class, just like the generate resource command would do. The difference is that these commands won't add DTO or entity files we won't need – for now, at least.

Before we move on, let's configure the `AuthModule` class. In the `src/auth/auth.module.ts` file, paste the following content:

```
@Module({
  providers: [AuthService],
  imports: [
    UsersModule,
    JwtModule.registerAsync({
      inject: [ConfigService],
      useFactory: async (configService: ConfigService) => ({
        secret: configService.get<string>('JWT_SECRET'),
        signOptions: { expiresIn: '24h' },
```

```
        global: true,
      }),
    }),
  ],
  controllers: [AuthController],
})
export class AuthModule {}
```

Here, we make sure we import all the necessary modules, such as `UsersModule` and `JwtModule`. `JwtModule` is imported from the native `@nestjs/jwt`. It will help us generate the `accessToken` and verify their validity on protected routes (we will talk about this in detail later).

Moving on to the authentication service file, let's first install the required packages. We will use `bcrypt` (`https://www.npmjs.com/package/bcrypt`), a popular tool, to encrypt users' passwords:

```
$ yarn add bcrypt
$ yarn add @types/bcrypt --save-dev
```

With the package installed, let's update the `auth.service` file with the following content:

```
@Injectable()
export class AuthService {
  constructor(
    private readonly userService: UsersService,
    private jwtService: JwtService,
  ) {}
  async login(username: string, password: string) {
    try {
      const user =
        await this.userService.getUserByUsername(username);
      if (await this.verifyPassword(
        user,
        password,
        user.password
      )) {
        delete user.password;
        const accessToken =
          await this.jwtService.signAsync
        ({
          sub: user.id,
          username: user.username,
        });
        return {
          message: 'Login successful',
          data: {
```

```
          ...user,
          accessToken,
        },
      };
    }
    return {
      message: 'Invalid username or password',
      data: null,
    };
  } catch (error) {
    return error;
  }
}

async signup(createUserDto: CreateUserDto) {
  try {
    const hashedPassword =
      this.hashPassword(createUserDto.password);
    const newUser: CreateUserDto = {
      ...createUserDto,
      password: hashedPassword,
    };

    return await this.userService.create(newUser);
  } catch (error) {
    return error;
  }
}

hashPassword(password: string) {
  return bcrypt.hashSync(password, 10);
}

async verifyPassword(
  user: User,
  password: string,
  hashedPassword: string
) {
  return user && (await bcrypt.compare(
    password, hashedPassword
  ));
  }
}
```

In the preceding code, we have implemented a few useful methods. One of those is `verifyPassword()` – which takes the user instance, the password, and the `hashedPassword`, then checks whether the provided user is not null. Then we compare the stored hashed password with the plain test password passed in the request using `bcrypt`'s compare function. If the password matches the hash stored, it will return `true`. Otherwise, it will return `false`. This needs to be used in the user service's login function. It's also important to use the `hashPassword()` function, which takes a plain string password and returns the hashed value of it using `bcrypt`'s `hashSync()` function. This will be used in the signup function to store a hashed value instead of the hard-coded `hashedPassword` we are currently storing. Note that we also moved the login and signup functions from `userService` to `authService`, which makes more sense.

Then we have the `login()` and `signup()` methods. For the first one, given a username and a plain password, it first checks whether the user exists in the database. It then compares the user's password, stored as a hash in the database, to the provided plain password and checks whether there is a match thanks to the `verifyPassword()` method. The login method also attaches an `accessToken` to the returned data object, thanks to the `signAsync` method from `jwtService`. The second one receives a `createUserDto` object, then calls the `create()` method from the `UsersService` class to persist the new user's information in the database. Note that from now on, when we create a new user, we no longer save the password as plain text. Instead, we save it as a hashed string thanks to the `hashPasswo()` method.

Also, note that we are injecting a `userService` entity in the constructor of the `AuthService` class. This means that the following is true:

- We need to import the `UserModule` class in the imports array of the `AuthModule`
- We then need to export the `UserService` provider from the `UserModule` module configuration or use it in the `providers` array in the `AuthModule`

Both methods work. Feel free to choose according to your preferences.

> **Facing any trouble so far?**
>
> Make sure you check out the `feat/auth` branch from the repository project and compare it to your implementation.

Authentication controllers

Now that we have proper login and signup methods in the service file, let's implement their route handlers. We can do that by pasting the following content in the src/auth/auth.controller. ts file:

```
@Controller('auth')
export class AuthController {
  constructor(private readonly authService: AuthService) {}

  @Post('signup')
  signup(@Body() createUserDto: CreateUserDto) {
    return this.authService.signup(createUserDto);
  }

  @Post('login')
  login(@Body() loginUserDto: LoginUserDto) {
    const { username, password } = loginUserDto;
    return this.authService.login(username, password);
  }
}
```

With the preceding implementation (don't forget to add necessary imports to the file), we have created two main authentication route handlers: the signup and the login. Both are POST requests. They expect the createUserDto and the loginUserDto objects, respectively. For the first one, we will use the same object located in the src/users/dto/create-user.dto.ts file. For the second one, let's create a new object. Since the login is explicitly related to the authentication feature, let's create a login-user.dto.ts file under the src/auth/dto folder with the following content:

```
import { PickType } from '@nestjs/mapped-types';
import {
  CreateUserDto
} from 'src/users/dto/create-user.dto';

export class LoginUserDto extends PickType(CreateUserDto, [
  'username',
  'password',
] as const) {}
```

In the preceding code, we use the PickType utility type from @nestjs/mapped-types to create a class with only the username and the password expected from the CreateUserDto object. Now, feel free to change the login function's signature from async login(username: string, password: string) to async login(loginUser: LoginUserDto).

Now that we have all the DTOs we wanted, and the route handlers in place, let's test the whole signup/login flow. We'll start by creating a new user, then logging in to the system using their username and password. Note that both login and signup endpoints are /auth/login and auth/signup. We can now delete the user/create endpoint from the UserController, since it doesn't treat passwords as we expected.

Following the preceding guide, you should be able to create a new user and log them into the system. You should note that passwords coming from the database are no longer plain texts and that on login, we attach an accessToken string to the response. This should look like *Figure 12.12*:

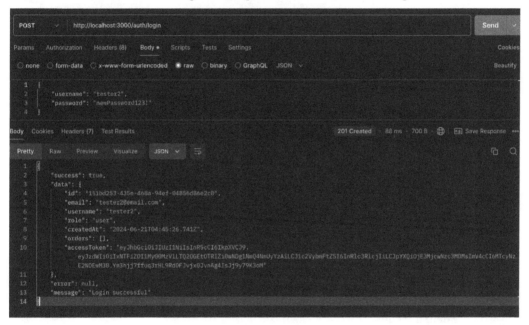

Figure 12.12: Login user with an accessToken

The authToken string will help us verify whether the user performing a request is authenticated on protected routes.

Authentication guard

Now that the authenticated user is getting their accessToken, it's time to improve the application's security by protecting sensitive endpoints. For example, not everyone should be able to create a product. Users should at least be connected with a valid accessToken, and probably have the ADMIN role. Also, an unauthenticated user should not be able to place an order or update its status.

To achieve this, we should create a **Guard** and bind it to the desired route handlers. In the `src/auth/auth.guard.ts` file, paste the following content:

```
@Injectable()
export class AuthGuard implements CanActivate {
  constructor(
    private jwtService: JwtService,
    private readonly configService: ConfigService,
  ) {}

  async canActivate(context: ExecutionContext):
    Promise<boolean>
  {
    const request = context.switchToHttp().getRequest();
    const token = this.extractTokenFromHeader(request);
    if (!token) {
      throw new UnauthorizedException();
    }
    try {
      const payload =
        await this.jwtService.verifyAsync(token, {
          secret:
            this.configService.get<string>('JWT_SECRET'),
        });
      request['user'] = payload;
    } catch {
      throw new UnauthorizedException();
    }
    return true;
  }

  private extractTokenFromHeader(request: Request):
    string | undefined
  {
    const [type, token] =
      request.headers.authorization?.split(' ') ?? [];
    return type === 'Bearer' ? token : undefined;
  }
}
```

This Guard implements the CanActivate class. Its canActivate() method takes the execution context that has access to the request object, and checks whether there is any token passed in the request's header.

If not, we directly throw an `UnauthorizedException` exception. Otherwise, we check whether the token is still valid using the JWT's `verifyAsync()` method. Then if everything is as expected, we return `true` so that the request can be handled by the handler.

> **Your turn**
>
> Now that we have the authentication guard, use the `@UseGuard()` decorator to protect the endpoints listed earlier. Go further, implementing the authorization check to ensure that only connected users with the ADMIN role can create a product. The code can be found in the chapter's repository.

By following the preceding guide, we can make sure that the basic features are implemented securely. Feel free to implement the reviews feature as a hands-on exercise.

Summary

In this chapter, we embarked on building an e-commerce application with NestJS, reinforcing our skills in REST API development, testing, data modeling, and integrating real databases. We tackled the following key areas.

We delved into the essential features and functionalities required for a robust e-commerce platform, ensuring a comprehensive understanding of user and business needs.

Then we designed a scalable architecture and defined our data models, laying the foundation for a well-structured application.

We developed RESTful endpoints for managing products, orders, and payments, ensuring a seamless flow of data and operations.

Finally, we implemented secure user authentication and authorization mechanisms using JWT, enhancing the application's security and user management capabilities.

Throughout this chapter, we integrated `PostgreSQL` for database management, moving beyond in-memory databases to tackle real-world challenges. By applying theoretical security considerations in a practical scenario, we solidified our understanding of creating secure and efficient applications.

With a solid grasp of REST API development and real-world application architecture, you're now ready to take on a new challenge. In the next chapter, we will explore building a real-world use case using GraphQL API. This will further expand your skills in API development, providing you with a deeper understanding of modern web technologies.

Get ready to dive into the world of GraphQL and explore its potential for creating efficient and flexible APIs. See you in the next chapter!

Get This Book's PDF Version and Exclusive Extras

Scan the QR code (or go to packtpub.com/unlock). Search for this book by name, confirm the edition, and then follow the steps on the page.

Note: Keep your invoice handly. Purchase made directly from packt don't require one.

13

Case Study 2 – Social Networking Platform

Welcome to our second use case, where we will build a real-life GraphQL application. Just like we did in the previous chapter, in this one, we will go through all the design and implementation processes, almost like we would in real-world application development.

In this chapter, we will apply our basic understanding of how GraphQL works with NestJS to build a **social networking platform** (**SNP**). Due to the complex and forever-evolving data structure of SNPs, GraphQL is often considered the best option to build it, while avoiding over-fetching or under-fetching, which are common issues associated with REST APIs.

We will use **NoSQL** databases due to the high volume of daily data in an SNP, intensive read-write operations, and the need for high availability and scalability. NoSQL databases are well-suited for these challenges. In our second case study, we will use **MongoDB** to build a scalable API for an SNP.

Let's give our SNP a name. How about *NectMe*? Does it sound good? We should not worry about the name; the most important thing now is to get the **minimum viable product** (**MVP**) ready for our end users.

Here are the topics we'll be covering in this chapter:

- Understanding the requirements of a social networking platform
- Designing the application structure for social networking
- Implementing GraphQL APIs for users, posts, and interactions
- Managing user relationships and social features
- Posting real-time updates and notifications in a social networking context

Ready to challenge yourself? Let's get started.

Technical requirements

For this chapter, ensure you have your local environment ready following the steps in *Chapter 3*. All the source code used to build the project can be found at `https://github.com/PacktPublishing/Scalable-Application-Development-with-NestJS/tree/main/ch13`; make sure you check it from time to time to compare it with your own implementation.

Understanding the requirements of a social networking platform

Before diving into coding, it's always important to understand the requirements for what we are willing to build and understand our target and our scope so we don't build less or more than what should be built. In this section, let's identify the needs from the user's perspective (target) and additional requirements (scope).

Users' needs

While not trying to clone Facebook or Twitter (X), we need to understand how a basic SNP should work. As a user of the platform, I want to be able to do the following:

- Log in securely to the system
- Navigate through the different pages and sections of the application easily
- Write and publish content (posts); for the MVP, we'll only allow text posts
- See other people's posts depending on my interests and be able to react to those posts through comments and likes, or save them for later reading
- Update my preferences anytime I want

For now, these sets of requirements are going to lead to our decision-making. Since we are using GraphQL and a NoSQL database, changing the requirements and the implementation in the future won't be a problem. We should be able to do it easily as the application grows. For example, adding support for posting other media such as images, videos, and so on should not be too hard, since the database schema can change repeatedly.

Functional requirements

Here are some of the main functions our application should support:

- **User account management**: The authentication flow from registration to authorization to perform some actions; for example, only users with an account in our system and logged in should be able to comment or publish content on the platform, while the rest of them can have read-only access to less important content

- **Post management**: The application should support some operations related to posts, such as the ability to publish (create), edit (update), or delete a post. The application should be resilient enough to manage the cascade effect when deleting a post with a certain number of comments and reactions attached to it. A soft-deletion kind of mechanism is a must.

- **Comment management**: Similarly, a comment is a kind of post, and should inherit all operations from its parent (post).

- **Reactions management**: Any post (or comment) can be linked to a certain number of reactions. A reaction can either be a like or an upvote, for an MVP.

- **Preference management**: Each user should be able to deliberately subscribe to certain kinds of content they want to see in their main thread. We should have operations that will allow users to update their preferences anytime they want.

- **Notification management**: Depending on the user's preferences, we should be able to have custom notifications sent to users anytime a certain event happens in their area of interest, such as a "like" on their post, a new post from their subscribed topic, and so on.

Based on the preceding requirements, we should be able to define the current scope and improve it anytime in the future, leveraging the scalability benefit of GraphQL APIs and NoSQL databases.

Non-functional requirements

Apart from the functional requirements we listed previously, our application should be resilient enough to satisfy the following non-functional requirements:

- **Performance**: Our application should be performant enough to serve clients' needs.

- **Security**: It should be secure for our clients, and it should avoid exposing sensitive information such as private posts, user passwords, and so on. Mechanisms such as authentication and authorization should be robust.

- **System availability**: While this aspect will be treated in depth in the DevOps parts, we should take this requirement into consideration to allow the system to be able to deal with the growing number of requests our application will be getting in the future.

- **Documentation**: Since we are working on the server side, we should give our clients well-written documentation that will allow them to play around with the available operations.

While this is simply a non-exhaustive list of requirements, stakeholders (clients, engineers, and product managers) should keep working together on reviewing it, allowing everyone to be at the same pace. For our example, we will focus on the non-functional requirements that we have just shown.

With the requirements in place, we can hand over the job to architects to plan for us... I just remembered... we're the architects :); let's work on designing our application in the next section.

Designing the application structure for social networking

In the previous chapter, this phase consisted of deciding which HTTP operations we needed to include in the application and how the server should react to the related requests. In the context of a GraphQL application, most of the time, we expose a single HTTP operation, POST, at the /graphql endpoint. This simplifies our job in this section; however, we should focus on how the data should look in our system, opening doors for future improvements, the object model, relationships between objects, the schema design, and the API design.

Object model

In GraphQL applications, the object model plays a critical role in defining how data is structured and accessed. This model defines the types of data in our system and how these types are interrelated. Based on the requirements outlined previously, we can design an object model for our SNP, *NectMe*. Here's an overview of the key objects and their relationships.

User

The User object represents an individual using the platform. Each user will have attributes such as the following:

- id: Unique identifier for the user
- username: The name chosen by the user
- email: The user's email address, used for login and notifications
- password: Hashed password for authentication
- bio: A short biography provided by the user
- preferences: User's content preferences
- createdAt: Timestamp of when the user account was created
- updatedAt: Timestamp of the last update to the user account

Post

The Post object represents a piece of content created by a user. Attributes include the following:

- id: Unique identifier for the post
- author: The user who created the post
- content: The text content of the post
- createdAt: Timestamp of when the post was created
- updatedAt: Timestamp of the last update to the post

- `comments`: List of `Comment` objects related to the post
- `reactions`: List of `Reaction` objects related to the post
- `isDeleted`: Boolean flag for soft deletion

Comment

The `Comment` object is a type of post that is associated with another post. Attributes include the following:

- `id`: Unique identifier for the comment
- `post`: The post to which this comment belongs
- `author`: The user who created the comment
- `content`: The text content of the comment
- `createdAt`: Timestamp of when the comment was created
- `updatedAt`: Timestamp of the last update to the comment
- `reactions`: List of `Reaction` objects related to the comment
- `isDeleted`: Boolean flag for soft deletion

Reaction

The `Reaction` object represents a user's reaction to a post or comment. Attributes include the following:

- `id`: Unique identifier for the reaction
- `user`: The user who reacted
- `post`: The post associated with the reaction (optional)
- `comment`: The comment associated with the reaction (optional)
- `type`: The type of reaction (e.g., like or upvote)
- `createdAt`: Timestamp of when the reaction was created

Preference

The `Preference` object represents a user's content preferences. Attributes include the following:

- `id`: Unique identifier for the preference
- `user`: The user associated with the preference
- `categories`: List of categories or topics the user is interested in
- `createdAt`: Timestamp of when the preference was created
- `updatedAt`: Timestamp of the last update to the preference

Notification

The Notification object represents a system-generated notification for a user. Attributes include the following:

- id: Unique identifier for the notification
- user: The user to whom the notification is sent
- content: The text content of the notification
- createdAt: Timestamp of when the notification was created
- read: Boolean flag indicating whether the notification has been read

Relationships between objects

Below are some of the most important relationships to implement:

- A user can create multiple posts
- A user can create multiple comments on posts
- A user can react to multiple posts and comments
- A user can have one set of preferences
- A user can receive multiple notifications
- A post can have multiple comments and reactions
- A comment can have multiple reactions

By defining these objects and their relationships, we create a robust data structure that can efficiently support the core functionalities of our SNP. This structure also provides the flexibility to scale and adapt as new features and requirements emerge.

Database schema design

With our object model defined, we need to map these objects to a database schema. Using MongoDB, our NoSQL database of choice, we can design collections to store these objects. MongoDB's flexible schema design allows us to store related data together, making it easier to query and scale.

Collections

In the context of NoSQL databases, a collection is a set of documents with a similar shape and function. This is the equivalent of tables in SQL databases. For our application, here are the collections we will build with:

- **Users collection:**
  - Stores user information including authentication details and preferences
  - Embeds subdocuments for preferences
  - Indexes on `email` for efficient querying

- **Posts collection:**
  - Stores posts created by users
  - Embeds subdocuments for comments and reactions
  - Indexes on `author` and `createdAt` for efficient querying

- **Comments collection:**
  - Stores comments associated with posts
  - References to the parent post and author
  - Indexes on `post`, `author`, and `createdAt` for efficient querying

- **Reactions collection:**
  - Stores reactions to posts and comments
  - References to the user, post, or comment
  - Indexes on `user`, `post`, and `comment` for efficient querying

- **Notifications collection:**
  - Stores notifications for users
  - References to the user
  - Indexes on `user` and `createdAt` for efficient querying

Schema flexibility

One of the key benefits of using MongoDB is its schema flexibility. As our application grows, we can easily update the schema to include new features such as support for multimedia in posts or additional reaction types. This flexibility allows us to adapt quickly to changing requirements without significant restructuring.

API design

With our object model and database schema in place, we can design the GraphQL API to interact with these objects. The API will define queries and mutations to perform CRUD operations on our data.

Queries

Queries are read-only operations in the context of GraphQL, and here are the most important ones:

- `getUser`: Retrieves user details by ID or username
- `getPost`: Retrieves post details by ID
- `getComments`: Retrieves comments for a specific post
- `getReactions`: Retrieves reactions for a specific post or comment

Mutations

Mutations are read-and-write operations that update the database; they are like the setters we had in the previous chapter. Here are the most important ones:

- `createUser`: Registers a new user
- `updateUser`: Updates user details and preferences
- `createPost`: Creates a new post
- `updatePost`: Updates post content
- `deletePost`: Soft deletes a post
- `createComment`: Adds a comment to a post
- `updateComment`: Updates comment content
- `deleteComment`: Soft deletes a comment
- `addReaction`: Adds a reaction to a post or comment
- `removeReaction`: Removes a reaction from a post or comment
- `markNotificationRead`: Marks a notification as read

By defining these queries and mutations, we create a comprehensive API that allows clients to interact with the system in a flexible and efficient manner.

With the object model, database schema, and API design in place, we are ready to start implementing the GraphQL APIs for users, posts, and interactions in the next section. Let's get started.

Implementing GraphQL APIs for users, posts, and interactions

Implementing GraphQL APIs for users, posts, and interactions involves setting up a NestJS project, defining schemas and **Data Transfer Object** (**DTO**)s, and creating resolvers to handle GraphQL queries and mutations. This process ensures our application can manage users, posts, and interactions efficiently.

In the upcoming sections, let's set up the project and build the main modules for our application.

Setting up the project

To get started, we need to set up our NestJS project and install the necessary dependencies for GraphQL and MongoDB. Let's do so by following these simple steps:

1. First, initialize a new NestJS project using the Nest CLI:

    ```
    $ npm i -g @nestjs/cli
    $ nest new nect-me
    $ cd nect-me
    ```

    This sets up a new NestJS project named nect-me; remember, you can choose any name that sounds good to you.

2. Next, install the required dependencies for GraphQL and MongoDB integration:

    ```
    $ npm install @nestjs/graphql graphql-tools graphql apollo-
    server-express mongoose @nestjs/mongoose
    ```

    These dependencies include the NestJS GraphQL module (https://docs.nestjs.com/graphql/quick-start), Apollo Server (https://www.apollographql.com/docs/apollo-server), and Mongoose for MongoDB (https://mongoosejs.com/docs/).

3. In src/app.module.ts, configure the GraphQL and Mongoose modules:

    ```
    import { Module } from '@nestjs/common';
    import { GraphQLModule } from '@nestjs/graphql';
    import { MongooseModule } from '@nestjs/mongoose';
    import { join } from 'path';

    @Module({
      imports: [
        GraphQLModule.forRoot({
          autoSchemaFile: join(process.cwd(),
          'src/schema.gql'),
        }),
    ```

```
    MongooseModule.forRoot(
      'mongodb://localhost/nectme'
    ),
  ],
})
export class AppModule {}
```

This configuration sets up Apollo Server for GraphQL and connects to a MongoDB database.

Now, let's implement the `Users` module, which will include schema definitions, DTOs, and resolvers.

Creating the Users module

We start by defining the `User` schema, creating DTOs for data transfer, and setting up resolvers to handle GraphQL operations:

1. In `src/users/schemas/user.schema.ts`, define the `User` schema using Mongoose decorators:

    ```
    import {
      Prop,
      Schema,
      SchemaFactory
    } from '@nestjs/mongoose';
    import { Document } from 'mongoose';

    @Schema()
    export class User extends Document {
      @Prop({ required: true, unique: true })
      username: string;

      @Prop({ required: true, unique: true })
      email: string;

      @Prop({ required: true })
      password: string;

      @Prop()
      bio: string;

      @Prop({ type: [String] })
      preferences: string[];

      @Prop({ default: Date.now })
    ```

```
    createdAt: Date;

    @Prop({ default: Date.now })
    updatedAt: Date;
}

export const UserSchema =
    SchemaFactory.createForClass(User);
```

This schema defines the `User` model with properties such as `username`, `email`, `password`, `bio`, `preferences`, `createdAt`, and `updatedAt`.

We also used some Mongoose-specific decorators such as `@Prop()` and `@Schema()`; these are the equivalent of `@Column()` and `@Entity()` for TypeORM, which we explored in the previous chapter.

2. In `src/users/dto/create-user.dto.ts`, create a DTO for creating a user:

```
import { Field, InputType } from '@nestjs/graphql';

@InputType()
export class CreateUserDto {
  @Field()
  username: string;

  @Field()
  email: string;

  @Field()
  password: string;

  @Field({ nullable: true })
  bio?: string;
}
```

This DTO defines the structure for user creation input, including optional bio. We are using some GraphQL-specific decorators, which we explored in *Chapter 6*; don't hesitate to refer to it if this looks confusing.

3. Next, we create a resolver to handle GraphQL queries and mutations related to users. In `src/users/users.resolver.ts`, add the following:

```
import {
  Resolver,
  Query,
  Mutation,
```

```
    Args
  } from '@nestjs/graphql';
  import { UsersService } from './users.service';
  import { CreateUserDto } from './dto/create-user.dto';
  import { User } from './schemas/user.schema';

  @Resolver(of => User)
  export class UsersResolver {
    constructor(
      private readonly usersService: UsersService
    ) {}

    @Query(returns => [User])
    async users() {
      return this.usersService.findAll();
    }

    @Mutation(returns => User)
    async createUser(
      @Args('createUserDto') createUserDto:
      CreateUserDto
    ) {
      return this.usersService.create(createUserDto);
    }
  }
```

This resolver handles the `users` query to fetch all users and the `createUser` mutation to create a new user.

4. In `src/users/users.service.ts`, implement the `User` service to interact with the database:

```
  import { Injectable } from '@nestjs/common';
  import { InjectModel } from '@nestjs/mongoose';
  import { Model } from 'mongoose';
  import { User } from './schemas/user.schema';
  import { CreateUserDto } from './dto/create-user.dto';

  @Injectable()
  export class UsersService {
    constructor(
      @InjectModel (User.name) private userModel:
      Model<User>
    ) {}
```

```
async findAll(): Promise<User[]> {
  return this.userModel.find().exec();
}

async create(createUserDto: CreateUserDto):
  Promise<User>
{
  const createdUser =
    new this.userModel(createUserDto);
  return createdUser.save();
}
}
```

This service provides methods to find all users and create a new user in the MongoDB database.

5. Finally, register the User module in src/app.module.ts:

```
import { Module } from '@nestjs/common';
import { GraphQLModule } from '@nestjs/graphql';
import { MongooseModule } from '@nestjs/mongoose';
import { join } from 'path';
import { UsersModule } from './users/users.module';

@Module({
  imports: [
    GraphQLModule.forRoot({
      autoSchemaFile: join(process.cwd(),
      'src/schema.gql'),
    }),
    MongooseModule.forRoot(
      'mongodb://localhost/nectme'
    ),
    UsersModule,
  ],
})
export class AppModule {}
```

Now that the User module is set up, let's move on to implementing the Post and Interaction modules. To reinforce your understanding, we should follow all the steps together and play with the code as we get deeper.

Now, let's continue with the implementation of the Posts module.

Creating the Posts module

Now that we've set up the User module, let's move on to creating the Post module. This will include defining the Post schema, creating DTOs for data transfer, setting up the resolver, and implementing the service to interact with the database:

1. In `src/posts/schemas/post.schema.ts`, define the Post schema using Mongoose decorators:

```
import {
  Prop,
  Schema,
  SchemaFactory
} from '@nestjs/mongoose';
import { Document } from 'mongoose';
import {
  User
} from '../../users/schemas/user.schema';

@Schema()
export class Post extends Document {
  @Prop({ type: String, required: true })
  content: string;

  @Prop({ type: Date, default: Date.now })
  createdAt: Date;

  @Prop({ type: Date, default: Date.now })
  updatedAt: Date;

  @Prop({ type: Boolean, default: false })
  isDeleted: boolean;

  @Prop({ type: String, ref: 'User', required: true })
  author: User;
}

export const PostSchema =
  SchemaFactory.createForClass(Post);
```

This schema defines the Post model with properties such as content, createdAt, updatedAt, isDeleted, and author.

2. In `src/posts/dto/create-post.dto.ts`, create a DTO for creating a post:

```
import { Field, InputType } from '@nestjs/graphql';

@InputType()
export class CreatePostDto {
  @Field()
  content: string;

  @Field()
  authorId: string;
}
```

This DTO defines the structure for post creation input, including `content` and `authorId`.

3. Next, we create a resolver to handle GraphQL queries and mutations related to posts. In `src/posts/posts.resolver.ts`, add the following:

```
import {
  Resolver,
  Query,
  Mutation,
  Args
} from '@nestjs/graphql';
import { PostsService } from './posts.service';
import { CreatePostDto } from './dto/create-post.dto';
import { Post } from './schemas/post.schema';

@Resolver(of => Post)
export class PostsResolver {
  constructor(
    private readonly postsService: PostsService
  ) {}

  @Query(returns => [Post])
  async posts() {
    return this.postsService.findAll();
  }

  @Mutation(returns => Post)
  async createPost(
    @Args('createPostDto') createPostDto:
    CreatePostDto
  ) {
```

```
      return this.postsService.create(createPostDto);
  }
}
```

This resolver handles the `posts` query to fetch all posts and the `createPost` mutation to create a new post.

4. In `src/posts/posts.service.ts`, implement the `Post` service to interact with the database:

```
import { Injectable } from '@nestjs/common';
import { InjectModel } from '@nestjs/mongoose';
import { Model } from 'mongoose';
import { Post } from './schemas/post.schema';
import { CreatePostDto } from './dto/create-post.dto';

@Injectable()
export class PostsService {
  constructor(
    @InjectModel(Post.name) private postModel:
    Model<Post>
  ) {}

  async findAll(): Promise<Post[]> {
    return this.postModel.find().exec();
  }

  async create(
    createPostDto: CreatePostDto
  ): Promise<Post> {
    const createdPost =
      new this.postModel(createPostDto);
    return createdPost.save();
  }
}
```

This service provides methods to find all posts and create a new post in the MongoDB database.

5. Finally, register the `Post` module in `src/app.module.ts`:

```
import { Module } from '@nestjs/common';
import { GraphQLModule } from '@nestjs/graphql';
import { MongooseModule } from '@nestjs/mongoose';
import { join } from 'path';
import { UsersModule } from './users/users.module';
import { PostsModule } from './posts/posts.module';
```

```
@Module({
  imports: [
    GraphQLModule.forRoot({
      autoSchemaFile: join(process.cwd(),
      'src/schema.gql'),
    }),
    MongooseModule.forRoot(
      'mongodb://localhost/nectme'
    ),
    UsersModule,
    PostsModule,
  ],
})
export class AppModule {}
```

By completing these steps, we have set up a basic Post module in NestJS with GraphQL and MongoDB.

Creating the Interaction module

The Interaction module will handle operations related to comments and reactions. We'll define the schemas, create DTOs, and set up resolvers and services for managing comments and reactions:

1. In src/comments/schemas/comment.schema.ts, define the Comment schema using Mongoose decorators:

```
import {
  Prop,
  Schema,
  SchemaFactory
} from '@nestjs/mongoose';
import { Document } from 'mongoose';
import {
  User
} from '../../users/schemas/user.schema';
import {
  Post
} from '../../posts/schemas/post.schema';

@Schema()
export class Comment extends Document {
  @Prop({ type: String, required: true })
  content: string;
```

```
@Prop({ type: Date, default: Date.now })
createdAt: Date;

@Prop({ type: Date, default: Date.now })
updatedAt: Date;

@Prop({ type: Boolean, default: false })
isDeleted: boolean;

@Prop({ type: String, ref: 'User', required: true })
author: User;

@Prop({ type: String, ref: 'Post', required: true })
post: Post;
}

export const CommentSchema =
  SchemaFactory.createForClass(Comment);
```

This schema defines the `Comment` model with properties such as `content`, `createdAt`, `updatedAt`, `isDeleted`, `author`, and `post`.

2.   In `src/comments/dto/create-comment.dto.ts`, create a DTO for creating a comment:

```
import { Field, InputType } from '@nestjs/graphql';

@InputType()
export class CreateCommentDto {
  @Field()
  content: string;

  @Field()
  authorId: string;

  @Field()
  postId: string;
}
```

This DTO defines the structure for comment creation input, including `content`, `authorId`, and `postId`.

3. Next, we create a resolver to handle GraphQL queries and mutations related to comments. In `src/comments/comments.resolver.ts`, add the following:

```
import {
  Resolver,
  Query,
  Mutation,
  Args
} from '@nestjs/graphql';
import { CommentsService } from './comments.service';
import {
  CreateCommentDto
} from './dto/create-comment.dto';
import { Comment } from './schemas/comment.schema';

@Resolver(of => Comment)
export class CommentsResolver {
  constructor(
    private readonly commentsService: CommentsService
  ) {}

  @Query(returns => [Comment])
  async comments() {
    return this.commentsService.findAll();
  }

  @Mutation(returns => Comment)
  async createComment(
    @Args('createCommentDto') createCommentDto:
    CreateCommentDto
  ) {
    return this.commentsService.create(
      createCommentDto
    );
  }
}
```

This resolver handles the `comments` query to fetch all comments and the `createComment` mutation to create a new comment.

4. In `src/comments/comments.service.ts`, implement the `Comment` service to interact with the database:

```
import { Injectable } from '@nestjs/common';
import { InjectModel } from '@nestjs/mongoose';
```

```
import { Model } from 'mongoose';
import { Comment } from './schemas/comment.schema';
import {
  CreateCommentDto
} from './dto/create-comment.dto';

@Injectable()
export class CommentsService {
  constructor(
    @InjectModel(Comment.name) private commentModel:
    Model<Comment>
  ) {}

  async findAll(): Promise<Comment[]> {
    return this.commentModel.find().exec();
  }

  async create(createCommentDto: CreateCommentDto):
    Promise<Comment>
  {
    const createdComment =
      new this.commentModel(createCommentDto);
    return createdComment.save();
  }
}
```

This service provides methods to find all comments and create a new comment in the MongoDB database.

5. Finally, register the Comments module in `src/app.module.ts`:

```
import { Module } from '@nestjs/common';
import { GraphQLModule } from '@nestjs/graphql';
import { MongooseModule } from '@nestjs/mongoose';
import { join } from 'path';
import { UsersModule } from './users/users.module';
import { PostsModule } from './posts/posts.module';
import {
  CommentsModule
} from './comments/comments.module';

@Module({
  imports: [
    GraphQLModule.forRoot({
      autoSchemaFile: join(process.cwd(),
```

```
        'src/schema.gql'),
    }),
    MongooseModule.forRoot(
        'mongodb://localhost/nectme'
    ),
    UsersModule,
    PostsModule,
    CommentsModule,
  ],
})
export class AppModule {}
```

By completing these steps, we have set up a basic `Comments` module in NestJS with GraphQL and MongoDB.

Creating the Reactions module

The `Reactions` module will handle operations related to reactions (likes and upvotes). We'll define the schema, create DTOs, and set up resolvers and services for managing reactions.

1. In `src/reactions/schemas/reaction.schema.ts`, define the `Reaction` schema using Mongoose decorators:

    ```
    import {
      Prop,
      Schema,
      SchemaFactory
    } from '@nestjs/mongoose';
    import { Document } from 'mongoose';
    import {
      User
    } from '../../users/schemas/user.schema';
    import {
      Post
    } from '../../posts/schemas/post.schema';

    @Schema()
    export class Reaction extends Document {
      @Prop({
        type: String,
        required: true,
        enum: ['LIKE', 'UPVOTE']
      })
      type: string;
    ```

```
@Prop({ type: Date, default: Date.now })
createdAt: Date;

@Prop({ type: String, ref: 'User', required: true })
user: User;

@Prop({ type: String, ref: 'Post', required: true })
post: Post;
}

export const ReactionSchema =
    SchemaFactory.createForClass(Reaction);
```

This schema defines the Reaction model with properties such as type, createdAt, user, and post.

2. In src/reactions/dto/create-reaction.dto.ts, create a DTO for creating a reaction:

```
import { Field, InputType } from '@nestjs/graphql';

@InputType()
export class CreateReactionDto {
  @Field()
  type: string;

  @Field()
  userId: string;

  @Field()
  postId: string;
}
```

This DTO defines the structure for reaction creation input, including type, userId, and postId.

3. Next, we create a resolver to handle GraphQL queries and mutations related to reactions. In src/reactions/reactions.resolver.ts, add the following:

```
import {
  Resolver,
  Query,
  Mutation,
  Args
} from '@nestjs/graphql';
```

```
import {
  ReactionsService
} from './reactions.service';
import {
  CreateReactionDto
} from './dto/create-reaction.dto';
import { Reaction } from './schemas/reaction.schema';

@Resolver(of => Reaction)
export class ReactionsResolver {
  constructor(private readonly reactionsService:
    ReactionsService
  ) {}

  @Query(returns => [Reaction])
  async reactions() {
    return this.reactionsService.findAll();
  }

  @Mutation(returns => Reaction)
  async createReaction(
    @Args('createReactionDto') createReactionDto:
    CreateReactionDto
  ) {
    return this.reactionsService.create(
      createReactionDto
    );
  }
}
```

This resolver handles the `reactions` query to fetch all reactions and the `createReaction` mutation to create a new reaction.

4. In `src/reactions/reactions.service.ts`, implement the `Reaction` service to interact with the database:

```
import { Injectable } from '@nestjs/common';
import { InjectModel } from '@nestjs/mongoose';
import { Model } from 'mongoose';
import { Reaction } from './schemas/reaction.schema';
import {
  CreateReactionDto
} from './dto/create-reaction.dto';
```

```
@Injectable()
export class ReactionsService {
  constructor(
    @InjectModel(Reaction.name) private reactionModel:
    Model<Reaction>
  ) {}

  async findAll(): Promise<Reaction[]> {
    return this.reactionModel.find().exec();
  }

  async create(createReactionDto: CreateReactionDto):
    Promise<Reaction>
  {
    const createdReaction =
      new this.reactionModel(createReactionDto);
    return createdReaction.save();
  }
}
```

This service provides methods to find all reactions and create a new reaction in the MongoDB database.

5. Finally, register the `Reaction` module in `src/app.module.ts`:

```
import { Module } from '@nestjs/common';
import { GraphQLModule } from '@nestjs/graphql';
import { MongooseModule } from '@nestjs/mongoose';
import { join } from 'path';
import { UsersModule } from './users/users.module';
import { PostsModule } from './posts/posts.module';
import {
  CommentsModule
} from './comments/comments.module';
import {
  ReactionsModule
} from './reactions/reactions.module';

@Module({
  imports: [
    GraphQLModule.forRoot({
      autoSchemaFile: join(process.cwd(),
      'src/schema.gql'),
    }),
```

```
    MongooseModule.forRoot(
      'mongodb://localhost/nectme'
    ),
    UsersModule,
    PostsModule,
    CommentsModule,
    ReactionsModule,
  ],
})
export class AppModule {}
```

By completing these steps, we have set up a basic `Reaction` module in NestJS with GraphQL and MongoDB.

With these modules in place, we've laid the groundwork for a robust SNP using NestJS, GraphQL, and MongoDB. Each module handles its own set of operations, ensuring our application is modular, scalable, and maintainable.

With the `Reaction` module fully implemented, we now have a solid foundation for users to interact with posts through likes and upvotes. This functionality adds a layer of engagement to our SNP, enabling users to express their opinions on content quickly. Next, we will delve into expanding the platform's capabilities by introducing user relationships and social features, enhancing the overall user experience, and fostering a more connected community.

User relationships and social features

In this section, we'll explore how to manage user relationships and integrate social features into your SNP. The goal is to enhance user interactions by allowing them to follow each other, establish friendships, and manage various social activities such as sending messages, sharing posts, and participating in groups.

Adding social features

Here, we have the most important social features:

- **Friendship management**:

  - Allow users to send, accept, and decline friend requests

  - Implement a way to list friends and manage friendship statuses (pending, accepted, or blocked)

- **Following system**:

  - Enable users to follow other users and be followed

  - Display a feed of posts from followed users

- **Messaging**:

  - Implement a private messaging system where users can send and receive messages

  - Consider adding real-time messaging capabilities with WebSockets

- **Groups and events**:

  - Allow users to create and join groups based on interests

  - Implement event creation and management within groups

Implementing these features

To implement these features, we will have to follow these steps:

- **Schema and DTO changes**:

  - Update your schemas to include necessary fields for friends, followers, and groups

  - Create new DTOs for friend requests, messages, and group management

- **Resolvers and services**:

  - Implement resolvers for managing friend requests, following/unfollowing users, and messaging

  - Extend your services to handle the logic for these new features

- **Database models**:

  - Update your MongoDB models to include relationships between users, messages, and groups

  - Consider using references and embedding documents for efficient querying

- **GraphQL queries and mutations**:

  - Create new queries and mutations to fetch friends, followers, messages, and groups

  - Ensure proper authorization and validation for these operations

---

Try this on your side

Follow the steps below as a hands-on exercise:

1. Add a `friendRequests` field to the `User` schema to track incoming and outgoing friend requests.

2. Create DTOs for sending and responding to friend requests.

3. Implement resolvers and services to handle sending, accepting, and rejecting friend requests.

4. Test your implementation by creating GraphQL queries and mutations to manage friend requests.

By extending your SNP with these features, you can create a more engaging and interactive platform for your users. The flexibility of GraphQL and the scalability of MongoDB will help you manage the evolving data structure and user interactions efficiently.

In the next section, let's build an interesting feature that will bring more life to our application: real-time updates.

Posting real-time updates and notifications in a social networking context

Real-time updates and notifications are crucial components of a modern SNP. They keep users engaged by providing immediate feedback and updates on activities they care about. In this section, we'll explore how to implement real-time updates and notifications in our SNP using NestJS and GraphQL **subscriptions**.

Real-time updates can be achieved using GraphQL subscriptions. Subscriptions are a way to push data from the server to the client whenever a specific event occurs. In our SNP, we can use subscriptions to notify users about new posts, comments, or reactions:

1. First, we need to set up GraphQL subscriptions in our NestJS application. This involves configuring the WebSocket transport and creating subscription resolvers:

    I. To configure WebSocket transport, modify `src/app.module.ts` to include WebSocket transport:

```
import { Module } from '@nestjs/common';
import { GraphQLModule } from '@nestjs/graphql';
import { MongooseModule } from '@nestjs/mongoose';
import { join } from 'path';
import { UsersModule } from './users/users.module';
import { PostsModule } from './posts/posts.module';
import {
  CommentsModule
} from './comments/comments.module';
import {
  ReactionsModule
} from './reactions/reactions.module';

@Module({
  imports: [
    GraphQLModule.forRoot({
      autoSchemaFile: join(process.cwd(),
      'src/schema.gql'),
      subscriptions: {
```

```
      'graphql-ws': {
        onConnect: (context) => {
          // Handle connection
        },
        onDisconnect: (context) => {
          // Handle disconnection
        },
      },
    },
  }),
  MongooseModule.forRoot(
    'mongodb://localhost/nectme'
  ),
  UsersModule,
  PostsModule,
  CommentsModule,
  ReactionsModule,
 ],
})
export class AppModule {}
```

II.   Next, create subscription resolvers to handle real-time updates. For example, let's create a subscription for new posts. In `src/posts/posts.resolver.ts`, add the subscription resolver:

```
import {
  Resolver,
  Query,
  Mutation,
  Args,
  Subscription
} from '@nestjs/graphql';
import { PostsService } from './posts.service';
import { CreatePostDto } from './dto/create-post.dto';
import { Post } from './schemas/post.schema';
import { PubSub } from 'graphql-subscriptions';

const pubSub = new PubSub();

@Resolver(of => Post)
export class PostsResolver {
  constructor(
    private readonly postsService: PostsService
```

```
) {}

  @Query(returns => [Post])
  async posts() {
    return this.postsService.findAll();
  }

  @Mutation(returns => Post)
  async createPost(
    @Args('createPostDto') createPostDto:
    CreatePostDto
  ) {
    const newPost =
      await this.postsService.create(createPostDto);
    pubSub.publish(
      'postAdded', { postAdded: newPost }
    );
    return newPost;
  }

  @Subscription(returns => Post)
  postAdded() {
    return pubSub.asyncIterator('postAdded');
  }
}
}
```

2. The next step is to implement notifications. We can send notifications to alert users about various events, such as new comments on their posts, new followers, or reactions to their posts:

   I.   First, define the Notification schema. In src/notifications/schemas/ notification.schema.ts, add the following:

```
import {
  Prop,
  Schema,
  SchemaFactory
} from '@nestjs/mongoose';
import { Document } from 'mongoose';
import {
  User
} from '../../users/schemas/user.schema';

@Schema()
export class Notification extends Document {
```

```
@Prop({ required: true })
message: string;

@Prop({ type: Date, default: Date.now })
createdAt: Date;

@Prop({ type: String, ref: 'User', required: true })
recipient: User;

@Prop({ type: Boolean, default: false })
read: boolean;
}

export const NotificationSchema =
  SchemaFactory.createForClass(Notification);
```

II.   Create a DTO for notifications. In `src/notifications/dto/create-notification.dto.ts`, add this:

```
import { Field, InputType } from '@nestjs/graphql';

@InputType()
export class CreateNotificationDto {
  @Field()
  message: string;

  @Field()
  recipientId: string;
}
```

III.   Then, create a resolver for notifications. In `src/notifications/notifications.resolver.ts`, add the following:

```
import {
  Resolver,
  Mutation,
  Args,
  Subscription
} from '@nestjs/graphql';
import {
  NotificationsService
} from './notifications.service';
import {
  CreateNotificationDto
```

```
} from './dto/create-notification.dto';
import {
  Notification
} from './schemas/notification.schema';
import { PubSub } from 'graphql-subscriptions';

const pubSub = new PubSub();

@Resolver(of => Notification)
export class NotificationsResolver {
  constructor(
    private readonly notificationsService:
    NotificationsService
  ) {}

  @Mutation(returns => Notification)
  async createNotification(
    @Args('createNotificationDto')
    createNotificationDto: CreateNotificationDto
  ) {
    const newNotification =
      await this.notificationsService.create(
        createNotificationDto
      );
    pubSub.publish(
      'notificationAdded',
      { notificationAdded: newNotification }
    );
    return newNotification;
  }

  @Subscription(returns => Notification, {
    filter: (payload, variables) =>
      payload.notificationAdded.recipientId ===
        variables.recipientId,
  })
  notificationAdded(@Args('recipientId') recipientId:
    string)
  {
    return pubSub.asyncIterator('notificationAdded');
  }
}
```

IV. Create a service for notifications in `src/notifications/notifications.service.ts`:

```
import { Injectable } from '@nestjs/common';
import { InjectModel } from '@nestjs/mongoose';
import { Model } from 'mongoose';
import {
  Notification
} from './schemas/notification.schema';
import {
  CreateNotificationDto
} from './dto/create-notification.dto';

@Injectable()
export class NotificationsService {
  constructor(
    @InjectModel(Notification.name) private
    notificationModel: Model<Notification>
  ) {}

  async create(createNotificationDto:
    CreateNotificationDto): Promise<Notification>
  {
    const createdNotification =
      new this.notificationModel(
        createNotificationDto
      );
    return createdNotification.save();
  }
}
```

V. Finally, register the `Notifications` module in `src/app.module.ts`:

```
import { Module } from '@nestjs/common';
import { GraphQLModule } from '@nestjs/graphql';
import { MongooseModule } from '@nestjs/mongoose';
import { join } from 'path';
import { UsersModule } from './users/users.module';
import { PostsModule } from './posts/posts.module';
import {
  CommentsModule
} from './comments/comments.module';
```

```
import {
  ReactionsModule
} from './reactions/reactions.module';
import {
  NotificationsModule
} from './notifications/notifications.module';

@Module({
  imports: [
    GraphQLModule.forRoot({
      autoSchemaFile: join(process.cwd(),
      'src/schema.gql'
    ),
      subscriptions: {
        'graphql-ws': {
          onConnect: (context) => {
            // Handle connection
          },
          onDisconnect: (context) => {
            // Handle disconnection
          },
        },
      },
    }),
    MongooseModule.forRoot(
      'mongodb://localhost/nectme'
    ),
    UsersModule,
    PostsModule,
    CommentsModule,
    ReactionsModule,
    NotificationsModule,
  ],
})
export class AppModule {}
```

By implementing real-time updates and notifications, we ensure that users remain engaged and informed about important activities within the platform. These features, powered by GraphQL subscriptions and the Notifications module, provide a dynamic user experience, keeping interactions fresh and immediate. With these components in place, our SNP offers a more responsive and interactive environment, further enhancing user satisfaction and retention.

Customizing notifications based on user preferences

In this section, we will enhance our notification system by customizing the notifications feed according to user preferences. This approach allows users to control which notifications they want to receive, improving their overall experience. Instead of an interactive exercise, let's walk through the implementation step by step.

Step 1 – Extend the User schema for preferences

We start by extending the User schema to include a preferences field, which will store the user's notification settings. These preferences may include categories such as new posts, comments, likes, and so on.

Here is the update that needs to be made on the users schema:

```
// src/users/schemas/user.schema.ts
import {
  Prop,
  Schema,
  SchemaFactory
} from '@nestjs/mongoose';
import { Document } from 'mongoose';

@Schema()
export class User extends Document {
  // Existing fields...
  @Prop({ type: Map, of: Boolean, default: {} })
  preferences: Map<string, boolean>;
}

export const UserSchema =
  SchemaFactory.createForClass(User);
```

Here, the preferences field is a map where the key is a string representing the notification category (e.g., newPosts or comments), and the value is a Boolean that indicates whether the user wants to receive notifications for that category.

Step 2 – Modify the notification logic to respect preferences

Next, we modify the createNotification method in NotificationsService to check user preferences before sending out notifications. This ensures that only relevant notifications, as specified by the user, are created.

To achieve it, let's paste the following code in the `notification.service.ts` file:

```
// src/notifications/notifications.service.ts
import { Injectable } from '@nestjs/common';
import { InjectModel } from '@nestjs/mongoose';
import { Model } from 'mongoose';
import {
  Notification
} from './schemas/notification.schema';
import { User } from '../users/schemas/user.schema';

@Injectable()
export class NotificationsService {
  constructor(
    @InjectModel(Notification.name) private
      notificationModel: Model<Notification>,
    @InjectModel(User.name) private userModel: Model<User>,
  ) {}

  async createNotification(userId: string,
    category: string, content: string)
  {
    const user =
      await this.userModel.findById(userId).exec();

    // Check user preferences
    if (user.preferences.get(category)) {
      const notification = new this.notificationModel(
        { userId, category, content }
      );
      return notification.save();
    }

    // If user preference is not set to true, do not create
    // notification
    return null;
  }
}
```

In this example, before creating a notification, we retrieve the user's preferences and only create the notification if the preference for the specified category is `true`.

Step 3 – Modify the subscription resolver

Next, we update the subscription resolver to filter notifications based on user preferences. This ensures that the user only receives real-time notifications for categories they are interested in.

Let's now update the subscription resolver:

```
// src/notifications/notifications.resolver.ts
import { Resolver, Subscription } from '@nestjs/graphql';
import { PubSub } from 'graphql-subscriptions';
import {
  NotificationsService
} from './notifications.service';

const pubSub = new PubSub();

@Resolver()
export class NotificationsResolver {
  constructor(
    private notificationsService: NotificationsService
  ) {}

  @Subscription(returns => Notification, {
    filter: (payload, variables, context) => {
      const userPreferences = context.user.preferences;
      return userPreferences.get(
        payload.notification.category) === true;
    }
  })
  notificationAdded() {
    return pubSub.asyncIterator('notificationAdded');
  }
}
```

Here, we use the `filter` function to check whether the notification category matches the user's preferences before pushing the notification to the user in real time.

Step 4 – Create a mutation for updating preferences

Lastly, we implement a GraphQL mutation that allows users to update their notification preferences.

This is how we add a `Preferences` mutation:

```
// src/users/users.resolver.ts
import { Resolver, Mutation, Args } from '@nestjs/graphql';
```

```
import { UsersService } from './users.service';
import { User } from './schemas/user.schema';

@Resolver(of => User)
export class UsersResolver {
  constructor(private usersService: UsersService) {}

  @Mutation(returns => User)
  async updatePreferences(
    @Args('userId') userId: string,
    @Args('preferences') preferences: Map<string, boolean>
  ): Promise<User> {
    return this.usersService.updatePreferences(userId,
      preferences);
  }
}
```

Then, we update `Preferences` in the `users.service.ts` file with the following code:

```
// src/users/users.service.ts
import { Injectable } from '@nestjs/common';
import { InjectModel } from '@nestjs/mongoose';
import { Model } from 'mongoose';
import { User } from './schemas/user.schema';

@Injectable()
export class UsersService {
  constructor(
    @InjectModel(User.name) private userModel:
    Model<User>
  ) {}

  async updatePreferences(
    userId: string,
    preferences: Map<string,
    boolean>
  ): Promise<User> {
    return this.userModel.findByIdAndUpdate(
      userId, { preferences }, { new: true }
    ).exec();
  }
}
```

This mutation allows users to update their notification preferences, and the updated preferences are saved in the database.

By following these steps, you have successfully implemented a fully functional notification system that customizes the notifications based on user preferences. This not only improves the user experience but also ensures that users only receive the notifications they care about.

Summary

We have reached the end of our second case study where we leveraged the use of GraphQL APIs and NoSQL databases.

We started with the requirements and adjusted the MVP based on them. The requirements led us to the design phase, where we defined the primary operations, data models, and schemas.

With a series of interactive exercises, we opened doors for improvement and left you space to improve with practice.

In the next chapter, we will explore how we can leverage the microservices architecture in real-world applications using NestJS. Excited about the next step? Let's conquer the microservices world together.

Get This Book's PDF Version and Exclusive Extras

UNLOCK NOW

Scan the QR code (or go to `packtpub.com/unlock`). Search for this book by name, confirm the edition, and then follow the steps on the page.

Note: Keep your invoice handly. Purchase made directly from packt don't require one.

14

Case Study 3 – Enterprise Resource Planning System

Welcome to our third case study, where we will build a real-life **enterprise resource planning (ERP)** system. Similarly to the previous chapters, in this one, we will go through the entire design and implementation process, as if we were developing a real-world application.

In this chapter, we will apply our understanding of how NestJS works to create an ERP system. ERP systems are essential for businesses to manage and integrate critical functions such as finance, human resources, supply chain, and customer relations. Using NestJS, we will build a modular, maintainable, and scalable ERP system that meets the dynamic needs of modern enterprises.

We will also leverage a microservices architecture to achieve scalability and modularity. This approach allows each component of the ERP system to evolve independently, ensuring robustness and flexibility. Additionally, we will explore techniques for data synchronization and consistency, which are crucial for maintaining the integrity and reliability of an ERP system. We will also address the challenges of managing complex business processes and workflows, providing practical solutions to streamline operations and enhance productivity.

Here are the topics we'll be covering in this chapter:

- Understanding the requirements of an ERP system
- Designing the system architecture for an ERP system
- Implementing microservices for scalability and modularity
- Data synchronization and consistency in an ERP context
- Handling complex business processes and workflows

Ready to build a real-life microservices architecture? Let's go.

Technical requirements

For this chapter, since we are going to build an actual microservices application, make sure you have your environment ready following *Chapter 3*.

You also need to go back to *Chapter 9* and *Chapter 10* for a theoretical understanding of the microservices architecture to be able to follow along while reading this case study.

We also have a GitHub repository (`https://github.com/PacktPublishing/Scalable-Application-Development-with-NestJS/tree/main/ch14`) with the whole code and different branches corresponding to headings and parts of this chapter; feel free to use it as a reference and compare it to your own version at any time of your reading ahead.

The code files for the chapters can be found at `https://github.com/PacktPublishing/Scalable-Application-Development-with-NestJS`.

Understanding the requirements of an ERP system

Before diving into the implementation of our ERP system, it's crucial to understand the requirements that will guide its development. This section will help us identify and outline the key functional, non-functional, and user requirements that our ERP system needs to meet. By understanding these requirements, we can ensure that the system we build will address the needs of its users and perform efficiently in a real-world environment.

Functional requirements

Functional requirements define the specific behavior or functions of the ERP system. These requirements outline what the system should do and how it should perform various tasks.

Core functionalities

The core functionalities of an ERP system typically include modules for managing finance, human resources, supply chain, and customer relations. Each of these modules must integrate seamlessly to provide a unified platform for business operations:

- **Finance**: Manage accounting, budgeting, financial reporting, and audits
- **Human resources**: Handle employee records, payroll, recruitment, and performance evaluations
- **Supply chain:** Oversee inventory management, procurement, order processing, and logistics
- **Customer relations**: Manage customer information, sales processes, and service requests

Module-specific requirements

Each module within the ERP system has specific requirements based on its functionality. These requirements ensure that each module operates effectively within the overall system. Let's have a look at these requirements:

- **Finance**: Support for multiple currencies, tax calculations, and financial compliance reporting
- **Human resources**: Employee self-service portal, benefits administration, and training management
- **Supply chain**: Real-time inventory tracking, supplier management, and automated reordering processes
- **Customer relations**: **Customer relationship management** (**CRM**), sales forecasting, and marketing automation

User roles and permissions

User roles and permissions are critical for ensuring that the right users have access to the appropriate functions within the ERP system. This enhances security and ensures that users can only perform tasks relevant to their roles. Here are the most important user roles for our application:

- *Admin*: Full access to all modules and settings
- *Manager*: Access to module-specific functions relevant to their department
- *Employee*: Limited access to their personal information and relevant work tasks

Reporting and analytics

Reporting and analytics are essential for decision-making and performance monitoring within an ERP system. The system should provide customizable reports and dashboards that offer insights into various business operations. Here are the most important ones:

- *Standard reports*: Predefined reports for common business metrics
- *Custom reports*: Ability to create tailored reports based on specific criteria
- *Dashboards*: Real-time data visualization tools for quick insights

Now that we know the functional requirements, it's time to jump on the non-functional requirements in the next section.

Non-functional requirements

Non-functional requirements define the system's operational attributes, such as performance, security, usability, and reliability. These requirements ensure that the system performs well and meets user expectations.

Performance and scalability

The ERP system must be able to handle a high volume of transactions and scale as the business grows. In this regard, some of the considerations would be the following:

- *Performance*: Fast response times for user interactions and batch processing
- *Scalability*: Ability to scale horizontally by adding more servers or vertically by enhancing existing server capabilities

Security

Security is a top priority for any ERP system due to the sensitive nature of the data it handles. The system needs to have strong security features to prevent unauthorized access and data leaks. Here's what to focus on:

- *Authentication*: Secure login mechanisms such as **multi-factor authentication (MFA)**
- *Authorization*: **Role-based access control (RBAC)** to restrict access to specific functions
- *Data encryption*: Make sure that data is encrypted when stored and when being transferred

Usability

The ERP system should be user-friendly, with an intuitive interface that minimizes the learning curve for users. Here are some of the most important usability requirements to keep an eye on:

- *User interface*: Clean and intuitive design with easy navigation
- *Accessibility*: Compliance with accessibility standards to accommodate all users
- *Help and support*: In-system help documentation and user support resources

Reliability and availability

The ERP system must be reliable and available to ensure continuous business operations without interruptions. So, we must consider the following:

- *Reliability*: Consistent performance without failures
- *Availability*: High availability with minimal downtime, supported by redundancy and failover mechanisms

User requirements

User requirements focus on the needs and expectations of the end users of the ERP system. Understanding these requirements helps to ensure that the system is user-centric and meets the specific needs of its intended audience.

User personas

Creating user personas helps to understand the different types of users who will interact with the ERP system. Each persona represents a typical user with specific needs and behaviors. Let's look at some of the common user personas:

- *Administrator Alice*: Needs comprehensive control over the entire system
- *Manager Mike*: Requires access to departmental data and reports
- *Employee Emma*: Wants easy access to personal information and work-related tasks

User stories and use cases

User stories and use cases provide detailed scenarios that describe how users will interact with the ERP system. These narratives help to clarify user expectations and guide the design of the system. We could consider the following narratives:

- *User story*: As an HR manager, I want to generate employee performance reports so that I can conduct annual reviews
- *Use case*: The system allows HR managers to filter employee data by performance metrics and generate comprehensive reports

By clearly defining the functional, non-functional, and user requirements, we lay a strong foundation for the development of our ERP system. Understanding these requirements ensures that we build a system that is not only functional and efficient but also user-friendly and secure. With these requirements in mind, we can now move on to designing the system architecture for our ERP system.

Designing the system architecture for an ERP system

Designing the system architecture is a critical step in building a robust and scalable ERP system. This section will guide you through the key architectural components and design principles necessary for creating an effective ERP system using NestJS. We will cover the high-level architecture overview, microservices design, database management, and communication patterns. By the end of this section, you will have a clear blueprint for your ERP system's architecture.

High-level architecture overview

The high-level architecture overview of an ERP system provides a bird's-eye view of the system's components and their interactions. This overview helps us understand the system's structure and the relationships between different modules.

The high-level architecture typically consists of several layers, including the presentation layer, business logic layer, data access layer, and database layer. Each layer plays a crucial role in the system's overall functionality:

- **Presentation layer**: This layer handles user interactions and displays information. It includes the user interface components such as web pages and mobile apps.

- **Business logic layer**: This layer contains the core business logic and rules that govern the system's operations. It processes user inputs, makes decisions, and interacts with the data access layer.

- **Data access layer**: This layer manages the communication between the business logic layer and the database. It includes repositories, data mappers, and **object-relational mapping (ORM)** tools.

- **Database layer**: This layer stores and retrieves data. It includes the **database management system (DBMS)** and the actual data storage.

With the architecture overview defined, let's dive into the real microservices architecture design in the next section.

Microservices architecture design

A **Microservices architecture** is essential for building scalable and maintainable ERP systems. This approach breaks the system into smaller, autonomous services, each of which can be developed, deployed, and scaled separately.

Each microservice is dedicated to a specific business function, such as finance, HR, or inventory management. This division of responsibilities improves modularity and enables teams to work on different services concurrently.

Here are the key aspects to keep an eye on when splitting a system into microservices:

- *Service decomposition*: Identify and define the individual microservices based on business functions. For example, you might have services for accounting, payroll, procurement, and CRM.

- *Service communication*: Establish communication patterns between microservices. Common patterns include RESTful APIs, gRPC, and message brokers such as RabbitMQ or Kafka.

- *Service discovery*: Implement service discovery mechanisms to enable the dynamic location of services. Tools such as Consul or Eureka can be used for this purpose.

- *Fault tolerance*: Design for fault tolerance by implementing retry mechanisms, circuit breakers, and fallback strategies.

This will guide our design thinking so we can create a better separation of concerns between microservices while keeping them tightly coupled, as discussed in *Chapter 4*. In the next heading, let's tackle one of the most important challenges in the microservices architecture: data management.

Database design and data management

Database design is a crucial aspect of ERP systems, as it determines how data is stored, accessed, and managed. A well-designed database ensures data consistency, integrity, and performance.

In a microservices architecture, each service can have its own database. This approach, known as database per service, enhances data isolation and reduces coupling between services.

For better database management, here are the key aspects to keep in mind:

- *Schema design*: Define the database schema for each microservice. Ensure that the schema is normalized to avoid data redundancy and maintain data integrity.

- *Data consistency*: Implement data consistency mechanisms such as eventual consistency or distributed transactions. Tools such as Saga or **two-phase commit** (**2PC**) can be used for managing distributed transactions.

- *Data storage*: Choose the appropriate type of database for each service. Options include relational databases (e.g., PostgreSQL and MySQL), NoSQL databases (e.g., MongoDB and Cassandra), and in-memory databases (e.g., Redis).

- *Data backup and recovery*: Implement backup and recovery strategies to ensure data durability and availability. Regular backups and automated recovery procedures are essential for preventing data loss.

After understanding data challenges, it's time to understand communication challenges and how to deal with them in the next section.

API gateway and communication patterns

An **API gateway** serves as the main entry point for all client requests in a microservices architecture. It handles request routing, composition, and protocol translation, simplifying client interactions with the system.

The API gateway pattern provides several benefits, including centralized authentication, rate limiting, and load balancing. It also abstracts the underlying microservices architecture from clients, making it easier to manage and evolve the system.

Here are the most important components of a good inter-service communication pattern:

- *API gateway*: Implement an API gateway using tools such as Kong, NGINX, or Amazon API Gateway. Configure the gateway to route requests to the appropriate microservices.

- *Request routing*: Define routing rules to map client requests to the corresponding microservice endpoints. Use path-based or host-based routing as needed.

- *Authentication and authorization*: Implement centralized authentication and authorization mechanisms at the API gateway level. Use OAuth2, JWT, or API keys for securing access.

- *Monitoring and logging*: Enable monitoring and logging at the API gateway to track request metrics, performance, and errors. Tools such as Prometheus, Grafana, and the **Elasticsearch, Logstash, and Kibana** (ELK) stack can be used for this purpose.

By designing a robust system architecture, we ensure that our ERP system is scalable, maintainable, and efficient. The high-level architecture provides a clear structure for the system, while microservices architecture enhances modularity and scalability. Proper database design ensures data integrity and performance, and the API gateway simplifies client interactions and centralizes key functions.

With this architecture in place, we are ready to move on to implementing microservices for scalability and modularity in our ERP system.

Implementing microservices for scalability and modularity

In this section, we will dive deeply into the implementation of microservices within our ERP system. We will cover creating individual microservices, setting up communication between them, ensuring scalability and modularity, and handling data consistency. By the end of this section, you will have a comprehensive understanding of how to build, deploy, and manage microservices in a NestJS application.

Creating individual microservices

Each microservice in our ERP system will be responsible for a specific business function, such as finance, HR, or inventory management. We will start by creating a simple microservice using NestJS.

Setting up a NestJS microservice

For simplicity, we will go for a monorepo structure we have already used in Chapters 10 and 11. Let's create one running the following command:

```
$ nest new api-gateway
```

Now, let's create a microservice for managing employee records. We will need to transform the initial structure into a Monorepo structure running the following command:

```
$ nest new app hr
```

This will update the structure of the project into a Monorepo, with an apps/ directory in the root containing both the api-gateway and hr applications.

Next, we'll install the necessary dependencies for a microservice in the root of the project using the following command:

```
$ yarn add @nestjs/microservices
```

We'll then set up the microservice in the HR project's main.ts file using the following code:

```
import { NestFactory } from '@nestjs/core';
import { AppModule } from './app.module';
import {
  MicroserviceOptions,
  Transport
} from '@nestjs/microservices';

async function bootstrap() {
  const app = await NestFactory.create(HrModule)
  app.connectMicroservice<MicroserviceOptions>({
    transport: Transport.TCP,
    options: {
      host: '127.0.0.1',
      port: 8001,
    },
  });
  app.startAllMicroservices();
  await app.listen(3001);
}
bootstrap();
```

In this setup, we've created a hybrid application and configured the HR microservice to use TCP transport on port 8001.

Creating a controller and service

Now, let's create a simple controller and service for managing employee records. First, we generate the necessary files:

```
$ nest generate controller employees
# select hr when prompted about the application
$ nest generate service employees
```

In `employees.controller.ts`, we define our controller:

```typescript
import { Controller } from '@nestjs/common';
import { MessagePattern } from '@nestjs/microservices';
import { EmployeesService } from './employees.service';
import { Employee } from './entities/employee.entity ';
@Controller('employees')
export class EmployeesController {
  constructor(
    private readonly employeesService: EmployeesService
  ) {}

  @Get()
  getEmployees() {
    return this.employeesService.getEmployees();
  }

  @Post()
  createEmployee(@Body() data: Employee) {
    return this.employeesService.createEmployee(data);
  }
}


// make sure you add the entity file under
// apps/hr/src/employees/entities/employee.entity.ts

export enum Department {

    HR = 'HR',
    IT = 'IT',
    Finance = 'Finance',
}

export class Employee {
    id: number;
    name: string;
    email: string;
    department: Department;
}
```

In the file above, we have two basic business logics and the appropriate Employee entity.

Now, in `employees.service.ts`, we define our service:

```
import { Injectable } from '@nestjs/common';

@Injectable()
export class EmployeesService {
  // an in-memory database - simulating a database per service
  // architecture
  private employees = [];


  createEmployee(employee: any) {
    this.employees.push(employee);
    return employee;
  }

  getEmployee(id: number) {
    return this.employees.find(emp => emp.id === id);
  }
}
```

With this setup, our HR microservice can create and retrieve employee records.

Before testing everything, remember we have an API Gateway that sits between clients and our services. This way we can implement a centralized authorization and authentication mechanism. This means that every HTTP request first queries the API Gateway before reaching out to the microservice concerned.

Let's implement this logic in the API Gateway. We need to install both `@nestjs/axios` and axios packages with the following command in the project's root:

```
$ yarn add @nestjs/axios axios
```

First, let's implement a logic that handles all the incoming HTTP requests in the `app.service.ts` file, add the following code:

```
import { HttpService } from '@nestjs/axios';
import { Injectable } from '@nestjs/common';
import { AxiosResponse } from 'axios';
import { Request, Response } from 'express';
import { lastValueFrom } from 'rxjs';

@Injectable()
export class AppService {
  // inject the httpService
  constructor(private readonly httpService: HttpService) {}
```

```
async handleRequest(
  req: Request,
  res: Response,
  endpoint: string,
  method: 'get' | 'post' | 'put' | 'delete',
  serviceUrl: string,
) {
  const route = `${serviceUrl}/${endpoint}`;

  try {
    const response: AxiosResponse = await lastValueFrom(
      this.httpService[method](route, req.body),
    );
    res.status(response.status).json(response.data);
  } catch (error) {
    res
      .status(error.response?.status ?? 500)
      .json(error.response?.data ?? error.message);
  }
}
}
```

In the code snippet above, the AppService class is designed to forward incoming HTTP requests from the API Gateway to other microservices. Here's how it works:

Dependency Injection: The HttpService from @nestjs/axios is injected into the AppService via the constructor, enabling the class to make HTTP requests.

- *Method Parameters:* The handleRequest method accepts several parameters:
- *req:* The incoming Request object from Express, containing request details.
- *res:* The Response object used to send responses back to the client.
- *endpoint:* A string representing the specific endpoint of the target service.
- *method:* A string specifying the HTTP method (get, post, put, delete).
- *serviceUrl:* The base URL of the service to which the request should be forwarded.
- *Constructing the target URL:* The route variable combines the serviceUrl and endpoint, creating the full URL for the target service's endpoint.
- *Forwarding the request:* Using the httpService and the method parameter, it sends the request to the target service. The lastValueFrom utility converts the Observable returned by httpService into a Promise, enabling async/await syntax.

Handling responses:

On success, it forwards the response from the target service back to the client with res.status(response.status).json(response.data).

If an error occurs, it catches it, extracts the status code and error message (if available), and returns them to the client. If no response data is present, it defaults to a 500 status with the error message.

This approach creates a dynamic handler in the API Gateway that can forward any request to any microservice by specifying the target serviceUrl and endpoint. It abstracts away direct calls to specific services, allowing the API Gateway to act as a flexible intermediary, streamlining communication and making the system more maintainable and modular.

Running the microservice

To run the HR microservice, execute the following command:

```
# to start the api-gateway
$ yarn start:dev
# to start the hr service
$ yarn start:dev hr
```

Now, we have a basic HR microservice running. Let's move on to setting up communication between microservices.

Setting up communication between microservices

Microservices in our ERP system need to communicate with each other to perform coordinated tasks. We will use TCP transport for inter-service communication.

Creating a client in another microservice

Let's assume we have another microservice for managing payroll. We'll set up communication between the HR and payroll microservices.

First, generate a new NestJS project for the payroll service:

```
$ nest new app payroll
```

Then, in payroll.service.ts, we create a client to communicate with the HR microservice:

```
import { Injectable } from '@nestjs/common';
import {
  ClientProxy,
  ClientProxyFactory,
  Transport
```

```
} from '@nestjs/microservices';

@Injectable()
export class PayrollService {
  private client: ClientProxy;

  constructor() {
    this.client = ClientProxyFactory.create({
      transport: Transport.TCP,
      options: {
        host: '127.0.0.1',
        port: 3001,
      },
    });
  }

  async createEmployeePayroll(employee: any) {
    const result = await this.client.send(
      { cmd: 'create_employee' },
      employee
    ).toPromise();
    // Further payroll processing logic here
    return result;
  }
}
```

In this setup, the payroll microservice is configured to send messages to the HR microservice over TCP transport.

Using the client in a controller

In payroll.controller.ts, we define a controller to use the client:

```
import { Controller, Post, Body } from '@nestjs/common';
import { PayrollService } from './payroll.service';

@Controller('payroll')
export class PayrollController {
  constructor(
    private readonly payrollService: PayrollService
  ) {}
```

```
@Post('create')
async createEmployeePayroll(@Body() employee: any) {
  return this.payrollService.createEmployeePayroll(
    employee
  );
}
}
```

In the preceding code snippet, we define a controller in the `payroll.controller.ts` file to handle payroll-related operations. The `PayrollController` class is annotated with the `@Controller('payroll')` decorator, which designates this controller as the handler for routes under the `/payroll` path.

Within the controller, we inject `PayrollService` through the constructor, making it accessible to the class. The `@Post('create')` decorator maps HTTP POST requests to the `/payroll/create` route to the `createEmployeePayroll` method. This method accepts an `employee` object from the request body (`@Body()`), which it then passes to the `PayrollService.createEmployeePayroll()` method for processing.

This setup is a basic example of organizing controller logic in a NestJS application, allowing for the separation of concerns by delegating business logic to a service class (`PayrollService`). This structure facilitates a clear and maintainable code base, making it easier to extend or modify payroll-related functionalities as needed.

Running the payroll microservice

To run the payroll microservice, execute the following command:

```
$ npm run start
```

Now, the payroll microservice can communicate with the HR microservice to create employee records and perform payroll processing.

Ensuring scalability and modularity

To ensure our ERP system can scale and remain modular, we need to implement best practices for microservices architecture.

Horizontal scaling

Horizontal scaling consists of adding more instances of a microservice to handle a higher level of traffic. We can achieve this using container orchestration tools such as Kubernetes or Docker Swarm.

Centralized configuration management

Centralized configuration management allows us to manage configurations for all microservices from a single location. Tools such as Consul, Spring Cloud Config, or Kubernetes ConfigMaps can be used for this purpose.

Monitoring and logging

Monitoring and logging are important for maintaining the health and performance of our microservices. Implement centralized logging using tools such as the ELK stack and monitoring with Prometheus and Grafana.

Service discovery

Service discovery allows microservices to dynamically discover and communicate with each other. Implement service discovery using tools such as Consul, Eureka, or Kubernetes.

Data consistency and synchronization

Maintaining **data consistency** across microservices is crucial for an ERP system. There are several approaches to handle this, as discussed in the subsequent sections.

Event-driven architecture

An **event-driven architecture** helps in maintaining data consistency by emitting events whenever there is a change in data. These events can be consumed by other microservices to update their data accordingly.

Implementing event-driven communication

In the HR microservice, emit an event when an employee is created:

```
import { Injectable } from '@nestjs/common';
import { EventEmitter2 } from '@nestjs/event-emitter';

@Injectable()
export class EmployeesService {
  private employees = [];

  constructor(private eventEmitter: EventEmitter2) {}

  createEmployee(employee: any) {
    this.employees.push(employee);
    this.eventEmitter.emit('employee.created', employee);
    return employee;
  }
}
```

```
getEmployee(id: number) {
  return this.employees.find(emp => emp.id === id);
}
}
```

In the payroll microservice, listen for the `employee.created` event:

```
import { Injectable, OnModuleInit } from '@nestjs/common';
import { EventEmitter2 } from '@nestjs/event-emitter';

@Injectable()
export class PayrollService implements OnModuleInit {
  constructor(private eventEmitter: EventEmitter2) {}

  onModuleInit() {
    this.eventEmitter.on('employee.created', (employee) => {
      // Handle employee created event
      this.createEmployeePayroll(employee);
    });
  }

  createEmployeePayroll(employee: any) {
    // Payroll processing logic here
  }
}
```

In this code snippet, we implement an event-driven architecture to ensure data consistency across microservices. `EmployeesService` in the HR microservice emits an event called `employee.created` whenever a new employee is added. This event can then be consumed by other microservices, such as `PayrollService`, which listens for the `employee.created` event and triggers the creation of the employee's payroll record. This approach allows for loose coupling between microservices, as each service can react to changes independently without direct communication between them.

This event-driven architecture lays the foundation for maintaining data consistency across our microservices. Next, we will explore how to handle distributed transactions to ensure that operations spanning multiple services remain reliable and consistent.

Handling distributed transactions

Distributed transactions ensure consistency across microservices. Tools such as Saga and 2PC can be used for managing distributed transactions.

Implementing a Saga pattern

In a **Saga pattern**, a series of local transactions are coordinated to ensure that either all succeed or compensatory actions are taken to roll back changes.

By following these practices, we ensure that our ERP system is scalable, modular, and maintainable. Each microservice can be developed, deployed, and scaled independently, allowing our system to evolve and adapt to changing business needs.

Example code for a complete microservice

Here is a complete example of a NestJS microservice setup with a focus on modularity and scalability.

Project structure

Here is the project structure each of our microservices will follow:

```
hr-service/
|-- src/
|    |-- employees/
|    |    |-- employees.controller.ts
|    |    |-- employees.service.ts
|    |-- main.ts
|-- package.json
|-- nest-cli.json
```

We will keep the structure straightforward and simple, as shown in the preceding code. We simply need a controller, a `service` file, and the `main.ts` file.

Next, the `main.ts` file will look like the following code snippet:

```
// main.ts
import { NestFactory } from '@nestjs/core';
import { AppModule } from './app.module';
import {
  MicroserviceOptions,
  Transport
} from '@nestjs/microservices';

async function bootstrap() {
  const app = await NestFactory.createMicroservice<
    MicroserviceOptions
  >(AppModule, {
    transport: Transport.TCP,
    options: {
```

```
      host: '127.0.0.1',
      port: 3001,
    },
  });
  await app.listen();
}
bootstrap();
```

In this code snippet, we set up a microservice in a NestJS application using TCP transport. The bootstrap() function initializes a microservice based on the AppModule class and configures it to listen on 127.0.0.1 at port 3001. The microservice is then started with the app.listen() method, making it ready to handle incoming requests and communicate with other services in the system.

Now, in the controller file, paste the following code:

```
// employees.controller.ts
import { Controller } from '@nestjs/common';
import { MessagePattern } from '@nestjs/microservices';
import { EmployeesService } from './employees.service';

@Controller()
export class EmployeesController {
  constructor(
    private readonly employeesService: EmployeesService
  ) {}

  @MessagePattern({ cmd: 'create_employee' })
  createEmployee(data: any) {
    return this.employeesService.createEmployee(data);
  }

  @MessagePattern({ cmd: 'get_employee' })
  getEmployee(id: number) {
    return this.employeesService.getEmployee(id);
  }
}
```

In this code snippet, EmployeesController is set up to handle messages in a NestJS microservice. The @MessagePattern decorators listen for specific commands, such as create_employee and get_employee. When a message with one of these commands is received, the corresponding method (createEmployee or getEmployee) is called, delegating the logic to EmployeesService to either create a new employee or retrieve an existing one.

Finally, in the `service` file, use the following code snippet:

```typescript
// employees.service.ts
import { Injectable } from '@nestjs/common';
import { EventEmitter2 } from '@nestjs/event-emitter';

@Injectable()
export class EmployeesService {
  private employees = [];

  constructor(private eventEmitter: EventEmitter2) {}

  createEmployee(employee: any) {
    this.employees.push(employee);
    this.eventEmitter.emit('employee.created', employee);
    return employee;
  }

  getEmployee(id: number) {
    return this.employees.find(emp => emp.id === id);
  }
}
```

In this code snippet, `EmployeesService` handles the core business logic related to employees. It maintains an in-memory list of employees and provides methods to create and retrieve employee records. When a new employee is created via `createEmployee`, the service not only adds the employee to the list but also emits an `'employee.created'` event using `EventEmitter2` to notify other parts of the system. The `getEmployee` method retrieves an employee by their ID.

With this setup, we've established a foundational structure for building a modular and scalable microservice using NestJS. Each component—the controller, service, and main entry point—plays a crucial role in ensuring the microservice operates efficiently and communicates effectively with other services.

Next, we'll explore how to Dockerize your microservices, providing a complete guide to containerizing and deploying them seamlessly.

Complete guide to Dockerizing microservices

Dockerizing microservices allows for easier deployment and scaling. The following is an example Docker setup for the HR microservice, starting with the `Dockerfile` file:

```dockerfile
# Dockerfile
# Use the official Node.js image.
# <https://hub.docker.com/_/node>
FROM node:18
```

```
# Create and change to the app directory.
WORKDIR /usr/src/app

# Copy application dependency manifests to the container
# image.
# A wildcard is used to ensure both package.json AND
# package-lock.json are copied.
COPY package*.json ./

# Install production dependencies.
RUN npm install --only=production

# Copy local code to the container image.
COPY . .

# Run the web service on container startup.
CMD [ "npm", "start" ]
```

In this code snippet, we define a Dockerfile file to containerize the HR microservice. The process begins by using an official Node.js image (node:18) as the base, which provides a pre-configured environment for running Node.js applications. The WORKDIR command creates and sets the working directory to /usr/src/app inside the container where the application code will reside. The COPY commands then copy the package.json and package-lock.json files to the container, followed by installing the production dependencies using npm install --only=production. After the dependencies are installed, the entire local code base is copied into the container. Finally, the CMD instruction specifies that the application should be started using npm start when the container is run.

Next, in the docker-compose.yml file, paste the following code:

```
version: '3.7'

services:
  hr-service:
    build: .
    ports:
      - "3001:3001"
    environment:
      - NODE_ENV=production
```

In this code snippet, we define a docker-compose.yml file to orchestrate the deployment of the HR microservice. Here, version specifies the version of the Docker Compose file format being used.

Under `services`, we define a service named `hr-service`, which is built using the Dockerfile in the current directory (`build:   .`). The `ports` section maps port `3001` on the host machine to port `3001` in the container, allowing external access to the service. The `environment` section sets the `NODE_ENV` environment variable to `production`, ensuring that the microservice runs in production mode within the container.

In this section on Dockerizing microservices, we've demonstrated how to effectively containerize the HR microservice using Docker and Docker Compose. By defining a Dockerfile and a `docker-compose.yml` file, we've laid the foundation for consistent, scalable, and portable deployment across different environments. This setup ensures that the HR microservice is ready to be deployed with ease, taking full advantage of Docker's capabilities.

Next, we'll explore how to deploy these Dockerized microservices to Kubernetes, enabling even greater scalability and management through container orchestration.

Deploying microservices to Kubernetes

Kubernetes provides powerful tools for deploying, scaling, and managing containerized applications.

The following is an example setup for deploying the HR microservice to Kubernetes:

```
# hr-service-deployment.yaml
apiVersion: apps/v1
kind: Deployment
metadata:
  name: hr-service
spec:
  replicas: 3
  selector:
    matchLabels:
      app: hr-service
  template:
    metadata:
      labels:
        app: hr-service
    spec:
      containers:
      - name: hr-service
        image: your-docker-repo/hr-service:latest
        ports:
        - containerPort: 3001
```

In this code snippet, we define a Kubernetes deployment for the HR microservice. Here, `apiVersion` and `kind` specify that this is a `Deployment` resource. The `metadata` section assigns a name to the deployment (`hr-service`). Under the `spec` section, we define that three replicas of this microservice should be created and managed. The `selector` and `template` sections ensure that the Pods created by this deployment are correctly labeled (`app: hr-service`), and the `containers` section specifies the Docker image to use (`your-docker-repo/hr-service:latest`) along with the port the container listens on (`3001`). This setup allows Kubernetes to automatically manage and scale the HR microservice across multiple instances.

Let's define a hr kubernete service with the following code snippet:

```
# hr-service-service.yaml
apiVersion: v1
kind: Service
metadata:
  name: hr-service
spec:
  selector:
    app: hr-service
  ports:
    - protocol: TCP
      port: 80
      targetPort: 3001
```

In this code snippet, we define a Kubernetes Service to expose the HR microservice to other services or external traffic. Let's delve into the code lines:

- `kind` is set to `Service`, and `metadata` gives it a name value (`hr-service`)
- The `spec` section includes a selector that matches the `app: hr-service` label from the deployment, ensuring the `hr` service routes traffic to the correct Pods
- The `ports` section maps port `80` on the service to port `3001` inside the container, allowing external clients to communicate with the microservice via the standard HTTP port

This section has covered the deployment of a microservice to Kubernetes, showcasing how Kubernetes can efficiently manage and scale containerized applications such as the HR microservice. By creating `Deployment` and `Service` resources, Kubernetes handles the complexities of scaling, load balancing, and service discovery, ensuring that your microservices are resilient and scalable.

Next, we'll delve into implementing security best practices to protect your microservices, ensuring they remain secure in production environments.

Implementing security best practices

Ensuring security in microservices is crucial. Here are some best practices:

- *Authentication and authorization*: Use OAuth2 and JWT for secure authentication and authorization across microservices. The following code shows an example of authentication:

```
import { Injectable } from '@nestjs/common';
import { JwtService } from '@nestjs/jwt';

@Injectable()
export class AuthService {
  constructor(private jwtService: JwtService) {}

  async validateUser(username: string, pass: string):
    Promise<any>
  {
    // Validate user logic
  }

  async login(user: any) {
    const payload = {
      username: user.username,
      sub: user.userId
    };
    return {
      access_token: this.jwtService.sign(payload),
    };
  }
}
```

In this code snippet, we define an `AuthService` class responsible for handling authentication logic within a NestJS application. The service is marked as `@Injectable`, making it available for dependency injection throughout the application.

The `AuthService` constructor injects an instance of `JwtService`, which is part of the `@nestjs/jwt` module and is used for creating and managing **JSON Web Tokens (JWTs)**.

The `validateUser` method is intended to contain the logic for validating a user based on their username and password. It returns a Promise that would typically resolve to the authenticated user's data if validation were successful.

The `login` method takes a `user` object as input and creates a JWT payload containing `username` and `userId` (sub is a standard claim in JWT representing the subject). The method then generates an access token using the `JwtService` sign method, returning it as part of an object. This access token can then be used by the client for authenticated requests.

- *Secure communication*: Use HTTPS and secure communication protocols between microservices. Here is an example of how you can secure an inter-service communication:

```
import { NestFactory } from '@nestjs/core';
import { AppModule } from './app.module';
import * as fs from 'fs';

async function bootstrap() {
  const httpsOptions = {
    key: fs.readFileSync('path/to/private-key.pem'),
    cert: fs.readFileSync(
      'path/to/public-certificate.pem'
    ),
  };
  const app = await NestFactory.create(
    AppModule, { httpsOptions }
  );
  await app.listen(3000);
}
bootstrap();
```

In this code snippet, we configure secure communication for a NestJS application by enabling HTTPS. The `NestFactory.create` method is used to create an instance of the application, and we pass an `httpsOptions` object to configure HTTPS.

The `httpsOptions` object contains the paths to the private key and public certificate files, which are read using `fs.readFileSync`. These files are essential for setting up a secure HTTPS connection. Here, `key` represents the server's private key, and `cert` represents the corresponding public SSL/TLS certificate.

Finally, the application is set to listen on port `3000`, ensuring that all communication to and from the service is encrypted using HTTPS, thus securing inter-service communication.

- *Rate limiting and throttling*: Implement rate limiting and throttling to protect microservices from abuse. The following shows a sample implementation:

```
import {
  Injectable,
  NestMiddleware
} from '@nestjs/common';
import * as rateLimit from 'express-rate-limit';

@Injectable()
export class RateLimiterMiddleware implements
  NestMiddleware
{
```

```
use(req: Request, res: Response, next: Function) {
  rateLimit({
    windowMs: 15 * 60 * 1000, // 15 minutes
    max: 100, // limit each IP to 100 requests per
              // windowMs
  })(req, res, next);
  }
}
```

In the preceding code, we add a limit of 100 requests from the same IP address in the last 15 minutes, which can be adjusted depending on the application user's needs.

By following this comprehensive guide, you can build, deploy, and manage microservices effectively in a NestJS application. This approach ensures that your ERP system is scalable, modular, secure, and maintainable, allowing it to adapt to changing business needs efficiently.

Data synchronization and consistency in an ERP context

In an ERP system, ensuring **data synchronization and consistency** across different modules and microservices is crucial for maintaining the integrity and reliability of the system. This section provides a comprehensive guide to achieving data synchronization and consistency in an ERP context, covering various strategies and best practices.

Understanding data consistency models

Before diving into the implementation, it's essential to understand the different data consistency models:

- *Strong consistency*: Guarantees that all nodes contain the same data at the same time
- *Eventual consistency*: Ensures that, given enough time, all nodes will converge to the same data state
- *Causal consistency*: Preserves the causal relationships between operations
- *Read-your-writes consistency*: Ensures that once a write is acknowledged, any subsequent read will reflect that write

In an ERP system, choosing the right consistency model depends on the specific requirements of each module.

Data synchronization strategies

There are several strategies to synchronize data across microservices in an ERP system. We'll discuss some of these strategies in the subsequent sections.

Event-driven architecture

In an event-driven architecture, microservices communicate by emitting and listening to events. This approach helps maintain data consistency by propagating changes across services in real time.

Implementing event-driven communication

Follow the steps below to implement an event-driven communication:

1. **Event emitter**: A service emits an event when there is a change in its data:

```
import { Injectable } from '@nestjs/common';
import { EventEmitter2 } from '@nestjs/event-emitter';

@Injectable()
export class InventoryService {
  constructor(private eventEmitter: EventEmitter2) {}

  updateStock(productId: number, quantity: number) {
    // Update stock logic
    this.eventEmitter.emit(
      'stock.updated', { productId, quantity }
    );
  }
}
```

2. **Event listener**: Another service listens to the event and updates its data accordingly:

```
import {
  Injectable,
  OnModuleInit
} from '@nestjs/common';
import { EventEmitter2 } from '@nestjs/event-emitter';

@Injectable()
export class OrderService implements OnModuleInit {
  constructor(private eventEmitter: EventEmitter2) {}

  onModuleInit() {
    this.eventEmitter.on('stock.updated', (event) => {
      // Handle stock updated event
      this.updateOrderStock(
        event.productId,
        event.quantity
      );
```

```
      });
    }

    updateOrderStock(
      productId: number,
      quantity: number
    ) {
      // Update order stock logic
    }
  }
```

Event-driven communication is needed where we have asynchronous operation interactions between services.

Now, let's see how to implement synchronous ones when needed in the next section.

Synchronous communication

Synchronous communication involves direct calls between services, ensuring that all services have the latest data before proceeding. This is often used for critical operations that require immediate consistency.

Implementing synchronous communication

Now, let's look at the steps for implementing synchronous communication:

1. **Client service**: A service that calls another service to get the latest data as shown in the code snippet below:

    ```
    import { Injectable } from '@nestjs/common';
    import {
      ClientProxy,
      ClientProxyFactory,
      Transport
    } from '@nestjs/microservices';

    @Injectable()
    export class BillingService {
      private client: ClientProxy;

      constructor() {
        this.client = ClientProxyFactory.create({
          transport: Transport.TCP,
          options: {
            host: '127.0.0.1',
            port: 3002,
    ```

```
      },
    });
  }

  async calculateTotal(orderId: number) {
    const order = await this.client.send(
      { cmd: 'get_order' },
      orderId
    ).toPromise();
    // Calculate total billing amount
  }
}
```

2. **Server service**: A service that responds to the request from the client service as implemented below:

```
import { Controller } from '@nestjs/common';
import {
  MessagePattern
} from '@nestjs/microservices';
import { OrderService } from './order.service';

@Controller()
export class OrderController {
  constructor(
    private readonly orderService: OrderService
  ) {}

  @MessagePattern({ cmd: 'get_order' })
  getOrder(orderId: number) {
    return this.orderService.getOrder(orderId);
  }
}
```

When a message or an event is handled by multiple services at a time, it becomes tricky to know whether they succeed or fail and then act accordingly. In the next section, we will explore how to implement distributed transactions between services.

Distributed transactions

Distributed transactions ensure that a series of operations across multiple services either all succeed or all fail. This is critical for maintaining consistency in operations that span multiple services.

Implementing the Saga pattern

The Saga pattern coordinates a series of local transactions across services, ensuring that either all transactions are completed successfully or compensating actions are taken to roll back changes. Let's look at the steps for implementing the Saga pattern:

1. **Orchestrator service**: This manages the flow of the saga:

    ```
    import { Injectable } from '@nestjs/common';
    import {
      ClientProxy,
      ClientProxyFactory,
      Transport
    } from '@nestjs/microservices';

    @Injectable()
    export class OrderOrchestratorService {
      private client: ClientProxy;

      constructor() {
        this.client = ClientProxyFactory.create({
          transport: Transport.TCP,
          options: {
            host: '127.0.0.1',
            port: 3003,
          },
        });
      }

      async createOrder(orderData: any) {
        try {
          const order = await this.client.send(
            { cmd: 'create_order' },
            orderData
          ).toPromise();
          await this.client.send(
            { cmd: 'reserve_stock' },
            Order
          ).toPromise();
          await this.client.send(
            { cmd: 'create_invoice' },
            Order
          ).toPromise();
        } catch (error) {
    ```

```
        // Compensating transactions
        await this.client.send(
          { cmd: 'cancel_order' },
          orderData
        ).toPromise();
      }
    }
  }
```

2. **Participating services**: These handle their respective local transactions:

```
import { Controller } from '@nestjs/common';
import {
  MessagePattern
} from '@nestjs/microservices';
import { OrderService } from './order.service';

@Controller()
export class OrderController {
  constructor(
    private readonly orderService: OrderService
  ) {}

  @MessagePattern({ cmd: 'create_order' })
  createOrder(data: any) {
    return this.orderService.createOrder(data);
  }

  @MessagePattern({ cmd: 'cancel_order' })
  cancelOrder(data: any) {
    return this.orderService.cancelOrder(data);
  }
}
```

Now that we have the theoretical aspects of communication patterns and challenges, let's see how to implement data synchronization in our case study in the following section.

Implementing data synchronization in an ERP system

For real-time data synchronization, use WebSockets or message brokers (e.g., RabbitMQ or Kafka) to propagate data changes instantly.

Using WebSockets

Let's look at the steps for using WebSockets:

1. **WebSocket gateway**: This handles WebSocket connections and events:

```
import {
  WebSocketGateway,
  SubscribeMessage,
  WebSocketServer
} from '@nestjs/websockets';
import { Server } from 'socket.io';

@WebSocketGateway()
export class EventsGateway {
  @WebSocketServer()
  server: Server;

  @SubscribeMessage('update')
  handleUpdate(client: any, payload: any): void {
    this.server.emit('update', payload);
  }
}
```

2. **Client service**: This connects to the WebSocket server and listens for updates:

```
import { Injectable } from '@nestjs/common';
import { Socket, io } from 'socket.io-client';

@Injectable()
export class NotificationService {
  private socket: Socket;

  constructor() {
    this.socket = io('<http://localhost:3000>');
    this.socket.on('update', (data) => {
      this.handleUpdate(data);
    });
  }

  handleUpdate(data: any) {
    // Handle real-time update
  }
}
```

In this code snippet, the `NotificationService` class is responsible for establishing a WebSocket connection with a server to receive real-time updates.

The `Socket` instance is created using the `io` function from the `socket.io-client` library, connecting to a WebSocket server at `http://localhost:3000`. Once connected, the service listens for incoming messages on the `update` event using the `socket.on` method. When an `update` event is received, the `handleUpdate` method is invoked to process the incoming data.

This setup allows the service to receive and handle real-time notifications or updates, which is essential for applications that need to stay synchronized with server-side changes or events.

Periodic data synchronization

For less critical data that does not require real-time updates, implement periodic synchronization using CRON jobs or scheduled tasks.

Using CRON jobs

The **scheduler service** runs periodic synchronization tasks:

```
import { Injectable } from '@nestjs/common';
import { Cron } from '@nestjs/schedule';

@Injectable()
export class SyncService {
  @Cron('0 * * * *') // Runs every hour
  handleCron() {
    // Synchronization logic
  }
}
```

We've explored how WebSockets and periodic synchronization can be effectively used to ensure that your application stays up to date with the latest data changes. Whether you need instant updates through WebSocket connections or less frequent synchronization via cron jobs, these techniques help maintain data freshness and responsiveness in your application.

Next, we'll dive into the best practices for data consistency, where we'll cover strategies to ensure that your data remains accurate and reliable across distributed systems.

Data consistency best practices

For data consistency, here are the best practices to follow:

- **Idempotency**: Ensure that operations are idempotent, meaning they can be performed multiple times without causing inconsistent results:

```
import { Injectable } from '@nestjs/common';

@Injectable()
export class PaymentService {
  private processedTransactions = new Set();

  processTransaction(transactionId: string,
    amount: number)
  {
    if (this.processedTransactions.has(transactionId))
    {
      return; // Transaction already processed
    }

    // Process the transaction
    this.processedTransactions.add(transactionId);
  }
}
```

In this code snippet, the `PaymentService` class demonstrates how to implement idempotency in a payment processing system. Idempotency ensures that even if the same operation is performed multiple times, the result remains consistent and no duplicate actions occur.

Here's how it works:

- The `processedTransactions` set keeps track of the transaction IDs that have already been processed

- The `processTransaction` method takes in a transaction id and an amount

- Before processing the transaction, the method checks whether the `transactionId` already exists in the `processedTransactions` set

- If the transaction ID is found, the method simply returns, indicating that the transaction has already been processed

- If the transaction ID is not found, the transaction is processed, and the transaction ID is added to the `processedTransactions` set to prevent future reprocessing

This approach helps maintain data consistency by preventing duplicate transactions, which is especially crucial in systems where the same transaction might be inadvertently submitted multiple times due to retries or other factors.

- **Versioning**: Use version numbers or timestamps to manage concurrent updates and resolve conflicts:

```
import { Injectable } from '@nestjs/common';

@Injectable()
export class DocumentService {
  private documents = [];

  updateDocument(docId: string,
    newVersion: number, data: any)
  {
    const doc = this.documents.find(
      d => d.id === docId
    );

    if (doc.version >= newVersion) {
      throw new Error('Version conflict');
    }

    doc.version = newVersion;
    doc.data = data;
  }
}
```

- **Distributed locks**: Use distributed locking mechanisms to prevent concurrent modifications and ensure data integrity:

```
import { Injectable } from '@nestjs/common';
import * as Redlock from 'redlock';

@Injectable()
export class LockService {
  private redlock: Redlock;

  constructor() {
    this.redlock = new Redlock([/* Redis clients */]);
  }

  async acquireLock(resource: string, ttl: number) {
    return this.redlock.lock(resource, ttl);
  }
}
```

```
    async releaseLock(lock: any) {
      return lock.unlock();
    }
  }
```

Ensuring data synchronization and consistency in an ERP system is vital for maintaining the reliability and integrity of the system. By implementing strategies such as event-driven architecture, synchronous communication, and distributed transactions, and following best practices such as idempotency, versioning, and distributed locks, you can achieve robust data synchronization and consistency across your microservices.

Handling complex business processes and workflows

Managing complex business processes and workflows is a critical aspect of an ERP system. This section provides a detailed guide on how to design, implement, and manage these processes using best practices and practical examples. We will cover workflow modeling, orchestration, automation, and error handling to ensure your ERP system can efficiently handle intricate business scenarios.

Understanding business processes and workflows

Business processes are sets of structured activities designed to achieve a specific business goal. Workflows represent the sequence of these activities and the flow of information between them. In an ERP system, handling complex workflows involves coordinating various tasks across multiple modules and services.

Here are the key components of a workflow:

- *Tasks*: Individual units of work within a process

- *Events*: Triggers that start, pause, or end tasks

- *Decisions*: Conditional logic that determines the path of the workflow

- *Actors*: Users or systems responsible for executing tasks

- *Artifacts*: Data or documents used and produced during the workflow

This overview of workflows in an ERP system provides a foundational understanding of how tasks, events, decisions, actors, and artifacts work together to achieve business goals. Each component plays a critical role in ensuring that processes are carried out efficiently and effectively.

Next, we'll delve into modeling business processes, where we'll explore how these components come together in a structured model to represent and optimize business operations.

Modeling business processes

Modeling business processes is the first step in handling complex workflows. Tools such as **Business Process Model and Notation (BPMN)** are commonly used for this purpose.

Let's see how we can create a BPMN diagram:

- *Identify the process*: Define the scope and objective of the process.
- *Map the tasks*: List all tasks involved in the process.
- *Define events and decisions*: Identify triggers and decision points.
- *Assign roles*: Specify the actors responsible for each task.
- *Document artifacts*: List the data and documents used in the process.

With the foundational steps of modeling business processes outlined (identifying processes, mapping tasks, defining events and decisions, assigning roles, and documenting artifacts), you can create a clear and structured BPMN diagram. This diagram will serve as a valuable blueprint for understanding and optimizing your workflow.

Figure 14.1 shows an example of a BPNM diagram in an e-commerce context:

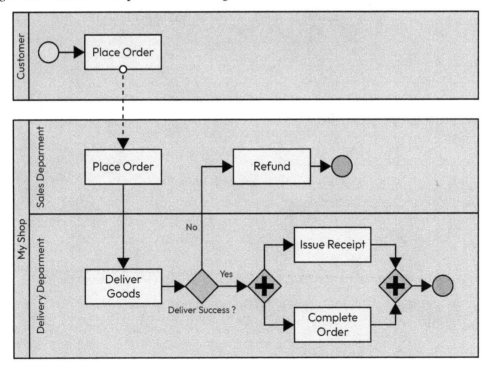

Figure 14.1 – Sample BNMP diagram (credit: https://www.visual-paradigm.com/)

Now, let's move on to orchestrating business processes, where we'll explore how to coordinate and manage these modeled processes to ensure smooth and efficient execution across different systems and teams.

Orchestrating business processes

Orchestration involves managing the execution of workflows, ensuring that tasks are completed in the correct sequence and data flows smoothly between them.

Implementing orchestration with NestJS

Here are the steps for implementing orchestration with NestJS:

1. **Workflow orchestrator service**: This manages the overall process and coordinates tasks:

```
import { Injectable } from '@nestjs/common';
import { TaskService } from './task.service';

@Injectable()
export class WorkflowOrchestratorService {
  constructor(
    private readonly taskService: TaskService
  ) {}

  async startWorkflow(data: any) {
    const step1Result =
      await this.taskService.executeStep1(data);
    const step2Result =
      await this.taskService.executeStep2(
        step1Result
      );
    await this.taskService.finalizeWorkflow(
      step2Result
    );
  }
}
```

2. **Task service**: This contains the logic for individual tasks within the workflow:

```
import { Injectable } from '@nestjs/common';

@Injectable()
export class TaskService {
  async executeStep1(data: any) {
    // Step 1 logic
```

```
    return step1Result;
  }

  async executeStep2(data: any) {
    // Step 2 logic
    return step2Result;
  }

  async finalizeWorkflow(data: any) {
    // Final step logic
  }
}
```

With the orchestration setup complete, you can now effectively coordinate complex workflows. Next, we'll explore automating business processes to enhance efficiency and minimize manual intervention.

Automating business processes

Automation involves using technology to perform tasks without human intervention, increasing efficiency and reducing errors.

Implementing automation with NestJS

Follow these steps to implement automation with NestJS:

1. **Scheduler service**: This automates the execution of tasks at predefined intervals:

   ```
   import { Injectable } from '@nestjs/common';
   import { Cron } from '@nestjs/schedule';

   @Injectable()
   export class AutomationService {
     @Cron('0 0 * * *') // Runs daily at midnight
     handleCron() {
       // Automation logic
     }
   }
   ```

2. **Event-driven automation**: This uses events to trigger automated tasks:

   ```
   import { Injectable } from '@nestjs/common';
   import { EventEmitter2 } from '@nestjs/event-emitter';

   @Injectable()
   export class AutomationService {
   ```

```
  constructor(private eventEmitter: EventEmitter2) {}

  automateProcess(data: any) {
    this.eventEmitter.emit('process.automate', data);
  }
}
```

Next, let's discover how to handle errors in your next workflows.

Error handling in workflows

Effective error handling is crucial for managing exceptions and ensuring the reliability of workflows.

Implementing error handling

Let's look at the steps for implementing error handling:

1. **Retry mechanism**: This automatically retries failed tasks:

```
import { Injectable } from '@nestjs/common';

@Injectable()
export class ErrorHandlingService {
  async retryTask(task: Function, retries: number) {
    let attempts = 0;
    while (attempts < retries) {
      try {
        await task();
        break;
      } catch (error) {
        attempts++;
        if (attempts === retries) {
          throw new Error(
            'Task failed after maximum retries'
          );
        }
      }
    }
  }
}
```

2. **Compensating transactions**: Roll back changes if an error occurs:

```
import { Injectable } from '@nestjs/common';

@Injectable()
export class CompensatingTransactionService {
  async compensate(data: any) {
    // Logic to rollback changes
  }
}
```

With automation in place, you can streamline your business processes, making them more efficient and reducing the risk of human error. As we move forward, we'll explore how to handle integration with external systems to enhance the capabilities of your ERP system by connecting it with other platforms and services.

Integrating with external systems

ERP systems often need to integrate with external systems to complete workflows, such as payment gateways, third-party APIs, or legacy systems.

Implementing external integrations

Follow these steps to implement external integration:

1. *HTTP integration*: Use HTTP clients to communicate with external APIs:

```
import {
  Injectable,
  HttpService
} from '@nestjs/common';

@Injectable()
export class ExternalIntegrationService {
  constructor(private httpService: HttpService) {}

  async callExternalApi(data: any) {
    const response =
      await this.httpService.post(
        '<https://api.example.com>',
        Data
      ).toPromise();
    return response.data;
  }
}
```

2.   *Message brokers*: Use message brokers such as RabbitMQ or Kafka for asynchronous communication:

```
import { Injectable } from '@nestjs/common';
import {
  ClientProxy,
  ClientProxyFactory,
  Transport
} from '@nestjs/microservices';

@Injectable()
export class ExternalIntegrationService {
  private client: ClientProxy;

  constructor() {
    this.client = ClientProxyFactory.create({
      transport: Transport.RMQ,
      options: {
        urls: ['amqp://localhost:5672'],
        queue: 'external_queue',
        queueOptions: {
          durable: false
        },
      },
    });
  }

  async sendMessage(data: any) {
    return this.client.send(
      'external.event', data
    ).toPromise();
  }
}
```

With the integration of external systems in place, your ERP system can now interact seamlessly with other platforms and services. Moving forward, we'll discuss monitoring to ensure that your integrations and overall system perform optimally.

Monitoring and managing workflows

Effective monitoring and management tools are essential for tracking workflow progress, identifying bottlenecks, and troubleshooting issues.

Implementing monitoring with NestJS

Here are the steps for implementing monitoring with NestJS:

1. *Logging*: Use logging to track workflow execution and errors:

```
import { Injectable, Logger } from '@nestjs/common';

@Injectable()
export class MonitoringService {
  private readonly logger =
    new Logger(MonitoringService.name);

  logWorkflowStart(workflowId: string) {
    this.logger.log(`Workflow ${workflowId} started`);
  }

  logWorkflowError(workflowId: string, error: Error) {
    this.logger.error(
      `Workflow ${workflowId} error:
      ${error.message}`
    );
  }

  logWorkflowCompletion(workflowId: string) {
    this.logger.log(
      `Workflow ${workflowId} completed`
    );
  }
}
```

2. *Metrics*: Use metrics to monitor workflow performance and health:

```
import { Injectable } from '@nestjs/common';
import { Gauge } from 'prom-client';

@Injectable()
export class MetricsService {
  private readonly workflowDuration = new Gauge({
    name: 'workflow_duration_seconds',
    help: 'Duration of workflow execution in seconds',
  });

  recordWorkflowDuration(seconds: number) {
    this.workflowDuration.set(seconds);
  }
}
```

Handling complex business processes and workflows in an ERP system involves careful planning, orchestration, automation, error handling, integration, and monitoring. By following the strategies and best practices outlined in this section, you can design and implement robust workflows that enhance the efficiency and reliability of your ERP system.

Summary

In this chapter, we embarked on the journey of building a real-life ERP system with NestJS, focusing on design, implementation, and best practices. We covered the following key areas.

We began by understanding the requirements of an ERP system, identifying the core functional and non-functional needs, and defining user roles and permissions to ensure the system meets business and user expectations.

Next, we designed the system architecture, leveraging microservices to achieve scalability and modularity. We explored the high-level architecture, database design, and communication patterns, ensuring a robust and efficient structure for our ERP system.

We then implemented microservices, focusing on creating scalable and maintainable services. We covered service decomposition, communication, and fault tolerance, providing practical code examples and best practices.

We delved into data synchronization and consistency, employing event-driven architecture, synchronous communication, and distributed transactions to maintain data integrity and reliability across microservices.

Finally, we tackled handling complex business processes and workflows, modeling workflows, orchestrating tasks, automating processes, and managing errors. We integrated external systems and implemented monitoring to ensure smooth and efficient operations.

Throughout this chapter, we solidified our understanding of building a comprehensive ERP system with NestJS, addressing real-world challenges, and applying best practices. With this foundation, you are now equipped to develop robust and scalable enterprise applications.

In the next chapter, we will explore a new use case, diving into advanced topics and further expanding your skills in modern web development. Get ready to take on the next challenge and continue your journey toward mastering NestJS and enterprise application development. See you in the next chapter!

Part 6:
Deployment, DevOps,
and Beyond

This part goes beyond and introduces you to the multiple ways in which you can deliver APIs built in NestJS, performance considerations, and the next steps to keep the skills you have gained up to date.

This part includes the following chapters:

- *Chapter 15, Deploying NestJS Applications*
- *Chapter 16, Embracing DevOps: Continuous Integration and Continuous Deployment for NestJS*
- *Chapter 17, NestJS Performance Optimization*
- *Chapter 18, NestJS Security Best Practices*

15

Deploying NestJS Applications

You've built your NestJS application, tested it, and ensured it's running smoothly. Now, it's time to take the next big step: ship it to the world. Welcome to the chapter where we transform your local development into a live, accessible service.

In this chapter, we'll guide you through the essential steps of deploying NestJS applications across various environments. Whether you're aiming for a local server setup or deploying to cloud platforms, we'll cover the necessary configurations and best practices. From ensuring security and performance optimization to handling environment-specific settings and monitoring, you'll gain the knowledge to launch your application to end users confidently.

We'll explore different deployment strategies, including the use of Docker for containerization and the various cloud platforms, such as AWS, Google Cloud, and more. Moreover, we'll discuss important post-deployment practices, such as monitoring, scaling, and securing your application in production.

For this chapter, here's what's on our agenda:

- Configuring a local server for production-like testing
- Deployment using Docker
- Deployment on cloud platforms
- Post-deployment best practices

By the end of this chapter, you'll not only be able to deploy your NestJS applications but also ensure they are secure, performant, and ready for the real world. Make sure you have your preferred deployment tools and cloud accounts set up as we dive into the world of deployment.

Let's begin this journey to make your application available to users everywhere.

Technical requirements

For this chapter, make sure you have your environment ready by following *Chapter 3*.

You must also refer back to *Chapter 12* for setting up your project.

Configuring a local server for production-like testing

Before we move on to the actual configuration, let's make sure we have our NestJS application ready.

Preparing your NestJS application for deployment

Before diving into the deployment process, it's essential to have a concrete project to work with. For this chapter, we will use the e-commerce application developed in *Chapter 12* as our reference use case. This REST API project provides a comprehensive base that can be applied to other projects in the future, making it an ideal starting point.

To follow along, you'll need to do the following:

- **Use the** *Chapter 12* **project**: We recommend using the e-commerce application from *Chapter 12* as it covers a broad range of functionalities, including REST API endpoints, database integration, and authentication mechanisms. If you've already worked through *Chapter 12*, ensure your project is up and running locally.

- **Clone the repository**: If you don't have the project ready or prefer to start fresh, you can clone the project from our book's GitHub repository. Please visit the following link to access the repository: `https://github.com/PacktPublishing/Scalable-Application-Development-with-NestJS/tree/main/ch12`. Ensure you have all dependencies installed and the application is running locally.

Having the project set up is crucial before we configure and prepare it for deployment. We'll cover essential tasks such as environment variable management, production build processes, and optimizing the application for deployment. If you encounter any challenges starting the project locally, make sure you have a look at *Chapter 7*, where we armed ourselves with debugging and testing knowledge.

Once you're ready with the project, we can proceed to prepare it for the deployment stages. Let's get started!

Now, we'll take a closer look at configuring a local server environment that mimics a production setup. This step is crucial for catching potential issues early and ensuring a smooth transition when deploying to actual production servers.

In this section, we will guide you through the following:

- Setting up a local server (NGINX, Apache, etc.)
- Configuring SSL for HTTPS
- Basic monitoring and logging

By the end of this section, you will have a more robust local environment that closely mirrors a production setup, enhancing your application's reliability and performance. Let's dive in and start by setting up a local server.

Setting up a local server (NGINX, Apache, etc.)

To create a production-like environment, we will set up a local server using NGINX. **NGINX** is a popular choice for serving applications, acting as a reverse proxy, and handling static content efficiently. Let's begin:

1. **Install NGINX:**

   Follow these steps to install NGINX locally:

   I.   On Ubuntu/Debian, use these commands:

   ```
   $ sudo apt update
   $ sudo apt install NGINX
   ```

   II.   On macOS, use Homebrew:

   ```
   $ brew install NGINX
   ```

   III. On Windows, follow this guide to get it installed: https://NGINX.org/en/docs/windows.html

2. **Configure NGINX:**

   With NGINX installed on your local machine, it's time to set it up by following these simple steps:

   I.   Open the NGINX configuration file

   II.   Use the following code to open your NGINX configuration file:

   ```
   $ sudo nano /etc/NGINX/sites-available/e-commerce-sample
   ```

   For macOS users, the NGINX configuration file is located at /usr/local/etc/NGINX/NGINX.conf for users with an Intel-based processor and at /opt/homebrew/etc/NGINX/NGINX.conf for those with one of the Apple silicon chips. Make sure you are editing the correct file depending on your hardware. Note that the configuration may vary depending on your operating system. For a different operating system than macOS, make sure you follow the NGINX official guide here: https://NGINX.org/en/docs/beginners_guide.html.

The preceding command will open the configuration file in an editor for you. Now, add the following configuration to serve your NestJS application and make sure this server block is added under the HTTP block for Apple users:

```
server {
    listen       80;
    server_name  localhost;

    location / {
        proxy_pass http://localhost:3000;
        proxy_http_version 1.1;
        proxy_set_header Upgrade $http_upgrade;
        proxy_set_header Connection 'upgrade';
        proxy_set_header Host $host;
        proxy_cache_bypass $http_upgrade;
    }
}
```

The preceding configuration file tells our NGINX proxy server which port to listen to (80) and the `location` / block tells NGINX what to do with any incoming request, which allows us to point the proxy port to our actual application using the `proxy_pass` parameter.

After the installation and configuration are completed, let's start to use NGINX in the next steps.

3. **Start NGINX**:

    I.   On Ubuntu/Debian, use the following command:

    ```
    $ sudo systemctl start NGINX
    ```

    II.   On macOS, use the following command:

    ```
    $ sudo NGINX
    ```

4. **Test the NGINX configuration**:

    Open a web browser and navigate to `http://localhost`. You should see your NestJS application running with the expected response, as shown in *Figure 15.1*.

Figure 15.1: NGINX server serving our NestJS application

With NGINX configured and your application running on a local server, you now have a basic production-like environment. However, in real-world production scenarios, securing communication between your server and users is crucial. That's where SSL comes into play.

Next, we'll take things a step further by configuring SSL for HTTPS to ensure encrypted and secure communication. This is particularly important for handling sensitive data, such as user information or payment transactions.

Configuring SSL for HTTPS

Securing your application with HTTPS is crucial for protecting data in transit and building user trust. We'll set up a self-signed SSL certificate for local testing. Let's start:

1. **Generate a self-signed SSL certificate**:

   To do that, run the following commands in your terminal:

   ```
   $ sudo openssl req -x509 -nodes -days 365 -newkey rsa:2048
   -keyout /etc/ssl/private/NGINX-selfsigned.key -out /etc/ssl/
   certs/NGINX-selfsigned.crt
   ```

2. **Configure NGINX for HTTPS**:

   To do that, modify the NGINX configuration file to include SSL settings:

   ```
   server {
       Listen 80;
       listen 443 ssl;
       server_name localhost;

       ssl_certificate
           /etc/ssl/certs/NGINX-selfsigned.crt;
       ssl_certificate_key
           /etc/ssl/private/NGINX-selfsigned.key;

       location / {
           proxy_pass http://localhost:3000;
           proxy_http_version 1.1;
           proxy_set_header Upgrade $http_upgrade;
           proxy_set_header Connection 'upgrade';
           proxy_set_header Host $host;
           proxy_cache_bypass $http_upgrade;
       }
   }
   ```

For macOS users, you may need to create new folders to store your key – following this article would help: `https://arjav-dave.medium.com/self-signed-ssl-NGINX-on-mac-part-3-ed484e7b6911`

3. **Restart NGINX**:

    Restart NGINX to apply the following changes:

    ```
    $ sudo systemctl restart NGINX
    # or
    $ sudo NGINX -s stop && sudo NGINX
    ```

4. **Test the HTTPS configuration**:

    To do that, open a web browser and navigate to `https://localhost`. You should see a warning about the self-signed certificate, as shown in *Figure 15.2*, which you can bypass for local testing.

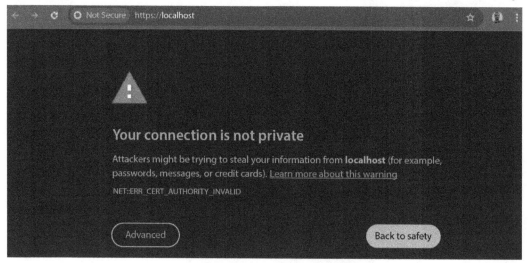

Figure 15.2: Starting the local server with SSL enabled

We have been able to start our application using NGINX locally and configure an SSL connection. Now let's see how we can monitor our application locally, mirroring the expected behavior in a production-like environment.

Basic monitoring and logging

Monitoring and logging are essential for diagnosing issues and understanding your application's behavior. We will now set up basic monitoring and logging using tools such as PM2 and built-in NGINX logs:

1. **Install PM2**:

    PM2 is a process manager for Node.js applications that includes built-in monitoring and logging. In your terminal, use the following command to install PM2 globally:

    ```
    $ npm install pm2 -g
    ```

2. **Start your application with PM2**:

    Start your NestJS application using PM2 by running the following command in the root of your application:

    ```
    $ pm2 start dist/main.js --name nest-app
    ```

    This command will start your NestJS application, as shown in *Figure 15.3*.

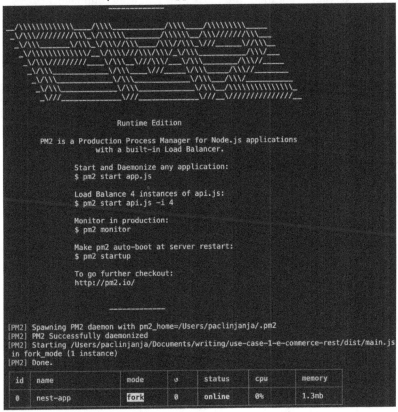

Figure 15.3: Using PM2 to start our NestJS application

3. **View logs**:

PM2 provides logs for your application. Run the following command in the root of your application:

```
$ pm2 logs nest-app
```

4. **NGINX logs**:

NGINX logs requests and errors. You can view these logs by running the following command anywhere in your terminal:

```
$ sudo tail -f /var/log/NGINX/access.log /var/log/NGINX/error.
log
```

5. **Monitor application performance**:

PM2 provides built-in performance monitoring, allowing you to monitor your application's status, memory usage, CPU consumption, and more in real time. This feature is especially useful when managing production systems, helping you maintain system health and identify issues early.

To monitor your application, you can use the following command:

```
$ pm2 monit
```

You have created a robust local production-like environment by setting up a local server with NGINX, configuring SSL for HTTPS, and implementing basic monitoring and logging. This setup will help you catch potential issues early and ensure your application is ready for seamless deployment to production servers.

Next, we'll move on to deploying your application to cloud services, where we will explore different platforms and their specific configurations. Stay tuned!

Deployment using Docker

In the previous sections, we configured a local server to mimic a production environment. Now, we'll take a more versatile approach by containerizing our NestJS application using Docker. Docker allows us to package our application and its dependencies into a portable container, ensuring consistent behavior across different environments, whether it's your local machine, a staging server, or a production.

In this section, we'll focus on deploying our sample application using Docker. We'll walk through the process of creating a Dockerfile, building a Docker image, and running it as a container. While we won't cover Docker basics in detail, we'll guide you to the official Docker documentation for any setup or background knowledge you may need.

Here's what we'll cover:

- Creating a Dockerfile for your NestJS application
- Building and running your Docker container
- Optimizing your Docker image for production

By the end of this section, you'll have a Dockerized version of your NestJS application that can be easily deployed to any environment. Let's get started with creating the Dockerfile.

Creating a Dockerfile for your NestJS application

A **Dockerfile** is essentially a set of commands that define how to build a Docker image. It outlines the base image, includes necessary dependencies, and provides instructions to configure and run the application within the container.

To create a Dockerfile, in the root directory of your NestJS project, create a new file named `Dockerfile` with the following content:

```
# Use an official Node.js runtime as a parent image
FROM node:16-alpine

# Set the working directory in the container
WORKDIR /usr/src/app

# Copy the package.json and package-lock.json files
COPY package*.json ./

# Install dependencies
RUN npm install --production

# Copy the rest of the application code
COPY . .

# Build the application
RUN npm run build

# Expose the port the app runs on
EXPOSE 3000

# Define the command to run the application
CMD ["node", "dist/main.js"]
```

In the preceding Dockerfile configuration, we have the following:

- **Base image**: We use the `node:16-alpine` image, which is a lightweight version of Node.js, ensuring a smaller Docker image size

- **Working directory**: The `WORKDIR` command sets the directory inside the container where commands will be run

- **Copying files**: `COPY package*.json ./` copies the package files, and `COPY . .` copies the entire project to the container

- **Install dependencies**: `RUN npm install --production` installs only production dependencies

- **Building the application**: `RUN npm run build` compiles the TypeScript code into JavaScript

- **Exposing ports**: The `EXPOSE 3000` command makes the application accessible on port 3000

- **Start command**: `CMD ["node", "dist/main.js"]` defines the command to start the application inside the container.

Now, let's run the container.

Building and running your Docker container

Once you've created your Dockerfile, the next step is to build the Docker image and run it as a container. Let's do it:

1. **Build the Docker image**:

   I.   Open your terminal, navigate to your project's root directory, and run the following command:

   ```
   $ docker build -t nestjs-app .
   ```

   II.   This command builds the Docker image and tags it as `nestjs-app`.

2. **Run the Docker container**:

   I.   After building the image, you can run it using this:

   ```
   $ docker run -p 3000:3000 nestjs-app
   ```

   II.   The `-p 3000:3000` flag maps port 3000 of the container to port 3000 on your local machine, making the application accessible at `http://localhost:3000`.

3. **Test the application**:

   Open a browser and navigate to `http://localhost:3000` to verify that your application is running inside the Docker container.

With your Docker container running successfully, the next step is to optimize it for production, focusing on reducing the image size, improving security, and streamlining performance. In the following section, we'll dive into best practices for creating a leaner, more efficient Docker image suitable for deployment in real-world environments.

Optimizing your Docker image for production

While the Dockerfile we created works well for local testing, there are a few optimizations we can make for a production environment:

- **Use multi-stage builds**:

  Multi-stage builds allow you to use a different base image for the build and runtime environments, reducing the final image size:

  ```
  # Build stage
  FROM node:16-alpine AS builder
  WORKDIR /usr/src/app
  COPY package*.json ./
  RUN npm install --production
  COPY . .
  RUN npm run build

  # Production stage
  FROM node:16-alpine
  WORKDIR /usr/src/app
  COPY --from=builder /usr/src/app .
  EXPOSE 3000
  CMD ["node", "dist/main.js"]
  ```

  In the code provided, we first use a build stage (`FROM node:16-alpine AS builder`) to compile the application. This stage installs dependencies, copies project files, and runs the `build` command. In the production stage (`FROM node:16-alpine`), only the compiled application from the build stage is copied into a fresh image, leaving out unnecessary build files and dependencies, which optimizes the image size for production.

- **Minimize layers**:

  Combine multiple `RUN` commands into one to minimize the number of layers in the image, reducing its size.

- **Security considerations**:

  Ensure that sensitive information, such as environment variables, is managed securely using Docker secrets or other secure methods.

By following the preceding list, you now have a Dockerized NestJS application that is optimized for deployment. This container can be easily deployed to various environments, from local machines to cloud services, ensuring consistency and reliability across the board.

In the next section, we'll explore deploying your Dockerized application to cloud platforms, where we'll walk through specific configurations and best practices for various cloud environments. Get ready to take your deployment skills to the next level!

Deployment on Cloud platforms

With your NestJS application now containerized using Docker, the next logical step is deploying it to a cloud platform. Cloud platforms offer scalable infrastructure, ensuring that your application can handle varying levels of traffic without requiring you to manage physical servers. In this section, we will walk through deploying our Dockerized sample application on popular cloud platforms such as AWS, **Google Cloud Platform** (**GCP**), and Microsoft Azure.

We'll focus on the essential steps to get your application up and running on these platforms. While we won't dive deep into cloud-specific details, we'll provide links to the official documentation for further learning.

Here's what we'll cover:

- Deploying to AWS Elastic Beanstalk
- Deploying to Google Cloud Run
- Deploying to Azure App Service

By the end of this section, you'll have a clear understanding of how to deploy your NestJS application to multiple cloud environments, allowing you to choose the best platform for your needs.

Deploying to AWS Elastic Beanstalk

AWS Elastic Beanstalk is a **platform-as-a-service** (**PaaS**) that simplifies the process of deploying and scaling web applications. It automatically handles infrastructure details such as load balancing, scaling, and monitoring.

Follow these steps to deploy on AWS:

1. **Prepare your application for deployment**:

    I.   Ensure your Dockerized application is working locally. If it's functioning correctly, it's ready for the cloud.

    II. Zip the entire project directory, including the Dockerfile and other necessary files.

2. **Create an Elastic Beanstalk environment**:

    I.   Log in to the AWS Management Console (`https://aws.amazon.com/console/`) and navigate to the Elastic Beanstalk service.

    II. Create a new environment, choose **Web Server Environment**, and select Docker as the platform.

    III. Upload the ZIP file of your application when prompted.

3. **Deploy your application**:

AWS will automatically detect the Dockerfile and build the Docker image as part of the deployment process.

After deployment, AWS Elastic Beanstalk will provide a URL where your application is accessible.

Deploying to Google Cloud Run

Google Cloud Run is a fully managed compute platform that automatically scales your containerized application. It abstracts away the infrastructure, allowing you to focus solely on your application.

Follow these steps to deploy your application on GCP:

1. **Containerize your application**:

Ensure your Docker image is ready. You can test it locally with `docker run -p 3000:3000 nestjs-app`.

2. Deploy to Cloud Run:

   I.   Install and configure the Google Cloud SDK if you haven't already.

   II. Push your Docker image to Google Container Registry:

   ```
   $ gcloud auth configure-docker
   $ docker tag nestjs-app gcr.io/your-project-id/nestjs-app
   $ docker push gcr.io/your-project-id/nestjs-app
   ```

   III. Deploy the image to Cloud Run:

   ```
   $ gcloud run deploy --image gcr.io/your-project-id/nestjs-app
   --platform managed
   ```

During the deployment, Cloud Run will provide a URL where your application can be accessed.

Deploying to Azure App Service

Azure App Service is a PaaS offering from Microsoft Azure that enables you to deploy web apps without managing infrastructure. It supports various programming languages and frameworks, including Docker.

Follow these instructions to deploy web applications on Azure:

1. **Prepare your Docker image**:

Ensure your Docker image is tagged and pushed to a container registry such as Docker Hub or Azure Container Registry.

2. **Deploy to Azure App Service**:

    I.   Log in to the Azure portal (`https://portal.azure.com/#home`) and create a new Web App resource.

    II.   Select Docker as the deployment source and provide the Docker image details.

    III. Azure App Service will pull the Docker image from the specified registry and deploy it.

3. **Access your application**:

    After deployment, Azure provides a URL where your application is accessible.

Now that you've seen how to deploy your NestJS application to different cloud platforms, you have the flexibility to choose the one that best fits your project's needs. Each platform has its own strengths, so consider factors such as cost, scalability, and ease of use when making your decision. In the next section, we'll discuss best practices for managing your deployed applications, including monitoring, logging, and scaling strategies. Let's continue optimizing our cloud deployments!

Post-deployment best practices

Congratulations on deploying your NestJS application! However, the work doesn't stop here. Ensuring that your application continues to perform well and remains secure is an ongoing process. This section will cover essential post-deployment best practices that will help you maintain, monitor, and optimize your application in a production environment.

Here's what we'll cover:

- Monitoring and logging
- Security and updates
- Backup and disaster recovery
- Scaling and load balancing

By the end of this section, you'll have a clear understanding of the steps required to keep your application running smoothly in production, minimizing downtime and protecting your data.

Monitoring and logging

Monitoring and **logging** are critical to understanding the health and performance of your application in production. They allow you to detect issues before they impact users and provide insights into how your application is being used.

In a production-like environment, follow this guide to implement monitoring in your application:

1. **Set up application monitoring**:

   I.   Use tools such as **Prometheus** and **Grafana** to monitor metrics such as CPU usage, memory consumption, and request rates.

   II.   Integrate **Application Performance Monitoring (APM)** solutions such as **New Relic** or **Datadog** to track application performance and identify bottlenecks.

2. **Implement logging**:

   I.   Configure structured logging using libraries such as **Winston** or **Pino** in your NestJS application. Ensure that logs are output in a format compatible with log management tools.

   II.   Use centralized logging solutions such as **ELK Stack**, also known as **Elasticsearch**, **Logstash**, **Kibana**, or **Splunk** to aggregate and analyze logs.

Security and updates

Maintaining the security of your application is crucial in a production environment. Regularly applying updates and patches, as well as following security best practices, can prevent vulnerabilities.

- **Regularly update dependencies**:

  - Use tools such as `npm audit` to identify and fix vulnerabilities in your project's dependencies.

  - Schedule regular updates for your Docker base images to ensure that they include the latest security patches.

- **Implement security best practices**:

  - Use HTTPS to encrypt data in transit, ensuring that sensitive information such as user credentials is protected.

  - Implement rate limiting and input validation to prevent common attacks such as DDoS and SQL injection.

- **Use environment variables securely**:

  Store sensitive information such as API keys and database credentials in environment variables. Ensure these variables are not hardcoded or exposed in your application's source code.

Backup and disaster recovery

No system is immune to failure, so it's essential to have a backup and disaster recovery plan in place. These plans ensure that your application can quickly recover from unexpected issues such as data loss, system failures, or cyber attacks.

You can do either of the following:

- **Implement regular backups**:

  - Use tools such as `pg_dump` for PostgreSQL to create regular backups of your application's database.

  - Store backups in a secure, off-site location using services such as Amazon S3 or Google Cloud Storage.

- **Develop a disaster recovery plan**:

  - Define **Recovery Time Objectives (RTOs)** and **Recovery Point Objectives (RPOs)** to set clear goals for system recovery in a disaster.

  - Test your disaster recovery plan regularly to ensure that backups can be restored quickly and accurately.

Scaling and load balancing

As your application grows, it's important to ensure that it can handle increased traffic and maintain high availability. **Scaling** and **load balancing** strategies help distribute traffic across multiple instances of your application, preventing overload on a single server.

To implement auto scaling, use cloud services such as **AWS Auto Scaling**, **Google Cloud Autoscaler**, or **Azure Scale Sets** to automatically adjust the number of application instances based on traffic demand.

Now, to set up load balancing, do the following:

- Configure a load balancer to distribute incoming requests across multiple application instances. Popular options include **AWS Elastic Load Balancing (ELB)**, **NGINX**, and **HAProxy**.

- Ensure that your load balancer is configured for health checks to automatically route traffic away from unhealthy instances.

By implementing these post-deployment best practices, you can ensure that your application remains reliable, secure, and performant in a production environment. Regular monitoring, security updates, and disaster recovery planning are key to maintaining the health of your application. With your application now deployed and properly managed, you're well-equipped to handle the demands of a production environment.

Summary

In this chapter, we've taken crucial steps to ensure that your NestJS application is not only deployed but also well-prepared for the demands of a production environment. By configuring a local server for production-like testing, deploying using Docker, and leveraging cloud platforms, you've learned how to deploy your application across different environments easily. We've also covered essential post-deployment best practices, including monitoring, logging, security, backups, and scaling, to maintain and optimize your application once it's live.

As we move forward, we must focus on automating these processes. In the next chapter, we'll dive into **Continuous Integration and Continuous Deployment (CI/CD)** pipelines, enabling you to streamline your deployment workflows, ensure code quality, and make your deployments faster and more reliable. Stay tuned as we take your application development process to the next level.

Further reading

To dive deeper into the material used and listed in this chapter, take your time to explore the official documentation and resources here:

- **Amazon S3 Backup Strategies**: `https://aws.amazon.com/backup-storage/`
- **PostgreSQL Backup Documentation**: `https://www.postgresql.org/docs/current/backup-dump.html`
- **npm audit Documentation**: `https://docs.npmjs.com/cli/v7/commands/npm-audit`
- **Prometheus Documentation**: `https://prometheus.io/docs/introduction/overview/`
- **ELK Stack Documentation**: `https://www.elastic.co/what-is/elk-stack`
- **Azure App Service Documentation**: `https://docs.microsoft.com/en-us/azure/app-service/`
- **Google Cloud Run Documentation**: `https://cloud.google.com/run/docs`
- **AWS Elastic Beanstalk Documentation**: `https://docs.aws.amazon.com/elasticbeanstalk/latest/dg/Welcome.html`
- **NGINX Load Balancing Documentation**: `https://docs.nginx.com/nginx/admin-guide/load-balancer/http-load-balancer/`
- **AWS Auto Scaling Documentation**: `https://docs.aws.amazon.com/autoscaling/`

Get This Book's PDF Version and Exclusive Extras

Scan the QR code (or go to `packtpub.com/unlock`). Search for this book by name, confirm the edition, and then follow the steps on the page.

Note: Keep your invoice handly. Purchase made directly from packt don't require one.

16

Embracing DevOps: Continuous Integration and Continuous Deployment for NestJS

You've successfully deployed your NestJS application and made it accessible worldwide. However, in a dynamic development environment, where software developers need to write, test, and debug code in real time to meet evolving project requirements, deployment is just the beginning. How do you ensure that your code is always ready for production? How do you avoid the pitfalls of manual deployments that can slow down your development process and introduce errors? Welcome to the chapter where we integrate **continuous integration** (**CI**) and **continuous deployment** (**CD**) into your workflow, automating and optimizing the path from code to deployment.

In this chapter, we'll explore how CI/CD practices can transform your development process by automating the testing, building, and deploying of your application. You'll learn about the tools for setting up CI/CD pipelines and how to implement them specifically for your NestJS projects. Whether you're working in a small team or a large enterprise, adopting CI/CD will allow you to deliver updates more quickly and with greater confidence.

Here's what we'll cover in this chapter:

- Understanding CI and CD
- Choosing your CI/CD tools
- Setting up a CI/CD pipeline for NestJS
- CI/CD best practices

By the end of this chapter, you'll have a robust understanding of how to incorporate CI/CD into your NestJS applications, ensuring that every change you make to your code base can be safely and automatically deployed. Prepare to take your deployment process to the next level as we embrace **DevOps** and build a streamlined, efficient workflow that can handle continuous delivery with ease.

Understanding continuous integration and continuous deployment

In this section, we'll introduce you to the world of CI and CD, two core practices in DevOps that help automate and streamline the development process. DevOps is a portmanteau of Development and Operations. It represents a set of practices that bring together software development (Dev) and IT operations (Ops) to shorten the development life cycle and provide continuous delivery with high software quality. Essentially, DevOps is about breaking down the silos between development and operations teams to enhance collaboration and productivity.

While this book isn't focused on DevOps, it's essential to understand how CI/CD can benefit your NestJS applications, especially after deploying them in the previous chapter.

Continuous integration

CI refers to the automated process of frequently merging code changes from various contributors into a central repository throughout the day. The goal of CI is to detect errors quickly, allowing teams to address issues as soon as they arise. In the context of your NestJS application, CI ensures that any new code added to the project is automatically tested and validated, reducing the likelihood of bugs making it into production.

Continuous deployment

CD takes the concept of CI one step further by automatically deploying every change that passes the CI process to production. This means that every time a new feature or bug fix is committed, it is automatically pushed to the live application after passing tests. This approach ensures that the latest version of your application is always available to users, minimizing manual intervention.

Why is CI/CD important for your NestJS application?

In the previous chapter, we successfully deployed a NestJS application. However, deploying manually can be time-consuming and error-prone. CI/CD automates this process, ensuring that your application is always up to date, tested, and ready for users. Implementing CI/CD in your project leads to faster development cycles, more reliable releases, and less stress for the development team.

Figure 16.1 illustrates what a basic CI/CD pipeline should look like:

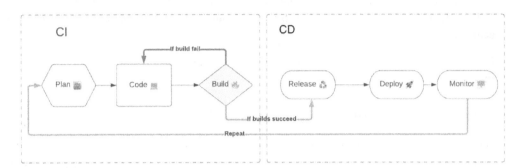

Figure 16.1 – CI/CD pipeline example

The diagram from *Figure 16.1* shows a basic CI/CD pipeline, where developers usually first plan. The plan is usually made through team meetings or meetings with the client. Then, a manager assigns tasks to developers before they start writing code and test everything locally. Next, developers need to make sure the changes made do not break any existing feature; this is done by building the project's bundle and running a series of tests. At this step, if anything fails, either the bundle throws an error or the tests (unit and/or integration and/or end-to-end), developers need to fix whatever bug the previous code introduced. Once the developer is confident with his builds, we need to release the changes so end users can start consuming the feature (if it was a new feature) or see the bug resolved (if it was a bug fix). We then need to deploy the changes, usually on different environments, before we start monitoring to check whether the change impacts the end user.

Now that you have a basic understanding of CI/CD and how it fits into DevOps, you're ready to explore the tools that make these practices possible. In the next section, we'll look at some of the most popular CI/CD tools available and how they can be integrated into your NestJS workflow. Let's dive into the tools that will help you automate and optimize your deployment process!

Choosing your CI/CD tools

With a solid understanding of CI/CD, the next step is to explore the tools that make these practices possible. CI/CD tools are software applications that automate the integration and deployment processes in your development workflow. These tools help ensure that your code is always in a deployable state, with changes automatically tested and deployed to production environments. By using these tools, you can reduce manual errors, improve collaboration, and increase the overall efficiency of your development team.

In this section, we'll introduce you to some of the most popular CI/CD tools that can be integrated into your NestJS projects. While this book isn't focused on in-depth DevOps training, knowing the right tools will help you automate and streamline your deployment process, leaving more time for actual development.

But before we introduce you to the popular CI/CD tools, let's give you some pointers that can help inform your selection of CI/CD tools.

Criteria to consider when selecting CI/CD tools

When it comes to choosing the right CI/CD tool for your NestJS application, there are several factors to consider. The decision largely depends on the specific needs of your project, your team's familiarity with certain tools, and the scale at which you plan to operate. Here are some criteria that can guide your choice:

- **Integration with existing tools**: If your team is already using certain version control systems, such as GitHub or GitLab, it makes sense to choose CI/CD tools that integrate seamlessly with them, such as GitHub Actions or GitLab CI/CD. This reduces the learning curve and allows for a more streamlined workflow.

- **Ease of setup and maintenance**: Consider how much time your team can dedicate to setting up and maintaining the CI/CD pipeline. Tools such as Travis CI and GitHub Actions are known for their simplicity and ease of use, making them ideal for teams that want to get started quickly without needing to manage extensive configurations.

- **Scalability**: If your project is expected to grow significantly in size and complexity, choosing a tool, such as Jenkins or CircleCI, that offers robust scalability and advanced features might be more appropriate. These tools can handle complex workflows and large teams, providing the necessary infrastructure to support growth.

- **Customization and flexibility**: Some projects may require custom workflows or integrations that only certain CI/CD tools can support. Jenkins, for example, is highly customizable with its extensive plugin ecosystem, making it suitable for projects that need tailored solutions.

- **Cost and resources**: Depending on your budget, some tools might be more suitable than others. For open source projects or those on a tight budget, Travis CI offers free services, while tools such as GitHub Actions and GitLab CI/CD provide free tiers with limitations. It's important to evaluate the cost implications of each tool, especially if you plan on scaling up.

- **Community support and documentation**: A tool with strong community support and comprehensive documentation can be invaluable, especially when troubleshooting issues. Popular tools such as Jenkins and GitHub Actions have large communities and extensive resources, which can help resolve issues quickly and efficiently.

By evaluating these criteria, you can make an informed decision on which CI/CD tool is the best fit for your NestJS application. Remember that the ideal tool may vary depending on the specifics of your project and your team's needs, so take the time to assess each option carefully.

Popular CI/CD tools

Here are the most popular CI/CD tools that can be used for your NestJS application:

- **Jenkins**: `https://www.jenkins.io/solutions/pipeline/`:

  Jenkins is one of the most widely used open source CI/CD tools. It offers extensive plugin support, making it highly customizable for various projects. Jenkins automates the process of building, testing, and deploying your application, ensuring that every change is properly validated before going live. However, Jenkins requires some setup and maintenance, which may be ideal for teams with more complex needs.

- **GitHub Actions**: `https://github.com/marketplace?type=actions`:

  GitHub Actions is a CI/CD tool integrated directly into GitHub, allowing you to automate your workflows right from your repository. It's particularly beneficial for projects already hosted on GitHub, as it offers seamless integration and a simple YAML-based configuration. With GitHub Actions, you can easily create workflows for building, testing, and deploying your NestJS applications, making it a great choice for teams looking for ease of use.

- **GitLab CI/CD**: `https://docs.gitlab.com/ee/ci/`:

  GitLab offers a built-in CI/CD pipeline that comes with its platform, making it a powerful tool for those using GitLab for version control. GitLab CI/CD allows you to create pipelines that automatically build, test, and deploy your code. It's particularly strong in its ability to handle large-scale projects and offers a robust set of features for CD.

- **CircleCI**: `https://circleci.com/`:

  CircleCI is another popular CI/CD tool known for its speed and scalability. It offers a cloud-hosted platform that simplifies setting up pipelines, especially for smaller teams or startups. CircleCI is known for its powerful integrations with various cloud providers and services, making it easy to deploy your NestJS application in a wide range of environments.

- **Travis CI**: `https://www.travis-ci.com/`:

  Travis CI is an easy-to-use CI/CD tool that integrates seamlessly with GitHub. It's a great option for open source projects, offering free CI/CD services to them. Travis CI is known for its simplicity and ease of setup, making it an excellent choice for smaller projects or teams that want to get up and running quickly.

While this section introduced you to some of the most popular CI/CD tools, mastering these tools requires hands-on practice and further research. Each tool has its strengths and use cases, so consider experimenting with them to see which best fits your workflow. Official documentation, community forums, and tutorials are great resources to deepen your understanding and build your CI/CD expertise.

Now that you've been introduced to various CI/CD tools, it's time to put this knowledge into practice. In the next section, we'll guide you through setting up a CI/CD pipeline for your NestJS application. This will bring together everything we've discussed so far, helping you automate and optimize your deployment process. Let's move forward and get our hands dirty with setting up your first CI/CD pipeline!

Setting up a CI/CD pipeline for NestJS

In this section, we'll guide you step by step through the process of setting up a CI/CD pipeline tailored for a NestJS application. Specifically, we'll use GitHub Actions, a powerful tool that integrates directly with your GitHub repository to automate your application's testing, building, and deployment. Whether you're managing a small project or deploying to a staging environment, automating these steps ensures consistent, error-free deployments and faster development cycles.

The CI/CD pipeline consists of several phases. Let's walk through the specific steps involved in setting up the pipeline:

1. **Code changes and code push**: Developers push their code changes to a specific branch (e.g., `feature/*`, `bugfix/*`, or `hotfix/*`).

2. **Pull request and automatic testing**: When a pull request (a proposal to merge a set of changes from one branch into another) is created, we trigger two key actions:

    - **Building of the code**: We use `yarn build` to compile the application
    - **Running of tests**: Both unit and end-to-end tests are executed to catch any errors early

3. **Automatic feedback**: If the build or tests fail, developers are immediately notified, allowing them to fix issues before a code review takes place.

4. **Staging deployment**: After passing all checks, the code is merged into the development branch. This automatically triggers a deployment to a staging environment; for demonstration purposes, we will use Render (`https://render.com/`), a free cloud application platform. This allows the **Quality Assurance (QA)** team to test the application before moving it to production.

5. **Production deployment**: Once the changes are approved in staging, the pipeline deploys the code to the production environment automatically.

Now that you have an overview of what a CI/CD pipeline looks like, let's write one in the next section.

Writing CI/CD actions in GitHub

Let's now get into the implementation details. We will use GitHub Actions, which is a free tool and easy to get started with.

Setting up GitHub Actions

To start, we need to define the actions that handle building and testing. We'll place these configurations in a `.github/workflows/` directory and create a `build.yaml` file as follows:

```
name: Build and Test Pipeline

on:
  pull_request:
    branches: ['develop']

jobs:
  build:
    runs-on: ubuntu-latest
    steps:
      - uses: actions/checkout@v3
      - name: Setup Node.js
        uses: actions/setup-node@v3
        with:
          node-version: '14'
      - run: yarn install
      - run: yarn build

  test:
    runs-on: ubuntu-latest
    steps:
      - uses: actions/checkout@v3
      - name: Setup Node.js
        uses: actions/setup-node@v3
        with:
          node-version: '14'
      - run: yarn install
      - run: yarn test
```

This configuration does the following:

- **Triggers on pull request**: The pipeline runs when a pull request is created on the develop branch

- **Builds job**: The build step ensures the project compiles by running yarn build

- **Tests job**: The test step runs the project's unit and end-to-end tests using yarn test

Dealing with environment variables

In most applications, environment variables (e.g., database connections and API keys) play a crucial role in both testing and deployment. To avoid failures due to missing environment variables, you can do either of the following:

- Inject environment variables directly into the GitHub repository secrets (under **Settings | Secrets and variables | Actions**). Then, click on the **New repository secret** button, as shown in *Figure 16.2*, and then fill out the form with the secret name and its value.

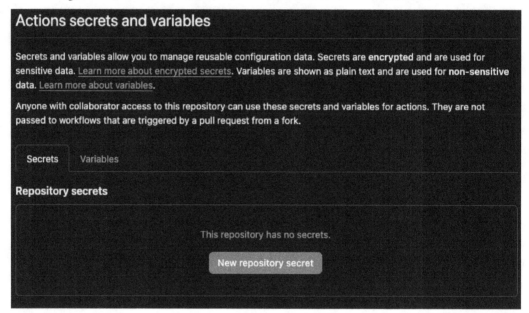

Figure 16.2 – Adding a new repository secret

- Use default fallback values in your code for testing environments, as shown here:

```
{
  secret: this.configService.get<string>('JWT_SECRET')
    || 'testSecret',
}
```

This ensures that even without injected environment variables, the tests can run successfully.

Since these secret variables are not hardcoded in the code base, when the CI/CD pipeline is running, it will use values injected directly in the repository's secrets section, which is the desired behavior (instead of exposing them to the code base). Now, let's see how we can deploy our code changes in the next section.

Deploying to staging

Once the CI actions pass, the next step is to deploy the application to a staging environment. Here's an example of how you can set deployment to Render by creating a `deploy.yaml` file:

```yaml
name: Deploy to Render
on:
  push:
    branches: ['develop']
jobs:
  deploy:
    runs-on: ubuntu-latest
    steps:
      - name: Trigger Render Deployment
        uses: sws2apps/render-deployment@main
        with:
          serviceId: ${{ secrets.RENDER_SERVICE_ID }}
          apiKey: ${{ secrets.RENDER_API_KEY }}
```

Here, we are targeting both the `develop` and `main` branches for staging and production environments, respectively. You'll need to inject your Render API keys and service ID as secrets in the repository as we did in the previous section.

For a production environment, here, we have a more complete version of the YAML file we can trigger whenever any code is merged into the main branch:

```yaml
name: Deploy on Production Server

on:
  push:
    branches:
      - main
jobs:
  deploy:
    runs-on: ubuntu-latest
    steps:
      - name: Checkout code
        uses: actions/checkout@v3
      - name: Setup Node.js
        uses: actions/setup-node@v3
        with:
          node-version: '18.x'
      - name: Install dependencies
        run: npm ci --ignore-scripts
      - name: Build application
```

```
        run: npm run build
    - name: Copy files to Production server
      uses: appleboy/scp-action@v0.1.4
      with:
        host: ${{ secrets.PROD_HOST }}
        username: ${{ secrets.PROD_USERNAME }}
        key: ${{ secrets.PROD_KEY }}
        port: ${{ secrets.PROD_PORT }}
        source:
          'dist/,
          package.json,
          package-lock.json,
          ecosystem.config.json,
          .npmrc,
          .npmignore'
        target: ${{secrets.PROD_LOCATION}}
    - name:
        SSH into Production and install dependencies and
        restart app
      uses: appleboy/ssh-action@v0.1.10
      with:
        host: ${{ secrets.PROD_HOST }}
        username: ${{ secrets.PROD_USERNAME }}
        key: ${{ secrets.PROD_KEY }}
        port: ${{ secrets.PROD_PORT }}
        script: |
          cd ${{secrets.PROD_LOCATION}}
          bash -ic
            'npm ci --ignore-scripts --only=production &&
            npm cache clean --force'
          bash -ic 'pm2 restart ecosystem.config.json'
```

This GitHub Actions workflow automates the deployment process to a production server every time code is pushed to the main branch, streamlining updates with minimal manual intervention. To set this up, save the following YAML file under `.github/workflows` (e.g., `deploy-production.yml`) in your repository.

The workflow performs several critical tasks:

- It checks out the latest code.

- It sets up Node.js to match the environment specified in your project.

- It installs dependencies, builds the application, and securely transfers the build files to the production server.

- Finally, it **Secure Shell** (**SSH**)s into the production environment, installs production-specific dependencies, clears the cache, and restarts the application using PM2.

This setup ensures your application deploys consistently and reliably, reducing deployment errors and simplifying the release process.

CI/CD best practices

As you begin to integrate CI/CD into your NestJS projects, it's crucial to adhere to best practices that ensure your pipeline is efficient, reliable, and scalable. Implementing these practices can significantly enhance the quality of your software, reduce deployment times, and minimize the risk of issues arising in production.

The following are some of the most important best practices for your CI/CD pipeline:

- **Version control integration**: At the heart of any CI/CD pipeline is a robust **version control system** (**VCS**), such as Git. Ensure that your CI/CD processes are tightly integrated with your VCS. This allows for automatic triggers of build and test processes whenever code changes are committed, helping to catch issues early in the development cycle. Consider using branch strategies such as Gitflow or trunk-based development to manage feature integration and releases smoothly.

- **Automated testing**: Automated testing is essential for maintaining code quality. Implement a variety of tests within your pipeline, including unit tests, integration tests, and end-to-end tests. Each code change should trigger these tests automatically and builds should only pass if all tests succeed. Additionally, consider using test coverage tools to ensure that a significant portion of your code base is tested.

- **Continuous code quality checks**: Incorporate tools for static code analysis, such as ESLint for JavaScript/TypeScript and SonarQube for broader code quality assessments. These tools can automatically check your code for potential issues, code smells, and security vulnerabilities. Integrating these checks into your CI pipeline ensures that code quality remains high and consistent across the entire project.

- **Environment parity**: To avoid the *it works on my machine* problem, strive for environment parity across development, staging, and production environments. Tools such as Docker and Kubernetes can help achieve this by ensuring that your application runs consistently in different environments. Your CI/CD pipeline should deploy to a staging environment that mirrors production as closely as possible, allowing you to catch potential deployment issues before they reach production.

- **Incremental and frequent deployments**: Frequent, smaller deployments are generally safer and easier to manage than large, infrequent ones. By continuously integrating and deploying code, you reduce the risk of conflicts and make it easier to identify the source of any issues that arise. Implementing feature toggles can also help you safely deploy new features without exposing them to users immediately.

- **Monitoring and logging**: Once your application is deployed, continuous monitoring and logging are critical. Integrate monitoring tools such as Prometheus, Grafana, or New Relic into your CI/CD pipeline to track the health of your application and infrastructure. Logs should be aggregated and monitored in real time, with alerts set up to notify the team of any critical issues. This proactive approach ensures that you can respond quickly to any problems in production.

- **Rollback strategies**: No matter how well you test your code, issues can still arise in production. Your CI/CD pipeline should include a rollback strategy that allows you to quickly revert to a previous stable version of your application if a deployment fails. This could involve keeping the last known good deployment artifacts or using version control to easily roll back code changes.

- **Security considerations**: Security should be an integral part of your CI/CD pipeline. Incorporate security scanning tools that check for vulnerabilities in your code, dependencies, and container images. Additionally, ensure that your deployment processes are secure by managing secrets properly, using secure communication protocols, and regularly reviewing access controls.

- **Documentation and transparency**: Maintaining clear and up-to-date documentation of your CI/CD processes is important for team collaboration and onboarding. This includes documenting the pipeline setup, deployment processes, and any custom scripts or configurations used. Additionally, ensure that build and deployment logs are easily accessible and transparent to the entire team, promoting a culture of shared responsibility.

- **Continuous improvement**: CI/CD is not a set-it-and-forget-it process. Continuously review and improve your pipeline based on feedback, new tools, and evolving project requirements. Regularly gather feedback from your team, analyze deployment metrics, and stay updated on industry best practices to ensure your CI/CD processes remain efficient and effective.

By following these best practices, you can build a CI/CD pipeline that not only accelerates your development process but also ensures that your NestJS applications are of the highest quality, secure, and ready for production. As you move forward, remember that the key to a successful CI/CD implementation is continuous learning and adaptation.

Summary

In this chapter, you've taken the first steps into the world of DevOps by exploring CI/CD and how they apply to your NestJS applications. We started by understanding the core concepts of CI/CD and why they are critical in modern software development. You learned about the various CI/CD tools, from Jenkins and GitLab CI/CD to CircleCI, each offering unique features to help streamline your development workflow.

We then moved on to setting up a CI/CD pipeline tailored for NestJS, focusing on automating the testing, building, and deployment of your applications. Best practices, including version control integration, automated testing, and environment parity, were emphasized to ensure your CI/CD pipeline is robust and reliable.

As you move forward, remember that mastering CI/CD is an ongoing process. The practices and tools introduced here are just the beginning. Continuous improvement and adaptation are key to keeping your pipeline aligned with the evolving needs of your projects.

In the next chapter, we'll dive deeper into advanced CI/CD techniques, including optimizing pipeline performance, integrating with cloud-based DevOps platforms, and implementing full-scale monitoring and alerting systems. Prepare to elevate your DevOps skills to the next level!

Get This Book's PDF Version and Exclusive Extras

UNLOCK NOW

Scan the QR code (or go to packtpub.com/unlock). Search for this book by name, confirm the edition, and then follow the steps on the page.

Note: Keep your invoice handly. Purchase made directly from packt don't require one.

17

NestJS Performance Optimization

You've built, deployed, and automated your NestJS application, making it robust and scalable. However, there's one more crucial step to ensure your application thrives in the real world: performance optimization. How fast does your application respond? How efficiently does it handle increasing traffic? How do you minimize resource usage while maximizing output? Welcome to the chapter where we focus on squeezing every bit of performance out of your NestJS application.

In this chapter, we'll explore a range of techniques and strategies for optimizing the performance of your NestJS applications. From code-level improvements to database optimizations and effective caching strategies, you'll learn how to make your applications faster, more efficient, and more reliable. Whether you're preparing for a surge in user traffic or simply aiming to provide a better user experience, performance optimization is key.

Here's what we'll cover in this chapter:

- Understanding performance optimization

- Code optimization techniques

- Database optimization techniques

- Caching strategies for NestJS

- Profiling and Load testing

- Best practices for performance optimization

By the end of this chapter, you'll have a toolkit of strategies to ensure your NestJS applications run at peak performance and are ready to handle the demands of production environments. Prepare to dive deep into the art of making your application not just functional but also exceptionally fast and efficient.

Technical requirements

The code files for the chapter can be found at `https://github.com/PacktPublishing/Scalable-Application-Development-with-NestJS`

Understanding performance optimization

Before diving into the technicalities of performance optimization, it's important to understand why it matters. Performance optimization is not just about making your application faster—it's about creating a seamless user experience, reducing costs, and ensuring your application can scale as your user base grows.

In the context of a NestJS application, performance optimization involves several key aspects: reducing response times, minimizing resource usage, ensuring efficient database interactions, and utilizing caching mechanisms effectively. It also encompasses writing clean, efficient code that executes quickly and using the right tools and techniques to monitor and optimize your application continuously.

When thinking about performance optimization, consider the following key areas:

- **Application efficiency**: How well does your code perform its tasks? Are there redundant processes that can be streamlined?

- **Scalability**: Can your application handle an increase in users without a decrease in performance?

- **Resource utilization**: Are you using system resources such as CPU, memory, and bandwidth efficiently?

- **User experience**: How quickly does your application respond to user requests? Is the experience smooth and consistent?

Understanding these aspects helps you make informed decisions about where to focus your optimization efforts.

By the end of this chapter, you'll not only understand the importance of performance optimization but also be equipped with strategies to improve the speed, efficiency, and reliability of your NestJS applications.

Now that you have a foundational understanding of performance optimization, it's time to delve deeper into the specific techniques that will make your NestJS application run more efficiently. In the next section, we'll start with code optimization techniques, where you'll learn how to write cleaner, faster, and more efficient code.

Code optimization techniques

Now that we understand the importance of performance optimization, let's start with one of the most critical areas: code optimization. Writing efficient code is fundamental to improving the overall performance of your NestJS application. Even small improvements in how your code is structured and executed can lead to significant gains in speed and resource usage.

In this section, we'll explore several techniques that will help you write cleaner, faster, and more maintainable code. The following techniques not only improve performance but also enhance the readability and scalability of your application.

Efficient data handling

In order to manage data efficiently, it's important to do the following:

- **Avoid unnecessary computations**: Minimize the use of expensive operations inside loops or frequently called functions. Calculate values once and reuse them when possible.

- **Optimize loops and iterations**: Ensure that loops are as efficient as possible. Consider using methods such as `.map()`, `.filter()`, and `.reduce()` to handle arrays in a more functional programming style, which can be more efficient and readable.

- **Limit data transfer**: Reduce the amount of data being sent between the server and the client. Use pagination, filtering, and sorting to ensure only necessary data is retrieved and sent.

- **Asynchronous programming**: When writing asynchronous code, we need to avoid failing into common traps with the following tips:

- **Use async/await wisely**: Properly implement asynchronous functions using `async/await` to avoid blocking the event loop. NestJS, built on top of Node.js, is designed to handle asynchronous operations efficiently, so leverage this to improve performance.

- **Parallelize independent tasks**: When possible, run independent tasks in parallel rather than sequentially. This can significantly reduce execution time for certain operations.

Reduce middleware and route complexity

You can reduce route and middleware complexity with the following tips:

- **Streamline middleware**: Only include middleware that is necessary for a specific route. Unnecessary middleware can add overhead to your requests.

- **Simplify routes**: Avoid overly complex routes that require significant processing. Simplify logic where possible, and break down complex routes into smaller, more manageable pieces.

Optimizing dependency management

When dealing with dependency injection, it's important to do the following:

- **Minimize dependencies**: Only include necessary packages and libraries. Each dependency adds to the startup time and memory usage of your application.

- **Use tree shaking**: For frontend code, use tree shaking to remove unused code from your bundles. This reduces the size of the application and speeds up load times.

Memory management

Memory is one of the big challenges when building server-side applications. It's important to help you do the following:

- **Avoid memory leaks**: Pay attention to memory management, especially in long-running processes. Identify and fix memory leaks that could degrade performance over time.

- **Use buffers and streams**: For handling large amounts of data, use Node.js buffers and streams to process data more efficiently and reduce memory usage.

These techniques provide a solid foundation for optimizing the performance of your code. Remember, the goal is not just to make your code faster but also to make it cleaner and more maintainable, which will pay off in the long run as your application grows.

With a better grasp of code optimization techniques, you're now equipped to write faster and more efficient code. However, optimizing your application's performance doesn't stop here. In the next section, we'll explore how to optimize your database interactions, which can have an even more significant impact on your application's overall performance. Let's dive into database optimization techniques and see how you can reduce query times and improve data handling in your NestJS application.

Database optimization techniques

As your NestJS application scales, the efficiency of your database interactions becomes increasingly crucial. Poorly optimized database queries and structures can significantly slow down your application, leading to bottlenecks that affect the user experience. In this section, we'll explore several techniques to optimize your database interactions, ensuring that your application remains fast and responsive as it grows.

Database optimization isn't just about writing efficient queries—it's about understanding the data structures, indexing, and caching strategies that can drastically reduce query times and improve overall performance. We'll cover a range of techniques from indexing to query optimization, each aimed at making your database interactions as efficient as possible.

Optimizing database queries

One of the first steps in optimizing your database is to review and refine your queries. Inefficient queries can lead to slow response times, especially when dealing with large datasets. Here are a few strategies to optimize your queries:

- **Avoiding select**: Selecting all columns from a table can be resource-intensive, especially if you only need a few fields. Specify only the columns you need to reduce the amount of data transferred and processed.

- **Optimizing joins**: When performing joins between tables, ensure that the join conditions are indexed and that the queries are written to minimize the amount of data being joined. Consider using subqueries or restructuring your database schema to reduce the need for complex joins.

Indexing

Indexes are one of the most powerful tools for improving query performance. By creating indexes on columns that are frequently used in `WHERE` clauses, `JOIN` conditions, or `ORDER BY` statements, you can significantly reduce the time it takes to retrieve data:

- **Primary and foreign keys**: Ensure that primary and foreign key columns are indexed, as these are often used in joins and lookups commands.

- **Composite indexes**: If you often query multiple columns together, consider using composite indexes, which cover multiple columns in a single index. This can further optimize your queries.

Database schema design

The way your database schema is structured can have a profound impact on performance. A well-designed schema will minimize redundancy and optimize data retrieval:

- **Normalization versus denormalization**: Normalization reduces data redundancy by dividing your data into smaller, related tables, which can improve data integrity and reduce storage costs. However, for performance reasons, denormalization—where data is duplicated in multiple tables—can sometimes be more efficient by reducing the number of joins needed for complex queries.

- **Partitioning**: For large tables, consider using partitioning, which divides the table into smaller, more manageable pieces. This can improve performance by limiting the amount of data that needs to be scanned for queries.

Caching strategies

Caching frequently accessed data can significantly reduce the load on your database. By storing the results of expensive queries in a cache, you can serve subsequent requests directly from the cache, greatly improving response times:

- **Query caching**: Implement query caching to store the results of commonly used queries. Tools such as Redis can be integrated with your NestJS application to manage cached data effectively.

- **Application-level caching**: Consider caching data at the application level, especially for data that doesn't change frequently. This can reduce the number of calls to the database and speed up your application.

By applying these database optimization techniques, you can ensure that your NestJS application scales efficiently and maintains high performance, even as the amount of data grows. Optimizing your database interactions will lead to faster load times, better user experiences, and a more robust application overall.

With a solid understanding of database optimization techniques, you're now equipped to make your data operations more efficient. However, our journey to performance excellence doesn't stop here. In the next section, we'll explore caching strategies, which can further enhance the speed and responsiveness of your NestJS application by reducing the load on your database. Let's move forward and dive into the world of caching!

Caching strategies for NestJS

In any high-performance application, caching is a critical component for optimizing speed and efficiency. Caching allows you to store frequently accessed data in memory, reducing the need to repeatedly retrieve it from slower storage mediums such as databases. In a NestJS application, leveraging caching effectively can significantly reduce response times, decrease database load, and improve overall user experience.

In this section, we'll explore different caching strategies you can implement in your NestJS applications. From simple in-memory caching to more complex distributed caching solutions, you'll learn how to cache data at various levels of your application to maximize performance.

In-memory caching with cache-manager

NestJS provides seamless integration with the cache-manager package, which allows you to implement in-memory caching quickly and efficiently. This type of caching is stored directly in the application's memory and is ideal for caching small, frequently accessed data that changes infrequently.

Here's how you can set up in-memory caching in a NestJS application:

```
import { CacheModule, Module } from '@nestjs/common';
import { APP_INTERCEPTOR } from '@nestjs/core';
import { CacheInterceptor } from '@nestjs/common';

@Module({
  imports: [
    CacheModule.register({
      ttl: 5, // seconds
      max: 100, // maximum number of items in cache
    }),
  ],
  providers: [
    {
      provide: APP_INTERCEPTOR,
      useClass: CacheInterceptor,
    },
  ],
})
export class AppModule {}
```

In the preceding code, we have the following:

- **Time-to-Live (TTL)**: This sets the duration (in seconds) that a cached item will remain in memory before it's automatically evicted. Adjust the TTL based on how often the data changes.

- **Max**: This limits the number of items that can be stored in the cache at any one time. This helps manage memory usage.

With this setup, any method in your application can be automatically cached by simply adding the @ Cacheable() decorator, drastically reducing load times for frequently requested data.

Distributed caching with Redis

For larger applications or those deployed across multiple servers, distributed caching using a service such as Redis is often more appropriate. Redis is an in-memory data store that can be used as a distributed cache, ensuring that cached data is consistent and available across all instances of your application.

Here's an example of how to configure Redis as a cache store in NestJS:

```
import { CacheModule, Module } from '@nestjs/common';
import * as redisStore from 'cache-manager-redis-store';

@Module({
  imports: [
    CacheModule.register({
      store: redisStore,
      host: 'localhost',
      port: 6379,
      ttl: 600, // 10 minutes
    }),
  ],
})
export class AppModule {}
```

In the preceding code snippet, here are the key components:

- **Store**: Specifies the cache store; in this case, Redis

- **Host and Port**: Configures the connection details for your Redis instance

- **TTL**: Determines how long the cached data will persist in Redis before it is evicted; adjust this based on the nature of the data and the frequency of updates

With Redis, your cache can be shared across multiple instances of your application, ensuring consistent performance regardless of the underlying infrastructure.

HTTP caching with @CacheKey and @CacheTTL

NestJS also provides decorators such as @CacheKey() and @CacheTTL() that offer more granular control over caching at the method level. These can be particularly useful for caching the results of specific API calls.

Here is an example:

```
import { Controller, Get } from '@nestjs/common';
import { CacheKey, CacheTTL } from '@nestjs/common';

@Controller('data')
export class DataController {
  @Get()
  @CacheKey('my-custom-key')
  @CacheTTL(300)
  findAll() {
    return this.dataService.findAll();
  }
}
```

In this code snippet, we have the following:

- @CacheKey: Assigns a custom key to the cached response, which can be useful when you need to cache similar data under different contexts
- @CacheTTL: Overrides the default TTL, allowing you to specify how long the result of this specific method should be cached

This level of control ensures that only the most critical data is cached, reducing unnecessary cache pollution and ensuring that your cache is as effective as possible.

Cache busting

Caching is powerful, but stale data can be a significant drawback if not managed properly. Cache busting refers to the process of invalidating or refreshing the cache when the underlying data changes. In NestJS, you can manually clear the cache when necessary using the CacheManager service:

```
import { CacheService } from '@nestjs/common';

@Injectable()
export class MyService {
  constructor(private cacheManager: CacheService) {}

  async updateData() {
    // Update data logic
```

```
      await this.cacheManager.del('my-custom-key');
   }
}
```

This method removes the cached data associated with the specified key, ensuring that the next request retrieves fresh data.

Using cache-busting strategies ensures that your users always receive up-to-date information without sacrificing the performance benefits of caching.

Caching is a powerful technique that can drastically improve the performance of your NestJS application. By using in-memory caching, distributed caching with Redis, and method-level caching controls, you can ensure that your application responds quickly, even under heavy load. However, remember to manage your cache effectively, using techniques such as cache busting to prevent stale data from affecting your users' experience. With these strategies, your NestJS application will be well-equipped to handle increased traffic and deliver a smooth, fast user experience.

Now that caching is optimized, let's dive into **profiling and load testing** to further ensure your application can perform reliably under varying demands.

Profiling and load testing

As you aim to optimize performance, the first step is understanding where your NestJS application can improve. Profiling and load testing help you identify bottlenecks, inefficient processes, and areas where optimization efforts will have the greatest impact. By examining your application under different loads, you can gain insights into response times, resource usage, and scalability limits.

In this section, we'll explore tools and techniques for profiling and load testing, allowing you to assess your application's performance accurately. You'll learn how to set up load tests to simulate real-world traffic, analyze performance metrics, and use profiling tools to dig into specific areas of your code. With this foundation, you'll be able to make informed decisions that improve the speed, reliability, and scalability of your application.

Profiling a NestJS application

Before diving into optimization, it's essential to identify which parts of your application may be slowing things down. Profiling helps us track where time and resources are being spent within an application, allowing us to make focused improvements. In this section, you'll use the e-commerce case study project from *Chapter 12* as a hands-on base for profiling. Profiling tools will help you explore your NestJS app's performance, especially as it handles more complex tasks such as asynchronous validation and password hashing.

By the end of this section, you'll know how to set up profiling tools, understand the metrics they provide, and pinpoint areas for optimization. Let's get started with setting up a simple profiler, analyzing code execution, and improving performance step-by-step.

Step 1 – setting up Node.js profiling tools

NestJS runs on top of Node.js, which has built-in profiling tools perfect for inspecting your app's performance. Let's begin with the Node.js built-in profiler and explore how it can be set up for our e-commerce project:

```
$ node --prof dist/main.js
```

This command starts your NestJS application with profiling enabled. It generates a `.log` file containing details about function calls, execution time, and memory allocation. Once you've generated the `.log` file, you can use the `node --prof-process` tool to analyze it:

```
$ node --prof-process isolate-0xNNNN.log > processed.txt
```

This output provides a breakdown of the runtime, highlighting areas of the code where the most processing time is spent. As you inspect the `processed.txt` file, pay special attention to calls to custom validation functions and password hashing operations, as these are often resource-intensive.

By profiling with Node's built-in tools, you can capture a broad view of how your application performs at runtime. The `.log` file shows function call frequency and execution time, helping to identify "hot spots"—areas of code that may benefit from optimization.

Step 2 – profiling database queries with PostgreSQL

Our e-commerce application uses PostgreSQL, and inefficient queries can lead to significant slowdowns. Start by enabling PostgreSQL's `auto_explain` module to get query execution details.

In your PostgreSQL configuration file, enable `auto_explain` and set the `log_min_duration_statement` parameter to specify the time threshold for logging slow queries (e.g., 100 ms):

```
# Enable the auto_explain module
shared_preload_libraries = 'auto_explain'
auto_explain.log_min_duration = '100ms'
```

Restart PostgreSQL, then check the logs after running your app, especially for complex validation routines and data-heavy processes.

The `auto_explain` logs will reveal query times and suggest which SQL queries are taking the longest. Since the e-commerce app has high data throughput, optimizing queries that take longer than 100 ms can significantly improve application responsiveness.

Step 3 – using the Clinic.js suite for advanced profiling

Clinic.js (`https://clinicjs.org/`) by NearForm provides detailed insights into Node.js applications. It includes tools such as Doctor, Bubbleprof, and Flame to examine bottlenecks, which can be highly effective in understanding complex logic. Here's hwo to start using it:

1. Install Clinic.js:

    ```
    $ npm install -g clinic
    ```

2. Run Clinic Doctor:

    ```
    $ clinic doctor -- node dist/main.js
    ```

3. Open the generated `.html` report in a browser. It provides visual cues on memory usage, CPU time, and asynchronous operations, which makes it especially helpful in areas such as password hashing and validation.

The visual reports show where asynchronous tasks may be stacking up, potentially causing delays. In a system with asynchronous validation, you might see these functions consuming significant resources, indicating a need to streamline or offload work.

Step 4 – analyzing code hot spots

As you follow the profiler reports, you'll identify "hot spots" where performance can be enhanced. For example, if password hashing appears frequently, consider adjusting the hash rounds for `bcrypt`:

```
// Use lower hash rounds for bcrypt in development
const saltRounds = process.env.NODE_ENV === 'production'
  ? 12
  : 8;
const hashedPassword = await bcrypt.hash(
  password,
  saltRounds
);
```

This approach maintains security in production while saving resources in development environments.

Profiling often shows high usage areas where minor adjustments can reduce processing time. By tuning `bcrypt` hash rounds based on the cnvironment, we retain production security while speeding up local development testing.

With a clearer view of application performance through profiling, the next step is to test how well it can handle increasing load. Load testing simulates user traffic, helping us assess the robustness of optimizations under stress. In the following section, we'll walk through setting up load tests to ensure your NestJS application remains responsive and reliable as demand grows.

Load testing a NestJS application

After identifying bottlenecks with profiling, the next step is to assess your application's resilience under high traffic with load testing. Load testing simulates real-world user interactions and measures how well your NestJS application manages heavy concurrent traffic, helping you identify areas for performance improvements. By the end of this section, you'll be able to set up and analyze load tests, using insights to enhance your application's capacity and reliability.

To keep things practical, we'll continue using the e-commerce project from *Chapter 12*, complete with PostgreSQL, custom validation, and password hashing. This setup is well-suited for demonstrating load testing under complex operations.

Step 1 – setting up a load testing tool

A popular tool for load-testing Node.js applications is Artillery. It integrates well with JavaScript, providing easy configurations for setting up high-concurrency scenarios. Here's how to set it up:

1. Install Artillery with the following command:

    ```
    $ npm install -g artillery
    ```

2. Create an Artillery config file. In your project root, create an `artillery-config.yml` file to configure the test duration, traffic rate, and requests:

```yaml
config:
  target: "http://localhost:3000"
  phases:
    - duration: 60
      arrivalRate: 20
scenarios:
  - flow:
      - get:
          url: "/api/products"
      - post:
          url: "/api/auth/register"
          json:
            username: "user-{{ $randomString }}"
            password: "Test@1234"
```

This configuration sends 20 requests per second for 60 seconds, targeting the `/products` and `/auth/signup` endpoints to simulate product retrieval and user registration, testing both read and write operations.

Step 2 – running and analyzing the load test

Run the test with the following:

```
$ artillery run artillery-config.yml
```

The real-time results will show metrics such as response time, throughput, and error rates. Here's a sample JSON structure for reference:

```json
{
  "scenariosCreated": 1200,
  "scenariosCompleted": 1180,
  "requestsCompleted": 2400,
  "latency": {
    "min": 50,
    "max": 800,
    "p95": 500
  },
  "errors": {
    "ECONNRESET": 5
  }
}
```

In the configuraton file above we have:

- Response time shows endpoint responsiveness
- Throughput measures successful requests per second
- Error rate tracks failed requests (e.g., ECONNRESET errors due to overload)

By reviewing these metrics, you can pinpoint optimizations such as adding database indexing, caching repetitive validations, or increasing the thread pool size for CPU-bound tasks.

After profiling and load testing, you've gained insights into your application's efficiency and potential areas for improvement. However, how can you ensure your application is consistently optimized as it grows? In the next section, we'll explore best practices for performance optimization, focusing on essential principles for maintaining speed, reliability, and scalability in production environments.

Best practices for performance optimization

Performance optimization is not a one-time task; it's an ongoing process that requires a strategic approach and careful consideration of multiple factors. As you continue to refine and enhance your NestJS application, adhering to best practices can help you maintain a high-performance application that scales effectively and delivers a superior user experience.

In this section, we'll cover key best practices for performance optimization in NestJS. These practices are designed to ensure that your application remains fast, efficient, and reliable as it evolves.

Monitor and benchmark regularly

Continuous monitoring and benchmarking are essential for identifying performance bottlenecks and ensuring that your application meets performance goals. Utilize monitoring tools such as Prometheus, Grafana, or Datadog to track key performance metrics such as response times, CPU usage, memory consumption, and request rates.

Here's an example:

```
import { Injectable, OnModuleInit } from '@nestjs/common';
import {
  register as promRegister,
  Counter
} from 'prom-client';

@Injectable()
export class MetricsService implements OnModuleInit {
  private readonly httpRequestsTotal: Counter<string>;

  onModuleInit() {
    this.httpRequestsTotal = new Counter({
      name: 'http_requests_total',
      help: 'Total number of HTTP requests',
      labelNames: ['method', 'status'],
    });
    promRegister.registerMetric(this.httpRequestsTotal);
  }
  incrementHttpRequestCount(method: string, status: string)
  {
    this.httpRequestsTotal.inc({ method, status });
  }
}
```

This example shows how you can use Prometheus with NestJS to monitor the total number of HTTP requests, segmented by method and status. By integrating monitoring directly into your application, you can continuously track performance metrics and identify trends or issues early.

Regular benchmarking should complement monitoring. Tools such as Artillery or Apache JMeter can simulate load on your application, helping you understand how it performs under stress. This allows you to proactively address performance issues before they affect your users.

Optimize resource allocation

Efficient resource allocation is critical for maintaining optimal performance. This involves tuning your application's use of CPU, memory, and I/O resources to match the demands of your workload:

- **Containerization**: If you're using Docker or Kubernetes, ensure your containers are properly sized and that you're not overcommitting resources. Leverage tools such as Kubernetes' **Horizontal Pod Autoscaler (HPA)** to automatically scale your application based on real-time metrics.

- **Process management**: For Node.js-based applications, using process managers such as PM2 can help you manage resource usage more effectively. PM2 allows you to cluster your application across multiple CPU cores, balancing the load and improving responsiveness.

Here's an example:

```
$ pm2 start dist/main.js -i max --max-memory-restart 200M
```

This PM2 command starts your NestJS application in cluster mode, using all available CPU cores (i max). The `-max-memory-restart` option ensures that if a process exceeds 200 MB of memory, it will be restarted, preventing memory leaks from degrading performance.

Leverage asynchronous programming and non-blocking I/O

NestJS, built on Node.js, excels at handling asynchronous operations and non-blocking I/O. Maximizing these features can greatly improve your application's performance, especially under high concurrency:

- **Async/await**: Always prefer `async/await` for handling asynchronous code, as it makes your code cleaner and easier to manage compared to using callbacks or `.then()` chains.

- **Non-blocking operations**: Ensure that operations, especially I/O-bound ones such as reading files or querying databases, are non-blocking. Use libraries or modules that support non-blocking operations to prevent your application from being slowed down by these tasks.

Here is an example:

```
import { Injectable } from '@nestjs/common';
import { readFile } from 'fs/promises';

@Injectable()
export class FileService {
  async readFileContent(filePath: string): Promise<string>
  {
    return await readFile(filePath, 'utf-8');
  }
}
```

This example shows how to use the `fs/promises` module to perform a non-blocking file read operation. By avoiding synchronous file operations, you can keep your application responsive even when dealing with large files or slow storage.

Minimize payload sizes

Reducing the size of the data exchanged between the client and server can significantly improve response times and reduce bandwidth usage. This involves optimizing both the request and response payloads:

- **Compression**: Implement response compression using middleware as compression. This reduces the size of your HTTP responses, making them faster to transfer over the network.

- **Serialization**: Use efficient serialization formats such as `ProtocolBuffers` or `MessagePack` instead of JSON for complex data structures, especially in high-performance or bandwidth-constrained environments.

Here is an example:

```
import {
  Module,
  MiddlewareConsumer
} from '@nestjs/common';
import * as compression from 'compression';

@Module({
  imports: [],
})
export class AppModule {
  configure(consumer: MiddlewareConsumer) {
    consumer
      .apply(compression())
      .forRoutes('*');
  }
}
```

The example demonstrates how to use the compression middleware in a NestJS application. This automatically compresses your HTTP responses, reducing their size and improving load times.

Implement efficient logging

Logging is essential for debugging and monitoring, but poorly configured logging can impact performance. Efficient logging practices ensure you capture necessary information without overwhelming your application or affecting response times.

Log levels

Set appropriate log levels (e.g., DEBUG, INFO, WARN, or ERROR) to control verbosity. In production, WARN or ERROR can reduce noise and improve performance, while DEBUG can be used in development for greater insight into application behavior.

Asynchronous logging

To avoid blocking the main thread, configure your logs to be asynchronous. This can be done using high-performance logging libraries such as pino, which is lightweight and suited for large applications.

Configuring Pino in a Production-ready environment

The following example demonstrates a production-ready pino configuration within a NestJS application. It includes a method to switch to pino-pretty for enhanced readability in non-production environments.

Configure pino in the AppConfig file

Add a getLoggerConfig function in your AppConfig file to set up pino with environment-specific configurations:

```
import { Params } from 'nestjs-pino';
import * as crypto from 'crypto';

export class AppConfig {
  public static getLoggerConfig(): Params {
    const { NODE_ENV, LOG_LEVEL, CLUSTERING } =
      process.env;

    return {
      exclude: [], // Exclude specific paths from logging
                   // if needed
      pinoHttp: {
        genReqId: () =>
          `${crypto.randomUUID()}/${
            Date.now().toString(36)
          }`, // Generate unique IDs for each request
        autoLogging: true, // Auto log HTTP
                           // requests/responses
        base: CLUSTERING === 'true'
          ? { pid: process.pid }
          : {}, // Include PID in logs if clustering
        customAttributeKeys: {
          responseTime: 'timeSpent'
        }, // Rename responseTime for clarity
```

```
        level: LOG_LEVEL ||
          (NODE_ENV === 'production'
            ? 'info'
            : 'trace'),
        serializers: {
          req(request) {
            return {
              method: request.method,
              url: request.url,
              id: request.id
            };
          },
          res(reply) {
            return { statusCode: reply.statusCode };
          },
        },
        transport: NODE_ENV !== 'production'
          ? {
              target: 'pino-pretty',
              options: {
                translateTime: 'SYS:yyyy-mm-dd HH:MM:ss'
              }
            }
          : null,
      },
    };
  }
}
```

This configuration does the following:

- Sets log levels based on the environment (production uses info, and development uses trace)
- Utilizes a `pino-pretty` transport in non-production environments for easier reading
- Adds custom `req` and `res` serializers to control logged request and response attributes

Integrate the logger in your AppModule class

In your AppModule class, switch the default logger to `pino` by using the `AppConfig` configuration:

```
import { Module } from '@nestjs/common';
import { LoggerModule } from 'nestjs-pino';
import { AppConfig } from './config/app.config';
```

```
@Module({
  imports: [
    LoggerModule.forRoot(AppConfig.getLoggerConfig()),
    // other modules
  ],
})
export class AppModule {}
```

This integration ensures that all HTTP requests and responses in your application are logged efficiently.

Using Logger in services

Within any service, utilize Nest's Logger class or `pino` directly for granular logging control:

```
import { Injectable, Logger } from '@nestjs/common';

@Injectable()
export class MyService {
  private readonly logger = new Logger(MyService.name);

  logSomethingImportant() {
    this.logger.log('Important operation executed');
  }
}
```

Adhering to best practices for performance optimization is key to maintaining a high-performance NestJS application. By continuously monitoring and benchmarking, optimizing resource allocation, leveraging asynchronous programming, minimizing payload sizes, and implementing efficient logging, you can ensure your application remains fast, scalable, and resilient. These practices will help you build applications that not only meet performance requirements but also provide an exceptional user experience as they grow and evolve.

Summary

In this chapter, we explored the crucial aspects of optimizing your NestJS application for peak performance. Starting with an understanding of performance optimization, we delved into various techniques to make your application faster, more efficient, and more scalable. From code-level improvements such as efficient data handling and asynchronous programming to database optimizations and effective caching strategies, you've learned how to enhance your application's responsiveness and reliability. Additionally, we covered best practices that ensure your application remains robust as it scales, including regular monitoring, resource optimization, and efficient logging.

With these tools and strategies, your NestJS application is now better equipped to handle the demands of production environments, providing a smooth and fast user experience. As you continue to refine your application, remember that performance optimization is an ongoing process—one that requires continuous attention and adaptation.

In the next chapter, we'll shift our focus to another critical area: security in NestJS. While performance ensures your application runs efficiently, security is essential to protect your application and its users from potential threats. Prepare to dive into best practices, techniques, and tools to safeguard your NestJS applications in the digital landscape.

18

NestJS Security Best Practices

You've built and optimized your NestJS application, making it fast, efficient, and scalable. However, there's another critical aspect to consider if you want your application to thrive in the real world: security. How well-protected is your application against threats? Are you confident that your users' data is safe? Welcome to the chapter where we'll focus on fortifying your NestJS application against potential security vulnerabilities.

In this chapter, we'll explore a comprehensive set of security best practices tailored specifically for NestJS applications. From securing your data and implementing robust authentication and authorization mechanisms to preventing common security threats, you'll learn how to protect your application from a wide range of risks. Whether you're safeguarding sensitive user information or ensuring your application can withstand potential attacks, security is not just an option—it's a necessity.

Here's what we'll cover in this chapter:

- Understanding application security
- Data security in NestJS
- Authentication and authorization in NestJS
- Preventing common security threats
- Security best practices in NestJS

By the end of this chapter, you'll have the knowledge and tools to secure your NestJS applications, making them resilient against threats and ensuring the safety of your users. Get ready to dive deep into the essential strategies that will help you build not only functional but also secure applications.

Technical requirements

The code files for the chapters can be found at `https://github.com/PacktPublishing/Scalable-Application-Development-with-NestJS`.

Understanding application security

When building modern web applications, security is not just an afterthought—it's a fundamental aspect of development. As applications grow more complex, so do the threats that target them. This section will guide you through the essentials of application security, helping you understand why it's critical, what risks you face, and how to start thinking about protecting your NestJS application.

The importance of application security

Security is vital for several reasons:

- **Protection of user data**: Users trust your application with their sensitive information, including personal details, payment data, and more. Failing to protect this data can lead to significant breaches, damaging both your reputation and your users' trust.

- **Legal compliance**: Regulations such as the **General Data Protection Regulation** (**GDPR**) (`https://gdpr-info.eu/`), **Health Insurance Portability and Accountability Act** (**HIPAA**) (`https://www.hhs.gov/hipaa/index.html`), and the **California Consumer Privacy Act** (**CCPA**) (`https://oag.ca.gov/privacy/ccpa`) require stringent security measures to protect user data. Non-compliance can result in hefty fines and legal consequences.

- **Business continuity**: A security breach can disrupt your operations, leading to downtime, financial loss, and long-term damage to your business.

Understanding these reasons underscores why security cannot be an afterthought but a core component of your development process.

Common security challenges

Web applications face a variety of security challenges. Some of the most common ones include the following:

- **Injection attacks**: Techniques such as SQL injection exploit vulnerabilities in your database queries, allowing attackers to manipulate or access data

- **Cross-Site Scripting** (**XSS**): Malicious scripts can be injected into your application, compromising user data or taking over sessions

- **Cross-Site Request Forgery** (**CSRF**): This type of attack tricks a user into executing unwanted actions on a different site where they are authenticated

- **Weak authentication and authorization**: Poorly implemented authentication can allow unauthorized access, while insufficient authorization checks can lead to privilege escalation.

- **Data exposure**: Sensitive data can be exposed through weak encryption, improper storage practices, or insufficient access controls.

Each of these challenges presents a significant risk to your application and requires targeted strategies to mitigate.

Risks of unsecured applications

Failing to secure your application can have some of the following severe consequences:

- **Data breaches**: Unauthorized access to sensitive information can lead to data leaks, financial fraud, and identity theft.

- **Financial loss**: Security incidents often come with direct costs, such as fines, remediation expenses, and lost revenue from downtime.

- **Reputational damage**: Trust is hard to rebuild once it's broken. A single security breach can cause lasting harm to your brand's reputation.

- **Legal ramifications**: Depending on the nature of the breach and the jurisdiction involved, your organization could face legal action, resulting in fines or other penalties.

Understanding these risks is the first step toward taking proactive measures to secure your application.

Defense-in-depth – a layered approach to security

Security is most effective when it is applied in layers, a concept known as **defense-in-depth**. This approach ensures that if one layer of defense is breached, additional layers still protect the application. The key components of a defense-in-depth strategy include the following:

- **Secure coding practices**: Writing code that is resilient to attacks, such as avoiding the use of unsafe functions, validating input, and using prepared statements for database queries, is crucial.

- **Data encryption**: Encrypting sensitive data both at rest and in transit to protect it from unauthorized access is important.

- **Authentication and authorization**: These are key security concepts in any application. Authentication verifies a user's identity, while authorization determines which resources they can access. Implementing robust authentication methods, such as **Multi-Factor Authentication (MFA)** (`https://aws.amazon.com/what-is/mfa/`), and ensuring that users have the correct access permissions

- **Regular audits and monitoring**: Continuously monitor your application for unusual activity and perform regular security audits to identify and fix vulnerabilities.

- **Incident response planning**: Preparing for potential breaches with a well-defined incident response plan to minimize damage and recover quickly is key.

By implementing a defense-in-depth strategy, you can create a robust security posture resilient against a wide range of attacks.

Understanding the importance of security and the challenges involved is crucial for any developer. As you build your NestJS applications, keeping security at the forefront will help you avoid the costly consequences of breaches and ensure that your applications are functional and secure. In the following sections, we'll explore specific strategies for securing your data, handling authentication and authorization, and preventing common security threats, helping you build applications your users can trust.

Data security in NestJS

In the digital age, data is one of the most valuable assets an organization can possess. Protecting this data is critical, not only to comply with legal and regulatory requirements but also to maintain user trust and safeguard your business operations. Data security in NestJS involves implementing strategies to protect data at every stage—during transmission, storage, and processing. In this section, we'll dive into best practices for securing data within your NestJS application.

Securing data in transit

Data in transit refers to any data actively moving from one location to another, such as across the internet or through a private network. Securing data in transit is essential to prevent unauthorized interception or tampering.

The following are a few strategies you may need to implement when securing data in your next NestJS applications:

- **Use HTTPS**: Ensure that all communications between the client and the server are encrypted using HTTPS. This prevents attackers from intercepting data transmitted over the network. In NestJS, this can be configured using TLS certificates:

```
import { NestFactory } from '@nestjs/core';
import { AppModule } from './app.module';
import * as fs from 'fs';

async function bootstrap() {
  const httpsOptions = {
    key: fs.readFileSync('path/to/private-key.pem'),
    cert: fs.readFileSync(
      'path/to/public-certificate.pem'
    ),
  };
  const app = await NestFactory.create(
    AppModule, { httpsOptions }
  );
  await app.listen(3000);
}
bootstrap();
```

The preceding code demonstrates how to enable HTTPS in a NestJS application by providing the necessary SSL/TLS certificates. This ensures that all data between the server and the client is encrypted.

- **Enable HTTP Strict Transport Security (HSTS)**: HSTS forces browsers to interact with your application only over HTTPS, reducing the risk of protocol downgrade attacks. Using `helmet` middleware, HSTS can be enabled in your NestJS application to enforce secure connections:

```
import * as helmet from 'helmet';
app.use(helmet.hsts());
```

In the preceding code snippet, `helmet.hsts()` is used to enforce HSTS, ensuring that the application is only accessible over HTTPS, and helping to prevent **Man-in-the-Middle (MitM)** attacks by instructing browsers to automatically use secure connections for future requests.

- **Encrypt sensitive data**: For highly sensitive data, consider encrypting it before transmission, adding an additional layer of security even if HTTPS is compromised. There are several packages that help achieve this, including the `crypto` (https://nodejs.org/api/crypto.html) package, which is going to be discussed in the next section.

Securing data at rest

Data at rest refers to data that is stored on a disk or database. Protecting this data is critical for preventing unauthorized access or breaches.

Here are some strategies you may need to consider:

- **Encrypt data in databases**: Ensure that sensitive data stored in your databases is encrypted. This can be done at the application level or using database-specific encryption features:

```
import * as crypto from 'crypto';

const algorithm = 'aes-256-ctr';
const secretKey = process.env.SECRET_KEY;

function encrypt(text: string) {
  const iv = crypto.randomBytes(16);
  const cipher = crypto.createCipheriv(
    algorithm,
    Buffer.from(secretKey, 'hex'),
    iv
  );
  const encrypted = Buffer.concat(
    [cipher.update(text), cipher.final()]
  );
  return iv.toString('hex') + ':' +
```

```
    encrypted.toString('hex');
}

function decrypt(text: string) {
  const [iv, encryptedText] = text.split(':');
  const decipher = crypto.createDecipheriv(
    algorithm, Buffer.from(secretKey, 'hex'),
    Buffer.from(iv, 'hex')
  );
  const decrypted = Buffer.concat(
    [decipher.update(Buffer.from(encryptedText,
    'hex')),
    decipher.final()]
  );
  return decrypted.toString();
}
```

In this code snippet, we demonstrate how to encrypt and decrypt data using the crypto module in your NestJS application. The `encrypt()` function first generates a random **initialization vector (IV)** using `crypto.randomBytes(16)`, which ensures each encryption has unique randomness. The text is then encrypted using the AES-256-CTR algorithm and a secret key stored in an environment variable. The encrypted data and the IV are concatenated and returned together, making the data secure.

On the other hand, the `decrypt()` function extracts the IV and the encrypted data, then reverses the encryption process by creating a decipher object with the same algorithm and key. This way, the original text can only be retrieved if the correct key is used.

This code demonstrates how encryption and decryption can be implemented in a secure manner, ensuring that sensitive data in your database remains protected even if the database is compromised.

- **Use secure storage mechanisms**: Avoid storing sensitive data in plain text. Use secure storage mechanisms such as environment variables, encrypted databases, or secure vaults for credentials and other sensitive information.

- **Implement data masking**: For less sensitive data that doesn't require full encryption, consider data masking techniques to obfuscate parts of the data. Common techniques include the following:

  - **Static masking**: Irreversibly replacing data with fictional values in non-production environments

  - **Dynamic masking**: Masking data in real-time for specific users or applications, while leaving the original data intact

  - **Tokenization**: Replacing sensitive data with tokens that have no exploitable value on their own

  - **Shuffling**: Randomly rearranging data within the same dataset, ensuring the original data cannot be easily reconstructed

Each of these techniques helps to ensure that even if the data is accessed, it cannot be fully understood without additional context.

Access control

Controlling who has access to data is a crucial aspect of data security. Implementing strict access controls helps prevent unauthorized access to sensitive data.

Here are the key strategies for access control:

- **Role-Based Access Control (RBAC)**: Implement RBAC to ensure that users can only access the data and resources necessary for their role. NestJS provides decorators such as `@Roles()` and guards such as `RoleGuard` to facilitate this. For example, see the code snippet that follows:

```
import {
  SetMetadata,
  Injectable,
  CanActivate,
  ExecutionContext
} from '@nestjs/common';
import { Reflector } from '@nestjs/core';
// Custom Roles decorator to assign roles to different
// routes
export const Roles = (
  ...roles: string[]
) => SetMetadata('roles', roles);
@Injectable()
export class RoleGuard implements CanActivate {
  constructor(private reflector: Reflector) {}

  canActivate(context: ExecutionContext): boolean {
    const requiredRoles = this.reflector.get<
      string[]
    >('roles', context.getHandler());
    if (!requiredRoles) {
      return true;
    }
    const { user } =
      context.switchToHttp().getRequest();
    return requiredRoles.some((role) =>
      user.roles?.includes(role)
    );
  }
}
```

In the preceding code snippet, the `Roles` decorator is used to assign roles to routes or handlers by setting metadata. `RoleGuard` checks the metadata for required roles and determines whether the user has permission to access the resource. You would apply `RoleGuard` to routes to ensure that only users with the correct roles can access certain functionalities:

```
import {
  Controller,
  Get,
  UseGuards
} from '@nestjs/common';

@Controller('users')
export class UserController {
  @Get('admin')
  @Roles('admin') // Only allow users with the 'admin'
                  // role
  @UseGuards(RoleGuard)
  getAdminData() {
    return 'Admin content';
  }
}
```

In this example, `RoleGuard` is applied to the `/users/admin` route, ensuring that only users with the admin role can access it.

- **Principle of least privilege**: Grant users the minimum level of access necessary for their tasks. This reduces the risk of unauthorized access and potential damage from compromised accounts.

- **Audit logging**: Keep detailed logs of data access and modifications. These logs are essential for detecting unauthorized access attempts and investigating security incidents.

Securing data is a critical aspect of application security that requires a multifaceted approach. By ensuring data is protected during transmission, properly encrypted when stored, and accessible only by authorized users, you can significantly reduce the risk of data breaches and other security incidents. With these strategies in place, your NestJS application will be better equipped to protect user data, maintain compliance with legal requirements, and uphold user trust. In the next section, let's move on to reviewing the authentication and authorization techniques in NestJS.

Authentication and authorization in NestJS

Authentication and authorization are critical components of any secure application, determining who can access your system and what they are permitted to do once inside. In previous chapters, we delved into implementing these mechanisms within various contexts, such as securing GraphQL APIs and protecting user data in an e-commerce application. Here, we'll revisit those principles, focusing on reinforcing your understanding and highlighting best practices that are essential for maintaining robust security in NestJS applications.

A quick review – authentication

Authentication is the process of verifying the identity of a user or system. In NestJS, this is typically achieved through a combination of strategies such as **JSON Web Tokens** (**JWT**), OAuth2, or basic authentication methods such as a username and password.

Before diving into specific practices, let's briefly review the authentication strategies you've already implemented in *Chapters 5* and *12*:

- **JWT authentication**: This is a common strategy whereby a JWT is issued after a successful login and used to authenticate subsequent requests. You've implemented this in both RESTful and GraphQL contexts, ensuring that only authenticated users can access protected routes or queries.

- **OAuth2**: For applications requiring integration with external identity providers (e.g., Google and Facebook), OAuth2 provides a robust mechanism for third-party authentication. This strategy allows users to log in using their existing accounts from these providers, simplifying user management and enhancing security.

- **Session-based authentication**: This traditional method involves storing session information on the server side and managing user sessions through cookies. While less common in modern APIs, it remains a viable option in certain scenarios, such as when handling sensitive transactions.

Understanding these strategies is crucial, as each comes with its own set of strengths and trade-offs. Ensuring you select the appropriate authentication method for your application's needs is a key step in securing your NestJS application.

Strengthening authorization mechanisms

Authorization determines what an authenticated user can do within the application. After a user's identity has been verified, it's vital to control access to resources based on roles, permissions, or other criteria. NestJS provides flexible mechanisms for managing these authorizations through guards, decorators, and custom strategies.

Let's recap the essential elements of authorization that you've implemented:

- **RBAC**: In previous chapters, you've implemented RBAC to restrict access based on the user's role (e.g., admin, user, and guest). This is often handled using custom decorators in NestJS, such as `@Roles()`, and guards that intercept requests to enforce these rules.

- **Custom guards and interceptors**: NestJS allows the creation of custom guards to enforce fine-grained control over what users can access. For example, you may have implemented guards to verify specific permissions or to ensure that users belong to a certain group or organization.

- **Policy-based authorization**: Beyond roles, policies provide another layer of control, allowing you to specify conditions under which certain actions can be performed. This might involve checking the ownership of a resource or evaluating custom business rules.

Ensuring that your authorization logic is comprehensive and consistently applied across your application is crucial for maintaining security. Inadequate authorization checks can lead to unauthorized data access or operations, potentially exposing sensitive information or allowing malicious actions.

Best practices for authentication and authorization

While you've already implemented various strategies for authentication and authorization, it's important to revisit and refine these practices regularly. Here are a few key considerations to keep in mind:

- **Regularly rotate and secure tokens**: For token-based authentication, ensure that tokens are regularly rotated and that they are securely stored. This reduces the risk of token theft and misuse.

- **Leverage MFA**: Consider adding MFA for sensitive operations or admin-level access, adding an extra layer of security beyond just passwords.

- **Centralize and automate role management**: Use centralized systems to manage roles and permissions and automate updates to reduce human error and ensure consistency.

- **Continuously monitor and audit access**: Implement logging and monitoring to track authentication and authorization events. Regular audits can help detect and respond to suspicious activity quickly.

By revisiting these core concepts of authentication and authorization, you've reinforced your understanding of securing access to your NestJS applications. These principles not only safeguard your system but also provide a strong foundation for building secure, user-centric applications.

In the next section, we'll delve into common security threats that your application may face and discuss how to prevent them. Understanding these threats is essential for staying ahead of potential attacks and ensuring that your NestJS application remains secure.

Preventing common security threats

In any web application, security threats are an ever-present concern. NestJS applications, like all others, are vulnerable to various attacks if not properly secured. Understanding these threats and how to mitigate them is crucial to maintaining the integrity, confidentiality, and availability of your application. In this section, we'll explore some of the most common security threats faced by web applications and discuss strategies to prevent them.

Overview of common security threats

Before diving into specific prevention techniques, let's briefly review the most common security threats you might encounter:

- **XSS**: This occurs when an attacker injects malicious scripts into content that other users view. These scripts can then execute in the context of the victim's browser, leading to unauthorized actions like stealing cookies or session tokens.

- **SQL injection**: SQL injection attacks occur when an attacker is able to execute arbitrary SQL queries on the database by exploiting vulnerabilities in the application's input handling. This can lead to data breaches, data loss, or unauthorized access to the database.

- **CSRF**: CSRF attacks trick a user into performing actions they did not intend to perform, such as submitting a form or clicking a link that results in an unauthorized request being sent from their browser.

- **Denial of Service (DoS) and Distributed Denial of Service (DDoS)**: These attacks aim to make your application unavailable by overwhelming it with a flood of requests, either from a single source (DoS) or multiple sources (DDoS).

- **MitM attacks**: In a MitM attack, the attacker intercepts and possibly alters communication between two parties without their knowledge. This can lead to data breaches, credential theft, and unauthorized access.

Each of these threats can have serious consequences if not properly addressed. Let's explore how you can prevent these attacks in your NestJS application.

XSS prevention

XSS attacks exploit vulnerabilities in your application's handling of user-generated content. To prevent XSS, you should do the following:

- **Sanitize user input**: Always sanitize user input to ensure that any potentially malicious scripts are removed before being rendered in the browser. Use libraries such as `DOMPurify` or the built-in tools provided by your templating engine to sanitize data.

- **Use context-aware escaping**: Escaping ensures that user input is rendered as plain text, not executable code. Depending on where the input is being used (HTML, JavaScript, or CSS), different types of escaping are needed to ensure security.

- **Implement Content Security Policy (CSP)**: CSP is an HTTP header that restricts how resources (such as JavaScript, images, and CSS) can be loaded and executed. Implementing a strong CSP can significantly reduce the risk of XSS by preventing the execution of unauthorized scripts.

SQL injection mitigation

SQL injection attacks can be devastating, compromising your entire database. To prevent SQL injection, do the following:

- **Use parameterized queries**: Always use parameterized queries or prepared statements when interacting with the database. This ensures that user input is treated as data, not executable code, preventing attackers from injecting malicious SQL.

- **Use ORM/ODM libraries**: By using **Object-Relational Mapping (ORM)** or **Object-Document Mapping (ODM)** libraries such as TypeORM or Mongoose, you abstract database interactions away from raw SQL, reducing the likelihood of SQL injection vulnerabilities.

- **Input validation**: Validate and sanitize all user inputs before they are processed or stored in the database. This adds an additional layer of security against injection attacks.

CSRF prevention

CSRF attacks trick authenticated users into performing actions they did not intend. To prevent CSRF, do the following:

- **Use CSRF tokens**: Implement CSRF tokens in your forms and verify these tokens server-side before processing requests. This ensures that only legitimate requests from your application are processed.

- **SameSite cookies**: Set your cookies to use the *SameSite* attribute, which restricts how cookies are sent with requests from external sites. This reduces the risk of CSRF by ensuring that cookies are only sent with requests originating from your site.

- **Verify HTTP Referer header**: As an additional precaution, verify the Referer header of incoming requests to ensure they originate from your own site.

Defending against DoS and DDoS attacks

DoS and DDoS attacks can cripple your application by overwhelming it with traffic. The following is a list of measures that can be implemented to migrate these attacks:

- **Rate limiting**: Implement rate limiting to restrict the number of requests a user can make within a certain time period. This helps prevent abuse by limiting the impact of automated attacks.

- **Use a Content Delivery Network (CDN)**: CDNs such as Cloudflare or AWS CloudFront distribute your traffic across multiple servers, making it harder for attackers to overwhelm your application with requests.

- **Deploy DDoS protection services**: Consider using dedicated DDoS protection services that can detect and mitigate large-scale attacks before they reach your application.

Protecting against MitM attacks

MitM attacks intercept and potentially alter communication between parties. Here are the different ways of preventing MitM attacks:

- **Enforce HTTPS**: Ensure that all data transmitted between the client and server is encrypted using HTTPS. This prevents attackers from eavesdropping on or tampering with the data in transit.

- **Use secure WebSockets**: If your application uses WebSockets, ensure they are secured with **wss://** to encrypt the data being transmitted.

- **Implement HSTS**: HSTS enforces the use of HTTPS, preventing browsers from making unencrypted requests to your application, which can be intercepted by attackers.

By understanding and implementing strategies to prevent these common security threats, you can significantly reduce the risk of your NestJS application being compromised. These practices are not just about preventing individual attacks but also about building a security-conscious mindset that anticipates potential vulnerabilities and addresses them proactively.

In the next section, we'll delve into security best practices that go beyond just preventing attacks. These practices will help you create a secure development life cycle, ensuring that security is integrated into every stage of your application's development and deployment.

Security best practices in NestJS

Securing a web application is not just about patching individual vulnerabilities; it's about adopting a holistic approach that integrates security into every aspect of the development and deployment life cycle. In this section, we'll discuss the best practices for ensuring that your NestJS application is secure, resilient, and ready to handle the challenges of the modern web.

Secure development practices

Security should be a fundamental part of the development process, not an afterthought. By adopting secure development practices, you can minimize the risk of vulnerabilities being introduced into your application:

- **Secure coding standards**: Follow established secure coding standards such as OWASP's guidelines to avoid common security pitfalls. Encourage your team to write clean, maintainable, and secure code.

- **Regular code reviews**: Implement a process for regular code reviews to catch potential security issues early. Peer reviews can help identify vulnerabilities that automated tools might miss.

- **Automated security testing**: Integrate automated security testing into your CI/CD pipeline. Tools such as Snyk, OWASP ZAP, or SonarQube can help you catch vulnerabilities as part of your build process.

- **Dependency management**: Regularly update your dependencies to ensure you are not using packages with known vulnerabilities. Use tools such as npm audit or Yarn audit to scan for insecure dependencies.

Secure configuration management

How your application is configured can significantly impact its security. Misconfigurations are one of the most common causes of security breaches:

- **Environment variables for sensitive data**: Store sensitive information such as API keys, database credentials, and tokens in environment variables rather than hardcoding them into your application. This prevents accidental exposure in your code base.

- **Secure default configurations**: Ensure that your application's default configurations are secure. Disable any unnecessary features, and ensure that your production configuration does not include development or debug settings.

- **Implement proper logging and monitoring**: Configure your application to log important security events such as authentication attempts, access control violations, and suspicious activities. Implement monitoring tools to alert you to potential security incidents in real time.

Access control and least privilege

Managing who has access to your application and its resources is a critical aspect of security. The principle of least privilege should guide your access control policies:

- **RBAC**: Implement RBAC to ensure that users only have the permissions necessary to perform their roles. Define clear roles and assign permissions accordingly.

- **Secure admin interfaces**: Restrict access to your application's administrative interfaces to authorized personnel only. Consider implementing IP whitelisting or MFA for added security.

- **Audit trails**: Maintain audit logs that record who accessed what resources and when. This can be invaluable for detecting and investigating security incidents.

Secure data handling

Protecting sensitive data is a key component of application security. Data breaches can have severe consequences, including legal and financial repercussions:

- **Data encryption**: Encrypt sensitive data both at rest and in transit. Use strong encryption algorithms and ensure that your encryption keys are securely managed.

- **Data masking and tokenization**: For sensitive data displayed in your application, consider data masking or tokenization to minimize exposure. This is particularly important for **personally identifiable information (PII)** or payment card information.

- **Secure API communications**: Ensure that all communication between your application and external APIs is encrypted and authenticated. Use API keys, OAuth tokens, or JWTs to secure your API endpoints.

Regular security audits and penetration testing

No matter how secure you think your application is, there's always a chance that something might slip through the cracks. Regular security audits and penetration testing can help you identify and fix these issues before they are exploited.

- **Conduct regular audits**: Schedule regular security audits to review your application's security posture. This should include code reviews, configuration checks, and assessments of your infrastructure.

- **Penetration testing**: Engage in penetration testing to simulate real-world attacks on your application. This can help you identify vulnerabilities that are difficult to detect through automated tools or code reviews alone.

- **Patch management**: Stay on top of security updates and patches for your software and infrastructure. Regularly apply patches to address known vulnerabilities.

Incident response planning

Even with the best security practices in place, incidents can still happen. Having a well-defined incident response plan is crucial for minimizing the impact of security breaches:

- **Develop an incident response plan**: Outline the steps to take in the event of a security breach, including roles and responsibilities, communication protocols, and steps to contain and remediate the incident.

- **Regularly test your plan**: Conduct drills or simulations to test your incident response plan. This helps ensure that your team is prepared to respond quickly and effectively in the event of a real incident.

- **Post-incident reviews**: After an incident, conduct a thorough review to understand what went wrong, how it was handled, and what improvements can be made to prevent future incidents.

By adopting these security best practices, you can significantly enhance the security posture of your NestJS application. These practices not only help protect your application from current threats but also prepare you to respond effectively to any security incidents that may arise.

Summary

As we close this final chapter, we reflect on the journey we've taken together, building a robust understanding of how to secure, scale, and optimize your NestJS applications. From crafting APIs to implementing microservices, handling asynchronous operations, and safeguarding your application's data, we've explored the intricacies of creating production-ready solutions.

In this chapter, we solidified essential security principles, learning to address application risks through encryption, access control, and proactive defense measures. These strategies empower you to defend your application against vulnerabilities and manage secure interactions across all your services.

The appendix contains a set of key takeaways and checklists that serve as a practical guide, summarizing the insights we've covered. It's designed to be a ready reference to support you as you deploy your own resilient, scalable applications. Thank you for taking this journey through NestJS with us—your dedication to building secure, high-performing applications is sure to pay dividends in your work ahead.

Get This Book's PDF Version and Exclusive Extras

UNLOCK NOW

Scan the QR code (or go to packtpub.com/unlock). Search for this book by name, confirm the edition, and then follow the steps on the page.

Note: Keep your invoice handly. Purchase made directly from packt don't require one.

Appendix
Concluding Remarks and Next Steps

As we reach the end of our journey through the world of NestJS, it's time to step back and reflect on what we've accomplished. You've learned how to build robust, scalable applications, mastered essential techniques, and tackled real-world challenges. However, your journey with NestJS doesn't have to end here. In this final chapter, we'll summarize the key lessons you've learned and guide you on where to go next.

Whether you're planning to deepen your expertise in NestJS, explore new technologies, or even contribute to the community, this chapter will serve as your roadmap. We'll discuss ways to continue your learning, contribute to open-source projects, and stay updated with the latest developments in the NestJS ecosystem.

Here's what we'll cover in this chapter:

- Key takeaways from the book
- Exploring the NestJS ecosystem further
- Keeping up with NestJS updates and best practices
- Other useful resources
- Avoiding common pitfalls
- Final words

By the end of this chapter, you'll have a clear path forward, equipped with the knowledge and resources to continue growing as a developer. This is not just the conclusion of a book but the beginning of your ongoing journey in the exciting world of software development. Let's take this final step together, ensuring you're ready for whatever comes next.

Key takeaways from the book

As you look back on your journey through this book, it's essential to reflect on the key concepts and skills you've developed. These takeaways are more than just a summary—they represent the foundational knowledge that will support your future projects and growth as a developer.

Mastering the NestJS core concepts

At the heart of your learning, you've mastered the core concepts that make NestJS such a powerful framework. You've explored modules, controllers, and providers, understanding how to structure applications in a way that's both modular and maintainable. This knowledge will be your guide as you build scalable and organized applications.

Building robust APIs with NestJS

You've gone beyond the basics to create RESTful APIs that are not only functional but also secure and efficient. You've learned how to implement advanced routing, handle requests and responses, and incorporate middleware to enhance the functionality of your applications. These skills are crucial for building back-end services that can handle real-world demands.

Implementing security best practices

Security is a cornerstone of any application, and you've learned how to implement best practices within the NestJS framework. From authentication and authorization to protecting your application against common threats, you've gained the tools to ensure that your applications are secure and resilient.

Embracing testing and validation

Testing and validation are key to delivering reliable software. You've learned how to write unit tests, integrate testing frameworks, and ensure data integrity through validation. These practices are essential for maintaining the quality and reliability of your applications as they grow in complexity.

Scaling applications for the real world

Finally, you've explored how to optimize and scale your applications. From performance optimization to handling large-scale deployments, you've acquired strategies that will help your applications thrive in production environments.

These key takeaways are the building blocks of your future success with NestJS. Keep them in mind as you continue to explore, experiment, and grow as a developer.

Exploring the NestJS ecosystem further

Now that you've built a solid foundation with NestJS, it's time to explore the broader ecosystem that surrounds it. NestJS isn't just a framework—it's a gateway to a vibrant and growing community of tools, libraries, and practices that can elevate your development experience.

Diving into official modules and libraries

NestJS offers a wide range of official modules that extend its capabilities, from GraphQL and WebSockets to microservices and more. By exploring these modules, you can expand your applications into new domains, leveraging the power of NestJS in areas such as real-time communication, distributed systems, and serverless architectures.

Integrating with third-party tools

The NestJS ecosystem is well-integrated with popular third-party tools and libraries. Whether it's integrating with databases such as MongoDB, ORM frameworks such as TypeORM, or messaging systems such as RabbitMQ, there's a wealth of options available. Familiarizing yourself with these integrations can help you build more versatile and powerful applications.

Contributing to the NestJS community

The NestJS community is active and ever-growing, offering opportunities for you to contribute, learn, and grow. Whether you're interested in contributing to the core framework, writing plugins, or sharing your knowledge through blogs and talks, getting involved can be incredibly rewarding. Engaging with the community can also keep you inspired and up-to-date with the latest trends and developments.

With the NestJS ecosystem covered, the next step is staying updated with the latest *NestJS updates and best practices*. This will help you maintain high performance and security, and leverage the latest features in your projects. Let's explore how to do that effectively in the upcoming section.

Keeping up with NestJS updates and best practices

In the fast-paced world of software development, staying updated is crucial. NestJS is continually evolving, with new features, updates, and best practices emerging regularly. Here's how you can stay on top of it all.

Following the official NestJS repository

The official NestJS GitHub repository is the primary source for updates, including new releases, bug fixes, and feature enhancements. By keeping an eye on the repository and subscribing to release notes, you'll be among the first to know about changes that could impact your projects.

Participating in NestJS conferences and meetups

NestJS conferences, webinars, and meetups are fantastic ways to learn about the latest developments directly from the core team and other experienced developers. These events often feature talks on best practices, case studies, and future roadmaps, providing you with insights that go beyond the documentation.

Continuous learning and experimentation

Best practices in software development are not static—they evolve as new challenges arise and technologies advance. By committing to continuous learning and experimentation, you can ensure that your skills and knowledge remain sharp. Whether it's through online courses, blogs, or side projects, make it a habit to keep exploring new ideas and techniques.

Staying informed with NestJS updates and best practices is key to keeping your projects efficient and up-to-date. By following the official GitHub repository, attending NestJS events, and engaging in continuous learning, you ensure that your development skills grow alongside the framework.

Other useful resources

Beyond the official documentation and community contributions, there are countless resources available to help you deepen your understanding of NestJS and related technologies. Here are a few recommendations to guide your further learning.

Books and online courses

Several books and online courses offer in-depth coverage of NestJS and its ecosystem. These resources are valuable for both beginners and advanced developers, offering structured learning paths and practical exercises. Platforms such as Udemy, Pluralsight, and Coursera host courses that can help you master specific aspects of NestJS.

Blogs and tutorials

The developer community is rich with blogs and tutorials that cover a wide range of topics, from basic NestJS tutorials to advanced use cases. Following influential developers and subscribing to their content can keep you informed about new techniques and real-world applications.

Official and community forums

If you ever run into challenges or need advice, the official NestJS Discord server and community forums are excellent places to seek help. Engaging with these platforms can provide you with quick answers to your questions and connect you with other developers facing similar challenges.

Real-world success stories with NestJS

While many companies prefer not to publicly disclose their tech stacks, some leading organizations have openly shared their success with NestJS. These real-world examples highlight the framework's ability to drive scalability, maintainability, and performance in large-scale applications:

- **adidas**: Revolutionized their architecture by using NestJS to create microservices that scale effortlessly, supporting their shift toward distributed systems
- **Neo4j**: Opted for NestJS to enhance data management and performance while handling complex data structures
- **Handelsblatt**: Leveraged NestJS for efficient server-side logic in the media production and distribution industry

For a more comprehensive list of companies using NestJS, explore the community-maintained GitHub issue (`https://github.com/nestjs/nest/issues/1006`) and the official documentation (`https://docs.nestjs.com/discover/companies`).

Avoiding common pitfalls

Building scalable applications is not just about adding more features or handling more users—it's about laying a solid foundation that can grow with your project. NestJS, with its modular architecture, gives you the tools to create scalable, maintainable systems, but to truly take advantage of this power, you must think carefully about your application's structure from the very beginning.

Before you write a single line of code, *take the time to architect your solution thoughtfully*. As we have seen in case study chapters, our application's structure should evolve in tandem with your goals for scalability, not as an afterthought. NestJS' modular design empowers you to build flexible and maintainable code bases, but this power only shines when you harness it with a solid architectural plan in mind.

To help you navigate these challenges, we've identified several common pitfalls developers face when building scalable applications. By understanding these, you'll be equipped to avoid them and fully leverage NestJS's capabilities for large-scale development.

Here are the most critical areas to focus on when architecting and building your NestJS application for scale:

- **Start with the architecture, not the code**: One of the most common mistakes developers make is diving straight into coding without thinking through the architectural blueprint of their application. When building applications designed to scale, your first task should always be designing a modular and decoupled architecture that allows for easy expansion. Ask yourself: how will new features be added? How can different parts of the application remain isolated but still communicate effectively? Let your architecture be the guide, so that when your application scales, you can do so too with minimal friction.

- **Master the Nest CLI**: Another powerful tool in your arsenal is the Nest CLI. When scaling applications, consistency is key. The Nest CLI helps maintain uniformity across your application's structure, allowing you to generate modules, controllers, and services that adhere to best practices. As your application grows, these generated files provide a clean, predictable structure, reducing technical debt. Don't underestimate the importance of this tool—using the CLI from the beginning ensures your project is ready for scale.

- **Avoid overcomplicating the design**: While it's tempting to create an elaborate architecture upfront, simplicity is your ally in the early stages. Keep your modules and services straightforward, and only introduce complexity when your application's scale requires it. By doing so, you avoid unnecessary overhead that can bog down development and complicate future maintenance.

- **Optimize dependency injection**: NestJS' dependency injection is a powerful feature, but improper management of dependencies can create issues as your application grows. Ensure that your dependencies are modular and avoid circular references. This helps maintain the scalability and flexibility of your services.

- **Make sure to test thoroughly**: It's easy to skip testing in the early stages, but this often leads to headaches down the road. Whether you're writing unit tests, integration tests, or e2e tests, remember that testing is the backbone of a reliable, scalable application. The larger your application becomes, the more critical testing will be to prevent bugs from creeping into production.

By keeping these principles in mind, you'll be well-equipped to avoid common scalability issues and maintain a clean, efficient code base as your application grows.

Final words

As we close this book, remember that the end of this chapter marks the beginning of your ongoing journey in software development. You've gained valuable skills, but the world of technology is ever-changing, and there's always more to learn.

Embrace lifelong learning

The knowledge you've gained is a strong foundation, but the best developers are those who never stop learning. Continue to challenge yourself, experiment with new ideas, and push the boundaries of what you can build with NestJS and beyond.

Stay connected with the community

The NestJS community is a rich resource—don't hesitate to stay engaged. Whether it's through contributing to open source projects, participating in discussions, or attending events, staying connected will keep you inspired and informed.

Your journey ahead

The skills you've developed will serve you well, whether you choose to deepen your expertise in NestJS or explore other technologies. Whatever path you choose, remember that each project, and each challenge, is an opportunity to grow. Keep building, keep experimenting, and most importantly, enjoy the journey.

Your future as a developer is bright, and this book is just the first step. Now, go out there and create something amazing. Happy building!

Unlock Your Exclusive Benefits

Your copy of this book includes the following exclusive benefit:

-  Next-gen Packt Reader
- 📄 DRM-free PDF/ePub downloads

Follow the guide below to unlock them. The process takes only a few minutes and needs to be completed once.

Unlock this Book's Free Benefits in 3 Easy Steps

Step 1

Keep your purchase invoice ready for *Step 3*. If you have a physical copy, scan it using your phone and save it as a PDF, JPG, or PNG.

For more help on finding your invoice, visit `https://www.packtpub.com/unlock-benefits/help`.

> **Note**
> If you bought this book directly from Packt, no invoice is required. After *Step 2*, you can access your exclusive content right away.

Step 2

Scan the QR code or go to `packtpub.com/unlock`.

On the page that opens (similar to *Figure X.1* on desktop), search for this book by name and select the correct edition.

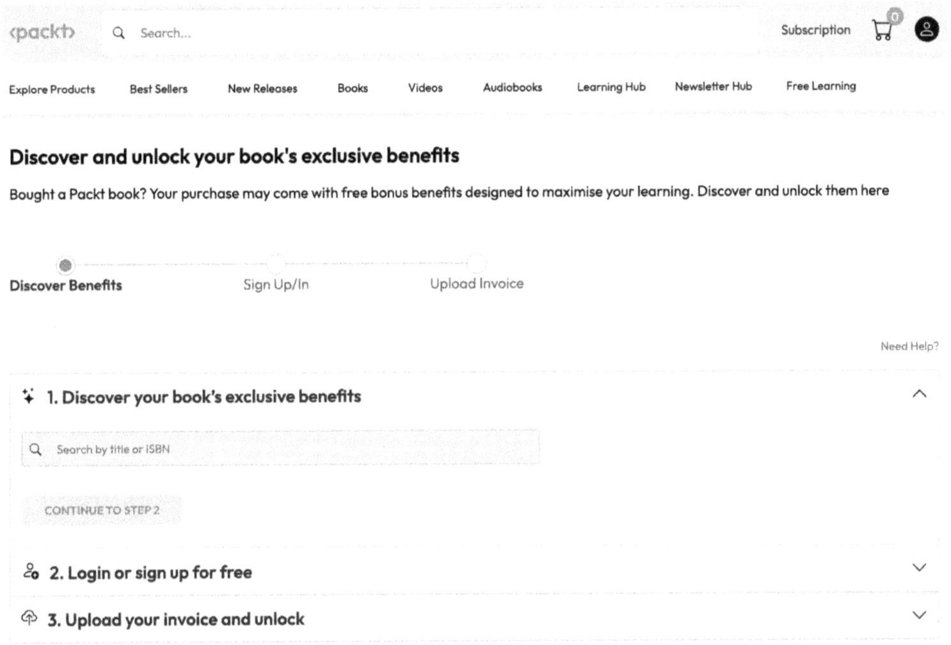

Figure 19.1: Packt unlock landing page on desktop

Step 3

After selecting your book, sign in to your Packt account or create one for free. Then upload your invoice (PDF, PNG, or JPG, up to 10 MB). Follow the on-screen instructions to finish the process.

Need help?

If you get stuck and need help, visit
`https://www.packtpub.com/unlock-benefits/help`
for a detailed FAQ on how to find your invoices and more. This QR code will take you to the help page.

> **Note**
> If you are still facing issues, reach out to `customercare@packt.com`.

Index

Symbols

A

W

Z

www.packtpub.com

Subscribe to our online digital library for full access to over 7,000 books and videos, as well as industry leading tools to help you plan your personal development and advance your career. For more information, please visit our website.

Why subscribe?

- Spend less time learning and more time coding with practical eBooks and Videos from over 4,000 industry professionals

- Improve your learning with Skill Plans built especially for you

- Get a free eBook or video every month

- Fully searchable for easy access to vital information

- Copy and paste, print, and bookmark content

Did you know that Packt offers eBook versions of every book published, with PDF and ePub files available? You can upgrade to the eBook version at packtpub.com and as a print book customer, you are entitled to a discount on the eBook copy. Get in touch with us at customercare@packtpub.com for more details.

At www.packtpub.com, you can also read a collection of free technical articles, sign up for a range of free newsletters, and receive exclusive discounts and offers on Packt books and eBooks.

Other Books You May Enjoy

If you enjoyed this book, you may be interested in these other books by Packt:

Effective Angular

Roberto Heckers

ISBN: 978-1-80512-553-2

- Create Nx monorepos ready to handle hundreds of Angular applications
- Reduce complexity in Angular with the standalone API, inject function, control flow, and Signals
- Effectively manage application state using Signals, RxJS, and NgRx
- Build dynamic components with projection, TemplateRef, and defer blocks
- Perform end-to-end and unit testing in Angular with Cypress and Jest
- Optimize Angular performance, prevent bad practices, and automate deployments

Modern Full-Stack React Projects

Daniel Bugl

ISBN: 978-1-83763-795-9

- Implement a backend using Express and MongoDB, and unit-test it with Jest

- Deploy full-stack web apps using Docker, set up CI/CD and end-to-end tests using Playwright

- Add authentication using JSON Web Tokens (JWT)

- Create a GraphQL backend and integrate it with a frontend using Apollo Client

- Build a chat app based on event-driven architecture using Socket.IO

- Facilitate Search Engine Optimization (SEO) and implement server-side rendering

- Use Next.js, an enterprise-ready full-stack framework, with React Server Components and Server Actions

Packt is searching for authors like you

If you're interested in becoming an author for Packt, please visit `authors.packtpub.com` and apply today. We have worked with thousands of developers and tech professionals, just like you, to help them share their insight with the global tech community. You can make a general application, apply for a specific hot topic that we are recruiting an author for, or submit your own idea.

Share Your Thoughts

Now you've finished *Scalable Application Development with NestJS*, we'd love to hear your thoughts! Scan the QR code below to go straight to the Amazon review page for this book and share your feedback or leave a review on the site that you purchased it from.

https://packt.link/r/1835468608

Your review is important to us and the tech community and will help us make sure we're delivering excellent quality content.